Land Use Problems and Conflicts

The causes, consequences and control of land use change have become topics of enormous importance in contemporary society. Not only is urban land use and sprawl a hot-button issue, but issues of rural land use have also been in the headlines. Policy makers and citizens are starting to realize that many environmental and economic issues have the question of land use at their very core.

Comprising papers from a conference sponsored by the Northeast Regional Center for Rural Development, *Land Use Problems and Conflicts* draws together some of the most up-to-date research and remaining research issues in this area. Sections are devoted to problems in the United States and Europe, consequences of such problems, land use-related data and alternative solutions to conflict.

With a lineup including some of the best scholarship on this subject to date, this volume will be of use to those studying environmental and land use issues in addition to policy makers, economists and other social scientists.

Stephan J. Goetz is director of The Northeast Regional Center for Rural Development at Pennsylvania State University and professor of agricultural and regional economics. **James S. Shortle** is University distinguished professor in the Department of Agricultural Economics and Rural Sociology at Pennsylvania State University. **John C. Bergstrom** is a professor in the Department of Agricultural and Applied Economics at the University of Georgia, Athens.

Routledge research in environmental economics

Land Use Problems and Conflicts

Causes, consequences and solutions

Edited by Stephan J. Goetz,
James S. Shortle and
John C. Bergstrom

Routledge
Taylor & Francis Group

LONDON AND NEW YORK

First published 2005
by Routledge
2 Park Square, Milton Park, Abingdon, Oxon OX14 4RN

Simultaneously published in the USA and Canada
by Routledge
270 Madison Ave, New York, NY 10016

Routledge is an imprint of the Taylor & Francis Group

Typeset in Bembo by Wearset Ltd, Boldon, Tyne and Wear
Printed and bound in Great Britain by MPG Books Ltd, Bodmin

British Library Cataloguing in Publication Data
A catalogue record for this book is available from the British Library

Library of Congress Cataloging in Publication Data
A catalog record for this book has been requested

ISBN 0-415-70028-0

Dedicated to the memory of Dr. David R. MacKenzie, whose vision and encouragement led to the conference that formed the basis of this work

Contents

Figures

Tables

Contributors

Charles W. Abdalla is associate professor of agricultural and environmental economics at Penn State University. His research and extension programs address public choices about natural resources and the environment.

David Abler is a professor of agricultural, environmental and regional economics and demography at Penn State University. His research interests include international trade, natural resource and environmental economics, and international economic development.

Mary C. Ahearn is a senior economist in the Resource Economic Division of USDA/ERS. Her research interests include improving the efficiency of farmland preservation programs, as well as farm structure and agricultural policies.

Anna Alberini is an assistant professor in the College of Agriculture and Natural Resources at the University of Maryland in College Park. Her research includes natural resource and environmental economics, econometrics and statistics.

Charles Barnard is an agricultural economist with the Economic Research Service, USDA, Washington, DC. His research focuses on land use and value issues, including the impact of urban influence on the farm sector.

Kathleen P. Bell is an assistant professor of resource economics and policy with the University of Maine in Orono. Her primary interests include environmental and natural resource economics as well as public economics and spatial econometrics.

John C. Bergstrom is professor of agricultural and applied economics at the University of Georgia in Athens. His research focuses on the economics of natural resources and land use.

Kevin J. Boyle is distinguished Maine professor and chair of the Department of Resource Economics and Policy at the University of Maine. His research is focused on understanding the public's preferences for environmental and ecological resources, and how people respond to environmental laws and regulations.

Steven Deller is a professor and extension economist in the Department of Agricultural and Applied Economics at the University of Wisconsin-Madison. His research and extension outreach education focus on regional economic structure and change; community economic development policies; and rural and small community public finance policies.

Stephan J. Goetz is professor of agricultural and regional economics and the director of The Northeast Regional Center for Rural Development at Penn State University. His research focuses on economic development, including the interrelationships between land use and regional development.

Nick D. Hanley is professor of economics at the University of Glasgow. His research interests are environmental economics, environmental valuation, cost-benefit analysis, agricultural economics, the economics of pollution control and the economics of sustainable development.

Ian Hodge is Reader in Rural Economy and Head of the Department of Land Economy at the University of Cambridge. His research interests are environmental management; rural development and land use; institutions and the environment; rural economic change, employment and disadvantage; and rural policy analysis and evaluation.

Thomas Johnson is Frank Miller professor of agricultural economics and director of the Community Policy Analysis Center at the University of Missouri in Columbia. His research focuses on economic development and public policy issues.

Mark B. Lapping is professor at the Edmund S. Muskie School of Public Service at the University of Southern Maine in Portland. The emphasis of much of his work lies in rural planning and development with a particular emphasis on problems confronting resource-based communities and regions.

Lawrence W. Libby is the Ohio State University's C. William Swank Professor of Rural–Urban Policy. His research program focuses on the economic consequences of alternative institutional devices for affecting patterns of resource use, with special emphasis on the rural–urban interface.

Lori Lynch is associate professor in the Department of Agricultural and Resource Economics at the University of Maryland. Her research focuses on public policy related to land use.

Elizabeth P. Marshall is assistant professor of agricultural and environmental economics at Penn State University. Her research integrates economic and ecological models to explore the demand for and the provision of open space within communities, and the implications of local land use decision making for regional landscape pattern and ecosystem services.

Catherine Meola is a Ph.D. student in the Department of Development Sociology at Cornell University. Her research interests include the inter-action of society and state in natural resource management, specifically regarding protected areas and gender equity.

Robert W. Paterson is a senior associate at Industrial Economics, Incorpor-ated in Cambridge, Massachusetts. His professional interests focus on the application of non-market valuation techniques to natural resource damage assessment and environmental policy.

Max J. Pfeffer is professor of development sociology and associate director, Cornell University Agricultural Experiment Station. His research program focuses on the relationship between conflicts of interests and values in modern society with an emphasis on the rural/urban fringe.

Richard C. Ready is assistant professor of agricultural and environmental economics at Penn State University. He works in the area of natural resource and environmental economics, including non-market valuation.

Andrew F. Seidl is associate professor of agricultural and resource eco-nomics and public policy extension specialist and a faculty affiliate of the Center for Research on the Colorado Economy (CRCE) at Colorado State University in Fort Collins. His recent research and outreach emphases include natural amenity-based rural development, outdoor recreation and tourism and agriculture, open lands preservation, and federal agricultural and resource policy.

James S. Shortle is distinguished professor of agricultural and environ-mental economics at Penn State University. His interests are primarily in the area of environmental and natural resource economics including the integration of economic and environmental information for environmental decision making; impacts of climate change; and the management of agri-cultural externalities.

Alvin D. Sokolow is public policy specialist in the University of California Cooperative Extension and a faculty member in the Department of Human and Community Development at UC Davis. His research con-cerns community governance, with a current focus on farmland protection and land use policy.

Richard C. Stedman is assistant professor of rural sociology at Penn State University. His research interests are based in the linkages between indi-vidual-level environmental attitudes, identity, and behavior, and larger scale societal and natural resource issues.

John Sydenstricker-Neto is an independent consultant in the area of environmental studies and a Ph.D. candidate in development sociology at Cornell University. His current work focuses on the relationships between social organization and land use/land cover change and developing social research methods integrating different paradigms and various research instruments.

Linda P. Wagenet is a senior extension associate in the Department of Development Sociology at Cornell University. Her research program focuses on environmental policy and management, especially as it relates to citizen participation in watershed management.

Fiona Watson is the director of the AHRB Research Center for Environmental History and a senior lecturer in history at the University of Stirling. Her broader research interests include woodland history and the history of the uplands, especially the complex relationship between the land, its owners and its users.

Michael P. Welsh is a senior economist with Christensen Associates. He specializes in the collection and analysis of customer preference data.

Acknowledgments

We are grateful for permission to use figures from the following sources: New York City Department of Environmental Protection, New York; Blackwell Publishing, Oxford; Elsevier Publications, United Kingdom.

This volume was supported in part by USDA/CSREES and The Northeast Regional Center for Rural Development at the Pennsylvania State University, University Park, PA; all opinions expressed are those of the individual authors. The workshop underlying this volume was organized by The Northeast Regional Center for Rural Development and endorsed by the National Association of State Universities and Land Grant Colleges (NASULGC), as well as the Transatlantic Partnership for Inter-University Cooperation in Education and Research for the Environment and Food Systems (TIC).

1 Contemporary land use problems and conflicts

Stephan J. Goetz, James S. Shortle and John C. Bergstrom

The causes, consequences, and control of land use change have become topics of enormous importance to contemporary society. Concern is perhaps most broadly evident in the attention to urban sprawl and the expressed desire for "smart growth." But land use issues in nonurban settings are also of significant interest. Rural issues include intensification of agricultural production in the form of large confined animal feeding operations; abandonment, afforestation, and desertification of agricultural lands; loss of wetlands to agricultural or other uses; fragmentation of forests by roads and second home developments; and the proper multiple-use management of public forests and range lands.

The reasons for societal interest in land use and land use change are many. Land use both reflects and determines where economic activity takes place, and where and how communities develop. Land use affects the built environment in which individuals live, work and recreate. It also affects the quality of the natural environment, with impacts on air quality, water quality, water supply, the costs of natural hazards such as flooding and earthquakes, the probabilities of hazards including flooding, and the functioning of terrestrial and aquatic ecosystems.

Fundamentally, land use becomes an important policy concern because it involves interdependencies among individuals and communities that have significant impacts on economic and social well being. More often than not, one person's land use decision affects the well being of other individuals. Examples include a new subdivision that blocks a scenic view; a farm operation on the rural–urban fringe that is adversely impacted by housing encroachment; increased traffic congestion that raises travel time to and from work; low-income families that are driven out of their homes by newcomers who cause property taxes to rise; and open or green space on one property that adds to a person's enjoyment of neighboring property.

The subject of land use is both broad and complex. The overwhelming breadth of the subject is evident from a long list of actual and perceived controversies that can attend land use decisions. For example, the conversion of land that produces food to land supporting housing development raises concerns about long-run domestic food security and availability of fresh, local food. Location of so-called "big-box" retailers, toxic waste sites, or confined animal feeding operations gives rise to the NIMBY (not-in-my-backyard) syndrome. Potential concerns over the environmental impacts of land use range from invasive species, endangered species preservation and ground-water filtration and recharge to flooding and surface water runoff from subur-ban parking lots. Undeveloped land uses such as open space, green space, parks and other natural areas are often said to provide economic, environ-mental and social benefits, enhancing community and individual quality of life, yet these relationships are poorly understood. Other topics associated directly or indirectly (and factually or mythically) with land use include right-to-farm laws, urban decay, "white flight," school quality, gentrification, traffic gridlock, urban gardens, asthma and health effects of pollution from cars, rising obesity rates, trailer homes, "McMansions," trophy homes, zoning, and so forth.

The subject of land use is complex in part because it usually involves com-peting public and private interests. Superimposed on the socioeconomic and physical land use/land cover attributes of a parcel of land are the land tenure and ownership characteristics and regulatory environment that govern land use, and the various tools state and local government use to influence land use decisions. These include zoning, easements, preferential taxation, and purchase or transfer of development rights. It is not uncommon for one branch of government to promote activities (such as industrial recruitment with attendant increases in pollution) that are in conflict with the goals of another branch of government (environmental protection).

As in other cases of social conflict, there are also multiple sides to any given land use story. A new highway fragments ecosystems, increases the amount of impervious surface, and may push the urban fringe out even further from the urban core. It also reduces the risk of traffic accidents and travel time of parents from their place of work, allowing them to spend more time with their children in a more spacious home situated on a larger lot than would otherwise be affordable. Sprawl that is viewed as wasteful and envi-ronmentally harmful by some is seen as economic development and a way to improve their standard of living by others. Zoning and other regulations that restrict land conversion for development purposes and result in higher housing prices can also restrict the amount of affordable housing available to low-income families. Along with food and clothing, housing or shelter is a basic human need, and how a nation uses its scarce land resources to the benefit of all members of society is a central measure of its economic devel-opment and quality of life. A growing society needs more housing to accom-modate population growth. But how new housing is best provided, and whose preferences are counted in the process, are important underlying ques-tions that are not often, or easily, answered. Growth can occur upwards in skyscrapers or outwards through sprawl. Which path is followed has import-ant implications for the local and regional economy, environment and society as a whole.

An increasing sense of urgency surrounds current land use decisions because of the high and perhaps prohibitive private and public costs of reversing these decisions. Both the magnitude and the patterns of current land uses are at issue. A 100-acre parcel can be subdivided into 100 housing units of one acre each, not counting space for roads and sidewalks and other easements. Or, the parcel can be developed by clustering the 100 homes into one 20-acre area and leaving the balance of the land in its natural state. Here the magnitude of development is the same in terms of the number of housing units created, but the pattern of development differs markedly, with the latter being potentially more environmentally- and traffic-"friendly." While some groups emphasize the relative scarcity of land with statements such as "they don't make land anymore," others point to the fact that only a small fraction of the world's total land base has been developed for housing purposes to date.

Among all of the causes or determinants of modern day land use in the United States, perhaps none is more important than the pronounced preference of Americans for large lots. As other countries develop around the world, this preference and yearning for more land devoted to housing per capita may become a worldwide pattern. American homeowners are voting with their dollars and their feet for these kinds of housing developments. While the decisions are perfectly sensible and rational for individual families, problems arise when these individual-level decisions are aggregated and their impacts on other members of society are measured. Individual decision makers often are unaware of how their actions contribute to the growing traffic congestion or other new problems in an area. In an interventionist sense, a certain need therefore exists to "save people from themselves." Furthermore, as soon as they have moved into an area, new residents often vehemently oppose further development – whether this is in a coastal retirement community, a mountain or lakeside vacation home development, or a rural or countryside housing development serving as a "bedroom community" to a nearby city.

Government interventions such as highway construction subsidies and mortgage interest rate deductions are widely believed to encourage residential locations on the urban fringe, although the importance of these interventions is in dispute (Glaeser and Kahn 2003). At the same time, a powerful construction industry growth machine is argued to drive current housing development patterns to the detriment of the urban poor, who also tend to be minorities (Jargowsky 2002; Savitch 2002). On the other hand, newer homes require less spending on maintenance initially, which can make it more feasible for young families to own a home (McCarthy *et al.* 2001).

Figure 1.1 provides an overview of the factors that affect land uses as well as the effects of alternative land uses on social, economic and environmental variables. According to economic theory, demand for land is a function of land price, consumer incomes, tastes and preferences, the number of consumers, and the availability of substitutes and complements for land. As already noted, consumers have a strong preference for large-lot housing developments and, equally important, they have the incomes needed to articulate their

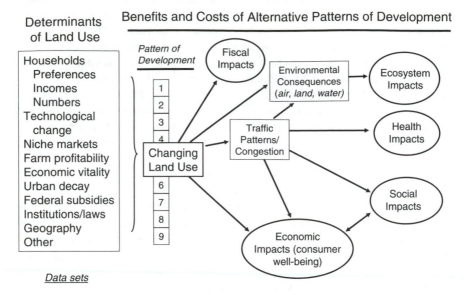

Figure 1.1 Determinants and consequences of land use (source: © 2004 The North-east Regional Center for Rural Development).

preferences in the market. During the 1990s in the United States, at least some of the gains in the stock market were used to purchase bigger and better housing units. Thus, consumers were voting unequivocally with their dollars for the types of homes and locations that builders were supplying.

A key and relatively recent sociodemographic trend has been the formation of smaller household units. In fact, in the United States single-person households were the fastest-growing demographic category during the last decade, for reasons that likely have both social and economic origins. In addition, changes in technology and the social organization of workplaces have allowed more workers to telecommute and to buy residences at greater distances from urban employment centers. This trend is often accelerated by the self-fulfilling prophecy of urban decay, which includes perceived and real deterioration in public services, such as education. Institutional differences and incentives, such as home rule, local propensity to engage in planning, mortgage interest deduction and subsidies for construction of interstate highways and other infrastructure contribute to differences in land use over space as well.

The profitability of farming affects the rate at which farmland is converted into housing developments as aging farmers choose between keeping their land in agriculture and cashing out their equity to retire. Farmers in some regions switch to higher-valued niche crops or engage in direct marketing to consumers in order to keep their farm in business. An increasing number of farmers and rural landowners are also engaging in agritourism and nature-based tourism to supplement their income. Finally, geography is also important in guiding land use. The prime farmland around cities is desirable for housing construction precisely because the land is flat, usually well-drained, and proximate to major consumer markets. In other words, the geographic features that make land suitable for farming also make it desirable for housing development. Geography also determines the economically feasible patterns of development. In the US West, for example, scarcity of water forces developers to build more compact housing settlements (Fulton *et al.* 2001). All of these multidisciplinary factors interact to produce given land use patterns, and make it necessary to draw on more than individual disciplines to understand land use trends and to address effectively problems that arise.

The complex causes of land use problems and conflicts described above can have varying land use impacts, depending on the pattern of housing development. As discussed earlier, both the amount of housing and the pattern in which land is consumed are important. The different possible patterns of development are symbolized in Figure 1.1 by the scale ranging from 1 to 9. The amount of land consumed per person increases from the urbanized (1) to the frontier or natural landscape (9), while population density falls accordingly. These latter concepts are described in Bergstrom (2001). Figure 1.1 also suggests that different land uses affect fiscal conditions of state and local governments; community social capital; consumer well being through housing affordability, traffic congestion and other factors; population health via pollution and stress caused by traffic bottlenecks; as well as ecosystems and the environment more generally.

To begin to address the complex sets of questions and issues surrounding land use problems and conflicts, The Northeast Regional Center for Rural Development sponsored a two-day workshop in Orlando, Florida. Because of the multidisciplinary nature of the land use issue, social science experts representing a number of disciplines were invited to attend. The primary objective of the workshop was to synthesize what is and what is not known about land use issues and conflicts from different disciplinary perspectives. From this synthesis a set of research priorities was identified and published in a summary proceedings (Goetz *et al.* 2002). The present volume contains the invited papers presented at the workshop, providing background information about the land use issues and conflicts discussed. The authors describe the causes of current land use patterns, the consequences of these patterns for the environment, society and the economy, selected land use valuation and measurement issues, and options for dealing with these problems.

The remainder of this book is divided into four parts and a conclusion. Part I presents overviews and various causes of land use problems and conflicts in the United States and in Europe. Part II presents selected consequences of land use problems and conflicts. Part III discusses land use-related data and empirical issues, including questions of valuing alternative land uses. Part IV presents alternative solutions to land use problems and conflicts, drawing on lessons from economics, sociology, psychology, planning and political science.

Part I

Land use problems and conflicts

Causes

2 Rural land use problems and policy options

Overview from a US perspective

Lawrence W. Libby

Introduction

The process and character of metropolitan expansion in the United States have been priority research and policy themes since at least the 1960s (Clawson 1971). In 1975 The Urban Land Institute published a seminal three-volume examination of growth management beginning with the assertion, "The ethic of growth in America is increasingly being challenged; no longer is it being accepted unquestioningly as a premise of progress. Its effects on the quality of life are widely debated, and its management and control are seen as essential elements of modern land use policy" (Scott 1975: 7).

Related to and yet distinct from concern about the pressures of physical growth has been interest in retaining farmland. Some of the impetus for farmland protection comes as a sidebar to growth management, but farmland retention policy has its own political and economic history.[1] There is more to growth management than protecting farmland or open space, and the economic forces shifting land out of farming run much deeper than pressure from urban uses.

This chapter considers the patterns of rural land use change in the US, the associated problems, and policy response. It concludes with judgments about future policy directions.

Land use change

Shifts in land use patterns are recorded in the National Resources Inventory (NRI) of USDA. It is a consistent and reliable national data set on how land is being used at selected points in time.[2] Current land use data are gathered from about 300,000 data points on non-federal lands of the 48 contiguous states plus Hawaii, based on satellite images with "groundtruthing" on a sampling basis. The NRI says little about *who* is on the land, focusing instead on categories of use that may be apparent from remote observation. It tracks conversion of specific areas from one use to another, as indicated in Table 2.1, which is published as part of the 1997 NRI.

As is apparent here, of the nearly 1.5 billion acres of non-federal land in

Table 2.1 Changes in land cover/land use between 1982 and 1997[a]

Land cover/land use in 1982	Land cover/land use in 1997 ('000 acres)								
	Cropland	CRP land[b]	Pastureland	Rangeland	Forest land	Other rural land	Developed land	Water areas and federal land	1982 total
Cropland	350,265	30,412	19,269	3,659	5,607	3,159	7,098	1,485	420,954
Pastureland	15,347	1,330	92,088	2,568	14,091	1,619	4,230	733	132,006
Rangeland	6,968	729	3,037	394,617	3,022	1,703	3,281	3,383	416,739
Forest land	2,037	129	4,168	2,099	380,343	1,755	10,279	2,528	403,338
Other rural land	1,387	93	1,014	719	2,768	42,713	727	228	49,648
Developed land	197	1	79	111	227	12	72,619	1	73,246
Water areas and federal land	798	3	337	2,204	898	181	18	443,761	448,198
1997 total	376,998	32,696	119,992	405,977	406,955	51,142	98,252	452,118	1,944,130

Source: Natural Resources Conservation Service, Table 5, 1997 Natural Resources Inventory, revised December 2000a.

Notes
a The 1982 land cover/land use totals are listed in the right-hand vertical column, titled "1982 total." The 1997 land cover/use totals are listed in the bottom horizontal row, titled "1997 total." The number at the intersection of rows and columns with the same land cover/land use designation represents acres that did not change from 1982 to 1997. Reading to the right or left of this number are the acres that were lost to another cover/use by 1997. Reading up or down from this number are the acres that were gained from another cover/use by 1997. Totals may not add up due to rounding error.
b CRP = Conservation Reserve Program.

the US, about 421 million acres were cropland in 1982. More than 70 million acres of 1982 cropland were converted to other uses by 1997, of which 30.4 million went into the Conservation Reserve Program (CRP), 19.3 million to pasture, 3.7 million to range, and 5.6 million to forest, and 7.1 million acres of cropland were developed in that 15-year period. A total of 26.7 million acres of land being used for other things in 1982 were cropland in 1997, for a net cropland reduction of 44 million acres. Much of the increase in cropland in that period came from reduced restrictions under the commodity programs of the 1996 Farm Bill and completion of CRP contracts, but the NRI also shows that 196,700 acres of "developed" land in 1982 were being cropped in 1997.[3]

Developed area increased by more than 34 percent between 1982 and 1997 in the US, with most of that increase coming in the eastern third of the nation, parts of Texas, and California. While there are recent exceptions, such as Colorado (Seidl 2004, chapter 5 this volume), much of the West remains unpressured by development and the cornbelt states of Iowa, Illinois, Missouri, and western Indiana had developed area increases of 10 to 20 percent.

Between 1992 and 1997, more than 11 million acres were urbanized across the US, three million of which were defined by USDA as prime farmland. The top ten states are shown in Table 2.2.

California, Texas and Florida have long been at the top of the development list, partly because of the climate and other natural amenities that attract people and partly because of economic growth. Georgia is a newcomer to the list, with Atlanta as the prime urban magnet in the South. The Carolinas are coastal and hilly states with moderate climates, Virginia has climate, coast and proximity to Washington, DC. North Carolina experienced a dramatic turn-around in population migration patterns in the 1990s as far more people

Table 2.2 Acres converted to urban use – top ten states

State	1992–1997 (thousand acres)
Texas	893.5
Georgia	851.9
Florida	825.2
California	553.4
Pennsylvania	545.1
North Carolina	506.6
Tennessee	401.9
Ohio	364.8
Michigan	364.1
South Carolina	362.0
Virginia	343.5

Source: Natural Resources Conservation Service, 1997 Natural Resources Inventory, revised December 2000b.

moved into rural areas than out of them (Renkow 2001). Ohio, Michigan and Pennsylvania are industrial states that have experienced an increase in developed area primarily as people have migrated from urban centers to live in smaller rural communities or in the open countryside. Commercial and retail services follow the people. None of these three states has seen significant population increases. All of the top ten states have important agricultural sectors that compete with higher paying development interests for the services of land.

For over 50 years, the Economic Research Service (ERS) of USDA has assembled data from several sources to give a more complete picture of use categories for the total US land base of 2.3 billion acres. Table 2.3 shows these in numbers for selected years starting in 1959.

Land has gone into and out of active cropping over the 1959–1997 period as prices and farm programs affected incentives for the farmer. The largest amount of active cropland existed in 1982 when there were few acreage restrictions in national policy, and active cropland was at its lowest just five years later when the CRP was in full operation. The largest proportionate increase over the entire period was for "special uses" that include transportation areas, parks and wildlife areas, wilderness, and rural and farm residences. Inclusion of Alaska in the ERS data set is evident in the "miscellaneous use" category that includes tundra, swamps, desert as well as urban or developed areas. Total urban area has increased from 47 million acres in 1980 to 66 million acres in 1997 (Vesterby and Krupa 2001: 21–22). ERS estimates that non-farm rural residences occupied 73 million acres in 1997, up from 56 million in 1980.

The increase in number of households is a better indicator of demand for development space than is population change. Rates of household formation reflect cultural trends and general economic conditions as people separate into smaller households for economic and social independence. Heimlich and Anderson (2001) point out that average household size has declined from 3.7 in 1950 to 2.6 in 2000, resulting in increased demand for houses, many of which are located at the urban fringe (see also Barnard 2004, chapter 4 this volume). While median lot size of new houses remains about 0.5 acres as new households look to town homes and condominiums, the average has increased to 2 acres, reflecting the trend toward 5- and 10-acre rural lots. Large lot housing is about half of new housing construction in rural areas and average lot size outside of metropolitan areas is nearly 3 acres (Heimlich and Anderson 2001).

Recent census data show the trend toward rural living. In Ohio, for example, more people are living in unincorporated townships than in large or small cities, and the increase in township residences between 1960 and 2000 – in excess of one third – has been substantial compared with the state's overall growth rate.

Development of farm and other rural land is small in proportion to total land being farmed in some manner. There is just no evidence that develop-

Table 2.3 Major uses of land, United States, 1959–1997

Land use	1959	1964	1969	1974	1978	1982	1987	1992	1997
	(million acres)								
Cropland	458	444	472	465	471	469	464	460	455
Cropland used for crops	359	335	333	361	369	383	331	338	349
Idle cropland	34	52	51	21	26	21	68	56	39
Grassland pasture and range[a]	633	640	604	598	587	597	591	591	580
Forest-use land[b]	728	732	723	718	703	655	648	648	642
Special use areas	123	144	141	147	158	270	279	281	286
Miscellaneous other land[c]	329	306	324	336	345	274	283	283	301
Total land area	2,271	2,266	2,264	2,264	2,264	2,265	2,265	2,263	2,264

Source: Adapted from Vesterby and Krupa (2001: 4).

Notes

a Other grassland pasture and nonforested range (excludes cropland used only for pasture and grazed forest land).
b Excludes forest land in parks and other special uses of land.
c Includes urban areas, areas in miscellaneous uses not inventoried, and areas of little surface use such as marshes, open swamps, bare rock areas, desert, and tundra.

ment threatens US food production capacity in the foreseeable future (Vesterby *et al.* 1994). But development patterns do affect the mix of services available from rural land and therefore are the focus of considerable policy attention.

Rationale for rural land policy

The reasons for policy intervention in the pattern and pace of rural land use change are diverse. These policies may have little observable impact on the macro categories of land use indicated in the NRI and other data sets. But they can make a profound difference in the quality of life at the margin, the interface between urban and rural land uses. People seek to reduce the frictions of unplanned land use conversion and to sustain or create a bundle of land services consistent with prevailing preferences. Whenever rules for land use change are adjusted in some way, some participants in the land market perceive a gain while others feel they are worse off. All of this depends on the starting point, of course, and perhaps those who perceive a loss were imposing cost on others under the old rules. Or, perhaps some land services were inadequately defined or reflected in the land market.

The frictions of growth

Arguably, the single phenomenon having the greatest impact on stress at the rural–urban interface is unplanned low-density residential development. The perceived amenities of a countryside home are a powerful force. Some of those single-family homes are in subdivisions with lot sizes of less than an acre; others are scattered on 5- or 10-acre parcels. People living in the countryside demand services that may not be available in the rural villages nearby. Franchise retail establishments are tuned to this increasing demand for food, fuel and health needs, and they are among the first to move out to the fringe to accommodate the demand. Too seldom is there adequate infrastructure to handle the increased load; consequently, costs for schools, roads, fire protection and other community services increase.

Scattered development patterns are predictable results of the incentives inherent in infrastructure financing systems in the US that accommodate, even encourage, building at the urban fringe or beyond rather than downtown or in planned high-density suburbs. Rusk (1999: 86) refers to "the sprawl machine" as the structure of subsidized mortgages for new detached single family homes, urban renewal programs that replace urban residences with high-rise office buildings, federal highway construction and sewer extensions that open new land for development. Richmond (2000: 10) puts it more directly: "Sprawl is the law of the land" in which housing subsidies favor single-family over multiple units and local zoning policies yield to any development, with little attention to guiding growth. Local governments depend on the property tax for services and the temptation to accommodate development is too great, even in the face of evidence that much of that development costs more to serve than it generates in local property taxes (see also Deller 2004, chapter 8 this volume). This leads to several friction points.

Congested roadways

Many of those who move to rural areas for the open spaces still expect to work and shop in a nearby city. New houses appear in the countryside with little prior attention to whether existing roads can handle the extra traffic. Transportation policies seem to emphasize responding to demand for more or wider roads, rather than trying to shape development patterns with roads or other forms of transit. Federal spending on highways for private automobiles far exceeds that for mass transit (US General Accounting Office 2000a). Not surprisingly, US travelers are far more dependent on private automobiles than travelers in any other developed nation.[4] "Road improvement" projects only add to the congestion and frustration as existing roadways are narrowed for the construction process that never seems to end. "Stuck in traffic" is the predominant state of being for people both within and outside of our metropolitan areas. Ulrich and colleagues at the Transportation Research Center at Texas A&M University have identified significant psychological impacts of the clutter and congestion of the suburban commute (Ulrich *et al.* 1991).

Cost of services

Many case studies throughout the US have documented the added cost of servicing dispersed rather than more concentrated populations. The general conclusion is that residences in low–density subdivisions or scattered parcels generate less in property tax revenue than it costs to provide them with roads, police and fire, and schools. Some communities have explicitly recognized this imbalance by trying to discourage new housing and encourage commercial development instead. The American Farmland Trust, a national non–profit group encouraging farmland protection and stewardship, has sponsored dozens of local cost of community services studies throughout the US and concludes that on average residential development requires $1.02 to $1.67 in service cost for every dollar in property tax revenue they generate, while commercial and industrial development cost $0.03 to $0.83 for a dollar in taxes (American Farmland Trust 1997).

These are admittedly partial analyses, omitting such other fiscal impacts as sales taxes, income generated by new residents and the related economic multiplier (Irwin and Kraybill 1999; Deller 2004, chapter 8 this volume), but they are useful comparisons for policy purposes. The lesson is that building new single-family homes on open land may be, and often is, a net drain on local property tax coffers. It is a matter to be carefully examined within each community dealing with development options. There are equity considerations as well. Existing residents find their taxes going up to add the waste treatment plant or widen the road to serve new homes at the periphery. Political strife is certain under those conditions (Downs 1994). Communities in several states have enacted "development impact fees" to shift the marginal cost of new development onto the new residences (Carrion and Libby 2000).

Competition among communities

With land policy and other decision authority vested primarily at the most local level in the US, communities inevitably compete with each other for location of tax-generating activities. They can offer various incentives, from free land to tax abatements, to get the right industrial firm. But communities also compete for residents, with open space, good schools, recreational facilities, security and other amenities. Many localities face the dilemma of preferring both a low-wage workforce for the potential industry and high-income residents who pay more taxes. Industries searching for a new location will often play the communities against each other, seeking the best possible deal. Existing business can get into the game as well, threatening to leave town if the terms are not right.

Economic segregation is the inevitable, though unintended, result of competition as communities enact zoning to establish more exclusive higher-income neighborhoods, isolated and protected from industry and lower-income neighborhoods. These higher-income areas frequently organize their own communities with local control to maintain a certain set of housing standards and quality of life. Zoning, subdivision rules and housing standards may create *de facto* exclusionary regulation that keeps those neighborhoods economically and racially homogeneous (Downs 1994). A lack of affordable housing for a diverse population led Montgomery County, Maryland, essentially a suburb of Washington, DC, to enact an ordinance in 1974 requiring that at least 20 percent of any new housing project be moderately priced housing units. The county would purchase one third of those units for low-income tenants. In return, the developer could increase housing density in the rest of the development project. In the past 25 years, developers have built nearly 11,000 moderately priced units in Montgomery County (Rusk 1999).

Urban disinvestment

A consequence of growth at the urban fringe is nearly always decline in the center. In 2002, Columbus, Ohio was feeling the effects of massive retail and residential growth at the periphery. Retail capacity in three huge malls built since 1987 simply redistributed sales from downtown to the suburbs. There was not enough spending power to keep all the stores in business. The large retail anchors had abandoned the city center for the new malls at the urban fringe. Other service firms flocked to the mall vicinity and residential developments followed. An aggressive annexation policy enabled Columbus to capture the tax revenue from those outlying malls, located many miles from the real center of the city, while losing revenue from the downtown. Columbus now faces the problems of inner-city decline that are so familiar to urban America.

There are racial and ethnic dimensions to the economic segregation in most US metropolitan areas (Rusk 1999). While these conditions exist in other developed nations as well, Jackson (2000) argues that the greater degree of income inequality and balkanization of government in the United States makes this problem more pronounced. Central city problems are clearly a friction point in the growth pattern of US metropolitan areas, though the extent, nature and policy implications of these problems are beyond the scope of this chapter.

The services of open land

Beyond the economic and social strain of relatively undirected growth are the positive services available from farmland and other open lands. These are key to the rationale for land policy in the US, particularly with respect to rural land.

Long-term food security

No serious policy analyst would assert that impending food scarcity is a defensible rationale for protecting US farmland. There is simply too much evidence to the contrary. But many voters support state and local farmland protection efforts with the intuitive sense that arable cropland has limits and the prudent course is to develop other lands and encourage farmers to continue farming. Food production technology continues to substitute for land and people engaged in farming, though experts differ on the potential. Waggoner *et al.* (1996) express great optimism about future production capacity, while Pimental and Giampietro (1994) have less confidence in the ability or willingness of farmers to employ those technologies in a timely way in the face of competition for water and our best farmland.

The food supply rationale is really about risk preference. Should we as a society assume that past trends in productivity increase will continue, or should we be more cautious with the physically limited supply of arable farmland? Many participants in the land policy debates gain utility from knowing that future generations will have a more secure food supply with thoughtful farmland policy. Protecting farmland has a short-run cost in the potential returns to an alternative use of those lands. According to Weitzman (1999: 29), a below market discount rate is warranted on actions that could imply a resource catastrophe, even if the probability is very low. He would employ the lower rate for the first 25 years, declining to 0 percent beyond 300 years. The consequence of underestimating the amount of farmland needed to feed future generations would likely be greater than the consequence of saving "too much" farmland. The precautionary principle so prominent in European environmental policy makes sense in this context (Foster *et al.* 2000).

Natural resource services

By its very nature, farmland produces ecosystem services that people value and seek to secure through policy. Most of these are economic public goods, non-rival in consumption and non-exclusive. One person's sense of well being from knowing that there is adequate bird habitat, species diversity or groundwater recharge does not reduce that service to other consumers. While direct exercise of effective demand for these services is generally not possible, there are organizations that will purchase lands for these non-exclusive services using funds donated by people who value the services. There are obvious free rider problems with any such public goods, though tax incentives do offer private benefit to those who contribute. Donors may also select those land purchase programs that match their preferences most closely, and where the benefits are most apparent, as with farmland within a particular state or even a particular farm that seems to have special signific-ance. Presumably donors gain more service or satisfaction from the land pur-chase than they would from an alternative use of those funds.

Several studies have attempted to estimate what the bundle of natural resource services from farmland would be worth if sold in a market. The most comprehensive analysis was by Costanza *et al.* (1997) in which the value of various ecosystem services of farm and other open land was estimated as the cost of providing those same services in some other way. Nutrient cycling, nitrogen fixation, soil formation, biological balance among species, growth medium for plants, and genetic diversity that may yield valuable medicines are among the services examined. Farmland can also mitigate flooding, provide a medium for pollination to assure plant reproduction, and reduce water pollution.

Active farmland generates various amenity services as well. Farms are key to a rural heritage for many people, and they will support farmland protection on that basis alone. "Ruralness" is not just the absence of city, with farmland a key part of what distinguishes city from country. Farms are important to a countryside that provides relief from the stresses of urban life. The opportun-ity to buy at a "farmers' market" is important to many voters and taxpayers. There is the sense that produce bought at a farm is somehow better than produce from a grocery store. People will incur cost and inconvenience to experience ruralness and we should assume that they value the ruralness more than the time and gasoline needed to get out there.

Some of these amenity services can be purchased. People often pay more for "farm fresh" produce at the farm, apparently getting some form of utility beyond the produce itself. Farms can be a recreation destination, through a bed and breakfast experience or the opportunity to hunt or hike for a fee. For example, M & M Hunting Lodge provides visitors to Delaware's eastern shore the chance to hunt geese and ducks on an old dairy farm (Matarese and Graham 1990). Urban tourists can contact Back Roads Adventures in Preston County, West Virginia for a guided tour of the farms, inns, crafts and folklore of the region, for a price. Farming is the main feature of the economic development plans in Loudoun County, Virginia. Their primary goal is to keep the 200,000-acre farm economy and encourage a varied farm tourism sector (Loudoun County, Virginia 1998). There are colorful brochures for self-guided specialty tours for the Christmas season, wineries, and fall foliage. Hunters pay up to $600 a day for access to prime whitetail deer habitat on the Hoover Farm in western Illinois. Deer like the corn stubble, and hunters like the deer (Miller 1999). There are similar examples in all farm states.

Several studies have estimated what people would be willing to pay to avoid development on specific farmland (Halstead 1984; Bergstrom *et al.* 1985; Beasley *et al.* 1986; Bergstrom and Ready 2004) as an indication of the value they place on the amenities of open land. At least some of the amenity associated with open farmland is an intrinsic value that people associate with healthy biological ecosystems themselves, beyond any definable "service" (Bergstrom 2004, chapter 6 this volume).

The policy response

There is clearly demand, some of it effective demand, revealed in purchase preferences, and some of it political demand, through the policy process, for the many services of farmland. People have also supported policies to reduce the frictions of development. The same basic set of legal options has been applied to both purposes. They draw on the full set of governmental powers, to regulate, to tax and to spend for public purpose.

Regulate the use of land

Enacting regulations on what uses are permitted within identified districts remains the primary policy option for local governments in the United States. Zoning has been part of local policy in cities, villages, counties and townships since it was deemed an acceptable application of police power in the late 1920s with *Euclid v. Ambler Realty*.[5] The zoning ordinance must establish that the public's health, safety and general welfare are protected by limiting uses of land within defined districts. In theory, any cost or inconvenience to the owner within a district is more than offset by the broader social benefit.

Other regulatory devices include sub-division controls, required sewer and water system connection, building permits and even growth moratoria. Local governments act, within state-enabling statutes, to establish the rules within which land can change use.

While nearly all municipalities in all 50 states use zoning to guide growth, only 24 states have zoning designed to protect agriculture. Of those 24, only

Hawaii has true state-wide zoning, while Oregon has required county agricultural zoning as part of the growth management plan; Maryland, California, Pennsylvania and Washington have active county-level programs (American Farmland Trust 1997: 51–53). The legal challenge with agricultural zoning is to establish a relationship to "public health, safety and general welfare," which are the bases for valid public purpose.[6] Some of those ordinances define "exclusive agricultural zones" within which only land use compatible with farming is permitted, while others rely on minimum lot sizes of 20 to 60 acres to discourage non-farm development.

The primary legal challenges of zoning, particularly in rural or suburban areas, turn on the "takings" clause of the US Constitution, concerns about exclusion and the personal right of mobility. The basic conclusion of regulatory takings cases is that unless all economic opportunity is eliminated by the ordinance, the restrictions are legal and compensation is not required (Cordes 1999). Several states have enacted property rights protection statutes to give citizens greater access to legal redress for alleged unfairness of zoning and other land use regulations that lower property value. These essentially side-step the Constitutional takings tests within limitations described in each ordinance (Cordes 1997). Only Florida and Texas spell out the extent of property value loss deemed to be unacceptable as a threshold for legal action (Libby 1997). The 18 or so other states require only that property rights impacts be an explicit part of the decision on enacting controls. Exclusion cases against zoning generally focus on the absence of affordable housing, economic, and therefore unintended racial discrimination, and they work on the equal protection or due process clauses of the 14th Amendment to the US Constitution (Lauber 1975).

Tax incentives

The various tax instruments for guiding growth and protecting open land either reduce the tax burden for land uses that have social value, or raise the cost of development to incorporate full social cost. Land uses that raise the capital cost of infrastructure in a developing area may be assessed an impact fee under state or local programs. Thus, a more efficient development pattern is encouraged by requiring those who raise the cost of infrastructure to bear that added cost (Peddle and Lewis 1996). The builder will try to pass those extra costs along in the purchase price of the home.[7] Other programs grant tax concessions for development in certain areas, through "tax increment financing" or selective tax abatements. These affect the pattern of development by giving advantage to siting in targeted downtown areas rather than in the suburbs or at the urban fringe.

All states have programs to tax farmland on a lower value than other land to encourage the farmer to stay on the land. These programs range from simple use value assessment, to use value with roll back if the eligible land is developed, to restrictive agreement as condition for use value assessment, to "circuit breaker" in which the farmer receives a state income tax refund if property tax exceeds a threshold percentage of household income (American Farmland Trust 1997). Special capital gains tax recapture provisions in several New England states require that a portion of the gain resulting from the development of open land go back to the state. The state then reclaims some of the cost of public infrastructure that contributed much of the land value captured by the owner in the sale for development.

Federal income and estate tax law makes it attractive for some farmers to donate their development rights to a state government agency or non-profit land trust. The value of those rights is a charitable donation against income if the transfer is permanent, and it affects the tax value of the estate at the time of transfer between generations.

These are incentives to guide rather than control growth. They work only to the extent that the value of the incentive, when added to farm income and other returns to the farmer, is greater than the value of the other land use options. Cost is borne by taxpayers who must offset the subsidy to land-owners. Studies of individual tax incentive programs suggest that they "buy some time" for farmland that may have development potential but have little long-term effect on development patterns unless seen as part of a package of regulatory and spending programs to influence private choices. Development rights donation, on the other hand, is permanent protection.

Spending

In effect, tax incentives represent spending by reducing revenues to govern-ment, but governments have also tried more direct ways to implement the perceived public interest in land use patterns – they buy the land outright, or the discretion necessary to have the desired land use. The United States has a vast system of national, state and local parks, wildlife areas, forests, refuges, wilderness areas and recreation areas owned and managed by government or by non-profit land trusts. Growth is controlled completely in such situations, or at least to the extent supported by agency policy.

Other programs purchase conservation or agricultural easements to permanently limit the ability of the owner to install a land use not consistent with the public interest. The owner retains essentially all use rights except the right to develop. These are voluntary sales by the owners with the idea of compensating the private landowner for the open space and ecological and amenity services provided for the broader public. Suffolk County, on Long Island, New York, implemented the first public program to purchase devel-opment rights to farmland in 1974. Maryland and several New England states began easement programs in the mid 1970s, several states were added in the early 1980s following the National Agricultural Land Study, and Ohio is the most recent addition in 2000. Nineteen states now authorize purchase of agricultural easements. Funds come from local sales or property tax initi-atives, targeted bond sales by the state and some federal dollars through the

Farmland Protection Program of the 1996 Farm Bill (American Farmland Trust 1997; Libby 2002).

Other spending programs encourage private actions that protect water quality and fragile ecosystems near active farms and take the most erosive land out of production. The Environmental Quality Incentive Program (EQIP) is part of the 1996 Farm Bill. It compensates the farmer for actions to reduce runoff. The Conservation Reserve and Wetland Reserve programs essentially lease environmentally important lands (Batie and Ervin 1999).

Future policy directions

Policy to manage growth and protect farm and other open lands is incremental and iterative at best. That is both the strength and frustration of the American political process. New programs are proposed, withdrawn, or just "run up the flag pole" to test the political winds. Stakeholders consider how the particular change in land market rules would affect their interests. Someone must articulate a specific vision of "the public interest" in the form of a concrete proposal before the process can begin. Several specific policy directions are apparent in these debates.

Regional action

The American institution of "home rule" is unique among developed nations. It is a source of strength in keeping authority close to the people, but typically does not handle well those phenomena, such as physical growth, that transcend local boundaries. Land use controls are local prerogatives within state-enabling authority. Transportation is an exception. The Intermodal Surface Transportation Efficiency Act of 1991 (ISTEA) acknowledged that transportation systems must be planned and implemented across localities. Air quality improvement is an important part of the rationale for regional attention to transportation systems by approved regional councils in all states. Because there is a clear link between human health and air quality, people can more readily see the need to override local authority for transportation planning than for other types of land use planning.

A 2000 national poll found that 80 percent of Americans support greater cooperation on growth management matters among local units of government (Smart Growth America 2000). People recognize that the effects of growth do not stop at the border. Only Portland, Oregon has real regional government with an elected council. Minneapolis-St. Paul has the Twin Cities Metropolitan Council appointed by the Governor. Ohio and other states have enabling laws for agreements among local jurisdictions on growth management, including the opportunity for tax sharing to get things done.

There will be more experiments in regional collaboration on growth issues in the years ahead. Some will deal with specific functions like housing and transportation, and others will be more comprehensive. Regionalism makes sense. It will not replace home rule, but will enhance it by enabling people to have greater influence over economic forces that cross local borders.

Directed public spending

It is clear that state spending for water and sewer, road improvement, parks, police and fire protection influences where businesses locate and where people want to live. Maryland's "smart growth initiative" emphasizes the relationship between discretionary spending and the pattern of development (Tregoning 2002). State funds for water and sewer, roads, schools, economic development and other services are directed toward "priority funding areas" and excluded from open land at the fringe. More states will undertake programs of directed spending to guide, rather than always accommodate, development.

More agricultural easement purchase authority, land law reform

Other states will join the 19 currently authorizing purchase of agricultural conservation easements. The authority comes when there are obvious reasons for it, when there is expressed concern for protecting farmland at the rural–urban fringe. Easement purchase programs are difficult to administer and pay for. But they have the intuitive appeal of a "user pays" approach to securing farmland amenities. These programs require consistent rules for defining the public's interest in spending for farmland development rights and establishing priorities among eligible farms. No state will take this on until there is clear benefit to be gained.

There will also be land policy reforms in several states, reducing the anomalies in zoning, annexation and subdivision law that frustrate thoughtful growth management. Subdivision control thresholds of 5, 10 or even 35 acres (Colorado) have unintended impacts on development patterns, but are embedded in the existing politics of land use change. There are other provisions as well, with many unique to a given state. Any set of land use rules shapes the land market; change in those rules will redistribute opportunity and those who lose in that shuffle will object. Policy reform should involve a comprehensive examination of the whole bundle of land use laws to capture the relationships among them and avoid creating more unintended results.

Require that new development pay its way

Development impact fees and exactions are increasingly popular ways to fund infrastructure. They also can improve chances that the needed facilities are available before new development goes in, thus affecting the pattern of development. This "user pays" approach to providing public services is increasingly attractive among local officials, planners, and economists as the fairest approach to distributing the cost of development. Fees have been particularly effective in Florida with its "concurrency rule" that all infrastructure be in place prior to development and in California, but they are being only slowly adopted in the northeastern states (Peddle and Lewis 1996). If installed in conjunction with a comprehensive development plan, these fees also can be versatile policy. Dimond (2000), a critic of interventionist growth management policies, argues that the best approach to guiding growth is to shift the full marginal cost of development infrastructure onto those demanding it, empower all citizens to exercise choice of location, and "get out of the way."

Federal support for local planning

Local governments will retain the initiative for land use planning and control, but a new source of federal funds is urgently needed. There has been little federal support in over 30 years and the basic infrastructure for rural planning needs to be overhauled. Few towns, villages or counties have professional planners. Even technical back-up in regional planning organizations is inadequate. Thoughtful planning is the most important element in improved policy. Planning gets people together to think and talk about their common future, and to collect and analyze relevant data in the process. There is clearly a national stake in effective local planning. We need a new version of Senator Henry Jackson's Land Use Planning and Policy Assistance Act of 1973. An urgent need exists for a member of Congress with leadership and vision who can respond to these issues.

Notes

1 Prominent in the policy history of growth management efforts in the United States is Section 701 of the 1954 Housing and Community Development Act. Through this program, $100 million were allocated each year to local governments for the development of comprehensive plans. Region-wide coordination of local planning was facilitated by the review procedures as part of OMB Budget Circular A-95 in the mid 1970s. Neither continued beyond 1980, and many local plans completed with 701 funds have never been updated. Washington Senator Henry Jackson proposed Federal funding for state comprehensive plans in 1973, but fear of "top down" planning killed the idea. Air and water quality concerns have driven interest in land use planning in more recent years, with regional coordination of local transportation plans to limit air quality problems and "208 plans" dealing with effects of land use on water quality. Farmland protection has been largely state and local, with action beginning in Maryland in 1956 with preferential assessment of farmland, exclusive agricultural zoning in California, Pennsylvania and Washington in the 1970s (now 21 states). Federal investment in farmland policy came in the form of a National Agricultural Land Study released in 1981, supported by USDA and the President's Council on Environmental Quality (Lehman 1995; Libby 2002). Housing and Urban Development (HUD) was the driving federal agency for early growth management, with USDA the primary federal presence for farmland policy questions. State agency leadership is similarly divided between growth management and farmland policy.
2 The data collection method changed with the 1982 NRI. Thus, time series comparisons are valid only for 1982, 1987, 1992 and 1997.

3 Developed land in the NRI includes large blocks of residential, commercial and industrial areas, prisons and other institutions, airports and other transportation facilities, as well as tracts of less than 10 acres surrounded by urban areas. It does not include the scattered residences on 5-acre, 10-acre or even larger parcels, but will capture most rural subdivisions.

4 In 1995, 84 percent of trips in the US were by private car and 3 percent by public transport, as compared to 64 percent and 14 percent, respectively, in England, and 36 percent and 11 percent in Sweden. Far more trips were on foot in Sweden (39 percent), France (30 percent) and England (12 percent) than in the US. This is explained in part by the more dispersed development patterns in the US (Lincoln Institute of Land Policy 1995: 7).

5 *Village of Euclid v. Ambler Realty Co.*, 272 US 365 (1926). Ambler Realty Company had charged that the very idea of zoning goes beyond the police power, and thus constitutes an unconstitutional "taking" of private property without compensation. The Supreme Court found that the stated purpose of zoning, to separate incompatible uses, did in fact further protection of the health, safety and general welfare of village residents. The case was made in terms of separating industrial and commercial activities from residential. The court further established a "presumption of validity" for zoning as a local legislative action. The burden was on the complainants to demonstrate lack of public purpose (Babcock and Bosselman 1975; Reiner 1975).

6 Ohio zoning enabling law for counties and townships omits the "general welfare" rationale, making true exclusive agricultural zoning virtually impossible.

7 Success in shifting the impact fee will depend on the elasticity of demand for housing. If the prospective homeowner has good substitutes for the home with the added fee, the developer will have to absorb the cost.

3 Land use problems

A European perspective

Nick D. Hanley and Fiona Watson

Introduction

In this short chapter, we intend to do three things. First, we will take a historical perspective of land use problems. Second, we will identify some causal factors of land use problems that reach back through recent history. Third, we will outline some recent solutions that have been put forward. Europe is large and very diverse in its land use history and problems. We will for the most part use the United Kingdom (UK) as an example of the European experience, rather than try to be geographically comprehensive. We will also focus almost exclusively on rural land use issues.

A short history of land use conflicts

The purpose of this section is to show that, over time, land use concerns and priorities change, molded as they are by changing cultural attitudes and market forces. We look at four snapshots – the 1750s, the 1850s, the 1950s, and the 1980s – before moving to the present day.

The 1750s

The agricultural revolution was in full swing in the UK in the 1750s. In general terms, land use was transforming from subsistence farming to commercial production, as science and the Enlightenment brought their focus to bear on agriculture. New improvement practices such as liming and planting clover to fix nitrogen were beginning to be taken up. In Scotland, large swaths of the rural population were displaced, and single-tenant farms were developed. In the uplands, people were increasingly replaced by sheep (Watson 2001).

The 1850s

In 1851, 54 percent of the population lived in towns and cities, with the countryside increasingly being seen as a food factory to fuel this industrialization. The rest of Europe followed a similar trend but lagged behind Britain at this point (Simmons 2001). The spread of railways enabled the beginnings of recreational use of the countryside, and coincided with the Romantic Movement's new spin on the rural idyll, exemplified in the writings of Wordsworth (1822) and Scott (1819, 2000), now that most people did not earn their livelihood by working on the land. Industrial and trading wealth allowed the development of large sporting estates, particularly in the north, with ecosystems being redesigned to support deer and grouse populations. Conflicts started to emerge over access to the countryside as a recreational resource for all. The "Battle of Glen Tilt," led by Edinburgh University professors, was one example (Smout 2000).

The 1950s

In the post-war era state intervention increased in most aspects of rural activity, as exemplified by the drive to repopulate more remote areas through forestry employment schemes. The introduction of National Parks legislation and the development of land use planning control mechanisms occurred, but neither of these had much protective impact on wildlife and landscape as it related to farming systems, which still occupied most of the rural environment. Policy arguments began over new forestry plantations in these National Parks and other scenic areas (especially the Lake District, which had become an icon of an idealized rural landscape, thanks to Wordsworth and his likeminded contemporaries), and over new roads (such as that which went through Glencoe in the Scottish Highlands). Agricultural production systems responded to the introduction of price supports (initially, as deficiency payments), setting into motion a process that would lead to conflicts between farming and wildlife interests later on. Arguments over the adverse environmental impacts of state-subsidized agricultural modernization on Exmoor led to the development of the "voluntary principle," which characterized almost all UK agri-environmental policy in years to come. Increasing challenges emerged throughout society to traditional sources of power and influence. The influence of the landowning class, through its close links with the Conservative Party, was affected by the success of the Labour Party in forming governments and pushing through agendas shaped by the demands of an urban, industrial workforce.

The 1980s

Hard evidence now emerged about the deleterious impact of modern farming systems and production levels on wildlife and landscape (Nature Conservancy Council 1983). Environmentalism as a political lobby began to grow. Farm incomes, which had boomed following entry into the European Union (EU) in the early 1970s, started a long-term decline. In 1985, the UK government agreed for the first time that agricultural ministry budgets could and should be used to pay for environmental outputs. Arguments arose about whether agricultural support was indeed the best way to safeguard employment in the countryside (e.g. the conflict between forestry and farming in the North Pennines).

2001

In 2001, the countryside, and agriculture in particular, found itself in a very different position than it had even 20 years ago. The foot-and-mouth disease outbreak in 2001, although labeled as a crisis for farming, showed the public and policy makers that the countryside is now more valuable for non-farming outputs such as tourism and recreation than for farming itself. This impression was borne out by the data: UK agriculture's Gross Value Added (GVA) in 2000 was around £6.6 billion, yet much of this reflects public subsidy.[1] In contrast, UK countryside tourism has a largely unsubsidized GVA of £9.3 billion. Farming could be seen as impeding the countryside from generating income from tourism. Along with the BSE disaster, foot-and-mouth disease also focused people's attention onto the nature of modern farming systems, which are increasingly questioned both in animal welfare and food safety terms. The idea that sustaining farm/agricultural system incomes is no longer necessary to sustain rural populations has been encouraged by the observation that although farm incomes continued to fall, rural employment and rural populations continued to rise (Keeble and Tyler 1995; Wakeford 2001).

The recent past has also provided evidence of an apparent loss and fragmentation of the traditionally strong political lobbying position of the farming industry. The Ministry of Agriculture itself disappeared in 2000, swallowed up in a new Department of the Environment, Food and Rural Affairs. A new food safety authority was launched, breaking the traditional governmental alliance between food producers and regulators. The state-subsidized farm advisory service was merged into a new Rural Development Service. At the EU level, Agenda 2000 saw agricultural policy placed in the wider framework of the Rural Development Regulation. In the UK, apparent political disenfranchisement of some groups in the countryside led to the emergence of a new lobby, the Countryside Alliance, an ill-at-ease coalition of diverse interests ranging from fuel prices to fox hunting and the disappearance of rural post offices.

Finally, the new century has seen the re-emergence of two sources of conflict with a long history. The first of these is access to the countryside for recreation. In England, the government recently passed a new act[2] allowing *de facto* access to "open" hill-land and moorland. In Scotland, arguments sprang up between farmers and other landowners and the access lobby (despite the fact that a voluntary accord had been signed by the two groups), over equivalent legislation. The Land Reform Act, which came into force in Scotland in 2003, succeeded in transferring *de facto* access rights to private land into law.

Bound up in this Scottish legislation is an attempt at the resolution of the second re-emerging issue – land reform. Concern has long been expressed about the way in which large areas of the Highlands can be sold on the open market, with local people having no say in the process and therefore in who would become their new landlord (Wightman 1996). Discussions about the Land Reform Bill in Scotland included the suggestion that locals be offered the first right to buy at a valuation assessed by the government, a price lower than that which could be obtained from the market. Needless to say, this was opposed by the landowning lobby, opposition that has continued since a limited right to buy was incorporated into the new Act. This idea was inspired by three recent cases in which large estates were "rescued" for locals from new private owners by charitable appeals (on the islands of Eigg and Gigha, and in the NW Highlands in Assynt). When it was eventually passed, the Act legislated for the right to limited community buy-outs of private estates, and the transfer of crofting land[3] into private hands under certain conditions.

Driving forces

Summing up the previous section, we may say that land use conflicts in the UK have historically centered on:

- conflicts between land use and environmental quality;
- conflicts between those who own land and those wishing to use it;
- political conflicts over the nature and extent of state support for agriculture; and
- conflicts about who owns land.

But what are the underlying factors behind these issues? Here we briefly note three such influences: market failure, policy failure and technical change.

With regard to market failure, it is well known that alternative land uses produce a wide range of external benefits and costs for which private agents are not rewarded or penalized by the market, and which affect the supply of rural public goods. Farming systems that destroy wildlife habitats, housing developments that reduce recreational access to the countryside, and forestry's impacts on water quality are familiar examples. Rural land uses also generate external benefits, however, such as the maintenance of "traditional" farm landscapes that are highly valued for their conservation and landscape interest. Unless governments intervene using regulation, economic incentives or voluntary mechanisms, the usual market failures will persist, with resultant conflicts and losses in social welfare.

Linked to market failure is policy failure. The Common Agricultural Policy is often held up as an example of one such failure (Bowers and Cheshire 1983). Production-related support payments increased output, yet also increased the incentives for farmers to change production systems in a way that increased environmental damages per unit of output. Despite this, employment in agriculture continued to fall, farm incomes went into long-term decline (after the early 1970s, with a few exceptions), and support payments became capitalized into land prices. This all happened at considerable cost to the consumer and taxpayer, which now stands at about £2 billion per year to the UK, or around £10 per week for a family of four (Muriel 2001).

The third underlying cause is technical change. Changes in how farmers farmed were foremost in popular explanations of why farming was coming increasingly into conflict with wildlife and landscape quality in the 1970s and 1980s, as seen for example in the writings of Bowers and Cheshire (1983) and Shoard (1980). Changes in pest and disease control options, changes in farm machinery and, more recently, the prospective widespread introduction of GM crops, have all been offered as examples of technological advances essentially at odds with maintaining natural capital. Other writers have pointed to the impact of technological change on social/community capital in rural areas (Hodge 2001; Pretty 1998). However, environmental historians point out that even bigger changes in rural technology have occurred in the past, bringing about huge changes in the appearance, biodiversity and economic systems operating in the countryside. The enclosure movement in England and the introduction of new sheep breeds to Scotland are good examples of past technology-driven shocks (Lenman 2001).

Current policy initiatives as partial solutions

Agriculture policy within the UK and European Union has clearly been a major driver of land use conflicts in the recent past, and reform of the Common Agricultural Policy (CAP) is often suggested as the most important factor in resolving these conflicts, especially those between farming and wildlife and landscape. Major recent and on-going EU-wide policy changes designed to reduce the extent of policy failure have been initiatives to de-link income support from production. One initiative is the increased emphasis on area payments rather than guaranteed prices (for example, under the Arable Areas Payments Scheme). Cross-compliance requirements that place environmental "due care" standards on upland livestock producers have also recently been put forward. In the UK, policy interventions are also being focused increasingly on the processing and marketing of food products in rural areas,[4] with the aim of increasing rural value-added. Advisory efforts are being targeted toward farm business diversification.

With regard to market failure and the externalities generated by agriculture, agri-environmental policy continues to become more influential. Agri-environmental schemes such as Environmentally Sensitive Areas and the Rural Stewardship Scheme are based on the voluntary or "provider gets" principle, whereby farmers may opt for per acre payments that reward improved environmental performance, such as in maintaining hedges or in managing hay meadows. Recent reforms to agri-environmental policy include a greater degree of spatial targeting: for instance, the Countryside Stewardship Scheme offers payments to farmers in specific areas to safeguard and extend the habitats of birds such as the stone curlew and cirl bunting.

Policy is thus designed to replace missing market rewards for the generation of environmental goods from agriculture. This implicit allocation of property rights to the farmer derives partly from the recognition that many valued habitats and species[5] in the UK (such as heathland and heather moorland) are highly artificial in that they depend on particular management regimes being in place that may be less profitable for the farmer than less nature-friendly alternatives. Total spending on agri-environmental schemes had risen to nearly £200 million per year by 2000, from about £85 million in 1996 when agri-environmental policy had just been initiated; this still represents only 6.5 percent of total public spending on agriculture. Research by economists (as summarized, for example, in Hanley *et al.* 1999) has shown that UK agri-environmental policy almost always generates benefits that are far in excess of costs.

However, the reform of the CAP alone will not solve all rural land use conflicts in the UK. Looking more widely, three recent initiatives are worthy of mention. First, attention in the EU has recently focused on conflicts over water management and use. The EU's Water Framework Directive, which came into force in 2001, will institute a system of compulsory catchment management planning at the river basin level throughout the EU. This will establish for the first time in the UK a framework for the integrated assessment and control of conflicting demands on water resources (e.g., for irrigation, for drinking water supply, for hydro power and for forestry). Implementing the Directive will also involve the use of economics to assess the costs and benefits of alternative water uses (and therefore land uses) as part of river basin management planning, and to establish whether lower objectives than the EU-wide default of "good ecological status" should be established for particular water bodies. Finally, full-cost pricing of water uses, which includes environmental costs, is provided for in the wording of the Directive.

Second, the UK government has sought to address the issue of development pressure on greenfield sites through the use of economic incentives to direct development onto brownfield sites. As a first step in this direction, work is underway to quantify in monetary terms the environmental externalities of developments on greenfield sites. If previous government policy on externalities is any guide, these estimates will subsequently form the basis of an environmental levy on greenfield site development.

Finally, rural development policy has now outgrown its agricultural straitjacket. As noted earlier, this is perhaps most obvious in the re-naming of the Ministry of Agriculture as the Department for Environment, Food and Rural Affairs. The recently launched Rural White Paper, and the English Rural Development Programme,[6] are noticeable for their non-agricultural focus, headlining instead measures such as regeneration programs for rural market towns, a rural tourism strategy, and a rural enterprise scheme. Agri-environmental schemes, and a wider suite of environmental measures (such as funding for national parks) are being brought into rural development programs in an effort toward "joined-up government."

Conclusion

This chapter has provided insights into both the nature of rural land use conflicts in the UK and some recent policy initiatives that address these conflicts. Perhaps the main focus of the recent past, namely the conflict between farming and wildlife and landscape, is being replaced by a broader debate about who owns the countryside, who should have a say in its future, and what we want from it. Farming is increasingly being seen as only one part, and a part of diminishing importance at that, in this debate. Certainly, the scope of rural development policy has broadened and become somewhat more integrated. Technological change has brought about a shift in the composition of rural populations and how they earn their living. Policy attention is increasingly focused on rural disadvantage/deprivation as a more general issue than declining farm incomes. This shift implies a different public policy focus, on issues such as public transport, training opportunities and rural job centers, than on guaranteed prices for wheat or per head payments for livestock.

Notes

1 One pound is worth approximately $1.80 (the editors).
2 The Countryside and Rights of Way Act (2000). See www.countryside.gov.uk/access.
3 Crofting is a form of small-scale farming operated in certain parts of the Highlands. Crofters do not own their land; it is owned either by the state or private landowners. The latter can pass tenancy rights on from parents to children. Typically, agricultural incomes from the croft must be supplemented with income from other sources. Crofters were given their particular tenurial rights under the 1886 Crofters' Holdings (Scotland) Act (see Cameron 1996).
4 This is specifically provided for in the Rural White Paper, *Our Countryside: The Future – A Fair Deal for Rural England* (Department of the Environment, Food and Rural Affairs 2000).
5 For example, Bignal and McCracken (1996) showed that the presence of ten European Union protected birds species depended on the continuation of low-intensity farming regimes.
6 Running from 2000 to 2006 with funds of £1.6 billion.

4 Employment growth, population growth and electronic technologies as determinants of land use

Charles Barnard[1]

Introduction

Spatial growth of cities and the accompanying pattern of development at their edges and in adjacent rural areas continue to generate debate concerning the costs of urban "sprawl" (Burgess and Bier 1998; Heimlich and Anderson 2001; Raup 1975; Vesterby and Heimlich 1991). During the 1970s, concern was most often expressed in terms of reduced national food production capacity associated with conversion of cropland to urban-related uses (Dunford 1983; Fischel 1982). More recently, concerns related to conversion of cropland to urban-related uses are expressed in the context of rural/urban conflicts, reduced quality and quantity of local food production, and losses of "rural amenities" (Hellerstein *et al.* 2002).

With the US population forecast to increase by as much as 93 percent over the next 50 years,[2] debate concerning land use on the rural/urban fringe, where city growth is concentrated, is likely to increase. Urban and built-up land[3] constitute only about 4 percent of the US land base, but the amount of land subject to urban influence (and hence subject to potential land use conflicts) is much larger. Barnard (2001), using population density data and geographers' gravity models, estimates that urban-influenced land accounts for as much as 17 percent of US farmland.

In the short term, land use problems and conflicts arising from urbanization occur at the rural/urban interface. Beyond the city edge, the interspersion of urban-related activities with farm production activities both fuels the conflict and sharpens the sprawl debate (Gardner 1994; Heimlich and Barnard 1992; Hellerstein *et al.* 2002; Larson *et al.* 2001; Lockeretz 1989; Lopez *et al.* 1988; Lopez *et al.* 1994). In the longer term, the urban spatial structure that evolves as a fringe is incorporated into a city ultimately determines the land area converted to urban use and generates the broader issues associated with tradeoffs between urban and rural land uses.

The land use conflicts and problems that underlie the sprawl debate ultimately stem from the structure and size of growing cities that are, in part, determined by population growth. Population growth translates into urban spatial growth through consumer residential choices and business employment/location decisions, both of which are influenced by technologies embedded in transportation, building construction, and communications infrastructure. Technological change has always been an omnipresent force underlying the evolving spatial structure and size of cities. But, beginning perhaps with the 1990s, an increased potential has arisen for innovations in digital microelectronics (particularly as manifested through new communications and information processing technologies) to alter urban structure and rural/urban land use tradeoffs.

The remainder of this chapter begins with a discussion of recent trends in land use beyond city edges. The forces powering those changes are examined first with respect to consumer residential choices and then with respect to business employment and location decisions. This section draws on Heimlich and Anderson (2001), who authored an Economic Research Service (ERS) report entitled "Development at the Urban Fringe and Beyond: Impacts on Agriculture and Rural Land." The next section examines the theoretical role of technology in shaping city structure, with special attention paid to evidence of the emerging impact of digital electronic technologies. The section highlights implications of these technologies for city structure, and thus the spatial extent of urban areas. A final section suggests avenues for further land use research.

Trends in the spatial growth of cities

The United States continues to experience a high rate of population growth, from 150 million to 281 million between 1950 and 2000. In its middle series projections, the Bureau of the Census predicts a population increase of more than 40 percent by 2050 – from 283 million in 2003 to 404 million in 2050 (US Census Bureau 2003). Contributing to high future population growth are longer life expectancy and high immigration levels.

But, while population growth may be the primary force, it is not the only force powering land use changes at the urban fringe, as is abundantly clear when one observes that changes in urban land consumption far exceed changes in population. Given that US population growth is essentially inevitable, cities (which now hold roughly 80 percent of the US population) can grow either upward or outward. Recent trends are decidedly outward. For instance, while the population of St Louis increased by 35 percent between 1950 and 1990, the city's area increased by 355 percent. Chicago's population increased 4 percent between 1990 and 2000, but over the same period, area devoted to housing increased 46 percent and commercial area increased 74 percent. In Ohio, population grew by 13 percent between 1960 and 1990, but urban land area increased by 64 percent (Ohio Farmland Preservation Task Force 1997 as cited in Burgess and Bier 1998: 3). In the United States as a whole, land consumption exceeded population growth between 1970 and 1990. Specifically, the amount of developed land in metro areas grew by 74 percent, while the population grew by 31 percent (US General Accounting Office 2000b).

The accelerated growth in suburban and exurban areas is, ironically, the result of trends toward both population concentration and deconcentration. The concentration of population from rural areas into ever-expanding urban centers was the most important development in population distribution in the first half of the twentieth century. Urbanized areas, including the central cities and adjacent, densely settled surrounding territory have grown in number from 106 to 465 since 1950, nearly quintupling in area to 47 million acres in 2000 (2 percent of total land area).[4]

But, in concordance with the movement of rural people into metro areas, the dense populations of central cities emptied out into the surrounding countryside. Population density in urbanized areas has dropped by half, from 8.4 to 4.2 people per acre over the last 60 years (US Census Bureau 2000; US Department of Housing and Urban Development 2000). "In the 1950s, 57 percent of MSA residents and 70 percent of MSA jobs were located in central cities; in 1960, the percentages were 49 and 63; in 1970, they were 43 and 55; in 1980, they were 40 and 50; in 1990, they were about 37 and 45" (Mieszkowski and Mills 1993: 135).

Most Americans, roughly 60 percent, now live in suburban areas. In the 25 largest metro areas, 75 percent of people live in suburban areas. In addition, the highest rates of population growth are occurring at the edges of metro areas (Figure 4.1). Population growth at metro fringes increased from 7.1 percent during 1982–1987 to over 10 percent during 1992–1997, while growth in metropolitan cores actually dropped. During the 1990s, more than 80 percent of new homes were built in suburbs (Hirschhorn 2000: 5).

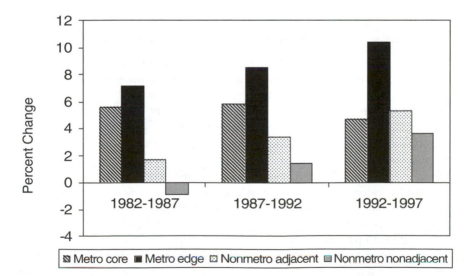

Figure 4.1 US population change, 1982–1997 (source: US Census Bureau, various years).

Links among population growth, employment growth, and land consumption

The forces that have driven spatial growth are quite well known and understood (Brueckner 2000). The primary driver is population growth but dynamic changes in household formation, consumer housing preferences, and business location combined to influence urban form and density and, thus, the amount of land consumed for urban-related purposes (Heimlich and Anderson 2001). Location choices, in turn, are affected by changes in transportation and communications technology. The macro economy, through its effects on employment, income, wealth, and interest rates, continues to add a cyclical influence. One might also point to the effects of public infrastructure investment, especially that related to transportation, which reduces the cost of commuting from outlying areas.

For ease of exposition, population growth (residential location) and employment (business location) are often discussed separately. But, city structure appears to be jointly determined by both residential and business location decisions. Movement of jobs to suburban locations, for instance, appears to be partly an effect and partly a cause of population growth in suburban locations (Thurston and Yezer 1994). People and jobs often move together, with people moving to areas where jobs are available and employers moving to areas with a large and skilled labor force. Increasingly, this means people and jobs move to outlying suburban areas. Sometimes, the question is cast as "whether jobs follow people or people follow jobs" (Kim 2002: 4). Although the literature has not reached a consensus, both of these relationships probably hold to some extent.

Forces translating population growth into urban land consumption

Population growth and relocation are not the sole determinants of urban land consumption. Perhaps as important a force is declining household size (Figure 4.2). Because the number of persons living in each housing unit has declined, more houses are now needed for the same number of people. Figure 4.2 shows that average household size dropped from 3.7 persons in 1950 to 2.6 in 2000, creating about 1 million new households each year. For the US, that translates into the same number of people now requiring 30 percent more housing than in 1950. In Maryland, for instance, population grew by 9 percent between 1990 and 1996, while the number of households increased by 19 percent (Hirschhorn 2000). Rhode Island provides another example: population grew by 4 percent from 1980 to 1997, while housing units increased by 15 percent (Hirschhorn 2000).

The amount of land ultimately consumed for developed uses is also determined by lot size. American consumers continue to demand larger residential space (including the housing lot) and more of the amenities associated with open space. Such attributes are more widely and cheaply available in subur-

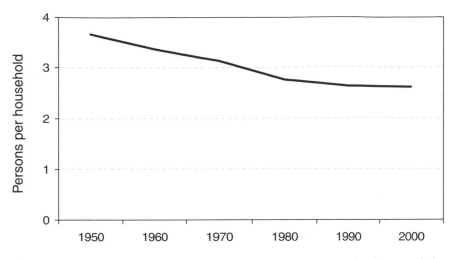

Figure 4.2 Average household size, 1950–2000 (source: Statistical Abstract of the United States, 2000).

ban and exurban locations. In addition, it may be that technological advances in information, communications, and transportation have "enabled" these demands to be satisfied over a much larger spatial area.

Growth in large lot development has been accelerating since the 1970s, and much of this has occurred in nonmetro rural areas beyond the urban fringe (Figure 4.3). A relatively small number of dwellings on the largest lot sizes account for vast acreage. Lot size itself seems to be strongly related to cycles in the general economy, which strongly influence income and wealth. The cyclical nature of annual additions to housing area is particularly evident for the largest lot category.

Only about 16 percent of the acreage used by houses built between 1994 and 1997 is located in existing urban areas within Metropolitan Statistical Areas (MSAs) defined by the Bureau of the Census. Much of this development is at relatively high densities, with the number of houses ranging from one to six per acre. Heimlich and Anderson (2001: 20) refer to this as "the continuing accretion of urban development at the fringes of existing urban areas in rural parts of metropolitan counties." Urbanized areas and urban places increased by about one million acres per year between 1960 and 1990.

Americans apparently hold strong preferences for the set of amenities associated with suburban and exurban living (Mieszkowski and Mills 1993: 136). Encouraged by relatively lower land prices in the suburbs, consumers have made consumption of large amounts of living space a key element of the American lifestyle. A large and increasing component of urban land consumption is accounted for by the proliferation of isolated, large-lot housing developments (one acre or more), which are generally occurring well beyond

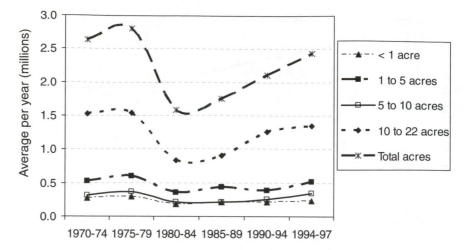

Figure 4.3 Gross annual additions to housing area, by lot size, 1970–1997 (source: ERS analysis of American Housing Survey, 1997 data).

Note
Data in chart are annualized.

the urban fringe in adjacent nonmetro counties. Nearly 80 percent of acreage used for recently constructed housing, about 2 million acres, is land outside urban areas or in nonmetro areas. Ninety-four percent of that land is in lots of one acre or more (Heimlich and Anderson 2001: 2). Exurban development often consists of scattered single houses on very large parcels (10 acres or more). Fifty-seven percent of the acreage used for recently constructed housing is on lots larger than 10 acres (Heimlich and Anderson 2001: 2).

Rural large-lot development is not a new phenomenon; it has dominated the development process during much of the time since World War II. But, over recent decades, an increasing fraction of land area used for single-family housing has been for the largest lot sizes (Hirschhorn 2000). According to data from the American Housing Survey, large-lot housing, as a proportion of new construction in rural areas, rose from 40 percent in 1980–1993 to 45 percent in 1994–1997 (US Census Bureau, US Department of Commerce and US Department of Housing and Urban Development 1999). Since 1994, the largest lot size category measured (10–22 acres) accounted for 55 percent of growth in area used for housing, and lots larger than one acre accounted for over 90 percent of land for new housing.

Other surveys also provide a clear indication that Americans have strong preferences for living in suburbs or outside metro areas. Seventy percent of those responding to Fannie Mae's 1997 National Housing Survey said they would prefer to live in a suburb near a large city, in a small town not near a city, or in a rural area (Federal Home Mortgage Association 1997). Only 9 percent of the respondents said they would prefer to live in a large city.

Furthermore, when asked where they would consider buying a home, 70 percent said they would consider buying a home in a suburb near a large city; only 39 percent said they would consider buying a home in the major city closest to their current residence. Preferences for buying single-family detached housing were stronger during the mid 1990s than a decade earlier. Surveys also provide evidence of US consumer preference for single-family detached houses surrounded on all sides by yards (Federal Home Mortgage Association 1996). In terms of buying preferences, single-family detached housing was more popular during the mid 1990s than it was a decade earlier.

Forces translating employment growth into urban land consumption

The pattern of business location and employment is also an important dimension of urban form, and thus has implications for land use change and consumption at the urban periphery. The traditional perception of a city is that of a central core of economic activity surrounded by "bedroom" suburbs from which residents commute to the core.[5] The urban form that inspired this simplified image of a city, if it ever existed, is gone. In the words of the US Congress, Office of Technology Assessment (1995: 99), "the historic dominance of the central city is giving way to a much more dispersed pattern of growth as economic activity spreads unevenly throughout the metropolitan areas in other nodes and centers."

In today's cities, economic activity is widely dispersed across the metropolitan area, with a larger percentage of employment located in suburban and exurban areas than in the central city. Businesses have relocated in large numbers to the suburbs and other outlying locations, revitalizing original bedroom suburbs into "edge cities" that are complete urban areas with major employment and retail centers. The core has become just another competitive node in a polycentric pattern of business activity.

According to a recent US Department of Housing and Urban Development (2000) report, 57 percent of metro jobs were located in the suburbs in 1997. Suburban jobs increased almost 18 percent between 1992 and 1997. In some cities, 85–90 percent of total metropolitan-area jobs are located in the suburbs (Hirschhorn 2000). Suburban areas now contain about 60 percent of office space nationwide, reflecting a 25 percent increase in suburban office space since 1970 (Hirschhorn 2000: 7). Gordon and Richardson (1995), upon comparing several sets of data, concluded that the trend toward decentralization of employment continues. They found that most job growth is still occurring in the outer suburbs, regardless of economic sector.

During the 1980s in particular, central business district (CBD) job growth was negligible or negative. Together, CBDs in the top ten cities (New York, Los Angeles, Chicago, Philadelphia, Dallas, San Francisco, Boston, Detroit, Washington and Houston) grew at barely over 1 percent per year in the period 1980–1986. But, job decentralization was uneven, with not all central-city economies losing jobs and the precise effect varying by sector.

The US Department of Housing and Urban Development (2000) reported that overall suburban job growth was approximately twice as high as that of cities (17.8 vs. 8.5 percent), with wholesale trade increasing six times faster in suburbs than in cities. Manufacturing jobs rose in suburbs by 7 percent and now account for 18 percent of all suburban employment. Manufacturing declined in cities, where it had been a major source of economic activity, with the gain going to suburbs. Virtually all central cities lost blue-collar jobs. Wholesaling, retailing, construction, and consumer services, which were once predominantly urban, are now primarily suburban. Service sector jobs in cities grew by 15.9 percent during this period compared with 26.4 percent in suburbs. Central cities, however, became more specialized in finance, advertising, accounting, law and other advanced services. These services rely more heavily on face-to-face contact and benefit from proximity to each other and to other industries.

The US Department of Housing and Urban Development (HUD) (2000) report concluded that much of the overall job growth during the 1990s was associated with so-called "New Economy" or high-technology industries in larger metro areas in all parts of the country. The HUD analysis was based on changes in occupational titles between 1992 and 1998. High-tech jobs were defined as including technology-intensive occupations in traditional industries as well as jobs in industries that are commonly identified as high-tech, including computer software development, biotechnology, and microelectronics. High-tech jobs, including the occupational classifications of telecommunications, science, and research and technology, accounted for 9.3 percent of job growth in the suburbs, and increased at twice the rate of 1992–1997 overall job growth in the suburbs. Most central cities gained high-tech jobs, but high-tech jobs in suburbs, on average, grew faster. A survey of mayors suggested that in most regions of the country high-tech jobs were growing 20–60 percent faster in suburbs than in cities (US Conference of Mayors and the National Association of Counties 2000). High technology, as an industry, also appears to exhibit a bias toward suburban and exurban locations, strengthening the overall trend in job growth at the urban fringe that characterized much of the last 50 years (US Department of Housing and Urban Development 2000) (see Figure 4.4).

Silicon Valley in California, Route 128 in Boston, and the Dulles Corridor near Washington, DC illustrate the tendency of "New Economy" firms to co-locate in corridors outside major cities (US Conference of Mayors and the National Association of Counties 2000). More recent high-tech corridors have begun to develop in rural areas even farther from central business districts. Loudoun County, Virginia, California's Central Valley, and southeastern New Hampshire are examples of such outlying employment-growth centers.

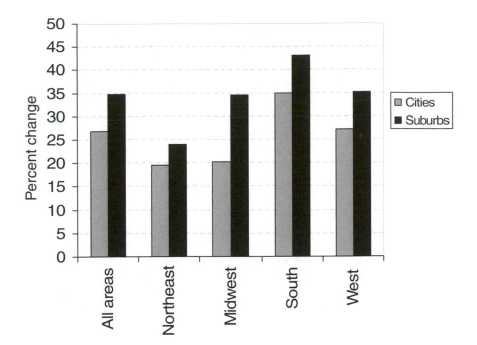

Figure 4.4 Proportion of high-tech jobs in cities and suburbs, 1992–1997 (source: US Department of Housing and Urban Development, 2000).

Rationale underlying suburbanization of population and employment

Urban spatial structure is the result of complex tradeoffs between the inevitable congestion costs of high-density settlements and the potential agglomeration benefits associated with that high-density (Gordon and Richardson 1997). High-rise, high-density buildings at the city core are expensive to construct and maintain, creating economic incentives for residents and businesses to disperse outward from the city center. Alternatively, firms located at the city center realize economic benefits through the increased accessibility, communications, and ease of face-to-face interaction that derives from locating in spatial concentration with other firms and workers (Anas *et al.* 1998). The economic benefits available at the urban core, often referred to as agglomeration economies, are supplemented by social and cultural advantages. Businesses and consumers seek conveniences, amenities, institutions, opportunities for learning and information, and infrastructure that can be found predominantly in metro areas (US Congress, Office of Technology Assessment 1995: 95).

The countervailing economic forces associated with location at the urban core exert pressures for either dispersion or agglomeration of residential and business locations. These forces thus have implications for the radial extent of cities, the interface between agricultural and urban land uses, and the amount of land subject to urban influence. Greater dispersion implies lower density and more land used for urban purposes while greater agglomeration implies greater density and less land used for urban purposes. At least until recently, the centrifugal forces that push cities toward a more dispersed urban form have been sufficiently countered by the benefits of agglomeration to ensure the continued existence of high–density urban cores.

Empirical studies of urban spatial structure are often cast in terms of the monocentric city model developed by Alonso (1960) and refined by Muth (1969), Mills (1972), and many others including Smith (1997). Fundamental to the monocentric city model is the idea that the "friction" costs of moving goods, people and information determine city form. The term friction costs refers to transport costs required to overcome the unavoidable effects of gravity and friction as people and physical goods are moved horizontally or vertically through space. For example, the costs of moving goods (or commuters, for that matter) to the central business district (CBD) increases as distance from the CBD increases. These friction costs countervail the agglomeration benefits and create incentives for residents and firms to locate away from the urban core.

Although it is based on limiting assumptions, the monocentric city model predicts that population density declines monotonically with distance from a (CBD).[6] Central to such models is the use of population and employment density gradients to empirically represent urban spatial structure (see Figure 4.5). Since density is defined as population (or employment) per unit of area or jobs per unit of area, density ultimately translates population and employment into the land area covered by cities. A lower population or employment density implies that more land is consumed for a given population or level of employment.

The role of technological change

Innovations in technology that reduce the costs of transportation and other costs of friction are known to modify the agglomeration/dispersion tradeoff. The effect of innovations that reduce horizontal friction is to flatten the rent and density gradients. The flattened gradients, in turn, reflect extension of urban development farther and farther from the CBD as urban spatial area consumes more land per unit of population or employment.

Flattening of density gradients is a worldwide phenomenon that has been underway over a long period of time (Gordon and Richardson 1997; Mieszkowski and Mills 1993). For centuries, rent and density gradients have become flatter, with the effect of extending the radius of cities farther from the CBD and increasing the land area of cities. Beginning with the development of streetcars and then the automobile, the trend in urban spatial growth

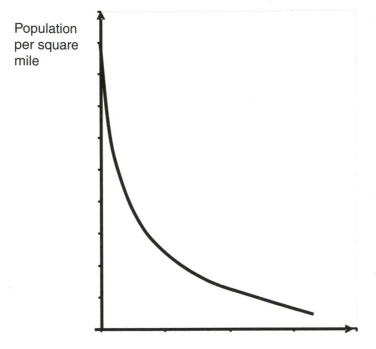

Population per square mile

Distance from CBD

Figure 4.5 Relationship of density to distance from CBD.

has accelerated toward a more spatially dispersed economy. According to Dyckman (1976), the effective radius of US cities in 1890 was approximately 2 miles, being limited largely by the necessity of primarily pedestrian access. By the 1970s, following development of public transit, widespread automobile ownership, and construction of urban freeway systems, the city edge was 20–24 miles beyond the CBD. During the 1980s, movement of a large number of jobs to what was the outer edge of the suburban ring had the effect of increasing the radius by an additional 50 miles.

New during the 1990s was the increased potential for innovations in digital microelectronics to alter urban structure and the rural/urban land use tradeoffs. Innovations in microelectronics directly altered computers, telecommunications, information, and transportation technologies, and indirectly reshaped America's cities (Lincoln Institute of Land Policy 2001). Society is currently experiencing the effects of widespread adoption of cellular (wireless) phones, pagers, facsimile machines, the Internet, and widely affordable 4-wheel drive and other all-terrain vehicles.[7] Yet, even more sophisticated microelectronic technologies are already being adopted by consumers, including high-definition digital images, high-speed Internet connections, and wireless computing and data transfer. All of these have the potential (at least conceptually) to further reduce the importance of urban spatial proximity, which has been a major reason for the existence of metro agglomerations.

These technological changes lower commuting and communications costs, and thus affect the jointly determined location decisions of households and firms. Yet, we know little definitively about the eventual effect of these technologies on land use, and whether these technologies are directly associated with apparent acceleration in the rate at which rural land is being converted to, and influenced by, urban-related uses. To a large extent, the counteracting forces of dispersion and agglomeration ultimately determine the land use effects of these technological innovations. Countering the centrifugal forces associated with lower commuting and communications costs are the opposing centripetal forces of agglomeration, whose dynamics are also changed in unpredictable ways by digital electronic innovation.

These technologies have changed the economics of business, residential, and recreation-related location decisions. Today, businesses and people are no longer tied economically and functionally to the cores of major metro areas. Increasingly, information and communications technologies allow social and commercial activities to occur much farther apart physically without loss of function. The result is a greatly expanded set of locational choices for both households and firms. Access to the CBD is no longer measured in terms of geographical distance. In the extreme case, perhaps as exemplified by tele-work, geographical distance might be irrelevant. Drucker (1989: 38) suggests that, in the near future, "office work, rather than office workers will do the traveling." Significant movement of data entry, software development and "help" centers to India exemplifies this trend. In addition, many activities that once required physical proximity to the central city are now moving from the city to the suburbs.

New technology also enables greater economies of scale by reducing the constraints of distance on business operations, letting them serve more customers and a wider area from fewer locations. Business service facilities have consolidated into fewer, larger service centers. The decreasing need for physical proximity and the consolidation of activity into larger operations both favor suburban locations on the edge of fast-growing metro areas.

The accelerated residential dispersion along metro fringes that was discussed earlier is likely to continue and to be enhanced by technological advances. With more and more jobs located on the edge of metro areas, employees have a larger range of residential choices, including exurban locations in nonmetro counties adjacent to metro areas. Commuting to a central city is no longer an absolute necessity, especially as telecommuting is adopted by a larger share of the workforce. Part-time telecommuting and commuting to tele-work centers, though, are likely to be more common than full-time telecommuting from home.

The suburbanization of business activity and the opportunity for tele-work means that more workers can choose to live in houses even farther from traditional urban cores. Because they can commute just to the metro edges (whether to a suburban job or a tele-work center), such employees are able to take advantage of the lower land prices available in exurban locations. Cheaper land prices, in turn, imply that consumers locating in exurban areas can afford even larger houses on even more acreage. The technological revolution in communications, information and transportation is likely to accentuate this ability (US Congress, Office of Technology Assistance 1995: 101). Technological innovation is also likely to facilitate the so-called "Jeffersonian rural lifestyle," which is the extreme case of a desire for exurban isolation (US Congress, Office of Technology Assistance 1995). Today, enabled by digital technology, such a lifestyle does not mean deprivation of urban amenities while living in rustic isolation. On the contrary, modern septic systems that substitute for urban sewer systems, satellite dishes that substitute for cable television, electronic home commerce that replaces in-store shopping and services, and other new information technologies bring a host of urban amenities into the most rural homes. Ability to maintain such a lifestyle is an important factor in the increased use of large lots in rural areas.

Knowledge-based and high-technology companies seem to have a particular penchant for locating in suburbs and edge cities rather than central-cities, perhaps due to the same cost-lowering effects that their own information, transportation, and communications innovations have created, and perhaps due to an accommodation of employee location preferences. Because of the knowledge-based nature of their products, and the knowledge-based nature of employee skills, New Economy companies and employees have unprecedented choice to live and work almost anywhere. In order to attract these highly skilled employees, New Economy businesses are now competing for knowledge-based talent on the basis of location amenities, often choosing campus-like job-sites that provide both tangible and intangible quality-of-life amenities. Sites with such arrays of amenities are more likely to be available in suburban or exurban areas. More traditional criteria, such as salary and cost of housing, now appear to be less important than quality of the environment (Hirschhorn 2000: 23).

Potential changes in land use attributable to innovations in communication and information-processing technologies

Gordon and Richardson (1997) argue that innovations in technology and falling transport and communications costs have eroded the agglomeration benefits that provide the incentive for centralized development. They postulate that, if unfettered by transportation and communications expense, people and businesses will increasingly choose to locate away from higher density areas in order to avoid the cost of congestion.

Just how footloose businesses and employees become depends on the share of business functions that can be transformed into electronic flows, the degree to which technological innovation overcomes the importance of face-to-face interaction among suppliers, customers and competitors, whether urban social and cultural amenities and agglomeration advantages remain important and, of course, the path of future technological change. At one extreme, assuming a sufficiently long period for adjustment and significant further innovation, one could envision an economy in which costs of friction are rendered insignificant. The implication is that city centers may no longer command substantial rent and land price premium. Location decisions can then be determined on the basis of other factors, including type and supply of amenities. This is not unrealistic: consider airline pilots who live in one city, but commute weekly to work (at zero expense on employing airlines) to a distant city. Also consider writers, editors, and others whose products are such that they do not require urban contact for long periods of time. Knowledge-based companies and their employees are just larger dimensions of the same phenomenon.

Ewing (1997) argues to the contrary, noting that while the centrifugal forces created by rapidly developing information technologies have enabled some types of activities to disperse, other functions, particularly high-level decision making, have remained centralized. Moreover, Ewing (1997: 112) believes that "electronic communications are (and probably always will be) imperfect substitutes for the kind of rapid face-to-face communications made possible by cities. There is a texture and subtlety to face-to-face exchanges that cannot be reproduced electronically." Glaeser (2000: 10–13), also arguing that cities will not disappear, notes that urban density holds advantages in its ability to move people which are enormously important. That advantage is critical in the service sector where personal interchange is required. In addition, he argues that the agglomeration of firms in dense urban areas allows people to change jobs without relocating their home.

The more likely scenario is that benefits from agglomeration, whether economic, social, or cultural, will be sufficient to maintain the existence of major metro areas. Continued existence of metro areas is essentially the scenario envisioned by recent government reports addressing the effect of information technologies on urban form. Nevertheless, these technologies will have a large impact on both urban and rural land use.

Although new electronic technologies will enable dispersal to rural areas, firms and residents are more likely to relocate both to lower-cost metro areas and to suburban and exurban locations within metro areas. The US Congress, Office of Technology Assessment (1995: 6), in its comprehensive review of the impact of communication and information technologies on human settlement patterns, concludes that "a limited number of high-amenity rural areas and rural areas at the periphery of metropolitan areas may experience significant growth" but "at least in the foreseeable future, most of the economy will be locating in metropolitan areas, perhaps not the largest, highest-cost metros, but the next tier of mid-sized metros."

Movement of population and employment among metro areas

In addition to the reshaping the structure of cities through internal relocation, new electronic technologies can also provide incentives for jobs and population to move between metro areas. These effects are often studied using models of city formation (Kim 2002).

New technologies are creating economies of scale in many services industries, leading to consolidated production centers that almost always locate in metro centers where larger, more diverse, and more skilled workforces are found. Access to customers is still important in many service industries, furthering the incentives for firms to expand in larger metro areas. Back office jobs, though relocatable, must have accessible air transportation. Metro areas are usually served by more airlines and flights tend to be cheaper. Access to regional postal facilities is still important for operations that process paper or collect funds, although less so as electronic commerce becomes more widespread. Technology has increased the importance of innovation and research, placing a higher premium on inter-firm cooperation, which is enhanced by locations in large or mid-size metro areas.

As technology allows more locational freedom, movement of people and firms to lower-cost, higher-amenity areas will reshape regional employment patterns. Partly due to typically lower wages, smaller and mid-size metro areas are likely to benefit disproportionately. These cost differentials among metro areas will continue to affect office relocation to low-cost regions until equilibrium is reached. Other characteristics of metro areas that will attract footloose industries are a large, skilled labor pool; frequent and cheap air transportation; availability of technical services; high-quality medical care; cultural and educational amenities; low cost of living; low crime, congestion, pollution; and access to open and green space (US Congress, Office of Technology Assessment 1995: 109, 117). These metro characteristics provide advantages to both industries and individuals.

In addition, many companies are locating at least part of their operations in suburban areas of small cities in less populated states. Long-distance and 800-number service centers are examples, as is Citigroup, locating its credit card processing facilities in Sioux Falls, South Dakota. Locations in the center of the United States have advantages in terms of both average distance and being in the central time zone.

In summary, little is actually known about the eventual effect of these technologies on urban settlement pattern and rural land consumption: these technologies are new, not fully adopted, and still evolving. At present, little research or empirical evidence exists to indicate that these technologies, in and of themselves, are creating widespread deconcentration to rural areas. It does not appear that a widespread migration of commercial and residential activity to rural areas will occur anytime soon. "Technological changes will most likely continue to facilitate this overall employment decentralization, which in turn permits even greater numbers of people to live in the outer suburbs and exurbs but be within commuting range of large employment sites" (US Congress, Office of Technology Assessment 1995: 195). Over time, though, as the physical barriers to communication and commerce continue to diminish, many factory and office location decisions may be made without consideration of proximity to an urban employment center. In such circumstances, even the polycentric urban development pattern characterized by edge cities may evolve into an urban form that is characterized by generalized dispersion of population and employment.

Conclusion

The trends discussed throughout this chapter raise questions about whether recent technological innovations that potentially alter development patterns signal significant impacts for production agriculture and for the landscape amenities that all rural land generates free of charge for consumers in the form of nonmarket public goods. Whether the outward growth of cities occurs in the form of inter-city relocation (i.e., movement to smaller metros) or in the form of intra-city relocation (i.e., movement to suburban and exurban locations), the development will be of an increasingly low-density, dispersed type. There appears to be widespread agreement that the conversion of rural land to urban-related uses is not of sufficient magnitude to endanger a cropland base adequate to meet foreseeable national food demand. This consensus holds despite the rapid development that has characterized the previous two or three decades. Thus, other issues constitute the primary concerns surrounding the development patterns arising from innovation in information and communications technologies.

First, current development patterns enabled by technological innovation involve conversion of increasing amounts of farmland, forestland, wetlands, and other forms of wildlife habitats to urban-related uses. Do these conversions, centered largely in the proximity of major metro areas, imply significant loss of important historical, cultural, and natural resources?

Second, do new, less dense, and more widely dispersed development patterns portend a particularly large loss of forestland and scenic amenities due to tele-work and recreational-type second homes in high amenity areas? Amenity-related housing growth, much of it related to tele-work or recreational and second-home development enabled by technological innovation, particularly affects scenic landscapes. A considerable amount of such development is not associated with population concentrations. Often, second home or recreational construction takes place in areas devoid of existing urban development. Though the effect of such development may not be as severe as that associated with high-density urban development, it may still contribute significantly to the real or perceived loss or degradation of rural amenities. Loss of such amenities may impose costs even on nonresidents, as consumers of the public goods associated with rural landscapes. For instance, one poorly designed residential development can diminish the quality of the viewshed of many consumers. This may be the case for substantial amounts of the development in the Intermountain West (Rosenberger and Walsh 1997).

Third, there may be significant but largely hidden costs to production agriculture that arise from the interspersion of agricultural and urban activities in a large, growing and permanent fringe. Following the trend of recent decades, urban development will continue to push outward beyond the suburbs, in a form that increasingly intersperses urban activities with farm activities in traditionally rural areas. If an increasing amount of that development occurs on large, isolated lots, or in isolated subdivisions and strip malls, then the interface between agricultural and urban land uses will expand.

This additional interface may impose external costs on production agriculture, brought about by conflicts between farmers and new suburban neighbors. Such conflicts often lead to constraints on farming activities, adding to costs already imposed on some farms when crop yields and profits deteriorate due to urban smog, theft and vandalism.

Notes

1 The views expressed here are those of the author, and not necessarily those of the Economic Research Service or the US Department of Agriculture.
2 US Census Bureau (2002) *Statistical Abstract of the United States*. High series projection accessed 13 June 2003 at: http://www.census.gov/prod/2003pubs/02statab/pop.pdf, table No. 3. The middle series projects a 43 percent increase.
3 Urban and built-up land is defined in the National Resources Inventory survey conducted periodically by the USDA Natural Resources and Conservation Service. See Heimlich and Anderson (2001: 10–11).
4 Basic data are from: http://www.census.gov/geo/www/ua/ua_mat;_100302.txt. Accessed 5 April 2004.
5 As discussed later in the chapter, this is a concept embedded in the monocentric city model. See Anas *et al.* 1998.
6 This model is essentially a model of the structure of the residential component of city structure, since it assumes that employment is concentrated at the city center. In other words, business location is exogenous to the model. Most recent work finds that city employment and population densities are jointly determined by location decisions of firms and households.
7 The list is much longer, of course, and includes video phones, computers, optical scanners, barcode readers, email, instant messaging, call-forwarding systems, voice messaging, pagers, local and wide-area networks, wireless communications and computing, fiber optics, data transfer protocols, digital switching, satellites and portable computers.

5 Failing markets and fragile institutions in land use

Colorado's experience

Andrew F. Seidl

Introduction

Land provides a complex mix of goods and services to society, which is dependent upon its use. Land use and management present a unique economic challenge due to land's fixed supply and location, the enormous variety of potential private and public uses, and the potential for important external effects and jointly produced goods and services resulting from land management choices. The economic complexity of land use decisions, particularly the potential for land use choices to have intended and unintended effects on neighboring landowners, communities and the broader society, has generated a web of private, public and mixed private/public actions to manage land toward private or public objectives. For example, land is bought and sold in real estate markets, but it is often encumbered by covenants or zoning regulations intended to limit the scope of land use alternatives available to its owner. Property rights are neither complete nor sacrosanct. Private individuals enter into land markets, as do profit-making corporations, public-representing local, state and national governments, and various types of constituency-serving nongovernmental organizations (e.g., churches and land trusts).

In this chapter, the uneasy evolution of institutions to manage land resources is discussed. Arguments are couched in terms of the incentives to convert land from spatially extensive uses (i.e., unmanaged, forested or many agricultural uses) to spatially intensive uses (i.e., residential or commercial/industrial) in search of evidence that markets fail to allocate land resources in a socially optimal manner. Society clearly benefits from public land management (e.g., national, state and local parks and forests). Here the focus is narrowed to discuss the conditions under which broader society benefits from or is hurt by the alternative uses of private lands, using the state of Colorado as a case study. Colorado is 66.3 million acres in area. About 59 percent of the state is privately owned and 32 million privately owned acres are classified as agricultural (Colorado Agricultural Statistics Service 2003), leaving about 10 percent of the state in residential, commercial or industrial development. Further, it is argued that alternative institutional structures implicitly or explicitly designed to move land markets toward social optimality have done so imperfectly. Colorado's experiences serve as illustration throughout the chapter and potential gaps in our current knowledge are emphasized.

Private goods attributes of private land management

Land and other features of land resources directly provide private benefits to people with direct access or claim to the land (e.g., landowners, land leasers, recreators with access rights). They may also provide private benefits (costs) to people with little or no direct influence on the manner in which land resources are managed (e.g., neighbors, community members). These private benefits (costs) may be reflected in local real estate prices, per capita tax burden and the quality of public services, or more general community quality-of-life features (e.g., automobile dependence, traffic congestion, air quality, water quality, landscape views, rural lifestyle, wildlife viewing, biological diversity). In some cases, the benefits (costs) are fully reflected in markets or managed by other institutions such that the net benefits of land management choices to society are maximized and there is no market failure. In other cases, they may not and so an argument for market or other institutional failure may be made.

The discussion of the private goods attributes of private land management is organized here into two sections: private (individual) impacts of private land use decisions and public (social) impacts of private decisions. First, it is argued that individual actions in real estate markets fail to reflect the true private costs and benefits from those actions to other individuals due to the inability of the market to fully capture landowner values and due to the spillover effects of landowner decisions on neighboring landowners. Then it is argued that individual action in real estate markets fails to reflect broader societal values and results in inefficient land allocation decisions from a broader societal perspective.

Benefits to claimants

The owner of a commercial operation benefits from the sale of the goods or services produced by the enterprise. Analogously, an agriculturist benefits from the sale of agricultural goods produced on her owned or leased land. Short-term land lease rates for agricultural land should reflect the expected benefits from the sale of agricultural products and the opportunity cost of deferring land conversion for a growing season. Global agricultural markets should exert downward pressure on agricultural land prices due to continued global increases in production and productivity and attendant low prices for most commonly produced agricultural commodities (Brueckner 2000; Heimlich and Anderson 2001).

Highly profitable agricultural land should be less prone to conversion than less profitable land (Brueckner and Fansler 1983). Moreover, distinct from other entrepreneurs, many agriculturists also derive real, if potentially nonpe-cuniary, benefits from their access to a large parcel of land that may include wildlife benefits, recreation benefits, rural lifestyle benefits, and attachment value, for example (Marshall *et al.* 2003). Agricultural lease rates should, therefore, be lower than the legitimate offer price for the sale of an agricul-tural property and the rate of agricultural land conversion cannot be predicted solely based upon its observable opportunity cost in agricultural versus altern-ative uses.

In areas of high population growth, agricultural profitability on spatially extensively managed lands will be less than the potential profits from more spatially intense land uses. Population growth and spatial urban growth are often, but not necessarily, related. Spatial urban growth is driven by three factors: increasing population and household numbers, increasing wealth and decreasing transportation costs (Heimlich and Anderson 2001; Mieszkowski and Mills 1993).

The state of Colorado, particularly the "Front Range" or "I-25 corridor," can serve as an illustration of these principal spatial growth factors. Colorado has the third fastest-growing population (30.6 percent from 1990–2000) (state of Colorado, Department of Local Affairs 2004) and the fifth highest per capita income ($33,455 in 2001) (US Department of Commerce, Bureau of Economic Analysis 2004) in the United States. The four fastest growing housing markets in the United States are located in north-central Colorado (Ft. Collins-Loveland, Greeley, Boulder-Longmont and Denver). Not only are state average incomes high, but they are unequally distributed between rural and urban areas. Colorado's agricultural sector earns about two thirds of the state's average per capita income (about $22,000 per person annually), indicative of the average returns to agricultural production, while Front Range urbanites account for about 82 percent of the income and about 75 percent of the population. In some, formerly rural, markets, average housing prices have outstripped increases in personal income by as much as 150 percent in recent years, indicating that commuting urbanites are entering rural land markets, building homes and bidding up land prices in formerly rural areas (Seidl 2002).

In part due to these factors, recent land use trends imply that urbanization in Colorado has occurred at a rate of approximately 28,000 acres per year (Colorado Agricultural Statistics Service 2003; Obermann *et al.* 2000), or about 3 acres per additional person, implying an increase in per capita con-sumption of land resources and, therefore, sprawl. One indicator of failure in state land markets is public opinion, and newspapers are one indicator of public opinion. Figure 5.1 illustrates the number of times the word "urban sprawl" has been mentioned in the *Denver Post* since 1993. It indicates a clear trend through 2000. Therefore, the question should at least be asked: has the sprawl problem been solved due to the marked change since that year?

Based upon purely private economic incentives, and assuming a positive

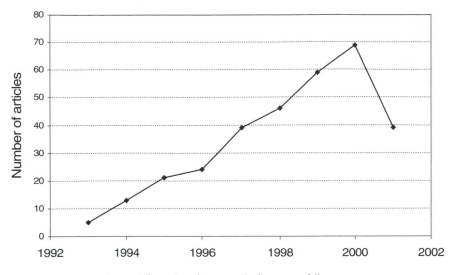

Figure 5.1 Denver Post articles using the term "urban sprawl."

rate of discount and accurate information about the slower rates of growth in the future, the rational rural landowner in Colorado's Front Range should probably sell her land sooner rather than later to residential or commercial uses and purchase a substitute parcel outside of the paths of growth. Rational, profit-maximizing farm-business owners face strong incentives to sell. Rational, utility-maximizing farmer–citizens face somewhat lower incentives to convert. These conditions do not necessarily imply that the real estate market fails to allocate land resources efficiently. However, state or local government action may be economically justified to guide incentives in the real estate market on distributional grounds, even if evidence is lacking on efficiency grounds.

Benefits to nonclaimants

People who lack direct access rights or property claims (here, nonclaimants) may gain an increase in property values due to their location adjacent to or nearby agricultural, native or open lands. On the other hand, they may experience countervailing decreases in property values due to agricultural odors and practices incompatible with residential use (e.g., pesticide spraying, late night harvesting). Analyses of the real estate effects of both positive and negative spillovers of agricultural and commercial or industrial uses number in the dozens (see, for example, Ready and Abdalla 2004, chapter 14 this volume). In sum, parcels adjacent to agricultural operations and open lands where there are positive spillovers experience an increase in value of approximately 9–23 percent (mean of 20 percent) of their total real estate value

(Crompton 2000). Depending upon the size and quality of the open space parcel and the amount of access allowed, properties within 500 to 2,000 feet enjoy measurable benefits to their real estate values, with about 80 percent of total benefit derived by properties within 500 feet of the open lands (Crompton 2000).

However, the nonclaimant has few market-based avenues to affect the flow of spillovers from neighboring properties. Since the claimant only has clear market incentives to provide for herself on her property, positive (negative) spillovers to nonclaimants will be underprovided (overprovided) by the real estate market. Greater understanding of the means to facilitate more efficient operation of the private real estate market in the face of positive and negative private spillover effects is needed.

Public goods attributes of land use

In the previous section, it was argued that real estate markets may or may not reflect the true private costs and benefits of alternative land uses due to potential positive and negative spillover effects and nonpecuniary benefits of landownership. In this section, it is argued that the broader scale public costs and benefits are similarly misrepresented by a relatively unfettered private real estate market. Evidence of the underprovision of these public goods and overprovision of public "bads" are provided through a discussion of "free-riding," income effects, travel costs and the fiscal impacts of private actions in real estate markets on broader societal well being.

Free-riding

Samuelson (1954) argues that goods and services with public good attributes would be underprovided from a social perspective due to incentives to under-represent individual preferences for these goods (free or easy ride). Public goods are characterized by difficult or costly exclusion of people from a good or service and the ability of many people to benefit from the good simultaneously without significantly diminishing the good's qualities or character. Police protection, public roadways, air quality and public radio are commonly cited goods or services that are more efficiently provided collectively than individually and that are prone to underprovision by individuals due to the incentives they face. Directly applied to land markets, open and green space, viewscapes, flood control, water quality, rural lifestyle, wildlife habitat, and wetlands, for example, will be underprovided from a social perspective.

Tiebout (1956) hypothesizes that people will choose to live where the mix of taxation and services befits their preferences. Within a region, this tatonnement process can contribute to spatial urban growth and suburban islands of economic preference homogeneity (Brueckner 2000). However, due to the relative irreversibility of many housing and construction decisions (capital fixity), the freedom to choose lies primarily with newcomers and not those who have already chosen to live in a community. Real estate markets are established by many small and relatively irreversible decisions (Heimlich and Anderson 2001). As such, community welfare is probably prone to the classical rent dissipation problems of open access resources.

Graves (2003) argues that sub-optimal provision of urban public goods (e.g., crime prevention, school quality, air quality) will result in the sub-optimal use of land in suburban development. Suburbs are viewed as imperfect private substitutes for urban public goods and land uses, since they provide lower crime and, ostensibly, higher school and air quality, but impose costs in the form of longer commuting times, greater fuel consumption and fewer choices of cultural amenities, for example. Thus, free-riding for both rural and urban public goods should result in sub-optimal land use, namely, lower intensity residential uses from an urban perspective and higher conversion pressure to higher intensity uses from a rural perspective.

Pre-emptive investment in urban public goods should best curtail incentives to suburbanize (Graves 2003). The changing incentive structure benefits those who can respond to financial incentives most easily and who have the most to gain or lose from action or inaction: the wealthy. Assuming that the demand for urban public goods increases with income (i.e., they are normal goods), the wealthy could be expected to return to the inner cities, pushing the less wealthy (those with lower opportunity costs) away from the center to absorb the negative attributes of suburban living. In Colorado, the high natural amenity mountain communities and the high cultural amenity redevelopment of lower downtown (Lo-Do) Denver reflect this, potentially economically superior, core–periphery development pattern. In the relatively low population mountain communities, crime rates do not vary substantially across housing choices and few school choices exist. As a result, parcel size, an imperfect substitute for public lands attributes, is the primary parcel choice feature to be weighed against travel time/convenience in the housing market. Lo-Do is an urban renewal success story. Once full of empty and dilapidated brick warehouses, rail yards, and people down on their luck, it is now the site of micro-breweries, steakhouses and sushi bars, riverside bicycle trails, Coors Field (the Rockies), the Pepsi Center (the Avalanche and Nuggets), Mile High Stadium (the Broncos and Rapids), lofts for the young and beautiful, and the highest priced real estate per square foot in the state.

Income effect

In addition, Graves (2003) argues that the income effects of public good preferences are neglected by Samuelson's thesis. That is, since the marginal influence of private preferences for public goods is zero, individuals with preferences for public goods relative to private goods will be rational in deciding to work less than would occur in the socially optimal provision of public goods even if Samuelsonian free-riding were somehow internalized.

Thus, individual rational behavior regarding work–leisure decisions is likely to exacerbate the underprovision of public goods in the absence of close substitutes. However, at least in Colorado there still appears to be a preponderance of revealed preference for imperfect substitutes for public goods in the form of sprawling 35-acre ranchettes, "McMansions" and "starter castles" and, therefore, people generating income at a rate that would not reflect muted work incentives.

Travel costs

The strength of these arguments relies, in part, on the notion that trips from a home to gain access to goods and services, and particularly work places, are costly. Travel can be privately costly in terms of time or money (Brueckner 2000). Despite western preferences for large gas-inefficient vehicles, improvements in vehicle fuel efficiency, Federal and state subsidization of roadways, and consistently low fuel prices provide little incentive to travel fewer miles (Brueckner 2000). Since no one can be excluded from public road use (i.e., it is managed as an open access resource), optimal commuting times are prone to the divergence of private and social costs known as traffic congestion. The failure of individuals to recognize the social costs of traffic congestion implies socially sub-optimal spatial dispersion of suburbs and excessive commuter miles (Wheaton 1998). Figure 5.2 clearly illustrates the

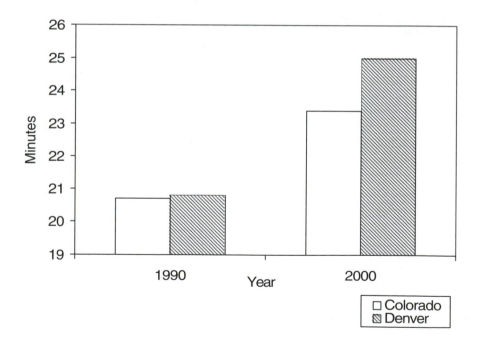

Figure 5.2 Average commute times for Colorado and Denver in 1990 and 2000.

increase in commute times in Denver (by 20 percent) and Colorado (by 13 percent) from 1990 to 2000.

Americans continue to work more and longer hours (International Labor Organization 2003). As a result, it would appear more likely that time to work would guide home location decisions. However, high-speed Internet access, telecommuting, and flex-hours allow people to work from home more conveniently and cell phones diminish the private cost of time spent commuting by allowing many people to work while they are en-route to their workplace (whether cell phone use also imposes additional social costs is another question). These factors decrease the strength of the spatial connection between work and home.

Sorting out the strength and direction of the influence of these technological and cultural changes raises empirical challenges. We do not really know whether (or under what conditions) people locate based upon the location of jobs, or whether jobs look for people, or if they are increasingly unrelated to one another (Thurston and Yezer 1994). In Colorado's mountain communities and on its Western Slope, second or vacation home purchasers and retirees drive high rates of population growth. These populations are not concerned with travel time to the workplace. Distinct preferences may imply different optimal spatial patterns of land use than are implied by the work-centered model.

Fiscal impacts

Private land use decisions made by individuals may have positive, neutral or negative impacts on community coffers. Land use decisions that create more revenues and, therefore, community goods and services than they require in community resources are desirable and those that do not are not. Per capita costs of common public services such as police protection, fire protection, ambulance services, school bussing, sewer and water provision, roadways and electric infrastructure increase with increasing spatial dispersion of development. Traffic congestion from excessive commuting miles, and increases in public infrastructure costs per capita provide evidence of non-optimal spatial urban growth (Brueckner 2000).

Though criticized on a number of fronts (see, for example, Deller 2004, chapter 8 this volume), about one hundred studies have indicated that residential development demands more community services than it provides in tax revenues (approximately $1.11 in services demanded per dollar of revenues generated, with a range of $1.03–1.67), in part due to relatively low residential tax rates. In contrast, agricultural ($0.31, $0.02–0.86) and commercial development ($0.29, $0.03–0.83) demand far less in community services than they provide in tax revenues (American Farmland Trust 2002; Heimlich and Anderson 2001), but for opposite reasons. Agriculture places very few demands on community services, but does not generate much tax revenue in relative terms. Commercial and industrial development may demand significant resources from the community, but generates substantial tax revenue to more than compensate for these demands, in part due to higher commercial tax rates. Evidence from Colorado indicates that agricultural land requires about $0.63 in services for each dollar of revenue contributed and low-density residential development requires about $1.65 in services for every dollar in revenue contributed (Coupal and Seidl 2003).

Tax revenues from agriculture are often low because the land is commonly taxed based upon its agricultural use value rather than its highest real estate valued ("highest and best") use. This lower tax rate encourages holding land in agricultural uses, but also decreases the cost of land speculation and reduces the incentive to make longer-term land use decisions. Whether such tax policies increase or decrease the long-term rate of land conversion has not yet been fully explored. Heimlich and Anderson (2001) estimate the cost of purchasing the development rights on cropland under the greatest conversion pressure over the next 30–50 years is $87–130 billion, and argue that if tax expenditures currently devoted to use-value assessment of agricultural properties were redirected to purchase development rights, almost one third of these lands could be protected.

In this section, it has been argued that private real estate markets fail to reflect public values and that they will allocate lands in such a way as to underprovide such valuable landscape attributes as viewshed, open and green space, wildlife habitat, flood control, and air and water quality. Moreover, private actions in imperfect land markets affect community service provision, suburbanization and community tax burdens. As with any market-driven resource allocation decision, those who are wealthier have greater ability to make choices about where they live and work. Therefore, it can be expected that the costs of nonoptimal land use choices are borne disproportionately by the less wealthy members of society. The next section addresses some of the ways in which formal and informal economic institutions have evolved to redress the failure of private real estate markets to better reflect these many types of public and private values.

Institutional innovation for land use

In recognition of the failure of land markets to fully reflect social values, collective action at a variety of scales emerged. Heimlich and Anderson (2001) estimate American households are willing to pay $1.4 billion to $26.6 billion per year, or $13.5 billion to $255.8 billion in present value terms, to conserve farmland and open space. Toward these ends a great variety of government and nongovernment actions has been taken. In this section, examples of the influence of government policies at various scales on land management decisions and the evolution of nongovernmental organizations as private collective actions to affect land use are discussed.

National scale

At the Federal level, Americans have chosen to tax themselves to create a system of national parks and protected areas reflecting substantial and general existence, bequest, option and nonconsumptive use value for this country's natural heritage. However, the vast majority of Federal lands are found in the western United States, where most voters reportedly opposed their establishment and conflict over land management priorities between Federal agencies and local residents abound.

Some 37 percent of Colorado is under Federal management (Obermann *et al.* 2000), implying that the scale of the public goods created on more than one third of Colorado lands extends to the nation as a whole. The mountain counties, which appear to follow the more economically efficient land use model described above, are commonly 75 percent to more than 90 percent held by Federal agencies. Colorado's ski companies have gained significant concessions to the seasonal use of Federal land and water rights. Pitkin (Aspen, Snowmass, Buttermilk, Aspen Highlands), Eagle (Vail, Beaver Creak, Arrowhead), Summit (Breckenridge, Copper Mountain, Keystone, Arapahoe Basin) and Routt (Steamboat) Counties also have the highest real estate values in the state and some of the highest in the country. It is not known to what extent national preferences for public lands and resources are subsidizing or taxing local preferences for economic development or lifestyles. Nor is it known to what extent public lands are complementary to or substitutes for private or more local scale governmental land activities in those regions. If they are substitutes, then government action to protect those lands may be crowding out (theoretically more efficient) private investment in similar activities in like locations.

The inheritance tax has been in place since the birth of the nation in order to limit the likelihood of the emergence of social classes. The Bush administration has set into motion the gradual elimination of this "death tax." Many farmers and ranchers strongly support this policy, arguing that agricultural lands assessed at their "highest and best use" as part of an estate would invoke a tax that would necessitate the sale and conversion of the property to that higher intensity use. However, the actual influence of this policy on the rate of land conversion is indeterminate. Under the inheritance tax, for agricultural operations of sufficient size to be affected by the policy, this generation's farmers and ranchers were forced to keep the land in agriculture by placing a conservation easement against the property or, by not taking this action, to convert to residential and commercial use upon passing their estate to their children. That is, the inheritance tax should only result in more land conversion when farmers and ranchers fail to engage in proper estate planning.

The ability to deduct interest paid on home mortgages from taxable income is another potentially perverse incentive in Federal income tax procedures. Since income tax is technically, if not practically, progressive, income tax deductions benefit the wealthy more than the poor, and deductions for interest paid on mortgages encourage larger mortgages. Since low-density suburban development tends to be oriented to higher-income individuals, it could be argued that this deduction encourages land conversion to residential uses.

Federal agricultural and resource policies have set aside low productivity and environmentally sensitive agricultural lands, keeping them out of both agriculture and residential development. Federal agricultural commodity programs and crop insurance increase the average profitability and reduce the downside risk of agriculture, and reduce the likelihood of short-term decision making that might increase the rate of agricultural land conversion due to temporary emergencies. Since the 1996 Farm Bill, 31,000 Colorado producers have received some $1.3 billion in Federal subsidies (Environmental Working Group 2001). More than $900 million of this support was for commodity programs, while about $350 million was in support of conservation-oriented programs. However, as Federal programs have increasingly become viewed as entitlements, the expected value of Federal assistance has been capitalized into lease and sale prices of agricultural lands, reducing the intended impact of the assistance programs.

Traditionally, Federal agricultural programs have targeted yields and planted acreages in efforts to ensure national food security. To the extent that national food security objectives are commensurate with local objectives for low-intensity land uses, little government failure should be in evidence. However, in the West, it is quite likely that large areas of native grasses and rangelands have been converted to cropland due to the unintended consequences (i.e., "perverse" incentives from a wildlife habitat perspective) created by Federal farm commodity programs (Conner *et al.* 2001; VanTassell *et al.* 2002).

State scale

In addition to Federal programs that reflect national objectives for low-intensity land use, all states have implemented complementary programs. The state of Colorado manages 5 percent of its 66.3 million acres (Obermann *et al.* 2000). Most of these lands are held in state parks and forests. The Colorado Division of Wildlife has been empowered to purchase and hold conservation easements on private lands in order to encourage management for wildlife habitat. Colorado has also created a trust fund (Great Outdoors Colorado or GOCO) from earmarked lottery funds to leverage local land preservation initiatives. The influence of these targeted matching funds on the quantity and dimensions of local demand for land preservation activities has not yet been studied, but it might be hypothesized that national or state objectives for land preservation activities are more often met than are local objectives when funds emanate from those greater spatial scales.

All states have right-to-farm legislation protecting agricultural producers from nuisance suits resulting from neighbor opposition to standard agricultural practices. Right-to-farm legislation probably reduces the pressure to convert for small– and medium–sized operations in high–growth areas. Where right–to–farm is not combined with agricultural districts or zoning, anecdotal evidence indicates that the implicit costs of doing business when surrounded by incompatible land uses can become intolerable (Edelman *et al.* 1999). Recent court decisions have held that operations that substantially increase their size subsequent to having non-agricultural neighbors, and large operations designated as commercial operations, are not typically protected by right–to–farm laws.

Local scale

Since planning and zoning is the responsibility of local governments, it is at the local level that many incentive and regulatory programs affecting land markets are initiated. Coloradoans typically favor private property rights over broader community-level rights. As a result, many local land use initiatives employ incentive-based voluntary programs to encourage the management of lands toward social objectives, including creating community buffers, providing wildlife habitat, flood control, an active agricultural economy, protecting the local natural heritage, and so forth. Tools employed include the donation, purchase, or trade of development rights, and fee simple purchase and bargain sales. At least 38 such local government programs are now active in Colorado, up from 25 in 1997. Local governmental programs have resulted in the protection of about 300,000 acres of Colorado open lands and working landscapes. Funding levels for local taxpayer-sponsored agricultural land and open space preservation programs have increased from an estimated $62 million in 1997 (Colorado Department of Agriculture 1997) to $115 million in 2001 (Colorado Conservation Trust 2001), implying that there appears to be a widely held public recognition of local land market failure to reflect public values.

Where local governmental agencies are involved in the real estate market, there is typically one bidder who represents the public's values (i.e., the demand side of the market is thin in revealing public willingness to pay) and comes in direct competition with the typically deeper market for weighing private objectives. The public's value will be compared to the willingness to pay for individual private objectives in order to determine who purchases the parcel. In examining several hundred market transactions engaged in by public agencies using a hedonic analytical framework, Loomis *et al.* (2002 and 2004) find that $13,800 was the average per acre price paid for a conservation easement on private lands by a local public agency in Colorado, often with matching funds from GOCO. Where water rights were included in the transaction, the price increased by $10,589 per acre. Fee simple purchase increased the price by $4,845, increases in county-level population by 1,000 residents increased the price paid by $30 per acre, and the presence of a wetland decreased the price paid by $7,534 per acre, likely due to supply side opportunity cost reductions.

Since public and private preferences for land attributes may differ, the public value for a parcel may be less than an individual's private value; they are essentially valuing distinct goods. However, the funding mechanisms for public programs do not accurately reflect individual willingness to pay for land attributes. Rather, they reflect the level of funding the polity would allow via the proposed mechanism, again resulting in sub-optimal support for public goods provision. Due to the tax structure in Colorado, either a mill levy or a sales tax is typically proposed. While a mill levy would probably compensate the public for private gains to owners of real estate bordering on community-purchased open space or easements, a sales tax is much more likely to provide a public subsidy to wealthier homeowners. Little information is available regarding who, in fact, shoulders the burden and reaps the benefits of agricultural land and open space preservation programs.

While regulatory approaches such as Urban Growth Boundaries have been used in many parts of the country (Ding *et al.* 1999), in the Intermountain West efforts to internalize the costs of new development and direct development using market signals are gaining popularity. Impact fees to account for the incremental costs of infrastructure (e.g., sewers, school facilities, roads, emergency services) to new development are used widely and can amount to several thousand dollars per new home (Altshuler and Gomez-Ibanez 1993; Brueckner 1997).

Properly crafted Transfer of Development Rights (TDR) programs can direct development to places where higher density is desired and away from places where it is undesirable without taxing existing residents unnecessarily. Developers purchase density credits from sending zones (decreasing develop-ment density) and apply them to receiving zones (increasing development density). Density credits should reflect the costs of infrastructure development and the price of the credits should reflect market signals for the returns to res-idential development. In Colorado, Boulder and Larimer Counties have TDR programs. TDR programs are best implemented in high-growth or highly isolated areas. Large, high-growth areas are needed in order to provide sufficient development rights transactions so that an efficient market can emerge. Isolated areas or high transportation costs are desirable because neighboring jurisdictions without TDR programs become targets of undesir-able leapfrog development when strong TDR programs are implemented within a jurisdiction.

Nongovernmental associations

At least 45 local, state, regional or national level nongovernmental organi-zations are active in Colorado land markets, accounting for about 350,000 of the 660,000 acres now permanently protected in the state. Presumably, people contribute time and money to nongovernmental organizations in order to express preferences for goods and services that have not been ade-quately represented by either the private real estate market or by government programs of various types.

Reflecting nationwide preferences for attributes of Colorado lands in addition to what has already been protected by Federal state and local agencies and private individuals, the Land Trust Alliance, the Nature Conservancy and the American Farmland Trust have been active in local land preservation activities within Colorado for a decade or more. Several state-level land trusts (e.g., Colorado Cattlemen's Land Trust, Colorado Working Lands, Colorado Conservation Trust) have been formed for similar reasons, but with somewhat different objectives.

However, by far the most common avenue for the expression of demand for land protection activities is at the local (e.g., county or municipal) level. Several explanations for the popularity of local action are feasible, including greater likelihood of access (i.e., use value rather than existence value), familiarity with the resources and political actors in question, and a sense of a greater influence in decision making. It is not unlikely that this excess demand for local land preservation activities stems from ineffectual governance with respect to these objectives of a portion of the polity. Government may not be sufficiently proactive in managing growth or may be inadequately prepared to respond to local growth challenges (Heimlich and Anderson 2001).

Anecdotal evidence suggests that local governance in Colorado's high-growth areas is often in the hands of those with the greatest vested interest in the community infrastructure – developers and real estate agents. These interests may not reflect all aspects of the community and may color land use planning and economic development decisions made by local government on behalf of their constituents. Exploring the appropriate role, efficiency and integration of governmental and nongovernmental organizations across scales of intervention and public goods aspects of land resources would provide useful insights into the information base in this arena.

Conclusion

In this chapter, a case for failing markets and fragile institutions in the management of US land resources has been made. The case was divided among a variety of potential sources of market and other institutional failures and illustrated by examples from the rapidly growing and increasingly wealthy state of Colorado. Potential sources of institutional failure are found in both private and public fora for preference revelation and at the local, regional, state and national scales. Throughout the preceding discussion, needs for the quantification of external effects and the development of tools to move efficiently toward socially optimal land use are evident. In land use research, multiple objectives among a variety of stakeholders, site specificity of lessons learned and the appropriateness of tools, thin markets, values that defy quantification, property rights, threshold effects, scale effects and blunt policy instruments complicate the research agenda and the effective application of research results.

6 Postproductivism and changing rural land use values and preferences

John C. Bergstrom

Introduction

Land has many, multifaceted values to people. Throughout history, the values provided to people by land and its relative scarcity have resulted in minor and major competitions for its possession, use and management. The struggle for survival leads to competition for land as an input for producing the basic necessities of life such as food, shelter and clothing. Conflicts over land to provide basic necessities for survival have occurred over and over again in past civilizations. These types of conflicts can be observed today in many underdeveloped parts of the world.

In most developed areas, market forces are doing an adequate job of allocating land to the production of necessities of life in a nonviolent manner. In agricultural land markets, for example, market-generated prices for food and fiber products play a pivotal role in determining how much land will be allocated to, say, corn and cotton production. Similarly, the demand for and supply of land for housing are captured in market prices and transactions that, in the absence of market distortions and restrictions, determine how much land in a region will be allocated to housing. Since von Thunen, economists have been quite familiar with and accepting of the market-driven allocation of land to different uses according to its "highest valued use."

If market prices and transactions capture and reflect all relevant values of land, allocation of land to its highest valued use via market forces should be automatic, assuming all other necessary assumptions hold. There are good theoretical reasons for believing that land markets adequately reflect the value of land as an input into the production of economic commodities in the nature of private goods such as food, fiber, timber, and mineral products. Land, however, provides additional services beyond the role as inputs in commercial production processes that are more in the nature of public goods. Certain types of land amenity values fall into this category. Economic theory suggests that the value of public good land services will not be adequately reflected in land markets. Other types of land amenity values will likely escape land markets altogether because of their incommensurable or intangible nature.

Economists typically do not venture outside of the commensurable land value terrain into the incommensurable or intangible land value terrain. Yet, as Crosson (1985) argued more than fifteen years ago, resolution of competing demands and interests in the use and allocation of land requires that the full scope of land values be taken into consideration. This theme is being repeated often in contemporary times, particularly in developed countries where land use conflicts increasingly are centered on the amenity values of land, rather than the value of land as an input into commercial economic production.

In the next section of this chapter, background discussion is provided regarding why we as a society seem to care so much about rural land values. Following this discussion, a framework for the empirical assessment of land values is presented, focusing on amenity values. Application of these values in the rural land management arena is then discussed. Some concluding thoughts are provided in the final section.

Rural land value: why do we care?

The struggle over defining the values of land to individuals and society has a long history. For example, in US history, Thomas Jefferson believed strongly that close ties with the land provided "character building" values that would result in the type of independent, moral, and productive citizens needed to support a growing, free democracy. At another area of the discussion was Alexander Hamilton, who did not completely share these sentiments with Jefferson. Hamilton viewed land values more narrowly as the use of land as an input into the economic engine needed to drive the new country. These differing perspectives on the value and importance of land to individuals and society, as well as differences of opinion on other issues, led Jefferson and Hamilton to advocate different and perhaps competing visions for the development of America (Crosson 1985; Hite and Dillman 1981).

The Hamiltonian view of land values apparently was more in line with a young, developing America. Throughout most of American history to date, including the history of economic thought, the predominant view of land has been as an input into commercial productive process just like any other input (Crosson 1985). In the world of economics, this traditional view of land values has been passed along from one generation of economists to the next primarily through the neoclassical production function. Using the neoclassical production function, one of the first lessons introductory economics instructors teach their charges is that land, along with labor and capital, provide the big three inputs for production of commercially valuable economic commodities. Values of land other than its marginal productivity in the production of food and fiber products, widgets, or some other commercial commodity are typically not discussed in standard college microeconomic theory courses.

The traditional view of land as a commercial input has contributed to a

historical emphasis in rural areas and rural/agricultural policy on "productivism." Productivism as applied to rural land implies a commitment to commercial production values supported by public policy. In the rural United
States, productivism has traditionally been the guiding force behind land use
policy and management (Lowe *et al.* 1993; Reed and Gill 1997). The results
of productivism can be seen throughout the rural landscape – in agricultural
operations producing an abundance of food and fiber products, private industrial forests where trees for lumber products are grown with utmost technical
precision, and large dams and reservoirs built to provide electricity to fuel all
manners of industrial production and output.

From an economic development perspective, productivism has been
extremely successful in America. In a relatively short historical time period,
America has transformed itself from a struggling, developing nation to a
highly developed "superpower" with unprecedented standards of living. In a
developing nation, or in remote rural areas of a developed nation, necessities
of life such as food, shelter, and clothing are often critically scarce. As a result,
there is high individual and societal demand for increased outputs of these
necessities with a corresponding high-derived demand for the use of land as a
commercial input. In this context, productivism naturally emerges as a means
for organizing and utilizing land and other inputs to deal with the scarcity of
necessities of life.

As a nation or rural area develops, two fundamental changes occur that put
pressure on the established emphasis on productivistic uses of rural land. First,
productivism helps to mitigate the scarcity problem related to necessities of
life to the point that it is no longer a major national or regional concern. In
the United States and many European nations, for example, an equally troub-
ling concern for individuals and society are the large surpluses of food and
fiber produced by the agricultural industry. Second, as a nation or rural area
develops, demand for noncommercial land values such as amenity values tend
to increase at a relatively greater rate than demand for more food and fiber
production. The reason from economic theory for these different demand
changes is that because they are in the nature of luxuries, the income elasticity of demand for noncommercial land values is greater than the income elasticity of demand for necessities such as food and fiber (Bromley and Hodge
1990).

Economists, rural sociologists, geographers and other observers of changes
in rural development patterns agree that many rural areas are moving into a
postproductivism era. This era is characterized by more diverse economic
activities and attitudes with respect to the use and allocation of land. A key
characteristic of a rural area experiencing postproductivism is a migration into
the area of new residents attracted by rural land amenities, and increased visi-
tation by nonresidents seeking recreational and leisure opportunities supported by rural land amenities. In addition to "on-site" benefits of rural land
amenities to rural area residents and visitors, postproductivism in a rural area
also receives support from "off-site" beneficiaries of rural land amenities.

These off-site beneficiaries include people in urban, suburban, and exurban areas who enjoy cleaner air and water supported by the countryside (Flynn and Marsden 1995; Lowe *et al.* 1993; Reed and Gill 1997; Troughton 1996).

Many people in rural areas of the United States remain geared toward productivism and represent the traditional stakeholders in rural policy. Accordingly, many local, state and federal institutions involved in rural development and policy continue to lean toward productivism. The new stakeholders in rural development and policy are the residents and nonresidents of rural areas who are more in the postproductivism camp. Institutions that serve the interests of the postproductivism stakeholders are not well developed. The presence of these different sets of stakeholders and the lack of institutions set up to handle and mediate the interests of both groups sets the stage for land value and property rights conflicts in need of resolution (Bromley and Hodge 1990; Reed and Gill 1997).

Rural land values: what are they?

When two parties do not see eye-to-eye on an issue, a first step toward an acceptable solution is for each group to have a better understanding of what is important or valuable to the other group. What are the various types of land values that may be of importance to productivists, postproductivists, or both? To address this question, the full scope of rural land values is discussed in this section, with an emphasis on amenity values.

An early influential paper on the subject of farmland values was written by Bruce Gardner and published in the *American Journal of Agricultural Economics* in 1977. Gardner (1977) delineated four major types of values provided jointly by farmland: (1) local and national food production; (2) provision of local jobs in the agricultural sector; (3) better and more organized development of urban and rural land; and (4) environmental amenities. Crosson (1985) provides further elaboration on farmland values in an article appropriately entitled, "Agricultural Land: A Question of Values." In this article, he first discusses the market values of farmland starting with the tremendous market value of food and fiber products produced on farmland. He also highlights the considerable employment benefits provided by jobs in the agricultural sector. Both Gardner (1977) and Crosson (1985) argue that private land markets adequately allocate farmland to the production of food and fiber products and the associated support of jobs in the agricultural sector.

Crosson (1985) also points out the market value of farmland for development purposes. In the absence of development subsidies, farmland is converted to residential, commercial, and industrial uses whenever the market value of the land in nonagricultural uses is higher than the market value of the land in agricultural uses. In the spirit of von Thunen, both Gardner (1977) and Crosson (1985) argue that private land markets adequately value and reallocate farmland from agricultural to nonagricultural uses.

Gardner's (1977) fourth category of farmland values, environmental amenities, was defined broadly as open space and other general amenities of farmland of an environmental and public good nature. Crosson (1985) included visual amenities provided by open space as a type of intangible value of farmland. Other intangible values of farmland, according to Crosson (1985), include wildlife habitat, "character building" values gleaned from rural life, and the value of a "sense of community" promoted by farming life. Gardner (1977) and Crosson (1985) agree that unlike market values derived from food and fiber production, employment, and development, the externality nature of the above amenity-type values means that private land markets are not likely to adequately allocate land to the support of these values.

A number of studies conducted mostly in the 1980s attempted to quantify the amenity-type values of farmland. Amenity-type values were defined somewhat differently by each study. Halstead (1984) referred generally to the "nonmarket value" of farmland, including wildlife habitat, scenic vistas, and recreation. Bergstrom *et al.* (1985) defined environmental amenities associated with farmland to include scenic value and the environmental qualities of agricultural land that generate nostalgic value. Nostalgic value is related to the virtues ascribed to living close to the land as advocated by Thomas Jefferson. Beasley *et al.* (1986) defined amenity values to include scenic values and historical values of farmland. Bowker and Didychuk (1994) refer to the "external benefits" of farmland that they define as including open space, scenic vistas, wildlife and traditional country life.

Rosenberger and Walsh (1997) define three categories of amenity-type values that they classify as nonmarket values of farmland: open space values, environmental amenities, and cultural heritage. Open space values include visual, recreational and therapeutic benefits. They define environmental amenities to include watershed protection, soil conservation, plant and animal habitat, and the biological diversity supported by these amenities. Cultural heritage value is defined as the value of farmland as part of the unique cultural or natural heritage or history of an area (Rosenberger and Walsh 1997).

Land and landscape amenities have also been a topic of considerable interest in the rural development, land planning, and environmental planning fields. Duffy-Deno (1997) and Reed and Gill (1997), for example, discuss the role of landscape amenities as such and scenic beauty and open spaces in attracting new residents and recreational visitors to rural areas. As with the economic valuation studies mentioned in the previous paragraph, a major concern in the land use and environmental planning literature is with the value of undeveloped land on the urban–rural fringe (e.g., greenbelts). Amenity-type values identified in the rural development and planning literature include recreational values, open space, scenic beauty, symbolic values, environmental quality and managing urban sprawl (Correll *et al.* 1978; Duffy-Deno 1997; Kline and Wichelns 1996a; Lee and Fujita 1997; Lee and Linneman 1998; Reed and Gill 1997; Young and Allen 1986).

Philosophers working primarily in the area of environmental ethics have identified and discussed values associated with nature that can be applied to rural land and landscapes. A general dichotomy of land values suggested by philosophers includes instrumental values and intrinsic values (Ferre 1988). Instrumental values of land are derived from the active or passive use of land to support or generate services that are useful or valuable to people, plants, animals, and ecological systems as a whole. Intrinsic values of land are the values of land that are independent of active or passive use by some other entity.

The source of intrinsic values is a rather deep ethical, philosophical, and theological question. Some schools of ethical/philosophical/theological thought identify the source of intrinsic values of land as the land itself. For example, Aldo Leopold's "land ethic" as outlined and discussed in his book, *The Sand County Almanac*, suggests that land values include the values of land elements such as plants and animals to themselves. Leopold's "land ethic" is an important foundation for modern schools of ethical thought that hold to the inherent value of the biotic and abiotic elements of land and landscapes to themselves, including biocentrism and ecocentrism (Oelschlaeger 1991). Consistent with biocentrism, the biocentric intrinsic value of land refers here to the value of living land elements to themselves. Consistent with ecocentrism, ecocentric intrinsic land value refers here to the value of living and nonliving land elements to themselves and to the land or landscape ecosystem as a whole.

Other schools of ethical/philosophical/theological thought identify the source of intrinsic values as God or other spiritual beings or entities. Judaism, Christianity, and Islam teach that God created the land and everything else in the universe. This creation has an inherent value to the creator that is apparent in common Judeo-Christian land and nature scriptures found in the Old Testament of the Bible (e.g., Psalm 104). Consistent with the idea of the inherent value of land and nature derived from its creator, theistic intrinsic land value refers here to the value of living and nonliving land elements to God independent of active or passive use by anyone or anything else on earth.

Buddism, Hinduism, and parts of Native American spiritualism teach that various types of spiritual beings inhabit the land and its elements. The presence of these spiritual beings provides value to land that is not dependent on active or passive use by anyone or anything else on earth. Thus arise, for example, "Sacred Groves" that are preserved by Hindus for the benefit of the spiritual beings that are believed to inhabit the grove of trees. The inherent value of living and nonliving land elements derived from a multitude of spiritual beings or entities is referred to here as pantheistic intrinsic land values.

Unlike intrinsic values, instrumental values of a particular land element are derived from the active or passive use of this element to generate, produce, or support some good or service useful and valuable to people or some other living or nonliving land element. Instrumental values can be divided up into noneconomic and economic instrumental values. Noneconomic instrumental values associated with land include biocentric instrumental land value and ecocentric instrumental land value. Biocentric instrumental land value is the value of land elements to plants and animals. For example, different types of soil have instrumental value to particular plants as sources of nutrients needed for life. Ecocentric instrumental land value is the value of land elements to all living and nonliving components of land ecosystems. For example, ecocentric instrumental land value would include the value of soil as a foundation for surface rock formations. The argument in philosophy and ecology circles is that the function of soil within the land ecosystem as a foundation for rock formations has value outside and independent of human activities that give rise to economic values.

Biocentric and ecocentric instrumental land values focus on the noneconomic instrumental values of land elements to biotic and abiotic components of land ecosystems. Noneconomic instrumental land values also include certain types of anthropocentric instrumental land values. Anthropocentric instrumental land values are derived from the active or passive use of land elements to generate, produce, or support goods or services of value to people. Philosophers such as Holmes Rolston and economists including Crosson, and Hite and Dillman identify a number of land values that can be classified as noneconomic anthropocentric instrumental land values. These values include particular types of aesthetic values, historical values, cultural values, security and stability values, mental health values, physical health values, and spiritual health or religious values (Crosson 1985; Hite and Dillman 1981; Rolston 1985).

Economists and philosophers have also identified a host of economic anthropocentric instrumental land values. Because economic values are always dependent on human preferences, the terms "economic" and "anthropocentric" in the label "economic anthropocentric instrumental land value" are redundant. Therefore, we can shorten the label somewhat to economic instrumental land values. Economic instrumental land values include a number of active use values, including material consumption value, recreational use value, on-site scenic appreciation value, and commensurable mental, physical, and spiritual health values involving on-site use. Economic instrumental land values also include a number of passive use values such as commensurable existence values, historical values, cultural values, job satisfaction values, security and stability values, off-site aesthetic appreciation values, off-site recreation and leisure values, and mental, physical, and spiritual health involving off-site passive use (Crosson 1985; Hite and Dillman 1981; Kline and Wichelns 1996b; Rolston 1985; Rosenberger and Walsh 1997). The various values of land from an interdisciplinary perspective are summarized in Figure 6.1.

Land function and value linkages

How can all of the various different potential types of land values summarized in Figure 6.1 be organized to facilitate empirical analysis and policy decisions

Support of local agricultural industry	Land input for recreational activities	Ecological life-support
Support of local resource extraction industry	Support of local tourism industry	Provision of genetic diversity
Support of local agricultural jobs	Provision of wildlife habitat	Intrinsic value
Support of local resource extraction jobs	Provision of open and green space	Existence value
Job satisfaction value	Provision of scenic views	Therapeutic value
Support of job security and stability	Support of aesthetic enjoyment	Physical health value
Support of community security and stability	Surface water storage	Religious/spiritual value
Support of national security and stability	Ground water recharge	Educational value
Provision of local food supplies	Natural water filtration	"Natural laboratory" value
Self-sufficiency in production of food items	Support of rural life values	Protection of cultural heritage
Dispersion of food production	Provision of character building opportunities	Nostalgic value
Continued production of unique food products	Support of national identity/ideals	Environmental amenities
Land input for residential development	Cultural symbolization value	Countryside amenities
Land input for commercial development	Historical value	Promotion of orderly development

Figure 6.1 Interdisciplinary rural land or landscape values.

related to rural land values and management? To accomplish this organization, it is useful to think of land as an asset with various functions, as illustrated in Figure 6.2. In the productivism tradition, the focus of rural land values and valuation has been on the use of land as a commercial input, such as an input into commercial agricultural production. For the most part, rural

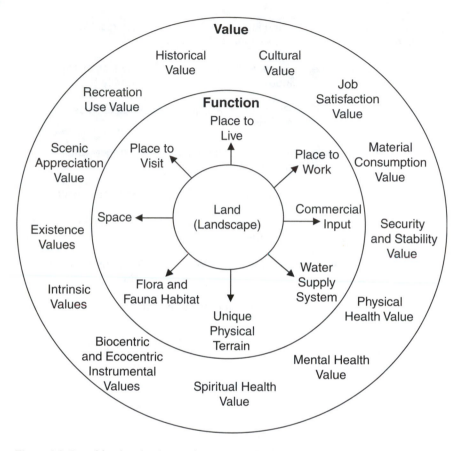

Figure 6.2 Rural land or landscape functions and values.

development policy in the United States has historically emphasized the goal of maximizing the commercial production use of rural land (Bromley and Hodge 1990; Reed and Gill 1997).

Land areas function as "places" that support what philosophers and sociologists refer to as "values of place" (Norton 1994). For residents, rural land areas, including farmland, function as places to live and work. In a rural area, these residents include long-time residents who work locally in traditional jobs in the agricultural, natural resource extraction and manufacturing sectors, and new residents who work in local or nonlocal nontraditional jobs in the recreation and tourism, high technology and business service sectors, or are retired and living off transfer payments from pension funds, retirement accounts and other nonlocal sources of income.

Land areas also provide places to visit. In many rural areas of the country, recreation and tourism catering to nonresident visitors are a booming business. Most of this recreation and tourism is nature-based – e.g., hunting and fishing, camping, hiking, boating, lake and river swimming, water skiing, off-road touring, snow skiing and snowmobiling. Agricultural-based tourism such as visiting "dude ranches" has been an established business activity in many parts of the US and is taking hold in other areas of the US.

Another broad function of land, especially in rural areas, is the provision of "space." Space here is defined from a human interaction perspective, as in the phrase "you're in my space." Specifically, space refers here to the physical distance between people as they engage in various life activities (e.g., work, play) and the interrelated frequency of interaction between people as they engage in these activities. One of the apparent reasons people enjoy visiting and living in rural areas is that rural land areas provide them with more space.

The provision of flora and fauna habitat is often identified as an important function of land by philosophers, ethicists, economists, ecologists, biologists, and other social and physical scientists. In recent years, the preservation of rural land and landscapes as habitat for endangered plant and animal species has been a contentious rural policy issue. Heated debate between and among residents and nonresidents of the Pacific Northwest over the preservation of old growth forest landscapes to provide habitat for the endangered spotted owl is a familiar example. In the southern United States, rural landowners have also been put under controversial land use restrictions if certain pine trees on their land happen to provide significant habitat for endangered red cockaded woodpeckers.

Another function of land and landscapes is provision of unique physical terrain. Physical terrain includes mountains, rolling hills, gorges, valleys, plains, marshes and beaches. Use and management of physical terrain features may also be a controversial area of rural land use policy at certain times and in certain regions of the United States. Clashes may arise, for instance, between and among residents and nonresidents of rural areas over the preservation and management of unique physical terrain features. Debates over mining and forestry practices (e.g., clear-cutting of trees, strip mining) that temporarily or permanently alter the physical terrain and appearance of a rural landscape are cases in point.

A major function of rural land areas is provision of a natural water supply system. With respect to water quantity, rural land areas support both a flow and stock of surface and subsurface water supplies through watershed runoff into rivers and lakes, and the seepage of surface water into subsurface aquifers. With respect to water quality, land elements (e.g., plants, soil) help to filter out chemicals in surface and subsurface water supplies that are potentially harmful to human, plant and animal health. The function of rural land as a natural water supply system is an especially important issue from a rural and urban development policy perspective.

The land functions shown in Figure 6.2 support the various land values discussed previously and listed in Figure 6.1. The function of land as providing commercial inputs primarily supports the value people derive from consuming commercial goods, or material consumption value. The function of land as a place to work also supports material consumption value as well as job satisfaction value, and security and stability value. The function of land as a place to live supports job satisfaction value, security and stability value, cultural value, historical value, recreation and leisure use value, aesthetic appreciation value, and mental, physical and spiritual health values. The function of land as a place to visit supports cultural value, historical value, recreation and leisure use value, aesthetic appreciation value, and mental, physical and spiritual health values.

The function of rural land and landscapes in providing "space," including "open and green space," support recreation and leisure use value, aesthetic appreciation value, existence values, intrinsic values, biocentric and ecocentric instrumental values, and mental, physical and spiritual health values. The functions of providing flora and fauna habitat, unique physical terrain, and a natural water supply system arguably have an important role in supporting all of the values shown in Figure 6.2.

Rural land value management

The preceding sections indicate that a broad array of commodity and amenity values are supported by rural land. Two relevant policy questions are: (1) what is the desired mix of value provided by a particular landscape or landscapes, and (2) how can this desired mix be achieved and maintained? Consider first a productivist rural area or landscape in which commodity values are the primary values of interest. Figure 6.3 illustrates the primary beneficiaries and institutional representation for this type of area or landscape.

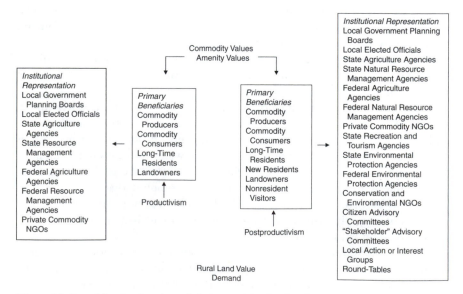

Figure 6.3 Rural land value, beneficiaries, and institutional representation.

Primary beneficiaries of commodity values in rural areas are commodity producers, commodity consumers, landowners, and long-time residents. These beneficiaries have traditionally had strong representation in local government planning boards, local elected officials, state agricultural agencies, state resource management agencies, federal agricultural agencies, federal resource management agencies, and private commodity nongovernmental organizations (NGOs).

When a rural area or landscape moves into postproductivism, there is demand for both landscape amenity and commodity values. Primary beneficiaries and institutional representation in this type of area or landscape are also illustrated in Figure 6.3. The demand for amenity values, in particular, adds new residents and nonresident visitors to the list of primary beneficiaries of landscape values. The demand for amenity values also results in government agencies and nongovernmental organizations (NGOs) that primarily represent the amenity value interests that become involved in landscape management in a rural area. Government agencies include local recreation and tourism development boards and state recreation and tourism agencies. NGOs include conservation and environmental organizations and local chambers of commerce in some areas.

A major challenge in rural areas experiencing postproductivism development is dealing with "value conflicts" between people whose interests are primarily with commodity values, and other people whose interests are primarily with amenity values. Commodity value interests are generally well represented in various land management institutions because of the private good nature of commodity values. There is a direct incentive for commodity producers, for example, to become involved in land management issues because their income and livelihood may depend upon it. Amenity value interests may not be as well represented in various land management institutions because of the public good nature of these values. A "free-rider" problem may occur, for example, if one person or group takes on the burden and costs of becoming involved in land management institutions to protect amenity value interests, and not everyone else in the community who enjoys nonrival, nonexclusive amenity values benefits from these actions (Bromley and Hodge 1990; Heimlich and Anderson 2001; Hellerstein *et al.* 2002; Organization for Economic Cooperation and Development 2001a; Reed and Gill 1997).

As a result of uneven representation in established land management institutions, new institutional arrangements may need to be developed for resolving value conflicts between commodity value and amenity value advocates in postproductivism rural areas. These new institutional arrangements may include more "bottom-up" organizations, including citizen advisory committees, stakeholder advisory committees, local action or interest groups, round tables and public forums. Many of the Federal land management agencies (e.g., US Department of Agriculture) have increased the use of stakeholder advisory committees, round tables and public forums in an attempt to resolve value conflicts between people who would like to maximize the use of national forests and rangelands for commodity values (e.g., timber harvesting, mining, grazing) and other people who would like to maximize the use of national forests and rangelands for recreation and other amenity values.

Summary and conclusion

People have a special attachment to land that spans a broad array of concerns and interests. These lead to a multitude of interdisciplinary values that people derive from land. Land or landscapes can be thought of as assets with a number of major functions. These functions include use as a commercial input, a natural water supply system, unique physical terrain, flora and fauna habitat, space, and a place in which to live, work and visit. Land or landscape functions support economic and noneconomic values ranging from material consumption value to nonuse values, including existence value and intrinsic value.

Two general categories of anthropocentric land or landscape values are commodity values and amenity values. Commodity values are derived from commercial commodities produced using land as a major input, including food and fiber products, timber products, mineral products and manufactured goods. Amenity values are derived directly from the land and have large non-consumptive or passive use components. Amenity values include recreational use value, scenic appreciation value, existence value, and certain types of cultural, historical, and health values.

Within a particular rural area or landscape, people residing inside or outside of that area or landscape will have different preferences for the current and future mix of rural land values (e.g., commodity vs. amenity values). Productivism, which has been a traditional focus of public policy in rural areas, focuses on commodity values. Many rural areas are moving into a postproductivism era that focuses on both commodity and amenity values. When a rural area moves from productivism to postproductivism, value conflicts often arise between individuals and groups whose primary interests are commodity values and individuals and groups whose primary interests are amenity values. Rural institutions for handling such conflicts may not be well established. There is a need to explore which institutions will be most effective in rural areas for moderating and solving value conflicts between people who desire different mixes of commodity and amenity values from land and landscapes.

Part II

A closer look at consequences of land use problems and conflicts

7 Urban development impacts on ecosystems

Elizabeth P. Marshall and James S. Shortle

Introduction

Once upon a time, when humans existed by hunting and gathering and were themselves prey, there was a "natural" landscape. Since then the Earth's surface, including the biota, topography, surface and groundwater, has been profoundly and irreversibly altered by the direct and indirect effects of human uses of the land (Sala *et al.* 2000; Vitousek *et al.* 1997; Wilson 1992). By some analyses, the transformation of the surface due to human activities approaches in magnitude the land cover transformations that have occurred during the transitions from glacial to interglacial climate (Meyer and Turner 1994; National Research Council 2001; Ramankutty and Foley 1999).

Changes in land use and land cover can have wide-ranging environmental consequences. These include loss of biodiversity, changes in emissions of trace gases affecting climate change, changes in hydrology and soil degradation (Meyer and Turner 1992). Moreover, changes in land use and land cover can influence vulnerability of people and places to environmental perturbations by, for example, influencing the spread of infectious diseases, interfering with the migration of species and affecting the risk of natural hazards (National Research Council 2001).

The environmental consequences of past and contemporary land uses are drawing significant attention. Deforestation and intensification of agriculture have, for example, received much notice as environmental threats. More recently, urbanization in general, and "urban sprawl" in particular, have been identified as significant environmental stressors (e.g., Kleppel *et al.* 2001; Vernberg *et al.* 1996; Vernberg and Vernberg 2001). No single definition of urban sprawl, or what distinguishes it from more traditional patterns of urbanization, exists (Burchell *et al.* 1998; Johnson 2001). Burchell *et al.* (1998, 2002) identify three essential characteristics implicit in most definitions of urban sprawl: low-density development, leapfrog development and unlimited outward expansion. A more colloquial definition provided by the United States Environmental Protection Agency (EPA) describes urban sprawl as "low density, automobile dependent development beyond the edge of service and employment areas" (US Environmental Protection Agency 2001a: 1).

This low-density development generally replaces existing acres of farmland, woodland and wetland and automobile-enabled leapfrog development creates seeds around which satellite communities grow. As the landscape becomes increasingly urbanized, the human system becomes more complex and the natural system becomes more simplified (Kleppel and De Voe 2000; Kleppel *et al.* 2001). Moreover, throughout the process of urbanization, ecologically disruptive elements (e.g., impervious surface areas, invasive species) are introduced.

The loss of ecosystem complexity and disruption of ecosystem structure results in a diminished capacity of the landscape to provide environmental services. This environmental degradation is part of what the EPA calls the "hidden debt" of urban sprawl (US Environmental Protection Agency 2001a). In this paper we introduce a conceptual framework for analyzing the environmental consequences of urbanization, provide a brief overview of research that has been conducted on those consequences and suggest a limited set of questions and issues for further research.

Environmental impacts of urban development and sprawl

The environmental impacts of sprawl development differ from those of high-density urban development because the low-density characteristic of sprawl results in a greater overall area being converted to urban use, and because the dispersed nature of sprawl development can create environmental problems above and beyond the impacts attributable to the magnitude of conversion. The predominant characteristics of urban sprawl, low-density and dispersed development, often operate in tandem, but they may have distinctly different effects in terms of environmental impacts. The outward expansion of cities in low-density concentric circles, for instance, may generate a bundle of environmental impacts that differs in composition from that generated by leapfrog development, which not only forms seeds for further sprawl but fragments remaining landscapes and requires a disproportionate amount of additional infrastructure development to support it.

The distinction between the two impacts can be seen to be that of impacts arising from the *magnitude* of conversion versus those arising from the *pattern* of conversion. The magnitude of conversion to urban area in a region can be measured with a simple aggregate indicator of some characteristic of the area converted. Analyzing pattern of conversion, on the other hand, recognizes that environmental impacts may vary with both relative location (i.e., position relative to other land uses) and absolute location, or position within a relevant natural unit such as a watershed or atmospheric inversion basin. Most of the research on the impacts of sprawl has focused on measures of magnitude of sprawl, though theory suggests that certain impacts, particularly those on habitat, may be particularly sensitive to the relative location of development. Because public policy designed to address the pattern of sprawl may look quite different from policy designed to address the magnitude of sprawl, it is important to differentiate between the effects and understand if, and how, they operate separately.

In an attempt to maintain a focus on the distinction between impacts related to magnitude and pattern of sprawl, we categorize impacts of sprawl into four categories: the effects of land conversion, the effects of land use change, the effects of landscape change and induced effects. The category "impacts of land conversion" captures environmental impacts that arise through the actual short-term process of land cover conversion. The remaining categories encompass long-term impacts that can be expected to arise within the system as a result of land use change. These categories address the changes in global and regional indicators of environmental quality that result from after the system has settled into a new state.

Within the remaining categories, the long-terms impacts are categorized as "the effects of land use change" if the impact is primarily generated within the converted parcel itself and is relatively insensitive to the parcel's absolute or relative location. These impacts may be understood and aggregated without reference to location or pattern of conversion. In contrast, "the effects of landscape change" arise precisely because a parcel's relative or absolute location means that its conversion will have a disproportionately larger environmental impact on some class of impacts than the conversion of a parcel of similar size in a different location. Although a sufficiently sophisticated understanding of landscape processes would likely conclude that location is always a significant variable in determining environmental impact, it might also allow us to demonstrate that there will always be some generalizable rules about tradeoffs between amount and location of urban conversion. In anticipation of an understanding of those tradeoffs, we develop a framework based on the distinction between impacts that predominantly arise through magnitude of conversion and those that arise through location of conversion.

The final long-term category of effects is "induced effects," which refer to those environmental effects that can be expected to arise as a result of human behavioral responses to the new landscape structure. Within each category, impacts may also be categorized as "precedent-specific" if the impact in question arises from the conversion of a particular pre-existing land cover, and therefore may be associated with urbanization only in certain cases. Table 7.1 provides an overview of the environmental impacts of urban sprawl.

The effects of land conversion

The effects of land conversion refer to the environmental impacts generated by the process of destruction and reconstruction involved in altering a land parcel's land cover and land use as well as in providing services and access to that parcel. These impacts may be relatively long term, but the window of time within which they are generated is limited to the period of

Table 7.1 Environmental impacts of urban sprawl

Mechanism of impact		Environmental impacts	Research needs
Conversion processes		Increased erosion Trace gas flux Soil compaction Introduction of non-native species	Quantification of impacts
Impacts of land-cover change	Increase in urban land cover	Increase in impervious surface – degraded water quality – increased flooding – increased variability in stream flow – increased erosion – urban heat island effect	Incorporation of location in impact analysis
	Decrease in pre-existing land cover	– loss of wetlands – loss of habitat area – loss of biomass sinks for atmospheric trace gases	Quantification of impacts Analysis of regional thresholds of effect
Impacts of landscape change		– loss of contiguous habitat – fragmentation of remaining habitat – loss of corridors, migration stops, or dispersability – increased edge – increased presence of non-native or invasive species – higher species mortality due to increased contact with humans	Identification of landscape metrics to characterize vulnerability of landscapes Analysis of spatial sensitivity of additional environmental impacts
Induced effects	Increased vehicle dependence	– air pollution; increased smog and greenhouse gas emissions – water pollution; increased deposition of air pollution – water pollution; polluted runoff and road maintenance – increased energy use – stimulated car production	Analysis of human behavioral interaction with landscape to explore ways of reducing VMT
	Other	– increased risk of abandoned brownfields – possible shift in agricultural production to marginal soils	

actual development. The most widely recognized impacts found in this category are the water and soil quality impacts of road and parcel construction, including increased soil erosion and runoff due to temporary loss of vegetative cover. This effect is exacerbated by the fact that construction inevitably results in soil compaction, which compromises the soil's ability to absorb water (Buol 1994). Grading of parcels for development also encourages invasion and establishment of non-native flora that might have been unable to compete with existing vegetation. The star mustard, an invasive European plant, is speculated to have arrived in Humboldt County, California, on a piece of construction equipment (National Wildlife Federation 2001).

Other precedent-specific effects may also arise as a result of clearing certain types of pre-existing land uses. Cutting a forest for development, for instance, may result in a quick release of the trace gases, including carbon dioxide, sequestered on that parcel. The more long-term impact of such conversion, however, lies in the long-term reduction of global sinks for these gases. This long-lasting effect will be discussed in the next section.

Land conversion's non-specific effects may be the easiest of sprawl's impacts to tackle because they are generated within a finite window of space and time and associated with particular activities. However, while easier to control, these short-term, flow-type impacts may not be the most important. In fact, what differentiates the environmental impacts of sprawl development from other types of development is likely to be found in the other, long-term and landscape-level impacts described below.

The effects of land-cover change

When a parcel of land is converted to urban uses, there are impacts that arise from increasing the urban land-surface cover, and there are impacts that arise from decreasing the amount of whatever cover was pre-existing. Although we limit this category to include only impacts that can be traced directly to the original conversion site, spillover impacts of that conversion may be felt at a much larger spatial scale. Meyer and Turner (1992) argue that altering the land surface and its biotic cover can have regional or global impacts through two different mechanisms. The first is by affecting a regionally or globally fluid system. In this case, impacts from a local conversion site flow to another site via some dispersion system such as air or water. The second mechanism is via aggregation, where enough sites are converted that their aggregate impact can be regionally or globally significant.

There is a substantial literature demonstrating that water quality is impacted by land cover (e.g., Allan *et al.* 1997; Herlihy *et al.* 1998; Jones *et al.* 2001; Roth *et al.* 1996). In urbanizing watersheds, a key water quality concern is the impact of impervious surface areas. A predominant characteristic of urban land surface cover is the prevalence of impervious surfaces. The environmental impacts associated with additional urban land surface cover can in large part be traced back to the resulting increase in impervious surface area. Impervious surfaces are constructed surfaces (i.e., rooftops, sidewalks, roads and parking lots) that are covered by impenetrable materials such as asphalt, cement or concrete and stone, and that therefore repel water and prevent water from infiltrating to the soil (Barnes *et al.* 2001). Transportation-related imperviousness (roads, driveways and parking lots) has been found to account for a greater percentage of impervious cover in many types of communities and may exert a greater hydrological impact as it is often directly linked to storm drain systems (Schueler 1994). Although the rooftop component of impervious surface area is often regulated through traditional density zoning measures, transportation-related imperviousness has been largely neglected by policy (Schueler 1994).

Altering the amount of impervious surface within a watershed has a multitude of environmental impacts; impervious surfaces alter local and regional hydrological cycles and water quality, and produce changes in local energy balances and micro-climates (Barnes *et al.* 2001). In a comprehensive review of the aquatic impacts of impervious cover, the Center for Watershed Protection categorizes those impacts as hydrologic impacts, physical impacts, water quality impacts and biological impacts (Center for Watershed Protection 2003). Impervious cover impacts the hydrologic cycle by altering the volume, pattern and timing of hydrologic flows at various points in the cycle. With an increase in impervious surface area, less precipitation infiltrates into the soil to recharge groundwater and more runs directly off into surface waters. Soil absorbs and stores stormwater, buffers water acidity, delivers nutrients to plant roots and serves as a conduit for groundwater recharge. When the top layer of soil is sealed off, these services are no longer provided. Increased volume of surface water runoff, increased magnitude and frequence of flooding events and decreased stream baseflow during dry periods have all been attributed to increased impervious cover in a watershed (Center for Watershed Protection 2003).

These changes in pattern and timing of water flows also lead to physical changes within the system. Increased stormwater runoff results in higher periodic stream flow, stream channel enlargement and incision, greater stream bank erosion and increased sedimentation in the stream channel (Center for Watershed Protection 2003; Schueler 1994; US Environmental Protection Agency 2001a). The water quality impacts of increased stormwater runoff can also be significant; reduced soil buffering means that urban contaminants (e.g., pesticides, deicers, trace metals and hydrocarbons), acid precipitation and nutrients (e.g., phosphorus and nitrogen) are carried more directly into surface water bodies, leading to higher peak acidity levels, an alteration of natural nutrient cycles, eutrophication and low stream oxygen levels (US Environmental Protection Agency 2001a). Stream temperature has also been found to be correlated to the imperviousness of the contributing watershed (Schueler 1994, citing Galli 1990).

Biological impacts arise from all of these other changes in the aquatic system. Stressors to biological systems that have been attributed to urbanization include the increased stream flow volumes, decreased base flows, increased sediments, loss of stream pools, increases in stream temperature, physical blockages and other changes to stream structure and reductions in water quality (Center for Watershed Protection 2003). These factors combine to significantly reduce habitat quality for stream macroinvertebrates (US Environmental Protection Agency 2001a). Research indicates that aquatic fish and insect communities respond in similar ways to the stream impacts typical of urbanization: egg and larvae survival decreases, total species diversity is reduced and species composition shifts toward more pollution-tolerant species (Center for Watershed Protection 2003; Weaver and Garman 1994). There is also evidence that changes in the hydrologic cycle compromise local wetland areas, with wetland insect community health and wetland plant density declining as impervious cover increases (Center for Watershed Protection 2003). Such wetland communities may rely heavily on groundwater during the dry spells between rains, and the detrimental impacts of urbanization play out through a number of factors such as reduced groundwater recharge, increased fluctuations in wetland water levels and changes in wetland water quality.

Numerous studies have attempted to identify thresholds in the relationship between impervious cover and various types of environmental impacts. A variety of studies indicate that 10 percent impervious cover represents an important threshold for many environmental impacts (Center for Watershed Protection 2003; Schueler 1995). The impervious cover model (ICM) developed by the Center for Watershed Protection assumes that most stream quality indicators decline when impervious cover exceeds 10 percent, and that severe stream degradation is expected when impervious cover exceeds 25 percent (Center for Watershed Protection 2003). Studies of the impacts of impervious surface for the Mid-Atlantic region of the United States indicate that changes in the biotic community in streams emerge when impervious surface is greater than about 3 percent of the watershed area, and that significant degradation of biotic community is observed when impervious surface reaches 10–15 percent or greater (Horner *et al.* 1996; May *et al.* 1997; Schueler and Gali 1992; US Environmental Protection Agency 1999; VanderWilt *et al.* 2003; Wang and Kanehl 2003). According to a study of suburban regions in the Chesapeake Bay area, impervious cover associated with residential development ranges from a mean of 10.6 percent for 2 acre lots to 27.8 percent for quarter acre lots, with townhome and multifamily residential development exceeding 40 percent imperviousness (Capiella and Brown 2001). One could interpret these numbers to mean that greater water quality protection is achievable with low-density development, but such a conclusion ignores the issue of scale: such low-density development spreads development over a much larger area and creates a demand for additional impervious roads to link dispersed communities. When analyzed at the regional or watershed scale, clustered high-density development will leave a larger percentage of the watershed in its natural condition and will decrease overall impervious cover (Kauffman *et al.* 2000).

Urbanization has also been linked to the "heat island effect," a phenomenon where temperatures within cities are higher than temperatures in surrounding areas. Research suggests that on a summer day, the average temperature in a US city is 3–5 degrees Fahrenheit warmer than surrounding areas, and that this temperature increase may account for 5 to 10 percent of urban peak electric demand (Chen 1994). This effect is due to the combined impacts of removing vegetation and replacing it with dark surfaces such as asphalt roads and dark roofs. The natural cooling effects of vegetative evapotranspiration are eliminated, while the sun-absorbing surfaces of roads and buildings heat up and raise the temperature of the air around them (Pomerantz 1999; Rosenfeld *et al.* 1996). Although this effect has been documented for large urban areas, it is unclear to what extent less concentrated forms of sprawl development generate such an effect.

Precedent-specific environmental impacts of urbanization arise due to the reduction in replaced land cover. The destruction and replacement of parcels bearing biomass has long been recognized to have atmospheric implications arising from changes in the flux and storage capacity for trace gases. When a forest parcel is replaced by an urban parcel, for instance, the region's ability to sequester the greenhouse gas CO_2 is reduced. The same effect would be observed to a lesser extent with the conversion of other natural systems with lower standing biomass. In aggregate, the effects of such conversions on atmospheric CO_2 levels may be substantial. Estimates suggest that the increase in atmospheric CO_2 from land cover change may be 10 to 50 percent of the increase due to industry and fossil fuel burning, which is a far more loudly denounced culprit (Penner 1994). Fluxes in other trace gases, some short-lived and some long-lived, have also been attributed to changes in land use, including the greenhouse gases methane and nitrous oxide, as well as sulfur dioxide and carbon monoxide.

Certain types of habitat have been found to be particularly vulnerable to development. The disappearance and degradation of wetlands in the United States has gained increasing attention over the last decade. It is estimated that between 1780 and 1980, 53 percent of the wetlands found in the lower 48 states, a total of 104 million acres, were lost (Dahl 1990). Net wetland losses have been declining since the 1970s but are still positive; between 1986 and 1997 wetland losses were estimated to average 58,500 acres per year (Dahl 2000). Over that period, development accounted for 51 percent of wetland loss, while loss to agriculture was only 26 percent (Dahl 2000). Between 1982 and 1992, those figures were estimated to be 57 percent and 20 percent, respectively (National Resources Conservation Service 1995). Additionally, policies to reverse wetland loss have focused primarily on wetland acreage rather than quality, and many remaining wetlands are plagued by the water quality issues mentioned above. Such loss and degradation compromises the services that wetlands have traditionally provided: removing nutrients, pesticides and sediments from surface water; absorbing the impact of storm tides and floods; replenishing groundwater; and providing critical breeding and feeding habitat for birds, fish and other wildlife (National Resources Conservation Service 1995).

When an urban area replaces a wetland, grassland, forest, or agricultural parcel, the viability of species that formerly occupied the parcel or adjacent parcels may be threatened. This impact occurs through two distinct mechanisms. One mechanism is a decline in the absolute amount of habitat available to support that species. The second is the effect of the loss of that parcel on the quality of remaining habitat. The two effects are conceptually quite different, as a small parcel of habitat may be a negligible portion of the total habitat area available, but at the same time it may represent a critical link or buffer such that its loss will have a significant effect on the quality of the habitat remaining in the landscape. This latter effect may far outweigh the importance of the land use change, or habitat loss, on one specific parcel.

Only the first of these two effects should be considered under the category "effects of land cover change." The latter habitat quality effect represents an impact that would fall under the heading "effects of landscape change." In documenting the magnitude of urbanization's impact on species viability, however, this distinction is not often made, as separating the effects would require an intimate understanding of a species' natural history. Therefore, we report evidence on the combined effects of urbanization, and emphasize the importance of recognizing the different mechanisms of impact in future applied research.

Habitat loss has been found to be the primary cause of species decline and endangerment on the mainland United States (Czech *et al.* 2000; Wilcove *et al.* 1998; Wilson 1992). The categories of habitat destruction examined by these studies include agricultural conversion, road construction and maintenance, water development and drainage projects and land conversion for urban and commercial development (Wilcove *et al.* 1998). A list of species pushed to the brink of extinction in large part due to urban sprawl looks like a "Who's Who" of the endangered species act. Of 877 species federally listed as threatened or endangered as of 1994, 275 were attributed primarily to urbanization (Czech *et al.* 2000). In California, one of the most rapidly urbanizing states in the United States, 66 percent of the federally listed threatened or endangered species were attributed to urbanization (National Wildlife Federation 2001), including the San Joaquin kit fox, the Santa Ana mountain lion and the Bay checkerspot butterfly.

As mentioned above, the magnitude of habitat directly lost to urbanization represents only the first wave of impacts that can be expected from land conversion. Urbanization can result in a cascade of secondary effects on habitat quality, including increased fragmentation of remaining habitat, increased exposure to habitat edge effects and introduction of non-native species. These effects are discussed in greater detail below.

The effects of landscape change

If a parcel is removed from a habitat matrix, the remaining habitat will be subjected to external forces that could alter its ability to support the species in question. Urbanization may therefore result in ecological spillovers that alter the landscape's ability to support species in a manner that supercedes loss of a single parcel. We categorize these impacts as effects of landscape change. As mentioned above, urbanization can have land-cover change effects through its reduction in the absolute amount of habitat available, but it can also have wider impacts on the landscape surrounding it that may ultimately more substantially impact species viability. In particular, urbanization results in fragmentation of existing habitat and an accompanying increase in the amount of habitat edge, and increased exposure to edge and non-native species. Habitat fragmentation has often been identified in the literature as a principal threat to a region's biodiversity (Noss and Cooperrider 1995; Wilcox and Murphy 1985).

Habitat fragmentation is produced both by the removal of natural habitat for development, and through the construction of roads, power lines, pipelines, etc., to support the new development. Spillover effects of this new development compromise not only the quality of the remaining habitat but also the accessibility of the remaining habitat. Effects on surrounding habitat quality generally proliferate via the "edge effect." The edge effect refers to the shifts that occur in micro-climate at habitat boundaries; such shifts generate alterations in species composition at habitat boundaries, and often favor exotic species at the expense of native or forest-interior species (Heimlich and Anderson 2001). The encroachment of non-native species at the habitat border results in a further effective loss of habitat for forest-interior species, which may be in direct competition with edge species that have evolved to exploit forest-interior species. Studies of bird populations consistently report correlations between nest predation and brood parasitism and habitat fragmentation (Donovan *et al.* 1997; Robinson *et al.* 1995). The brown-headed cowbird, a brood parasite, has been implicated in the decline of such species as the Kirtland's warbler and the willow flycatcher; the competitive success of this generalist edge species is likely increased by the expansion of its habitat, which brings it into closer proximity to its host species. Even seemingly benign habitat disruptions such as power line corridors can act as a powerful conduit for the invasion of edge and non-native species. Interaction with non-native species has also been found to be a major cause of species endangerment in the United States (Czech *et al.* 2000).

Fragmentation of habitat also limits species' ability to access the habitat that remains to them. Roads form a significant barrier, as many species exhibit an aversion to roads, and some, such as the black bear, cannot cross highways with guard rails (Heimlich and Anderson 2001). Road presence, construction and maintenance have been associated with the endangerment of 94 species nationwide (Czech *et al.* 2000). Roads may also impact species mortality directly; cars and trucks now rank among the main causes of death for pups of the endangered San Joaquin kit fox, and research in Florida suggests that road kills are the primary cause of death for most large mammal species there (Heimlich and Anderson 2001; National Wildlife Federation 2001).

The magnitude of the environmental effects of landscape change can be seen to depend in large part on the interaction that existed between land uses prior to development. In landscapes composed originally of fragmented land uses, the marginal impact of further fragmentation may be minimal. However, in relatively undisturbed landscapes, the impacts generated by even a small amount of disturbance (e.g., through road or bridge building) may be substantial. The impacts of landscape change are therefore highly sensitive to the relative location of development within an existing development matrix.

It is likely that there are other environmental effects whose impacts are determined in large part by location. Unfortunately, there are far more questions about the importance of location than there are answers. Are watersheds more vulnerable to the effects of impervious surfaces on ridges or in the valleys themselves, for instance? It is reasonable to expect that absolute location of land-cover change may play an important role in differentiating water-quality impacts, but we could find little evidence with which to corroborate this theory. The research is currently lacking, but the recent explosive development of simulated landscape modeling is a promising move toward spatially explicit impact analysis.

Induced effects of landscape change

Sprawl-style development induces a pattern of human behavior that generates additional environmental impacts. These impacts, which arise from the landscape occupants' behavioral response to the new landscape form, are categorized as "induced effects of landscape change." Perhaps the most widely denounced aspect of urban sprawl development is the increase in vehicle miles traveled that is believed to accompany the widening distances between locations of residence, work, play and consumption. Between 1980 and 1997, total vehicle miles traveled in the United States rose 63 percent; over that period the annual growth rate in vehicle miles traveled (3.1 percent) was triple that of the population growth rate (1 percent) (US Environmental Protection Agency 2001a).

This disproportionate growth in distance traveled has been attributed by many authors to homeowners' preferences for less dense neighborhoods and workplaces (Downs 1992). In fact, several forces are at work, including the effects of changing demographics and the changing status of women in the workforce (National Personal Transportation Survey 1995). Changes in land use patterns are found to be a significant factor as well, however, with average commute distances increasing by 37 percent between 1983 and 1995, and daily vehicle miles traveled per driver increasing from 28.5 miles to 32.1

miles between 1990 and 1995 (National Personal Transportation Survey 1995, 1999). Due to changes in measurement and methodology, National Personal Transportation Survey (NPTS) results prior to 1990 and post-1990 are not comparable, but the 1990 NPTS survey found that between 1983 and 1990, average per-person trip distances increased by 38 percent and number of trips made per person increased by 25 percent (US Environmental Protection Agency 2001a).

The environmental impacts associated with increased vehicle miles traveled are many and familiar. Exhaust emissions are responsible for increased atmospheric levels of carbon monoxide, sulfur dioxide, particulate matter, hazardous air pollutants, ozone, nitrogen dioxide and lead, among other things. The degradation of air quality arising from exhaust emissions has local health effects as well as global climate effects; the transportation sector is currently responsible for 32 percent of US carbon dioxide emissions, and carbon emissions from transportation are projected to increase by 47.5 percent between 1996 and 2020 (US Environmental Protection Agency 2001a). Vehicle travel also generates the greenhouse gases nitrous oxide and methane (US Environmental Protection Agency 2001a).

Regional water quality is further degraded directly by polluted road runoff and the application of road maintenance materials (salting and de-icing compounds, for instance), as well as indirectly through the deposition of air pollution. Estimates suggest that atmospheric nitrogen may be responsible for 5–50 percent of the total loading to the Chesapeake Bay (with most estimates around 30 percent), and estimates of atmospheric loadings of metals range from 95 percent in the case of lead to 10 percent for cadmium (US Environmental Protection Agency 2001b). Although research has not yet traced these atmospheric pollutants back to their source, it is reasonable to suspect mobile sources as significant contributors. Depending on how far back along the chain of causality one progresses, environmental impacts associated with increased fuel provision, such as oil spills and leaking underground storage tanks, as well as motor vehicle manufacture, could be implicated.

Sprawl development, or rather the ability to engage in sprawl development, may have other consequences that are best considered under the category of "induced" effects. A failure to recognize the full costs of sprawl may result in an increased risk of abandoning rather than mitigating brownfields, for instance. Another charge levied against urban sprawl is that it results in the loss of prime agricultural farmland (American Farmland Trust 1994). Although the highly debated implications for aggregate productivity or food security are not considered in this chapter, if the loss of prime agricultural farmland results eventually in increased reliance on soil types that are less suitable for cultivation, we may experience additional environmental impacts related to intensive use of inputs and increased erosion (Imhoff *et al.* 1998).

Conclusion and future research

Other authors have proposed research agendas to address the costs, environmental and otherwise, of urban sprawl (Burchell *et al.* 2002; Johnson 2001; Pennsylvania Twenty-first Century Environment Commission 1998). We add to those agendas a call for research on the importance of "location, location, location." The spatial aspect of sprawl's impact is important in terms of understanding the magnitude of the biophysical environmental impacts, but it is equally critical because sprawl impacts, and is impacted by, a co-evolving socioeconomic system (see Table 7.1, page 82). Understanding the feedback between systems will be crucial to the design of effective policies for managing sprawl. To what extent do choices for location of residence affect the environmental impact of that development? At what point, and under what conditions, can conversion of that parcel affect landscape-level processes and thresholds? How can that conversion and its aggregate effects be expected to impact back upon the community that made those development choices in the first place? What about impact on other communities that were not involved in the decisions to develop? Does the dynamic of development choices, together with the environmental change that results, lead to an "acceptable" equilibrium between development and environmental quality, or do the system dynamics lead inevitably to degradation and further sprawl? What policies might successfully maintain the system at some intermediate point? The possible questions are, of course, endless; what is critical to future research is the recognition that, while understanding detailed mechanisms of both the biophysical and the socioeconomic mechanisms is important, understanding the interaction between the systems is equally important. We have identified several specific areas of research that will help us move toward that end.

Predicting the ecological consequences of development

- It is clear that urban development alters ecosystems in ways that adversely affect primary productivity, nutrient cycling, resilience, biodiversity and other indicators of aquatic and terrestrial ecosystem structure and function (i.e., health), and a loss of ecosystem services. However, while it is possible to describe changes that have accompanied past development, the scientific basis for predicting the ecological consequences of future development or evaluating the ecological consequences of policies to protect ecosystems is limited. Stressor-response effects are often not well understood, making the consequences of future changes in urban stressor levels uncertain.
- Indicators used to predict the environmental impact of sprawl have traditionally been aggregate measures such as percent of impervious surface or total vehicle miles traveled in a region. Future research should focus in addition on metrics of landscape and development pattern that may be useful in describing how impacted a region is by development as well as predicting how it would respond to future development.

Choosing futures and restructuring patterns of growth

- "Community-based" environmental policy is in vogue, and is appropriate for addressing some local-scale urban environmental externalities. However, much remains to be learned about how to inform citizens of environmental risks, and methods of engaging them in the evaluation and selection of actions.

- Land use controls are typically exercised by local governments, but local political jurisdictions generally do not correspond to the space in which the impacts of local decisions are made. In consequence, decisions that make sense at a local level may have adverse consequences when aggregated. Alternatively, local decisions that are intended to have "good" environmental consequences may be rendered ineffective when environmental outcomes depend on large landscape scale processes that extend beyond the boundaries of the community. How does the scale at which communities make land use decisions affect their pattern of development and therefore the environmental impacts they can expect to see from development? Can coordination of land use decision making be demonstrated to have more benefits for certain types of impacts than for others?

- Communities have a menu of policy instruments for addressing the various issues created by urban development, and for re-structuring growth along preferred paths. However, there is limited economic research to guide policy choices. While the literature on the choice and design of policy instruments for environmental externalities is vast, the context assumed is usually quite limited. The urban environmental externality problem offers multiple stressors emanating from point and non-point sources, affecting a range of ecosystem types over a range of spatial scales, stochastic variations, and both acute and cumulative impacts. This mix alone poses significant theoretical and empirical challenges for the design and evaluation of policy instruments. But the problem is significantly complicated by the fact that the urban environment is one in which a mix of public and private goods are jointly produced, making for a complex web of market and nonmarket interactions that must be addressed in a multiple objective comprehensive design. Community experiences are instructive but may not reveal general lessons. Dynamic simulation experiments using spatially explicit models that couple economic and ecological components offer a method for obtaining robust results.

Landscapes are in constant motion. In our discussion of environmental impacts of sprawl, we have focused on the "global flows" of air and water mentioned above, as well as the animal and plant migration that occurs as species pass through or around matrices of land uses in an attempt to find the resources they need for survival and reproduction. Development moves

across the land surface as well, of course, in response to decisions communities and individuals make about appropriate rates and patterns of land conversion. These decisions are made within the existing environmental context,
but every time a parcel is converted, the entire environmental landscape
adjusts and either new natural pathways of movement of air and water are
created, or, in the case of species extinction, the movement itself is stilled.
The result is a change in environmental context, perhaps a development
response, and eventually a new set of decisions about rates and pattern of land
conversion. Effective land-management policies will emerge when we have
the information needed to move beyond a myopic approach to land use to
anticipate and accommodate the future impacts of today's policies.

8 Urban growth, rural land conversion and the fiscal well-being of local municipalities

Steven Deller[1]

Introduction

As urban areas grow in terms of population, income and wealth, the value of the land surrounding these places increases. Returns to developing the land for housing and commercial enterprises exceed the returns to farming. Some of the most productive agricultural areas become attractive sites for development (Morris 1998). Prior to the 1960s, the conversion of farmland was considered part of the natural process of spatial economic growth. Rapid suburbanization of cities due in part to the completion of the interstate highway system and the draw of suburban lifestyles caused many environmentalists to question the wisdom of allowing unregulated growth. As observed by Rome (2001), the 1960s and 1970s witnessed the emergence of two conflicting mega trends: first, massive migration to the suburbs and high amenity exsuburban rural areas and second, the rise of the environmental movement.

Throughout the 1960s and early 1970s environmentalists and others concerned with rapid unregulated growth argued for more restraints due to nebulous environmental concerns, broad quality of life issues and concerns over the demise of the family farm. While the general public was aware of these issues, there was little for local decision makers to use to offset the positive economic impacts emphasized by developers and the strong sense of private property ownership rights. The tone of the discussion shifted rapidly in 1974 with the release of the "Cost of Sprawl" study prepared by the Real Estate Research Corporation (RERC) (Real Estate Research Corporation 1974a) for the US Department of Housing and Urban Development. For the first time the public was made aware of differential fiscal impacts on local governments from alternative land use patterns. The major conclusion of this study was that "for a fixed number of households, 'sprawl' is the most expensive form of residential development ... [t]his cost difference is particularly significant for that proportion of total costs which is likely to be borne by local governments" (Real Estate Research Corporation 1974a: 7).

In a follow-up study in Wisconsin, the Real Estate Research Corporation (1974b) analyzed the cost implications of accommodating projected future growth under different development scenarios. The study compared the public costs associated with accommodating a forecasted statewide population increase of almost one million persons under three different growth scenarios: compact, high-density "containment;" "suburban extension;" and "exurban dispersion." On the basis of the study, RERC (7) concluded that "[i]f saving money on community facilities is important to citizens and local government officials, an increase in density and a reduction in leapfrogging will save significant sums." Environmentalists and concerned planners who before the RERC studies had been able to point to qualitative concerns about unregulated growth now had tangible "hard" evidence upon which to plead their case.

More recent examples of studies supporting the notion that planning and growth management can save taxpayers money include the work of researchers at Rutgers University's Center for Urban Policy Research (CUPR). The CUPR study (1992) estimated the public costs that would result from following the New Jersey growth management plan compared to unregulated growth. The Rutgers researchers found that over a twenty-year period, $1.3 billion in infrastructure costs could be saved. More remarkable about the Rutgers study is that the New Jersey growth management plan did not limit the amount of growth to occur but rather simply altered the pattern, density and location of development. While the CUPR study covered a range of environmental and social issues, the fiscal calculation attracted by far the greatest publicity and public comment. Other large-scale studies that have drawn significant attention in the planning arena and the public's eye include the Builders Association of the Twin Cities study (1996), the Kelly (1993) study of the Maryland "Vision" plan, and the DuPage County Planning Department study (1992) of the rapid growth west of Chicago. In each case, the low-density growth that is most often associated with "sprawl," in which a given amount of population and business growth consumes larger amounts of land, has significantly higher capital costs borne by local governments.

Within the academic literature, the work of Ladd (1990, 1994 and 1998) and her colleagues represents perhaps the most systematic and rigorous analysis of alternative growth patterns. In her 1990 study, for example, Ladd examined 248 large counties and found that those with higher rates of growth, and larger increases in tax-paying new development, had higher levels of public expenditure and higher tax rates than slower growing communities. The work of Ladd and other economists associated with the Lincoln Institute of Land Policy has consistently found that more rapidly growing areas tend to have greater increases in expenditures and tax burden than slower growing areas. These results are intuitive because rapidly growing areas require greater and faster investments in new infrastructure and government services not previously supplied. While Ladd points out that her work is not intended to assess the impacts of one type of development over another, it has been viewed as supporting evidence for the advocates of managed or, more recently, "smart growth."

As noted by Bunnell (1997, 1998), fiscal impact assessment has moved from unbiased information used in the public debate over land use and growth patterns into the realm of advocacy against unmanaged growth and for farmland and open space preservation. Planners working in the field quickly learned of the findings of the DuPage County study in a special Planning Advisory Service Memo (American Planning Association 1991) headlined "Does Development Really Pay for Itself?" Similarly, a 16-page report issued by the Sierra Club's Midwest Office titled "Sprawl Costs Us All – How Uncontrolled Sprawl Increases Your Property Taxes and Threatens Your Quality of Life" presents findings from a number of fiscal impact studies which show that development is fiscally "unbeneficial" to local governments and therefore should be severely limited (Hulsey 1996). It argues that a Property Tax Impact Statement should be required when any new development is proposed. "With the Property Tax Impact Statement, we will know up front what we will be paying for and we will decide if this development is beneficial or detrimental to the community" (Hulsey 1996: 13).

Perhaps the clearest example of the use of fiscal impact studies to support an advocacy argument related to growth management is the American Farmland Trust's (AFT) sponsorship and promotion of Cost of Community Services (COCS) studies. The AFT offers an alternative to the widely used methods of fiscal impact assessment provided by Burchell and Listokin (1978, 1980 and 1994) and Burchell *et al.* (1985). The COCS approach assesses a community's overall balance sheet of revenues and expenditures at any given point in time and attempts to determine the proportion of municipal revenues and expenditures attributed to major categories of land. The final product of a COCS study is a set of ratios expressing the proportion of revenues and costs for various land uses. The ease of interpretation and the promotion of the COCS approach by the American Farmland Trust have thrust it into the mainstream of America's thinking about the fiscal impacts of alternative land use patterns. The success of the AFT's COCS studies can be viewed in the "new conventional wisdom" that it has created: "everyone knows housing development doesn't pay for itself but commercial development does."

But this conclusion is not without some rigorous evidence. Danielson and Wolpert (1991) examined the growth of 365 contiguous municipalities in northern New Jersey during the 1980s. They assessed whether growth in employment and population affected several indices of fiscal and non-fiscal benefits. In general, they concluded that employment growth benefited local communities while population growth was largely detrimental. With specific regard to fiscal impacts, employment growth significantly lowered property tax rates while raising local government revenues per capita.

In the end, however, the new conventional wisdom has resulted in a unique scramble for fiscally productive tax bases that can produce undesirable and bizarre patterns of land use. Many communities seek to attract industrial and commercial developments but ignore the housing needs of employees,

especially those with low incomes and large families. Taken to its logical conclusion, the new conventional wisdom being touted by many people within
the land use planning community and fostered by AFT COCS-type studies
could lead to a world with farms, but no farmers and businesses, without
employees: a community of farms and businesses, but no residents.

The remainder of this chapter has four sections. First, a review of what
impact assessment is and is not, and the potential confusion that impact assessment can cause is provided. Then the AFT COCS approach is critically
reviewed. Third, a case study examining the economic and fiscal impact of
five alternative land use options is provided. Using a conjoined
input–output/econometric model of Wisconsin counties, five alternative
forms of economic development (i.e., land uses) are compared and contrasted. The chapter closes by outlining one potential research agenda.

Impact assessment: what it is and is not

When a community undertakes an impact assessment, it must consider several
elements of the assessment, including what it is and what it is not. These elements include an understanding that impact assessment is a process that:

- comprehensively evaluates the consequences of development on a
  community;
- provides extensive documentation of the anticipated related economic,
  fiscal, environmental, and social impacts of a proposed development;
- makes use of existing information where possible;
- employs techniques to gather additional, new information, where necessary; and
- provides a framework to integrate data, models, spatial and statistical
  analysis and the impacts of alternatives.

What is vital to this view of impact assessment is that it is a process through
which a community gathers and reflects on information about the proposed
development. Within the community development literature the idea of sustainable development hinges on grassroots development and adoption of specific proposals. While outside consultants can play an important role in
providing technical expertise, the community should not be held hostage to
the opinions of the developer or outside advocates. An understanding and
appreciation of the process of impact assessment is almost as important as the
technical merits of the assessment itself.

The benefits of impact assessment are wide-ranging and include the
following:

- Impact assessment is designed to enhance sound land use management at
  the local level and includes a number of important characteristics, not
  just fiscal impacts.

- Impact assessment provides an opportunity for communities to gain advance understanding of a particular development so that they may plan to both efficiently meet new service demands and avoid potential environmental or social costs.

But impact assessment is only beneficial if it leads to sound decisions such that the development minimizes adverse environmental impacts, is suitable for the location, makes efficient use of existing community infrastructure and services, accounts for community costs in the broadest context, is the product of broad public consensus, and is consistent with the community's economic, cultural and regional character. Impact assessment is particularly beneficial if the proposed development is large, unique or precedent setting and may have a substantial impact on a community's financial, environmental and cultural resources. But in the end, the decision to allow or dismiss the proposed development must be founded in the community's vision of itself. Elements of a "proper" impact assessment should include:

- evaluations of both the positive and negative impacts of the proposed development in all of the elements that a community defines as important in its vision of itself;
- focus on the significant impacts, not on the nominal effects of the proposed development. In other words, impact assessment should draw attention away from "red herring" issues and onto the noteworthy impacts;
- consideration of the direct as well as the indirect impacts of the proposed development;
- an assessment process that gives high priority to community values, long-term goals and self-vision when assessing impacts;
- an impact assessment that involves the community in evaluating impacts, especially when considering social and cultural impacts.

While impacts should be comprehensive and draw on local knowledge when at all possible, there are several things it will not do:

- Impact assessment does not provide *the* answer.
- It will not account for the possibility of spill-over into other communities.
- It should not be used to evaluate community values and/or vision of itself.
- It tends not to be cumulative in that impact assessment evaluates proposed development on a case-by-case basis.

Because impact assessment, when properly conducted, includes a wide range of both quantitative and qualitative information, it is important to realize that impact assessment in and of itself cannot provide the answer. While impact assessment should be comprehensive, covering a range of issues, it should not be confused with cost-benefit analysis. Impact assessment is a process that draws information into the decision making process whereas cost-benefit analysis is an attempt to quantify all costs and benefits of the proposed development. Seldom does a community have the time, energy or resources to conduct a full cost-benefit study for every proposed development.

A successful impact assessment, particularly the decision that comes at the end of the process, hinges on the notion that the community has an up-to-date and well thought-out vision and comprehensive plan in place. The plan should guide the impact assessment to focus on issues relevant to the community. In addition, the plan should outline the weights the community places on elements of the impact assessment. Without a vision or comprehensive plan in place, the impact assessment itself can inadvertently steer the decision making process. In the extreme, the impact assessment can dictate the community's vision of itself. The latter makes for poor public policy in terms of matching policy with the wishes and desires of local residents.

While, in theory, impact assessments should consider the longer cumulative impacts of a proposed development on the community, in practice impact assessments tend to focus on individual development proposals on a case-by-case basis. In the absence of a long-term comprehensive plan or vision of the community, short-term decisions on the basis of impact assessment can result in poor long-term policies. In essence, the cumulative collection of short-term decisions can take the community in a direction it may not deem desirable in the long run. In addition, the decisions of any individual community seldom consider the impact of the proposed development within the context of the larger urban area. A reasonable decision by any one community at a given point in time may have unpredictable consequences on the larger urban area.

For example, within the planning literature land use patterns described as leapfrogging are generally considered to have negative fiscal impacts (Real Estate Research Corporation 1974b). Monocentric urban density analysis, however, points out the shortcomings of short-term views of urban structure. Peiser (1989), for example, empirically demonstrates that areas that are skipped over and subsequently developed are developed at higher land use densities than they would have been had they not been skipped over. Peiser (1989: 197) notes that "[t]he driving forces behind the hypothesis are that land values on vacant in-fill parcels increase faster than land values at the urban fringe, and therefore developers must build at higher densities to achieve the same level of return." Ohls and Pines (1975) further suggest that skipping over central city locations to build low-density housing at the fringe is efficient from a regional perspective by saving central locations for more intensive uses. In the end, impact assessment properly conducted can provide invaluable information into the decision making process notwithstanding some of the shortcomings discussed above. Incomplete, poorly executed or conducted within an advocacy setting, impact assessment can result in poor public policy.

Cost of community service studies

One collection of studies that has contributed the most to the current confusion over the economic and fiscal impact of alternative land use patterns is the AFT COCS studies. While often referred to as fiscal impact analysis, the COCS method allows the community to assess its fiscal position at any one point in time in terms of demands placed on the locality by different land use categories. The studies are snapshots of the net fiscal costs of differential land uses. They are snapshots in that they measure one year at a time and do not make projections into the future. The COCS approach compares annual revenues to annual expenditures on public services for various land uses. Local revenues and expenditures are appropriated to major categories of land use, and the result is a set of ratios purporting to show the proportional relationship of revenues and expenditures for different land uses at one point in time.

Kelsey (1996) expresses a common formulation of the ratio as:

$$ratio_u = \frac{\Sigma((taxsd_{ut} + nontaxsd_{ur}) + (taxmcd_{ut} + nontaxmcd_{ur}))}{\Sigma(expendsd_{uj} + expendmcd_{uj})}$$

where:

$ratio_u$ = ratio of revenues to expenditures for land use u

$taxsd_{ut}$ = school district revenue from tax t and land use u

$nontaxsd_{ur}$ = school district revenue from non-tax source r and land use u

$taxmcd_{ut}$ = municipal revenue from tax t and land use u

$nontaxmcd_{ur}$ = municipal revenue from non-tax source r and land use u

$expendsd_{uj}$ = school district expenditure j related to land use u

$expendmcd_{uj}$ = municipal expenditure j related to land use u.

The ratio is said to provide an easy-to-understand measure of the net fiscal impact from a particular land use. When net fiscal impact is neutral (i.e., expenditures exactly equal revenues) the ratio will be 1:1. If expenditures exceed revenues, then the ratio will be less than one. The ratio is generally calculated on four different types of land uses: residential, commercial, industrial and farmland.

The critical part of these studies is the determination of which revenues and expenditures should be allocated to what types of land use and in what proportions. Some allocation decisions are straightforward, such as property tax revenues. Determining the allocation of certain expenditures can be accomplished through detailed analysis of community records, such as the number of fire department calls to alternative land uses or refuse collection based on tonnage collected from different land uses.

Allocating other expenditures is more difficult, if not completely arbitrary, such as the general administrative costs of running the local government. Here the AFT suggests using the percentage of all tax revenues arising from each land use as a default. For example, if residential properties account for 50 percent of property taxes, 50 percent of all non-directly allocable revenues and expenditures are attributed to residential land.

In the end, the allocation of revenues and expenditures depends on the availability and completeness of local records, the willingness of local staff and officials to participate in interviews and help in the allocation process, and the objectivity of the analyst conducting the analysis. This latter point is vital because inherent in the COCS approach is that judgment calls on the part of the analyst are inevitable. As argued by Bunnell (1997, 1998) in the current environment of using fiscal impact assessment in an advocacy setting, the objectivity of analysts has been called into question.

COCS studies consistently show that for residential land the cost of service ratio is greater than one. The averages of ratios of previous studies range from about $1.05 to $1.50 for residential development for every dollar of revenue generated (Table 8.1). COCS ratios for commercial and industrial properties are typically below one, with costs ranging between 30 and 65 cents for every dollar of revenue generated. For agricultural land and open space, ratios are typically smaller, ranging from 10 to 15 cents for every dollar of revenue generated. COCS studies across the board have concluded that farmland and open space provide more revenue to a community than is incurred in expenditures, resulting in a net fiscal benefit to a community.

COCS studies, however, are fraught with problems and critics often discount them because of the many underlying assumptions. Most notable, the conventional studies often fail to acknowledge that the residential category includes the homes of most people who farm or work on farms in the study area. This means that the costs associated with servicing farmers, resident agricultural workers and their families are apportioned to the residential category and many kinds of costs, such as street maintenance, garbage collection or protective services are not assigned to any agricultural uses. As a result of this approach, the overall costs associated with agriculture and other natural resource industries will necessarily be low or nonexistent. Since the traditional AFT methods discount the human service costs associated with agricultural activities, conventional COCS ratios may not provide a clear picture of the different fiscal impacts associated with farming versus residential land uses.

Gross land use categories

By averaging across land types, key distinctions between different land uses within the same category are lost and thus the method may unintentionally influence the conclusions about which development policies and subsequent land use patterns are cost-effective from a fiscal perspective. For example, the aggregate group of residential use makes no distinction among mobile homes, single-family dwellings, apartment buildings or smaller retirement homes. Additionally, the method gives no insight into the differences between small and low-intensity manufacturing development and large-scale operations, or

Table 8.1 Cost of community service studies

	Residential (with farm homes)	Combined commercial and industrial	Farmland, forest and open lands	Study source
Connecticut				
Bolton	1:1.05	1:0.23	1:0.50	Geisler, 1998
Durham	1:1.07	1:0.27	1:0.23	Southern New England Forest Consortium, 1995
Farmington	1:1.33	1:0.32	1:0.31	Southern New England Forest Consortium, 1995
Hebron	1:1.06	1:0.47	1:0.43	AFT, 1986
Litchfield	1:1.11	1:0.34	1:0.34	Southern New England Forest Consortium, 1995
Pomfret	1:1.06	1:0.27	1:0.86	Southern New England Forest Consortium, 1995
Idaho				
Canyon County	1:1.08	1:0.79	1:0.54	Hartmans and Meyer, 1997
Cassia County	1:1.19	1:0.87	1:0.41	Hartmans and Meyer, 1997
Kentucky				
Lexington-Fayette	1:1.64	1:0.22	1:0.93	AFT, 1999
Maine				
Bethel	1:1.29	1:0.59	1:0.06	Good, Antioch New England Graduate School, 1994
Maryland				
Carroll County	1:1.15	1:0.48	1:0.45	Carroll County Department of Management and Budget, 1994
Cecil County	1:1.12	1:0.28	1:0.37	Cecil County Office of Economic Development, 1994
Frederick County	1:1.14	1:0.50	1:0.53	AFT, 1997
Massachusetts				
Agawam	1:1.05	1:0.44	1:0.31	AFT, 1992
Becket	1:1.02	1:0.83	1:0.72	Southern New England Forest Consortium, 1995
Deerfield	1:1.16	1:0.38	1:0.29	AFT, 1992
Franklin	1:1.02	1:0.58	1:0.40	Southern New England Forest Consortium, 1995
Gill	1:1.15	1:0.43	1:0.38	AFT, 1992
Leverett	1:1.15	1:0.29	1:0.25	Southern New England Forest Consortium, 1995
Middleboro	1:1.08	1:0.47	1:0.70	AFT, 2001
Southborough	1:1.03	1:0.26	1:0.45	Adams and Hines, 1997
Westford	1:1.15	1:0.53	1:0.39	Southern New England Forest Consortium, 1995
Williamstown	1:1.11	1:0.34	1:0.40	Hazler *et al.*, 1992
Michigan				
Scio Township	1:1.40	1:0.28	1:0.62	University of Michigan, 1994

Table 8.1 Continued

	Residential (with farm homes)	Combined commercial and industrial	Farmland, forest and open lands	Study source
Minnesota				
Farmington	1:1.02	1:0.79	1:0.77	AFT, 1994
Lake Elmo	1:1.07	1:0.20	1:0.27	AFT, 1994
Independence	1:1.03	1:0.19	1:0.47	AFT, 1994
Montana				
Carbon County	1:1.60	1:0.21	1:0.34	Prinzing, 1999
Gallatin County	1:1.45	1:0.16	1:0.25	Haggerty, 1996
Flathead County	1:1.23	1:0.26	1:0.34	Citizens for a Better Flathead, 1999
New Hampshire				
Deerfield	1:1.15	1:0.22	1:0.35	Auger, 1994
Dover	1:1.15	1:0.63	1:0.94	Kingsley *et al.*, 1993
Exeter	1:1.07	1:0.40	1:0.82	Niebling, 1997
Fremont	1:1.04	1:0.94	1:0.36	Auger, 1994
Groton	1:1.01	1:0.12	1:0.88	New Hampshire Wildlife Federation, 2001
Stratham	1:1.15	1:0.19	1:0.40	Auger, 1994
Lyme	1:1.05	1:0.28	1:0.23	Pickard, 2000
New Jersey				
Freehold	1:1.51	1:0.17	1:0.33	AFT, 1998
Holmdel	1:1.38	1:0.21	1:0.66	AFT, 1998
Middletown	1:1.14	1:0.34	1:0.36	AFT, 1998
Upper Freehold	1:1.18	1:0.20	1:0.35	AFT, 1998
Wall	1:1.28	1:0.30	1:0.54	AFT, 1998
New York				
Amenia	1:1.23	1:0.25	1:0.17	Bucknall, 1989
Beekman	1:1.12	1:0.18	1:0.48	AFT, 1989
Dix	1:1.51	1:0.27	1:0.31	Schuyler County League of Women Voters, 1993
Farmington	1:1.22	1:0.27	1:0.72	Kinsman *et al.*, 1991
Fishkill	1:1.23	1:0.31	1:0.74	Bucknall, 1989
Hector	1:1.30	1:0.15	1:0.28	Schuyler County League of Women Voters, 1993
Kinderhook	1:1.05	1:0.21	1:0.17	Concerned Citizens of Kinderhook, 1996
Montour	1:1.50	1:0.28	1:0.29	Schuyler County League of Women Voters, 1992
Northeast	1:1.36	1:0.29	1:0.21	AFT, 1989
Reading	1:1.88	1:0.26	1:0.32	Schuyler County League of Women Voters, 1992
Red Hook	1:1.11	1:0.20	1:0.22	Bucknall, 1989

continued

Table 8.1 Continued

	Residential (with farm homes)	Combined commercial and industrial	Farmland, forest and open lands	Study source
Ohio				
Madison (V)	1:1.67	1:0.20	1:0.38	AFT and Lake County Ohio SWCD, 1993
Madison (T)	1:1.40	1:0.25	1:0.30	AFT and Lake County Ohio SWCD, 1993
Shalersville	1:1.58	1:0.17	1:0.31	Portage County Regional Planning Commission, 1997
Pennsylvania				
Allegheny (T)	1:1.06	1:0.14	1:0.13	Kelsey, 1997
Bedminster (T)	1:1.12	1:0.05	1:0.04	Kelsey, 1997
Bethel (T)	1:1.08	1:0.17	1:0.06	Kelsey, 1992
Bingham (T)	1:1.56	1:0.16	1:0.15	Kelsey, 1994
Buckingham (T)	1:1.04	1:0.15	1:0.08	Kelsey, 1996
Carroll (T)	1:1.03	1:0.06	1:0.02	Kelsey, 1992
Maiden Creek (T)	1:1.28	1:0.11	1:0.06	Kelsey, 1998
Richmond (T)	1:1.24	1:0.09	1:0.04	Kelsey, 1998
Stewardson (T)	1:2.11	1:0.23	1:0.31	Kelsey, 1994
Straban (T)	1:1.10	1:0.16	1:0.06	Kelsey, 1992
Sweden (T)	1:1.38	1:0.07	1:0.08	Kelsey, 1994
Rhode Island				
Hopkinton	1:1.08	1:0.31	1:0.31	Southern New England Forest Consortium, 1995
Little Compton	1:1.05	1:0.56	1:0.37	Southern New England Forest Consortium, 1995
Portsmouth	1:1.16	1:0.27	1:0.39	Johnston, 1997
West Greenwich	1:1.46	1:0.40	1:0.46	Southern New England Forest Consortium, 1995
Texas				
Hays County	1:1.26	1:0.30	1:0.33	AFT, 2000
Utah				
Cache County	1:1.27	1:0.25	1:0.57	Snyder and Ferguson, 1994
Sevier County	1:1.11	1:0.31	1:0.99	Snyder and Ferguson, 1994
Utah County	1:1.23	1:0.26	1:0.82	Snyder and Ferguson, 1994
Virginia				
Augusta County	1:1.22	1:0.20	1:0.80	Valley Conservation Council, 1997
Clarke County	1:1.26	1:0.21	1:0.15	Piedmont Environmental Council, 1994
Northampton County	1:1.13	1:0.97	1:0.23	AFT, 1999
Washington				
Skagit County	1:1.25	1:0.30	1:0.51	AFT, 1999

Table 8.1 Continued

	Residential (with farm homes)	Combined commercial and industrial	Farmland, forest and open lands	Study source
Wisconsin				
Dunn	1:1.06	1:0.29	1:0.18	Town of Dunn, 1994
Dunn	1:1.02	1:0.55	1:0.15	Wisconsin Land Use Research Program, 1999
Perry	1:1.20	1:1.04	1:0.41	Wisconsin Land Use Research Program, 1999
Westport	1:1.11	1:0.31	1:0.13	Wisconsin Land Use Research Program, 1999

Source: Edwards and Jackson-Smith (2000).

different types of agricultural operations such as intensive large-scale confined livestock operations and open crop fields. One could state that the method is subject to aggregation bias where all residential property is treated the same, as is all manufacturing, commercial or agricultural land.

Consider, for example, two different types of residential development, both using 100 acres of land. One development has three to four acre lots with 5,000 square foot homes. The other development is a mobile home park with low-income renting policies. Clearly, the fiscal impact of these two developments will be vastly different, but the COCS approach generally treats the two as the same. Plainly stated, the level of specificity in COCS is sufficiently gross that little insight into fiscal impacts is gained.

Basis measure bias

Because COCS uses a gross dollar basis to make comparisons, intensity of land use is lost. In COCS studies farmland and open spaces appear to have the most favorable fiscal impact. This is because the ratios are estimated on a dollar basis. If the ratios were calculated on a per-acre basis, industrial and commercial land would seem much more important. One acre of industrial land on average will contribute much more to the tax base than one acre of agricultural land. For example, it may take 1,000 acres of farmland to generate the same property tax revenues as one acre of high-end commercial office space. The fact that actual land use patterns are not used distorts the analysis. Here, methodological flaws in COCS predetermine the study's outcome.

Capacity to develop is ignored

The notion of excess capacity in the provision of local public services is vital to understanding the impact of any particular development. For example, a sewer treatment plant operating at 80 percent capacity may be able to absorb

100 new single-family dwellings with little if any additional costs. The 101st dwelling, however, may exceed the capacity of the treatment plant and expensive expansions may be required. In this example, the first 100 dwellings more than paid for themselves, but the 101st did not. This error is commonly seen when averaging analysis is used in situations where marginal analysis is in fact appropriate.

Economies of scale are ignored

Local public services carry a high fixed cost and have been documented to exhibit economies of scale. As a community grows these fixed costs can be spread over more residents and per-resident costs decline. For example, a community with road maintenance responsibilities must have a minimum of equipment regardless of road mileage. In smaller communities, equipment sits idle and is very expensive. In larger communities, that same equipment can be used more fully and the fixed costs can be spread over more residents. Again, this error is commonly seen when using averaging analysis when marginal analysis is preferred.

Nature of public goods is ignored

Public goods are very different from private goods. Private goods are characterized as rival and excludable. If one person consumes an apple, another cannot consume the same apple. Consumers are rivals for private goods. Consumers can also be excluded from private goods through market mechanisms, most notably price. Most consumers are excluded from the market for Ferrari automobiles because of price. Public goods, however, are non-rival and non-excludable. If an effective police department deters crime, all residents of the community consume that public service simultaneously. Nor can any one resident be excluded from the sense of security the police provide. COCS treat public goods and services as if they are private in nature. In a public setting, adding a new industrial park or residential development will not deter prior residents or new residents from continuing to enjoy the same level of the public service. At some point, however, congestion in the consumption of the public good will prevail and additional investments (expenditures) for the good will be required. Here congestion is similar to capacity discussed above.

In addition to these specific shortcomings, the results of COCS studies are often interpreted incorrectly. For example, although a general class of land use may be associated with a net fiscal benefit or loss, it is also true that any individual piece of property may have an impact that can be significantly different from the overall averages. Finally, fiscal impact assessment and COCS studies in particular can be criticized as a tool for local decision making on the grounds that, in contrast to social cost-benefit analysis, they focus attention on a narrow view of benefits and costs. Benefits of development are measured only in terms of the additional revenues that accrue to the local government. Similarly, costs include only those that affect local governments.

As noted by Ladd (1998), most economists agree that fiscal impact assessment as advocated by the American Farmland Trust is a narrowly defined and incomplete cost-benefit analysis, and consequently cannot by itself provide appropriate signals about whether a new development should be allowed. Because local residents care so much about their tax burdens, however, such analysis will often be requested. With the new conventional wisdom dominating land use discussion, the call for analysis may not even be forthcoming. At best, fiscal impact analysis should be regarded as an input into a more comprehensive analysis of the costs and benefits of new development.

The AFT COCS literature has, however, shone a very public spotlight onto a serious set of questions that local decision makers and concerned citizens should be asking. While the specific methods have been challenged along with the policy implications of AFT COCS, they have caused many to question the reasonableness of some proposed developments. The AFT COCS has opened the door not only for fiscal and economic impact assessment, but has raised the awareness of local citizens. The challenge now is to provide local citizens with the best information that the social sciences can bring to bear.

The impact of alternative land uses

This chapter now presents and uses a comprehensive regional economic modeling system to explore the variation in socioeconomic and fiscal impacts of alternative economic development options within a land use framework. Five alternative development proposals are compared and contrasted, including: a high- and middle-income residential development, a commercial retail development a service-based development and a manufacturing development. Issues concerning consistency in scenario development are explored, as are issues that arise in comparing simulation results. A case study approach is adopted for ease of comparison using Walworth County in southeastern Wisconsin.

The economic and fiscal impacts of different types of economic growth events and corresponding land use patterns on local economies is modeled using an integrated (or conjoined) input–output (IO)/econometric modeling framework. This Wisconsin Economic Impact Modeling System or WEIMS (Deller and Shields 1996; Deller and Shields 1998; Shields 1998; Shields *et al.* 2000) resembles other regional models constructed for policy simulations, including Kort and Cartwright (1981) for US states; Conway (1990) for Washington state; Coomes *et al.* (1991) for the Louisville Standard Metropolitan Statistical Areas (SMSA); Treyz *et al.* (1992) for user-defined regions; and Rey (1994) for San Diego.

The conjoined models, the input–output (IO) component, are used to determine industry outputs and primary factor demands. The econometric component estimates final demands, factor prices, and primary factor supplies. The aim is to retain the sectoral detail afforded by IO techniques and close the model with a system of endogenous econometric relationships (Dewhurst and West 1990).

As noted above, many studies looking at the impact of alternative land use patterns are limited because they offer only partial analysis. Using an integrated approach to assess the economic and fiscal impact of alternative land use patterns is a marked improvement over these previous studies because it moves toward the holistic approach that is often lacking in this literature. In particular, our approach recognizes the economic relationships among all agents in the economy, thus providing a better understanding of far-reaching impacts.

The WEIMS is a complex model, consisting of more than 50 stochastic equations. Because many details of the complete model are not relevant for this study, discussion is limited to the demographic and fiscal modules. A graphical overview of the system is presented in Figure 8.1. Six modules compose the model: (1) production, (2) labor, (3) demographics, (4) retail, (5) housing and (6) local government (fiscal). All modules, save the production module, consist of a series of stochastic econometric equations. To capture interrelationships, the modules are linked by one or more endogenous variables. Similar to other models of its type, the WEIMS model recognizes two sources of demand, external and local. While county growth is driven primarily by export production, the model also contains a number of local policy variables that allow users to model locally induced demand shocks.

Intermediate production relationships in the local economy are examined in the input–output component. The IO model provides a detailed family of production functions that rely on a number of fairly strong assumptions. A common way to initiate a policy simulation in the WEIMS is to specify a demand shock – the scenario often involves reducing or increasing output for a single industry. The IO core is used to estimate changes in output by industry due to changes in final demand.

The labor market components of the model are linked to the production sector via industry output as determined by the production module. Part one of the labor module is used to estimate industrial employment and wages while part two examines unemployment, commuting patterns, population (including migration), total personal income and income distribution responses to the initial change in economic activity.

The remaining induced demand modules incorporate information provided by the labor market modules. Local retail sales depend on personal income, population and commuting patterns. Income and population change, among other factors, drive the local housing market. Key forecasts from the housing sector include housing starts and property values. Income, population, and income distribution drive local government expenditures and rev-

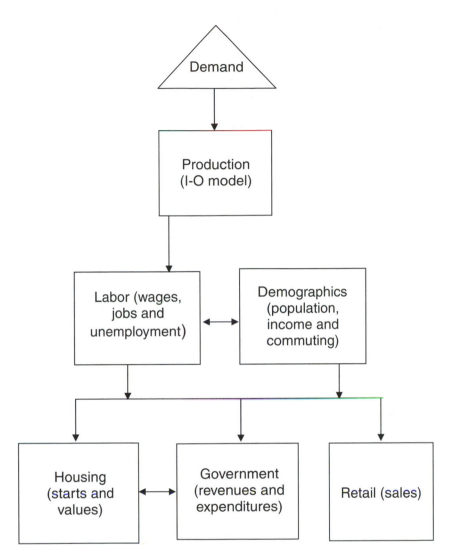

Figure 8.1 The Wisconsin Economic Impact Modeling System.

enues. Local government is also closely integrated with the local housing sector through property values (i.e., the property tax base).

To date WEIMS has been used to assess the economic and fiscal impact of retirement migration (Shields *et al.* 1999; Stallmann *et al.* 1999), the effects of commuting on local retail markets (Shields and Deller 1998), the operation of a state prison (Deller 1999b) and a public airport (Deller and Koles 1999). In addition, the modeling system has served as the foundation for an extension outreach educational program aimed at helping local officials better understand the economics of alternative policies and events (Deller and Shields 1998).

The case study and scenarios

For the purpose of this case study, five alternative land use patterns are examined within the context of alternative economic development options. The scenarios are designed to be as compatible as possible but sufficiently different to allow for contrasts between alternative policy options. The hypothetical scenarios center on a 100-acre parcel of land on the edge of a representative community. It is assumed that the public construction costs (e.g., new road construction, water and sewer line extensions, etc.) are comparable across the five development options. Therefore, the comparisons emphasize changes in operational expenditures and revenues of the hypothetical developments. In addition, a minimal number of assumptions are made about the structure of each scenario, allowing the greatest flexibility for the model and comparisons.

The five alternative scenarios include: (1) commercial retail development, specifically a general merchandise-type store such as a Wal-Mart or K-Mart; (2) a service development, specifically a health care facility or small hospital; (3) a manufacturing facility that is consistent with the study area (a food processing facility, specifically a condiment-making plant); (4) a residential development marketed at households earning more than $75,000 annually (high income); and (5) a residential development targeted at households earning $35,000 annually (middle income). Each development is assumed to employ 100 persons paying prevailing wages. The two residential developments are assumed to include 100 homes each. For consistency in comparisons, it is assumed that all of the retail, service and manufacturing jobs are taken from in-commuters while each of the 100 workers associated with the residential developments out-commute. While this latter assumption represents an extreme oversimplification, it is required in this experimental framework to ensure comparability across scenarios.

As outlined above, each scenario is constructed to be readily implemented by IMPLAN, the input–output component of WEIMS. In turn, the general merchandise sectors (IMPLAN sector 449), hospital sector (IMPLAN sector 492) and condiment food processing sectors (IMPLAN sector 69) are shocked by 100 jobs. For the residential scenarios, income was injected into the local economy using the expenditure patterns for the high- and middle-income households. For the high-income case, $7.5 million is injected into the region, while for the middle-income $3.5 million is injected. The expenditure pattern reflects the spending patterns that each of these new households represents (see Wagner *et al.* 1992 for details). For population estimates, each household is assumed to be composed of one worker and two and one half persons.

The region used for this experiment is Walworth County in the southeastern portion of Wisconsin. Walworth County has a population of about 88,000 persons with a per household income of slightly less than $62,000. Perhaps best known for the recreational area of Lake Geneva, it has historically been a weekend retreat for higher-income residents of Chicago. Today, the southern part of the county, which borders on the Illinois–Wisconsin state line, is starting to experience the exsuburban growth pressures from the north-northwest growth of metro Chicago. The northern and western parts of the county are traditional agricultural with fairly large-scale (relative to Wisconsin) crop production farms. Scattered throughout the county is a large and growing Hispanic population that supports a number of low- to average-paying manufacturing jobs. In short, Walworth County represents a community that has a balance of economic activity and, as the Chicago metro area grows from the south and the Milwaukee metro area from the northeast, an area that will be facing increased demands for alternative land uses.

Scenario results

The results of the simulation are presented in Tables 8.2 through 8.5. The estimated changes in industrial demand from the input–output model (IMPLAN) are provided in Table 8.2. Immediately, significant differences are obvious in the scale and variation in impacts across the five scenarios. The middle-income residential development has the smallest total impact on industrial output at only $1.5 million, a level significantly below the $3.5 million in injected income. This loss of economic activity comes from effective margining of retail expenditures and non-local spending associated with out-commuters (Shields and Deller 1998). The commercial retail development impacted total regional activities by $3.7 million in industrial output, followed by the high-income residential development at $4.4 million, and the hospital development at $8.4 million in industrial output. The manufacturing scenario, however, generated a significantly higher change in industrial output: 100 jobs in the food processing sector generated $41 million in additional industry sales. This dramatic difference can be attributed to high output per worker in this particular sector. Care must be taken because this disproportionately large impact for manufacturing will affect the rest of the analysis.

The econometric components of WEIMS indicate that the change in employment levels will range from 27 jobs with the middle-income residential development to 352 for the manufacturing scenario (Table 8.3). Eighty jobs are generated for the high-income scenario, only 110 for the commercial retail development and 174 for the hospital scenario. The difference in the two residential developments seems reasonable given the assumption of 100 percent out-commuting and differences in income levels and spending patterns. The 100 hospital jobs resulting in 174 total jobs imply an employment multiplier of 1.74, which is reasonable. The small increase in additional jobs from the retail development, with an implied employment multiplier of only 1.10, reflects the lower pay scale often offered at general merchandise type stores and the leakage of profits from the area. The 100 additional jobs

Table 8.2 Industry output impacts

	Retail: general merchandise ($)	Manufacturing: food processing ($)	Services: hospital ($)	Residential: high income ($)	Residential: middle income ($)
Agriculture	11,073	594,022	39,873	63,596	24,813
Mining	0	0	0	0	0
Construction	37,194	332,762	91,662	124,072	37,060
Manufacturing	91,915	32,970,794	187,176	195,181	70,633
Transportation, communications and public utilities	65,819	1,858,257	186,075	262,877	96,686
Trade	2,997,778	2,405,768	566,242	1,198,233	423,743
Finance, insurance and real estate	251,944	1,187,299	669,846	1,287,400	401,346
Services	248,046	1,820,859	6,569,279	1,184,897	389,536
Government	33,330	171,835	101,019	127,752	47,844
Total	3,737,099	41,341,596	8,411,172	4,444,008	1,491,661

Source: WEIMS, simulation of 100 new jobs or households.

Table 8.3 Employment impacts

	Retail: general merchandise	Manufacturing: food processing	Services: hospital	Residential: high income	Residential: middle income
Agriculture	0	11	1	1	0
Mining	0	0	0	0	0
Construction	0	2	1	1	0
Manufacturing	1	197	1	1	0
Transportation, Communications and public utilities	1	17	2	2	1
Trade	100	72	17	36	13
Finance, insurance and real estate	2	8	5	9	3
Services	5	40	144	26	9
Government	1	5	3	4	1
Total	110	352	174	80	27

Source: WEIMS, simulation of 100 new jobs or households.

in food processing manufacturing translate into 352 total jobs for an implied multiplier of 3.52, an estimate that is unreasonably high.

Since no structure is imposed within the various scenarios on the location of persons taking jobs created, other than that all workers from the residential development out-commute, the model is given complete flexibility. Changes in population range from 139 persons for the retail development to 447 persons for the manufacturing scenario (Table 8.4). The residential developments result in population increases of 351 and 285 persons for the high- and middle-income scenarios, respectively.

There are also changes in the level of unemployment and net commuting patterns. Across all five scenarios, the number of unemployed persons decreases from between five for the middle-income residential development to 54 for the manufacturing development (Table 8.4). In terms of unemployment rates, these declines in the number of unemployed translate into modest reductions in the unemployment rate from about 2.6 to 2.5 percent. In each of the scenarios there is a noticeable change in commuting patterns from an increase in out-commuting across all five, and modest reductions in in-commuting, save for the manufacturing scenario. The balance of the jobs is taken by in-migrants.

The changes in commuting patterns are best explained within WEIMS by relative changes in regional wages (per capita income) and housing prices. The econometric results of WEIMS suggest that increases in housing prices (median house values) relative to housing prices in surrounding counties raise the tendency of new jobs to be taken by in-commuters as opposed to in-migrants. The econometric results also suggest that changes in local wages relative to wages in surrounding counties affect net commuting patterns. In

Table 8.4 Labor and housing market impacts

	Retail: general merchandise	Manufacturing: food processing	Services: hospital	Residential: high income	Residential: middle income
Population	139	447	219	351	285
Per capita income	−$7.54	$22.78	−$5.45	−$9.17	−$42.13
Total income	$2,582,479	$8,318,355	$4,069,254	$6,520,651	$5,285,151
Unemployment	−19	−54	−29	−13	−5
In-commuters	−18	111	−5	−5	−17
Out-commuters	42	91	60	72	52
Median house value	$10.76	$170.16	$35.55	$17.90	−$65.32
New housing permit value	−$10.69	$32.31	−$7.73	−$13.00	−$59.76
Increase in new construction	18	59	29	46	37

Source: WEIMS, simulation of 100 new jobs or households.

four of the five scenarios, per capita income declined, ranging from $42 for the middle-income scenario to a modest decline of slightly more than $5 for the hospital scenario. Interestingly, the general merchandise retail scenario saw a decline of about $7.50, which is a smaller decline than for either residential developments. The manufacturing scenario results in an increase of almost $23 in per capita income. But even the largest absolute change in per capita income is only 0.23 percent of the original level.

Based on the housing module of WEIMS there are small changes in median housing values (Table 8.4), which feed into commuting patterns. In four of the five scenarios, the median price of housing increased by almost $11 for the retail scenario to $170 for the manufacturing scenario. Only the middle-income residential development saw a decrease in market values, with a $65 decline. But with an original median house value of nearly $68,000, these represent less than a 1 percent change. Still, this is a sufficient change to influence commuting flows described above. Also reported in Table 8.4 are simulated changes in the value of new residential construction (new housing permit value) and the change in the rate of flow of new housing construction (increase in new construction). It is important to note that these latter measures do not directly reflect the two residential development scenarios, but rather the level of ripple or multiplier effects from the initial shock (scenario).

While the changes in income and housing values may appear to be small, specifically less than one half a percent, these variables drive the labor market module of WEIMS. It is in the latter module that absolute changes in population are derived and "getting population right" is critical in assessing fiscal impacts. The econometric results, numerous applications of WEIMS and other CPAN-like models (e.g., Deller 1999a) all suggest that the level and magnitude of impact assessment hinges on correctly estimated population changes. In the end, population changes drive the impacts.

The fiscal impacts of the five alternative economic development options, and corresponding land use patterns, are reported in Table 8.5. Consistent with the rest of the analysis, the food processing manufacturing scenario has the largest increase in local government expenditures at about $350,000, exclusive of K-12 public schools. General government administration expenditure is the largest single category of expenditures followed by expenditures on safety-related items including police and fire protection. The smallest increase for the manufacturing example is health and human services, with only a $7,000 increase. The small increase in the latter category is a direct result of the estimated increase in per capita income and the relatively large decrease in the number of unemployed. Total revenues are estimated to increase by over $800,000, hinting at a net positive impact. Care must be taken, however, because the expenditures estimated here do not include any capital expenditures (e.g., road construction, sewer and water lines, etc.) or the costs of servicing any debt incurred to finance the capital items.

The high- and middle-income residential developments increase total local expenditures by $317,000 and $231,000, respectively. For the high-income

Table 8.5 Fiscal expenditure and revenue impacts

	Retail: general merchandise ($)	Manufacturing: food processing ($)	Services: hospital ($)	Residential: high income ($)	Residential: middle income ($)
Expenditure impacts					
Health and human services	7,123	6,930	9,057	58,971	53,699
Government administration	36,562	102,777	55,668	66,494	54,578
Safety services	22,746	92,175	38,493	89,654	64,928
Road maintenance	8,774	49,034	16,689	26,535	6,017
Solid waste and sanitation	9,251	37,528	15,660	25,050	14,367
Cultural and amenities	19,610	67,167	31,504	50,424	37,867
Total	104,066	355,611	167,071	317,128	231,456
Revenue impacts					
Intergovernmental aids/revenues	32,271	115,304	52,495	112,931	76,927
Property taxes	208,152	700,908	332,753	531,513	419,976
Total	240,423	816,212	385,248	644,444	496,903

Source: WEIMS, simulation of 100 new jobs or households.

scenario, expenditure on policy and fire protective services is the single largest category increase at almost $90,000, and for the middle-income residential development protective service expenditures increased by almost $65,000. It is most interesting to note that the two types of residential developments do not produce parallel expenditure impacts. For example, the protective expenditure increase for the middle-income residential development is about three-quarters that of the high-income scenario. But road maintenance expenditures, at $26,000 for the high-income case, are almost four times higher than the middle-income residential development. Health and human services expenditures are nearly the same for both types of development ranging from about $54,000 to $59,000. As with the manufacturing example, total revenues are expected to increase by about $645,000 for the high-income development and almost $500,000 for the middle-income. In both cases, the developments appear to more than pay for themselves. It is particularly important to note that in addition to capital expenditures not being captured, these analyses do not include public schools.

The retail development places modest demands on local public services, with an estimated increase of just over $100,000, yet it generates revenues of $240,000. The service development, in this case a modest size hospital, increases local government expenditures by $167,000 and revenues by $385,000. Again, both the general merchandise-type development and the hospital development more than pay for themselves.

For each of the five different types of economic development options, and corresponding land use decisions, the demand for services provided by local governments increases. But given the size of local government in the case study area (Walworth County, Wisconsin), the increases represent less than one half of 1 percent; these are modest impacts given the relative size of the county. Increases in revenue outpace increases in expenditures by 2 to 2.3 times in every scenario. For this county example, development does seem to pay for itself if congestion in services is not an issue.

From a local decision making perspective each economic development scenario has positive and negative aspects. For example, the manufacturing development will have the greatest impact in terms of jobs and income, but will increase local government expenditures the most. On the other hand, the manufacturing development may have a net revenue windfall of $460,000. But will the manufacturing development impact the community to such an extent that the character of the community may be altered? Four of the five scenarios have a positive net fiscal impact, yet per capita income declines, albeit modestly. Only one development scenario, manufacturing, has a modest positive impact on median housing value and the middle-income residential development actually lowers median housing value. Other than the manufacturing example, which may be overstated with an implicit employment multiplier of 3.4, each of the scenarios has both positive (e.g., fiscal) and negative (e.g., per capita income) economic impacts. In the end, local officials must balance multiple and often contradictory economic impacts.

An outline of a research agenda

Part of the difficulty in making decisions about alternative development proposals and corresponding land uses is the inherent complexity of each decision. It is human nature to try to simplify complex issues into more manageable problems. Further, if we can be offered a simple solution or answer to these oversimplified problems, all the better. Fiscal impact assessment, and Cost of Community Services studies in particular, can offer what appear to be black-and-white answers to complex issues. Indeed, COCS have provided a "rule of thumb" that is often applied blindly to a range of development alternatives. As outlined in detail above, COCS studies are not only inherently flawed, but they also narrowly focus attention on only the fiscal element of impact assessment. In light of this critical assessment, several research agenda items can be advanced:

- A sampling of communities for which COCS ratios have been calculated should be the focus of a selection of in-depth, broad-based studies. Using a range of impact assessment methods, four hypothetical development scenarios should be rigorously examined.
- A collection of community impact assessment modeling tools covering a range of impact areas (e.g., economic, fiscal and environmental) that are based on rigorous theory and empirical dimensions needs to be developed. These tools can then be used to systematically examine the impact of alternative development patterns. The work of the Community Policy Analysis Network (CPAN) is an example of this type of effort.
- More rigorous methods of modeling the elusive notion of quality of life need to be explored. If it can be proxied and modeled, then impacts of alternative development patterns on quality of life could potentially be assessed.
- Spatial modeling that is now possible in light of geographic information systems (GIS) technologies needs to be focused on assessing the true impacts of alternative development patterns. In addition to modeling impacts, insights into what drives growth and the policies that affect growth can be gained.
- Develop clearer links between public service provision levels and government expenditure patterns. Due to the lack of a better method, impact studies link services provisions directly to expenditures: more spending is equated with better services.
- Explore the potential insights that game theory can provide on the "winners and losers" of alternative development proposals.
- Develop stronger links between alternative development patterns and land use decisions to notions of fiscal stress and health.

In the end, the results of the most rigorously crafted and executed research program cannot have the desired effects if there is not a complementary outreach educational program. In the advocacy environment in which much of the public discussion takes place today, even the best research on this area may be collecting dust on the shelves of university libraries.

Conclusion

As urban fringe and high amenity rural areas experience increased pressure for the development of open spaces, local officials are asking increasingly more complex questions concerning the economic and fiscal impact of alternative land uses. These officials often seek simple answers to their complex questions. Regrettably, simple answers are not available, and rules of thumb that have been advanced by advocates of Cost of Community Services studies are widely misused and often wrong. Each community is unique, as is each development proposal. Indeed, the same proposed development on opposite sides of the same community may have vastly different impacts because the current provision of infrastructure and other public services will differ.

The analysis presented in this chapter is intended to (1) critique the current approaches to conducting impact assessment of alternative land uses, (2) offer an example of how complex impact assessments can be, (3) provide a range of impacts for reasonable alternative development options, and, finally, (4) offer a research agenda to advance our ability to provide local decision makers with the best information possible.

Note

1 Support for this work was provided by the University of Wisconsin Agricultural Experiment Station, the University of Wisconsin-Madison, and The Northeast Regional Center for Rural Development, Penn State University. All opinions expressed in this essay reflect those of the author and not necessarily the University of Wisconsin. All errors of commission or omission are the responsibility of the author.

9 Sense of place as an integrated framework for understanding human impacts of land use change

Richard C. Stedman

Introduction

This chapter introduces sense of place as a theoretical and operational framework for understanding human social and psychological effects of land use change. Human concerns about land use change often focus on potential impacts on environmental quality: this discourse has been legitimized and reinforced through institutional structure (e.g., laws such as the US Clean Water Act) and ecological science that quantitatively measures water chemistry impacts from increased nutrient loadings; wildlife population impacts from conversion of habitat to human habitation; and air quality impacts resulting from auto emissions as suburban residents commute longer distances to jobs in urban centers, for example.

Impacts on some aspects of human quality of life, such as economic well being, are also readily measured through indicators such as per capita income, real estate values and unemployment rates (see other chapters in this volume). Harder to justify through conventional science are impacts of changing land use practices on less tangible aspects of human quality of life: satisfaction and attachment to place; valued social relationships; aesthetic value; and participation in favorite activities. Because they are harder to measure, these aspects have often been neglected as potential discursive strategies for opposing changing land use practices. Quite simply, it is easier to oppose land uses when there is hard evidence that these practices will have tangible, measurable, objective and widespread impacts. "Environmental impacts" may at times represent a defensive discourse strategy, or code, for this larger set of impacts. However, articulations of the impacts of sprawl solely in terms of the environment are potentially challenged if land use changes do not result in the environmental impacts that are suggested (see Marshall and Shortle 2004, chapter 7 this volume). For example, the conversion of input intensive row cropping to low-density residential development (sprawl) may not necessarily have adverse effects on water quality (Carpenter *et al.* 1998). Opponents of land use change are potentially taking a risk by placing all of their eggs in the environmental quality basket: if expected environmental impacts are not encountered, proponents of these arguments stand on shaky ground. What is needed is a framework for organizing the human intangible impacts in such a way that they are measurable in a systematic fashion, and more defensible through conventional hypothesis-driven science. As such, these effects may carry more credibility in dialogues about impacts of changing land use practices. This chapter articulates sense of place as such a framework, and presents a short case study of its application.

Introducing sense of place

Common to the rapidly proliferating definitions of sense of place is a three-component view that links the physical environment, human behaviors and social or psychological processes (Brandenburg and Carroll 1995). A place is a spatial setting that has been given meaning (Tuan 1977) based on human experience, social relationships, emotions and thoughts. A three-component view of sense of place predominates: places include the physical setting, human activities and social and psychological processes rooted there (Brandenburg and Carrol 1995; Relph 1976, 1997).

Sense of place as "squishy"

Sense of place theory and research can be divided into positivistic and phenomenological approaches (Lalli 1992; Shamai 1991). Of these, the latter tradition, which emphasizes the particularistic nature of place (specific to the individual, the group, the setting), has tended to dominate. Place theorists (e.g., Relph 1976; Tuan 1977) either align themselves with this approach or eschew formal hypotheses-testing in research. Proponents of the holistic, phenomenological nature of sense of place suggest that it cannot be broken down into specific, measurable components and then reassembled into multivariate models. Sense of place is a whole, more than the sum of its parts.

A social psychological framework

One may challenge the above conception. Considering sense of place in a more systematic fashion may increase the probability of sense of place-related concerns entering into the dialogue about land use. Previous suggestions have been made (Jorgensen and Stedman 2001; Stedman 2002) that suggest the utility of adopting the language- and hypothesis-testing approach found in conventional social psychology. In this approach, sense of place can be conceived as a collection of symbolic meanings, attachment and satisfaction with a spatial setting held by an individual or group. This conception suggests a social psychological model of human–environment interaction. Briefly, symbolic meanings about place can be translated into cognitions: descriptive statements of "what does this place mean to me?" rather than "how much does it mean?" Meanings are the cognitive building blocks of attitude (Bem 1970). They are combined with values or evaluative broad end states that lack a particular object, such as freedom, justice and equality (Rokeach 1970). Expectancy-value models posit that attitudes, or summary evaluative judgments, are the sum of beliefs about an object multiplied by the evaluation of each (Fishbein 1967; see Eagly and Chaiken 1993 for a cogent review). Key to these translations is that the physical setting and its attributes take on the role of object or locus for these descriptive and evaluative statements. This conception is advantageous to the project at hand because it offers clear terminology, empirically specifiable relationships between concepts, and established methodological approaches.

Applying the framework to potential impacts of land use change

Settings entail bundles of attributes that may have certain utilities, and potential for substitution. However, some of these attributes, such as the memories of past experiences, or symbolic values, are potentially less substitutable than others but nonetheless may be entered into a mental calculus about potential substitutability of that setting (Thibaut and Kelly 1959). Landscapes have meaning to people (Greider and Garkovich 1994), based on past experiences (Tuan 1977), but also potential future experiences. Conflict over land use may be conceived of as disagreement over the particular meanings embodied in the landscape: questions about "what kind of place is this?" and by extension, "what kind of place should it be?" Although some suggest that attachment to a place may provide a basis for collective action to preserve it (e.g., Cheng *et al.* 2003), these suggestions do not fully take into account the potential for conflicting meanings that may imply contrasting courses of action. Simply put, it may be just as important to understand what the setting means to an individual or group rather than how much it means. High levels of attachment per se may be the basis for acrimony rather than agreement, if cognitions differ. A social psychological framework that includes beliefs, values, and attitudes allows examination of these variables and their interrelationships in more detail, and consequently promotes prediction of what interests are promoted or impacted by certain land use strategies.

A case study: rapid second home development in northern Wisconsin

The sense of place approach was used to organize human response patterns to sprawl patterns of development in Vilas County, Wisconsin. Vilas County is a tourism-intensive and recreational home landscape: in 2000, 57.5 percent of all housing in Vilas County was classified as for seasonal, recreational, or occasional use, the highest proportion in the state, and tenth among all 3,108 counties in the contiguous 48 states in terms of the proportion of housing units that are seasonal. This phenomenon is lake-based: Vilas County has 1,320 lakes, more than any other county in Wisconsin (Wisconsin Department of Natural Resources 1991). A total of 14.3 percent of the surface area of the county is water. Disregarding the 321 ocean and Great Lakes coastal counties, this proportion of surface water ranks the county 21st among the remaining 2,789 counties in the 48 contiguous states.

Seasonal and year-round population has been growing rapidly. The permanent population of Vilas County grew from 8,894 in 1940 to 21,033 in 2000, an increase of 136 percent. During the same period, nonmetropolitan counties as a whole grew by just 30 percent. Development pressures have been especially intense around lakes. The Northern Wisconsin's Lakes and Shoreline Study (Wisconsin Department of Natural Resources 1996a) found a 60 percent increase in shore development density on selected lakes between 1960 and 1996. Development pressure was most intense on the biggest lakes (lakes over 200 acres held an average of 19 dwellings per mile of shoreline). New construction has resulted in a dramatic decline in vacant lakeshore property. The loss of shoreline is considered a priority issue in the WDNR Northern Initiatives work (Wisconsin Department of Natural Resources 1996b). Over half of the respondents to a Wisconsin Department of Natural Resources survey were "very concerned" about the loss of wild areas to development (60 percent), and shore development more specifically (55 percent). Several town planning documents in Vilas County echo these concerns. The town of Eagle River found that clean water, lakes and woods were most important to quality of life. These amenities are threatened by unplanned sprawl, inadequate shore land zoning, and recreational conflict. Similar results are found in planning documents from the towns of Manitowish Waters (1995), Arbor Vitae (Town of Arbor Vitae 1996), St. Germain (1997), and Eagle River (Town of Eagle River 1996).

Objections to these trends have typically been expressed in terms of concerns about environmental impacts. However, support for these assertions has been mixed. Meyer *et al.* (1997) examined the relationship between Vilas County lakeshore development and riparian zone vegetation, green frog distribution, breeding bird populations, bald eagle distribution and productivity and common loon productivity. They found that housing density was negatively related to vegetation, including tree canopy coverage in terrestrial buffer zones, shrub coverage along the water/land interface, and coarse woody debris. Similar to Clark *et al.* (1984), the number of breeding birds did not differ between developed and undeveloped lakes, although the species composition changed. There was no effect of development on bald eagle distribution and productivity, as bald eagles breeding near developed areas showed little sign of abandoning nests. A similar question with common loon productivity found no conclusive relationship (see also Heimberger *et al.* 1983).

There exists a potential paradox: opposition to shoreline development has been articulated as concern about potential environmental effects, but data speaking to these issues do not provide conclusive evidence that environmental harm is occurring. This research explores this paradox by offering a potential alternative conception: high levels of shoreline development may threaten landowner-preferred conceptions of place.

Research question and methods

The research examines landowner response to shoreline development patterns on their lake: how do they respond emotionally and cognitively to increased levels of shoreline development?[1] In particular, the sense of place model is illustrated as a way of organizing human response. What is the cognitive (symbolic meanings), and evaluative (satisfaction and attachment) impact of increased levels of shoreline development, that has been fostered by relatively unrestricted land use planning?

The research was conducted via a mail survey sent in 1999 to a stratified[2] random sample of 1,000 Vilas County property owners, drawn from the 1998 property tax rolls. The research utilized a three contact mailing procedure (initial mailing, postcard reminder and follow-up full mailing), resulting in a 72.1 percent response rate. Respondents were asked to describe and evaluate a particular lake of their own choosing. If their Vilas County property had lake frontage (as it did for 76 percent of the respondents) they were asked to answer the questions using the lake on which they owned property as their attitude object. Respondents who did not own lake frontage selected a lake that was near their property, visited often, or a favorite for another reason.

These data were then matched to several available databases characterizing Vilas County Lakes. One database, provided by the Vilas County government, includes all lakes in the county over 50 acres in size, or 275 lakes in total. In this chapter, only the data on the density of lakeshore development are presented. Development density was operationalized as the number of structures in the 100 meter shoreline buffer per mile of lake frontage, calculated using 1996 aerial photographs, where visible structures were identified using a stereoscope and mapped on lake GIS coverages.[3] Until very recent efforts to enact more restrictive lakeshore zoning, 100 feet of frontage were required to construct a seasonal or permanent home.

Results

This chapter presents only selected results to highlight the elements of the framework described above. To assess the impact of shoreline development on cognitions and evaluations, respondents were separated into groups based on the level of shoreline development of their lake. Means for each of these domains were compared (t-test for independent samples) between respondents on relatively highly developed lakes (more than 30 structures per total mile of lake frontage) versus those on relatively lightly developed lakes (less than 15 structures per mile of frontage). Respondents in the middle category are excluded from the analysis.

Cognitions

What meanings do respondents hold for their lakes? Respondents were asked to agree or disagree (on a five-point scale) with a number of lake descriptors.

To the majority of respondents, their lakes are places of high environmental quality to escape from civilization, and represent the "real up north." Fewer respondents agreed that their lakes are communities of neighbors, or like residential neighborhoods. Also, there were high levels of agreement with descriptors that emphasized high environmental quality (Table 9.1).

This simple analysis quickly reveals that level of lakeshore development exerts strong impacts on beliefs about one's lake. Respondents on more highly developed lakes were significantly less likely to consider them a pristine wilderness, places of high environmental quality, places to escape from civilization, scenic, peaceful, with clear water and abundant forests. They were more likely to think of their lakes as residential neighborhoods, crowded with shoreline development and recreationists, and polluted water. These differences in cognitions have measurable impacts on patterns of land use change: what happens to the landscape is not independent of human cognition.

Place attachment and satisfaction

Overall, respondents indicated high levels of attachment to their lake (as indicated on a seven-point scale, with 1 = strongly disagree and 7 = strongly agree), with over 70 percent agreeing with items such as "I can really be myself there," "I really miss it when I am away too long," and "I feel happiest when I am there" (Table 9.2).

Table 9.1 Lake cognitions

My lake is . . .	Mean	Less developed	More developed	Significance level (p)
A family place	4.29	4.29	4.28	ns
A pristine wilderness	3.30	3.61	2.72	0.001
A residential "neighborhood"	2.63	2.27	3.21	0.001
A place mostly for vacationers	3.08	2.99	3.15	ns
A place of high environmental quality	3.74	3.90	3.36	0.001
A place to escape from civilization	3.85	4.05	3.48	0.001
A community of neighbors	2.99	2.71	3.66	0.001
The "real up north"	3.84	3.95	3.50	0.001
Is extremely scenic	3.72	3.73	3.38	0.01
Shore is extremely developed	3.07	2.78	3.39	0.001
Has many recreationists using it	3.13	2.97	3.51	0.001
Is extremely peaceful	3.35	3.51	3.19	0.001
Water is extremely polluted	2.29	2.19	2.59	0.01
Is extremely crowded	2.67	2.41	3.01	0.001
Has extremely clear water	3.40	3.34	3.24	ns
Shore is extremely forested	3.39	3.62	3.17	0.001

Source: Author's calculations; based on a five point scale (5 = strongly agree, 1 = strongly disagree). ns = not significant.

Table 9.2 Place attachment

	Less developed	More developed	Significance level (p)
I feel that I can really be myself there	5.61	5.28	0.01
I feel happiest when I am there	5.35	5.14	ns
For the things I enjoy most, no other place can compare	4.78	4.65	ns
It is my favorite place to be	5.09	5.00	ns
As far as I am concerned, there are better places to be[a]	3.04	3.67	0.001
It reflects the type of person I am	5.04	4.76	ns
I really miss it when I am away too long	5.50	5.26	ns
It is the best place to do the things I enjoy	5.26	5.10	ns
Everything about it is a reflection of me	4.55	4.39	ns
Summed scale (alpha = 0.937)	5.12	4.87	ns

Notes
a Item asked in the negative; recoded for inclusion in the summed scale.
ns = not significant.

There are few differences in attachment between respondents on highly developed and lightly developed lakes, suggesting that although beliefs about what kind of place a lake is may change, identification with it as an important place remains relatively strong. In fact, it has been suggested that attachment is relatively difficult to affect for a variety of reasons, such as memories of past events, or a variety of defense mechanisms that are employed to protect preferred conception of place (Fitchen 1991; Stedman 2003).

Satisfaction with a lake is operationalized as an attitude, and is relatively distinct from attachment. Stedman (2002) showed these concepts were positively correlated, but the correlation was modest. Table 9.3 illustrates the

Table 9.3 Place satisfaction

	Less developed	More developed	Significance level (p)
Cost of property taxes	2.02	1.90	ns
Fishing quality	2.45	2.31	ns
Water quality	3.21	2.96	0.001
Solitude/peacefulness	3.32	2.88	0.001
Scenery	3.59	3.28	0.001
Number of users	2.92	2.58	0.001
Level of shore development	2.89	2.51	0.001
Populations of wildlife	3.14	2.86	0.001
Others' recreation activities	2.60	2.25	0.001
Summed scale (alpha = 0.846)	2.90	2.62	0.001

Note
ns = not significant.

effects of lakeshore development on satisfaction (measured on a four-point scale where 1 = extremely dissatisfied to 4 = extremely satisfied).

Tables 9.3 and 9.4 present evidence about the effect of lakeshore develop-ment on satisfaction, both as specific elements and as more overarching assessments. Respondents on the most developed lakes were significantly less satisfied with nearly every aspect of their lake, including water quality, soli-tude, scenery, number of users, amount of shore development, wildlife popu-lations and the recreational activities of other lake users. It is important that although some of these elements (especially water quality) have not been linked to shoreline development (i.e., environmental impacts), people believe that this linkage exists.

Respondents were also asked to evaluate the overall quality of their lake. A near normal distribution is observed: only 7.1 percent thought their lake was only in poor or fair condition, but even fewer (2.5 percent) described their lake as perfect (31.8 percent regarded its condition as "excellent"). These findings differ dramatically between more and less developed lakes: respondents on more densely developed lakes were about twice as likely as respondents on sparsely developed lakes to rate their lake as poor or fair, and only about half as likely to rate their lake as excellent or perfect (no respondent on a densely developed lake rated his or her lake as perfect). Clearly, the level of development on a lake is associated with less positive evaluations.

Relationships between variables

How do cognitions and evaluations interrelate? We have already observed that more developed lakes are associated with a different set of cognitions and also are less satisfying to respondents. Are these relations causal? This next section of the chapter examines interactions between cognitions and satisfac-tion via correlations and multivariate regression analyses (Table 9.5).

Nearly all of the belief items that differ by the level of lakeshore develop-ment are also strongly associated with satisfaction. In most cases, these differ-ences are robust. For example, lakes that are more satisfying are places of high environmental quality, $(r = 0.439)$, places to escape from civilization $(r = 0.401)$, and the "real up north" $(r = 0.468)$. In turn, lakes that are highly

Table 9.4 Overall lake rating

	All (%)	*Less developed (%)*	*More developed (%)*
Poor	1.2	0.5	1.9
Fair	5.9	4.9	10.4
Good	24.5	14.6	35.0
Very good	34.1	41.6	31.9
Excellent	31.8	35.1	20.9
Perfect	2.5	3.2	0.0

Table 9.5 Cognitions and satisfaction: correlations and OLS regression

My lake is...	Correlation	Significance level (p)	beta coefficient	t-statistic	Significance level (p)
A pristine wilderness	0.357	0.001	0.057	1.35	ns
A residential "neighborhood"	−0.173	0.001	−0.019	−0.46	ns
A place of high environmental quality	0.439	0.001	0.144	3.38	0.001
A place to escape from civilization	0.401	0.001	0.110	2.43	0.05
A community of neighbors	0.016	ns	0.015	0.38	ns
The "real up north"	0.468	0.001	0.181	4.01	0.001
Is extremely scenic	0.309	0.001	0.013	0.27	ns
Shore is extremely developed	−0.233	0.001	0.017	0.41	ns
Has many recreationists using it	−0.224	0.001	0.031	0.72	ns
Is extremely peaceful	0.379	0.001	0.073	1.51	ns
Water is extremely polluted	−0.377	0.001	−0.189	−4.56	0.001
Is extremely crowded	−0.338	0.001	0.010	0.18	ns
Shore is extremely forested	0.254	0.001	0.010	0.14	ns
Adjusted R^2	–	–	–	–	0.356

Note
ns = not significant.

developed are far less likely to be associated with these attributes and far more likely to be labeled as polluted and crowded, factors that are negatively associated with satisfaction (r's of -0.377 and -0.338, respectively).

The joint effects of these cognitions are entered simultaneously in an OLS regression. The cognitions that differ significantly between less developed and more developed lakes explain over one third (adjusted $R^2 = 0.356$) of the variation in the satisfaction scale. Four beliefs remain: lakes that are places of high environmental quality, places to escape from civilization, the "real up north," and do not have polluted water are more satisfying to respondents.

Summary and conclusion

The application of the sense of place framework demonstrates its utility for synthesizing and interpreting human response to changing land use patterns. Impacts of these changing land uses are not simply "environmental impacts." Rather, we can understand and predict intangible human response in a fairly systematic fashion. Ultimately, we value our landscapes as "places." To sustain landscapes, land use planning should understand the following variables and how they are distributed throughout the population: what people do (preferred activities and uses), landscape attributes and features, landscape meanings, and attachment and satisfaction. These variables are all related to each other in predictable ways.

A number of lessons have been learned using this framework. First, human social and psychological impacts are real and measurable. Those who oppose certain land use practices that result in sprawl-like patterns of development need not frame their arguments solely in terms of impacts on the physical environment. Human impacts are not limited to mere aesthetics, which are criticized as completely subjective and idiosyncratic, shallow, emphasizing the visually pretty, and not defensible through positivistic science. These types of impacts can be measured and predicted systematically, which may increase their legitimacy in political discourse and land use planning.

Second, meanings matter. Holding a given set of cognitions for a spatial setting appears to be crucial to evaluative domains, particularly satisfaction. Meanings, although descriptive of a setting, are not value neutral. Certain linked sets of meanings are clearly preferred to others. The setting in which this framework was applied has a relatively truncated set of meanings tied to environmental amenities: there is no viable countering set of cognitions in this case. Future research should apply this framework in settings with a more diverse set of potentially viable meanings. One example is a setting where there is conflict among tourism, preservation, and traditional resource-extractive activities such as logging or grazing. In these instances, the setting may lack a dominant set of meanings that is so overwhelmingly linked to overall levels of satisfaction. Rather, these relationships may be specific to particular stakeholder groups. For example, if a landscape is described in terms of meanings based on extractive-related employment (e.g., a place to earn a living, or a place to engage in traditional practices), this may foster satisfaction for some while serving as the source of great discomfort for others.

The "real" physical environment contributes to meanings. Setting attributes and potential experiences that require a certain set of attributes are the raw material for created meanings. It may be difficult to maintain preferred meanings in the face of land use changes that, for example, reduce open space, wildlife habitat or clean water. As demonstrated clearly by examining the differences between more and less developed lakes, meanings are not immune to threats to the physical landscape. The reader should also keep in mind that these differences in meanings and evaluations are obtained in a setting that embodies a small range of variation in the physical environment. All of the lakes in the setting, for example, support fishable populations of fish, and swimmable, but not drinkable, water. Importantly for this analysis, nearly all lakes had some level of shoreline development. That such robust findings were obtained simply by comparing respondents on lakes with fewer than 15 structures per mile with respondents on lakes with more than 30 structures per mile is telling. Settings that exhibit potentially greater variation in the biophysical environment (i.e., large, pristine wilderness areas versus industrial landscapes) will likely demonstrate the utility of the framework with more clarity, based on greater differentiation.

Finally, we can conceive of a model of sense of place-based planning. This research suggests that sense of place can and should enter into formal planning and zoning efforts. Although we cannot plan for satisfaction, we are already managing and planning for meanings, whether we realize it or not. Whenever planning or zoning decisions are made that favor one set of uses over another (e.g., zoning a parcel of land as agricultural, commercial or single-family residential), we make implicit statements about what kind of place we want the setting to be – what experiences people will have there, and what meanings they are likely to derive. The framework introduced here allows making these implicit assumptions explicit, and potentially revealing the sets of meanings that different stakeholders have, and by extension, whose meanings and attachments are likely to be supported or harmed by certain land use planning strategies.

Notes

1 Because this project lacks development density change data, change is instead approximated by comparing patterns of response on lakes with varying levels of development. While this is an imperfect substitute for change over time, it still provides important insights into the effects of development and land conversion.

2 This sample was stratified by gender to assure adequate representation of females. In the common case of joint property ownership, the male is nearly always listed first.

3 This variable reflects the total number of structures in the shoreline buffer, rather than the number of housing units. For example, a lakeshore home that also had a detached garage and boathouse would be recorded as three structures rather than

one. Thus, a conversion needs to be made from structures to dwellings, but as long as the ratio is constant across lakeshore properties, there is no need to do this. This assumption is followed in the research – there is no reason to assume, for example, that lakeshore property owners on a given lake are systematically more likely to have a different "building to dwelling" ratio than on any other lake. Another factor to consider is that 1996 data are somewhat dated, given the rapid pace of change in Vilas County. As well, the "within 300 feet" designation corresponds to the area covered by county shore land zoning, and includes some property that does not actually border the shore. Again, this is assumed to be a constant rather than variable source of error.

10 Socioeconomic and health outcomes of land use

Stephan J. Goetz[1]

Introduction

This wide-ranging chapter examines evidence about the impacts of current patterns of housing development or sprawl on two sets of variables: socioeconomic well being and health of the population. New home construction matters both in terms of its magnitude (how much) and its pattern – how it is distributed over space and where it is located relative to existing construction, for example. The primary land use measure of interest in this chapter is population density, because within economics this is an important predictor of productivity and well being. Readers interested in measures of sprawl related to neighborhood design and street arrangements should refer to Ewing *et al.* (2003a) and Sokolow 2004, chapter 18 this volume. This chapter touches only briefly on these measures as they relate to health consequences for the population.

The chapter is organized into three sections and a conclusion. The first section addresses the relationship between settlement patterns and economic outcomes, including population density and income, and the impact of new home construction on income. The second section examines sprawl and congestion, housing affordability, social capital and distributional effects of current housing development patterns. The last section focuses on health factors related to current housing choices, including air pollution, sedentary lifestyles and psychological factors, some of which we are only beginning to understand. It is important to keep in mind that the impacts of sprawl on various socioeconomic and health outcomes are often difficult to separate from the effects of urban lifestyles in general.

Settlement patterns and income

Population density and aggregate income

Agglomeration or clustering economies created in densely settled areas lead to higher per capita incomes and higher economic growth rates (Ciccone and Hall 1996; Glaeser 2000; Ihlanfeldt 1995; Rupasingha *et al.* 2000). The conventional explanation is that proximity facilitates exchange or spillovers among workers, thereby raising productivity and stimulating innovation (Anas *et al.* 1998). For example, spontaneous exchanges may occur when workers meet in a bar downtown after work. In addition, fixed transaction costs associated with face-to-face exchanges are lower in cities than in sparsely populated areas (Gaspar and Glaeser 1998). To the extent that sprawl reduces population density, society potentially loses due to lower productivity and output.

In terms of understanding the origins of population agglomeration, Rappaport and Sachs (2002) argue that productivity benefits, rather than natural amenities represented by the oceans, are primarily responsible for the increasingly bi-coastal population settlement pattern of the United States. They base this on a regression analysis that holds constant other natural factors and initial conditions that were inherently correlated with density of the population and economic activity. These relationships are slowly changing over time, according to the authors, as quality of life or amenity considerations are becoming more important.

What has not been sorted out in the literature is whether the positive effect of density occurs only with respect to location of employment or residence, or both. In particular, the productivity-enhancing benefits of agglomeration need to be compared with the productivity-reducing effects of traffic congestion and air pollution on health, both of which are discussed below. A relatively new literature in psychology suggests that the stress and aggression caused by traffic congestion can produce uncooperative and counterproductive behavior by workers (Hennessy 2003; Hennessy and Wiesenthal 1999), thereby offsetting productivity advantages associated with agglomeration. The fact that the costs to society associated with congestion are not borne or internalized by builders of new homes, and homebuyers, is at the core of many of the disputes over sprawl and how land "ought" to be used (Schmid 2003).

The events of September 11, 2001 caused businesses to reevaluate the benefits and costs of agglomeration, and many firms have left the densely settled area of Manhattan.[2] Even so, Glaeser and Shapiro (2002) argue that terrorism will likely have only a small effect on American cities. They suggest that war and terrorism raise transportation costs (e.g., for air travel and the United States mail system), thereby increasing the demand for density and offsetting the population's desire to disperse in response to attacks on population centers. Johnson and Kasarda (2003) offer the opposite conclusion, outlining factors that will potentially undermine the economic well being of cities in the future.

Finally, it is worth noting that density alone does not guarantee high incomes and productivity. This is perhaps nowhere more obvious than along the US–Mexico border, which also represents the line with the greatest per capita income differential of any region in the world. Nogales, Mexico, for example, is much more densely settled and poorer than Nogales, Arizona, highlighting the importance of institutional and other factors in explaining productivity differences.

New home construction and income

Researchers concerned with land use patterns have tended to focus more on the effect of income growth on housing expansion, than the reverse relationship. The importance of the latter relationship is evident from the fact that the Federal government uses new home construction as one leading economic indicator. The National Association of Home Builders (2002) asserts that the housing industry is without equal both in terms of economic stimulus provided and value-added to gross domestic product, and that national economic performance rises and falls with the sector. The Association further maintains that for every 1,000 single-family homes constructed, 2,448 jobs are created in the construction and related industries, with wages of about $79.4 million, and taxes and fees at all levels of government in excess of $42.5 million.

To investigate this question empirically for a single region, a simple Barro-type growth model was specified and estimated econometrically using data from 299 counties in the Northeast United States, covering the period 1990–1999. These counties vary in population density from remote and sparsely populated – three persons/mile^2 in Hamilton County, NY – to the densely settled urban core of New York City/County, with 53,173 persons/mile^2. The dependent variable was formulated as the logarithm of per capita income in 1999 relative to per capita income in 1990. Initial (1990) income per capita and the percent of population with a college degree, along with an interaction term for these variables, were the basic regressors. Population density was excluded from this regression because it is highly correlated with initial per capita income. Building permit activity over the period 1990–1999, as a percent of the existing housing stock in 1990, was added to the regressors following an instrumental variables estimation (see footnote to Table 10.1). This variable ranges from 0 in two West Virginia counties to 48.8 percent in Calvert, Maryland. Regression results are reported in Table 10.1.

The results in the first column reveal that higher rates of building activity depress the rate of income growth. This is statistically significant at the 10 percent level. Adding a quadratic term for building permits produces an inverted U-shaped relationship, in which a maximum is reached at 9.8 percent, compared with a sample average building permit rate of 8.1 percent. About 72 percent of the counties lie below this turning point, implying that most counties do in fact experience a faster income growth rate as building activity expands, while slightly more than one quarter do not. Therefore, while housing construction is associated with higher incomes and economic activity nationally, the situation in specific counties and regions varies and depends on the local supply linkages and propensities of businesses and households to spend locally, as might be expected.

Table 10.1 Income growth model with building permits variable, 1990–1999, Northeast United States

Variable	Coefficient (t-statistic)	
Intercept	0.396*** (16.0)	0.387*** (15.7)
Initial income ($10,000)	−0.037** (2.15)	−0.041** (2.35)
College education (in percent)	−0.19* (1.73)	−0.24** (2.17)
Income × education	0.19*** (3.66)	0.20*** (3.95)
Building permits (100s)	−0.108* (1.82)	0.25* (1.68)
Building permits (100s) squared		−0.012*** (2.35)
Adjusted R-squared	11.1%	12.3%

Note
Heteroscedasticity-consistent t-statistics; N = 299. The dependent variable is the logarithm of per capita income in 1999 to income in 1990. Building permits are instrumented on population and income growth, initial income and population density; the R-square value is 65.6 percent. Significant at the * = 10 percent, ** = 5 percent, *** = 1 percent level or lower.

Selected economic outcomes

Sprawl and congestion

The amount of time spent commuting determines a worker's effective income earned and leisure time, and quality of life generally. According to the Census Bureau, mean travel time to work increased by 13.8 percent nationally between 1990 and 2000, from 22.4 to 25.5 minutes (Reschovsky 2004: 5). Arguing that cars provide significant advantages in terms of saving commuters time, Glaeser and Kahn (2003: 21) point out that the median commuting time for workers using public transportation was 48 minutes in 2000 compared with only 24 minutes for workers who used their own car. They also state that average commuting time increases with the logarithm of population density, and use this to argue that sprawl is not a problem requiring government intervention (35).

Between 1980 and 1997, total vehicle miles traveled (VMT) in the United States increased by 3.1 percent annually, while the population grew by only 1 percent; considerable variation exists in these percentages across metro areas (see US Environmental Protection Agency 2001b: 20). The Federal Highway Administration estimates that VMT will increase by 53 percent over the next two decades, and it forecasts increasing travel delays for drivers (US Department of Transportation 1998: 60). However, there is some debate as to whether dispersion of the population has led to significant increases in commuting time (Gordon and Richardson 1994 and Gordon *et al.* 1991). Also, average highway speeds are increasing over time. At the same time, it is not clear that time spent commuting necessarily creates a disutility for all workers. Some workers may use the time to work, listen to books on tape, or shift mentally between work and home life.

Glaeser and Kahn's (2003) argument ignores the fact that congestion costs associated with driving – measured as the number of hours drivers are delayed due to traffic congestion and the cost of wasted fuel – are increasing uniformly around the country, even as the average population density of metro areas has fallen. Figure 10.1 illustrates this point nationally per peak road traveler, using data from the Texas Transportation Institute. On average, hours of delay increased from about 17 hours per driver to over 60 hours each year, or more than threefold. For peak and non-peak period travelers combined (i.e., all drivers), the average annual delay per person is 26 hours.

American cities can be separated into two groups, depending on whether their population density has increased or fallen over the last two decades. A key point is that average traffic delays are rising regardless of what is happening to population density. Figure 10.2 illustrates this pattern for two typical cities: Atlanta and Baltimore. In Atlanta, population density has risen, as it has in Albany, Hartford, Los Angeles and Portland, Oregon. At the same time, hours of delay in traffic per driver due to congestion increased in each of these cities. For example, delays in traffic increased from an average of 10 hours per capita in 1982 to 50 hours in 1999 in Atlanta, Georgia, which along with Los Angeles (with over 55 hours) has some of the longest delays in the nation.

Another set of cities, exemplified by Baltimore, experienced falling population density over time combined with rising hours of delay. Here, hours of

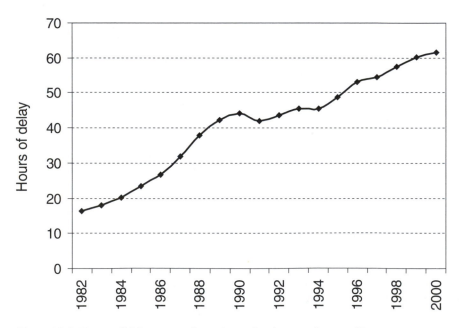

Figure 10.1 Hours of delay per peak road traveler, by year (source: Texas Transportation Institute, 2001).

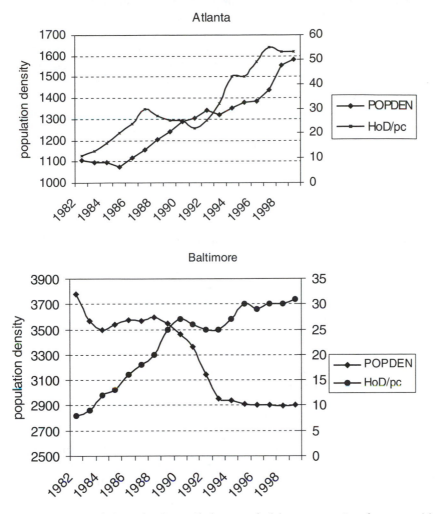

Figure 10.2 Population density and hours of delay per capita for two cities, 1982–1999 (source: Basic data are from the Texas Transportation Institute, 2001).

Note
POPDEN is population density, HoD/pc is hours of delay per capita.

delay increased from 10 hours in 1982 to 30 hours in 2000. Other cities in this group include Kansas City, Minneapolis/St. Paul (where density has recently stabilized) and New York City.

Furthermore, the relationship between hours of delay experienced and population density is not the same everywhere in the country. One might expect a greater population density to be associated with greater congestion and more delays (i.e., a positive correlation coefficient). The simple coefficient of correlation between density and delay is strongest and statistically different from zero in the US Northeast (0.678) and West (0.490), weaker in the Midwest (0.062), and – for reasons that are not obvious – slightly negative but not significant statistically in the metropolises of the South (−0.200). In other words, as population density increases in the Northeast and West (more people per square mile), so do the hours of delay that drivers experience. In the South and Midwest, on the other hand, no such relationship exists. These data need to be examined further to determine the influence of other physical characteristics of metro areas on delays. For example, annual average hours of delay decline with total population size of a metro area, from an average of over 40 hours per capita in the largest to 10 hours in the smallest metro areas (Texas Transportation Institute 2001).[3] It is noteworthy that Chicago and Portland had both the same population density and average hours of delay per capita in 1999.

Downs (1999: 969) points out that "the most important thing to understand about peak-hour traffic congestion is that once it has appeared in a region, it cannot be eliminated or even substantially reduced. There is no effective remedy for traffic congestion because it is essentially a balancing mechanism that enables firms and people to pursue key objectives other than minimizing commuting time." These objectives include capturing agglomeration economies by having workers at work during the same hours (as discussed above), which in turn contributes to congestion. Households, on the other hand, seek flexibility in choosing where to live and prefer low-density housing; want to engage in multi-purpose trips; prefer private motor vehicles; and also (ibid.) "want to separate their own family dwelling – and particularly public schools – spatially from other households with much lower income and social status, and often from people of different racial groups" (see also Anas *et al.* 1998: 1439).

Research described in Benfield *et al.* (1999: 76) suggests that "individuals driving suburban arterial strips may perceive their driving times to be 23 [percent] longer than their actual time; in contrast, when driving down traditional neighborhood streets, drivers may perceive their times to be 16 [percent] *less* than their actual time." Not surprisingly, other studies have shown that drivers of newer, more expensive cars derive greater satisfaction than do drivers of older cars, all else equal. More generally, relatively little is known about how commuters view tradeoffs between time spent in traffic versus leisure time or work time, and the extent to which they are able to work while driving.

According to Putnam (2000: 213), about 45 percent of respondents to one survey indicated that "driving is my time to think and enjoy being alone." Younger drivers were more likely to agree with this statement than older drivers. Other studies, in contrast, have found that commuting can raise stress levels, and cardiovascular and back problems (see below; also see Hennessy 2003; and Frumkin 2002: 18, citing Koslowsky *et al.* 1995). More research is needed on how time spent driving enters a household's or worker's utility function, and how it affects the total household time constraint.

Sprawl and housing affordability

Housing affordability has become an increasingly important issue in the last decade, and nowhere more so than in the Northeast United States (Goetz and Kelsey 2003). Fewer new homes were constructed nationally in the last decade per new resident than in either the 1970s or 1980s. Anecdotal evidence suggests that those on fixed incomes are especially threatened by rising home prices and property taxes, and more so in areas that offer appealing natural amenities, such as bodies of water, a pleasant climate, or interesting landscapes and topography.

Interventions that reduce the supply of land (and housing) potentially raise the cost of homeownership for individuals and families (Abbott 1997; Fishel 1997; Katz and Rosen 1987; for the opposite view, see Nelson *et al.* 2002). An inverse relationship between housing affordability and population density is evident in Figure 10.3: the lower the population density, or more sprawling the metro area, the higher the affordability index. This index is compiled quarterly by the National Association of Home Builders and it measures the share of homes in an area that can be purchased by families earning the area's median income.[4] The population density in Figure 10.3 is that compiled by the Texas Transportation Institute.

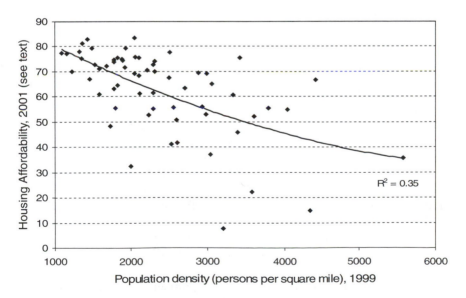

Figure 10.3 Housing affordability versus population density (source: Compiled by author using data from the Texas Transportation Institute and National Association of Home Builders).

Kahn (2001) reports that the gap between black and white households in the consumption of housing services – measured as the number of rooms, square footage and ownership – is narrower in areas that are more sprawling. He uses American Housing Survey (AHS) data from 1997 and ZIP Code-level jobs data to measure sprawl as the proportion of jobs that are located outside a 10-mile radius and within a 35-mile radius of the metro core's central business district. Based on his measure (Table 1: 79), Portland, Oregon, New York City and Anaheim, California are the least-sprawling cities, while Detroit, Tampa, Oakland, Atlanta and Chicago are the most-sprawling (in that order).

Kahn (2001: 84) concludes that "black households living in sprawled metropolitan areas live in larger housing units and are more likely to own a home than observationally equivalent identical black households in less sprawled areas. In addition, as the metropolitan area's sprawl level increases, the black/white housing gap closes for these measures of housing." He also cautions that the flight of businesses to suburbs, which often accompanies sprawl, reduces employment opportunities for minorities, leading to spatial mismatch. Consequently, a tradeoff arises between employment and housing opportunities for African-American families. This topic is discussed further below.

An important consideration is that newer homes require less initial maintenance expenditures and, conversely, older homes require more spending on upkeep and renovations to maintain property values. Thus, homeowners with lower disposable incomes may be better off moving into new subdivisions in sprawling neighborhoods on the fringes of cities (McCarthy *et al.* 2001).

Sprawl and social capital

Empirical studies show that social capital enhances economic growth and also leads to lower poverty rates (Rupasingha *et al.* 2000, 2002). Basically, the greater level of trust that is associated with social capital or civic capacity reduces transaction costs, thereby allowing more economic activity to take place, all else equal.[5] At the same time, some authors have argued that sprawl leads to declining social capital and neighborhood ties (Bressi 1994; Burchell *et al.* 1998; Calthorpe 1993; Ewing 1997). The common reason given is that modern suburbs provide fewer possibilities for social exchanges (Freeman 2001: 70) and the space provided by low-density housing also makes it unnecessary for homeowners to visit public green spaces.[6] Other researchers have examined the effect of crowding, or the sensation of being crowded on individuals' well being.

In his chapter on "Mobility and Sprawl," Putnam (2000: 213) presents a widely cited statistic according to which participation in civic activities – such as engaging in volunteer work or attending public gatherings – declines by 10 percent for every 10 extra minutes an individual spends commuting.

Putnam states that conventional demographic factors are controlled for in arriving at these figures, and that the results are robust across surveys, but it is not clear which factors these are, or what pertinent variables may have been excluded from the analysis.

Authors of the work reviewed by Freeman conclude that, in neighborhoods where cars are not the primary means of transportation, the "sense of community" is greater (Glynn 1981; Nasar and Julian 1995). Other authors have found that more urbanized, densely settled areas also exhibited lower levels of social capital. Fischer's (1982) work suggested that local ties were highest among residents of semi-rural places, followed by small-town residents, central city dwellers and suburbanites (in that order). Fischer controlled for basic demographic and socioeconomic features of the population studied, and defined social networks as consisting of those "people who most affected respondents' beliefs, actions and well-being" (288).

Freeman's (2001) regression analysis employed data from Atlanta, Los Angeles and Boston. He failed to uncover a statistically significant effect of residential density (and density squared) on social interaction among neighbors. Freeman defined "neighbor social ties" based on responses to the question, "from time to time, most people discuss important matters with other people. Looking back over the last six months, who are the people, other than those living in your household, with whom you discussed matters important to you?" (72). The larger the number of such people (up to a total of three), the greater the social ties in the community. Other regressors in his study included age, duration of residence, race, marital, employment and ownership status, as well as educational attainment and income. Freeman concludes that more work is needed on this topic, under different residential settings, and that surveys eliciting reasons for the selection of specific residential neighborhoods will be helpful. Freeman's own work could be expanded upon to examine the effects of any selection bias, as well as interactions between density and carpooling, for example.

Gordon and Richardson (2000: 10) maintain that sprawl has little if any effect on levels of social capital, or "today's social problems – crime, divorce, family disintegration, and illegitimate teenage pregnancy." They point to Fukuyama's (1999) observation that levels of social engagement have been declining across industrial countries around the world, so that sprawl may be a consequence rather than a cause of declining social capital levels. Gordon and Richardson (2000: 10) further assert that "'New Urbanism' is widely sold as a way to foster close-knit communities and general contentment. Yet no one knows the recipe for good or bad community formation, let alone an easy spatial fix." They refer to the fact that residents of central cities and suburbs take about the same number of social trips, and of similar duration, as evidence that sprawl has not reduced social interaction (14). Finally, Florida (2002) argues that individuals today prefer and seek out the anonymity that only modern suburbs can provide.

Sprawl and income distribution

The house pricing dynamics that trap especially African-American and poor households in inner cities are laid out compellingly by Jargowsky (2002). As white populations flee the cities to the suburbs, he argues, they take with them employment opportunities as well as important public and private resources or services such as day care operations. Lacking suitable transport, minorities face a spatial mismatch in terms of where employment opportunities reflecting their skills sets are located, and their residences. As the tax base erodes and school quality declines, the cycle of poverty is reinforced and poverty is perpetuated. Glaeser and Kahn (2003) point to the high cost of buying and owning a car as a major factor entrapping low-income households, and propose subsidizing cars for the poor as a remedy.

Katz (2000: 68) reports that while Philadelphia County, Pennsylvania contains only 12 percent of the state's population, it has nearly one half of the state's welfare recipients (48 percent). For Baltimore, the corresponding percentages are 13 and 56 percent. Here, growing concentration of poverty appears to be both a consequence and a cause of sprawl, usually in the form of white flight. A related phenomenon is that many of the older suburbs are now starting to experience similar forms of decay, producing widening belts of poverty and declining property values. At the same time, the gentrification that occurs when higher-income residents move back into cities also causes problems for low-income residents. Often these returning, higher-income residents are empty-nesters, or they send their children to private schools.

Gordon and Richardson (2000) contend that urban decay is basically a problem of low levels of human capital, and not sprawl *per se*. The problem with this argument is that it ignores the dynamics behind human capital investment decisions and opportunities. In particular, poorer regions often have educational systems of lower quality, which tend to produce students with lower educational achievement and aspirations, thereby perpetuating poverty. This has been studied as neighborhood effects, according to which children make investments in education based on the perceived returns, which tend to be low or altogether absent in neighborhoods without college graduates (Boarnet and Haughwout 2000; Case and Katz 1991; Cutler and Glaeser 1997; Goetz 1993; Wilson 1987). One manifestation of disinvestments in urban education is that Catholic schools have experienced significant enrollment declines.[7] Sprawl is widely cited as putting pressure on schools both in inner cities (lack of funding) and the suburban fringes (crowding). However, these relationships, and the importance of educational systems in migration decisions, have not been systematically quantified.

Health outcomes

Sprawl has been blamed for numerous health problems. Interdisciplinary research by health experts and planners is an important emerging research frontier (see, *inter alia*, Roper *et al.* 2003). Primarily because it increases reliance on automobiles, sprawling development contributes both to air and ground pollution as well as sedentary lifestyles that are blamed, among other things, for rising obesity. This section examines these health-related issues. An important challenge here remains that of separating the effects of sprawl on population health from the effects of urban lifestyles in general.

Current residential choices are believed to affect the population's health in a number of ways. These range from reduction in physical activity both because modern suburbs create automobile dependence and at the same time are pedestrian-unfriendly (Ewing *et al.* 2003a), to car crashes and pedestrian fatalities, road rage or mental stress, urban heat islands and air pollution (Frumkin 2002). Linking sprawl and public health, Frumkin writes (4) that questions surrounding land use, including sprawl, transportation issues and residential planning are increasingly and almost exclusively in the domain of urban planners and engineers, with experts in public health having only minor roles, if any. This theme was also stressed by Libby (2004, chapter 2 this volume), and the same is true of social scientists in non-planning fields generally. Frumkin (2002) contrasts the current situation with that in earlier centuries, when questions surrounding the design of cities and health of the public were virtually inseparable. He argues (27) that those concerned with public health need to more proactively engage in land use debates, especially in terms of housing impacts, while engineers, architects and planners need to increasingly realize that their work has important implications for public health, and that they should in turn call on health experts. Therefore, while public health and residential choices were once viewed as closely interconnected, that relationship has fallen apart over time. Now recognition is growing that these problems are complex and that they can only be resolved effectively through multidisciplinary approaches. Similarly, Jackson and Kochtitzky (2001, preface) maintain that choices involving land use affect the public's health as surely as do choices involving the preparation of food. And, in the latter case, government has a pronounced and explicit regulatory role.

One example where multidisciplinary work is useful is in dealing with the much maligned cul-de-sac that has become a hallmark of sprawl in some areas. Traffic engineers correctly point out that these "sacks" can cause congestion elsewhere in a subdivision. At the same time, this arrangement also has the effect of calming traffic in the street that has a dead end. The potential benefits of this traffic-calming in terms of lives of small children saved need to be weighed against the costs incurred elsewhere in the development as a result of the cul-de-sac. The role of social scientists in general, and economists in particular, is to measure and value all of the benefits and costs to society of specific projects, including those that are perhaps not immediately obvious. This is a broader mandate than that pursued by traffic engineers, for example, who seek only to transport individuals from point A to B in the least cost and safest manner.

Air quality issues

Along with the rising hours of congestion-induced delays discussed above come increasing quantities of fuel wasted as engines are idling. A recent report relating sprawl to air pollution, unhealthy lifestyles and poor health of the population received widespread coverage in major newspapers.[8] The report was co-authored by a medical doctor from the Centers for Disease Control (CDC) and published by the Sprawl Watch Clearinghouse (Jackson and Kochtitzky 2001). These authors cite (6) Congressional Research Service (National Council for Science and the Environment 1999) statistics on the contributions of motor vehicles to total carbon monoxide (58 percent), nitrogen oxide (30 percent), volatile organic compounds or VOCs (about 27 percent) and particulate matter (9 percent). Nitrogen oxide and VOCs in turn contribute to smog formation (US Environmental Protection Agency 1997).

Another widely cited Centers for Disease Control study relates the 22.5 percent reduction in Atlanta's morning traffic during the 1996 Summer Olympics to a 27.9 percent reduction in maximum ozone levels during the same period as well as a 41.6 percent decline in asthma-related medical emergencies (Figure 3 in Friedman *et al.* 2001). An Abt Associates (1999) study suggested that excess levels of ozone contributed to 130,000 asthma attacks in the District of Columbia, 86,000 in Baltimore and 27,000 in Richmond in 1999. Aside from this, studies relating residential patterns specifically to vehicle emissions are rare (Benfield *et al.* 1999: 56–60), although the Environmental Protection Agency (EPA) recently released two related reports on this subject (US Environmental Protection Agency 2001b, c).

Cars are clearly becoming more fuel-efficient over time, largely as a result of Corporate Average Fuel Economy (CAFÉ) standards, leading some researchers to claim that sprawl-related increases in driving are not an issue (e.g., Glaeser and Kahn 2001). These authors conducted a study of California, partitioning the state into the Los Angeles Basin and the remainder. Using air quality data from the California EPA Air Resources Board, they conclude that improvements in automobile fuel efficiency have more than compensated for increased driving. In particular, they find that in the LA Basin area the number of days each year that those living near monitoring stations were exposed to ambient ozone in excess of national standards dropped from 33 in the 1980s to only 5 in the 1990s.

A question that arises here is whether the experience of Los Angeles is transferable to other regions of the United States or the world, especially those not exposed to ocean breezes. During the 1990s, population density in the LA region has according to Texas Transportation Institute data also increased slightly, from 5,200 persons per square mile to 5,575. Thus, Los Angeles is not representative of those cities in which population density has fallen or housing development has sprawled the most over time. Another question revolves around what specific pollutant should be measured.

Recently the EPA has pointed to fine particular matter, or soot, as a major health threat from cars and power plants. And the agency specifically lists Southern California as an area where the amount of soot poses a threat to the population.

Former President Clinton's Task Force on Environmental Health Risks and Safety Risks to Children (2000) estimated that one quarter of all children in the United States are exposed to excess ozone levels. At least one quarter of these excess levels is in turn directly attributable to motor vehicle emissions. Childhood asthma cases are rising dramatically in the United States, with an increase to 5.5 million in 1995 from 2.3 million children affected in 1980.

Sedentary lifestyles

Obesity and diabetes are two other serious health concerns that are on the rise. While these medical problems are the result of a complex set of lifestyle and other factors, including overeating, many authors have pointed to the automobile dependence that results from sprawl as a major causal factor. In particular, Jackson and Kochtitzky (2001: 8–9) relate sedentary and automobile-dependent lifestyles associated with sprawl to adverse health impacts. While consistent statistics are not yet available, reports in the popular press citing CDC officials reveal growing numbers of Type II Diabetes (adult-onset) cases in children, for example. According to the National Center for Health Statistics, age-adjusted obesity rates (body mass index, or BMI, of 30 or more) for US adults aged 20–74 years doubled from 15 percent in 1976–1980 to 31 percent in 1999–2000, the most recent year for which data are available. The share of overweight population (BMI of 25 kg per square meter or more) over that period increased from 47 to 64 percent. Ewing *et al.* (2003b: 51) report that residents of the least-sprawling area in their study (the New York City boroughs) on average weighed 6.3 lbs less than did residents of the most-sprawling area, Geauga County, Ohio. This represents a difference in BMI of about 1 kg/m^2.

It is important to stress that residential choice and the attendant modes of transportation used are only a part of the general public health problem, and how important they are is unknown. One clue about the effect of residential choice on mode of transportation is provided by data on how children aged 5–15 years travel to school, as a function of how far away they live from the school. Using data from the 1995 National Personal Transportation Survey, the CDC reports that 31 percent of youth living within a one-mile radius of their school walk to school. Three percent use a bicycle, 14 percent a school bus and 51 percent travel by car. For youth living between one and two miles from their school, the share walking drops to 5 percent and that using a bicycle falls to 1 percent. Instead, 41 percent of these children use the school bus and 50 percent use a car.

Understanding the forces motivating individuals' choices among different modes of travel (bicycling, walking, driving), as well as participation in car-pools and purchasing of sports utility vehicles, is a fertile area for research by social scientists (see also Frumkin 2002: 7). The same is true of understanding the relationship between residential choices (sprawling subdivisions) and physical exercise, such as driving to the neighborhood gym for a workout on a treadmill. Econometric estimation issues such as selection bias pose serious challenges for empirical work, and it is important to take advantage of naturally occurring experiments where they arise. For example, residents of sprawling communities may have systematic but unmeasured characteristics that account for their higher (or lower) BMI, and they self-select themselves into these sprawling communities. The summer Olympics held in Atlanta, Georgia are an example of a natural experiment. During this time traffic flows into the city were sharply curtailed, allowing researchers to study the effect of traffic on various environmental and health-related measures. Other examples of natural experiments may include the redrawing of a school dis-trict boundary or the annexation of an outlying area by a city, and the closing of a local plant, that in turn leads to less pollution of the environment. Natural experiments are important in the social sciences, because it is often difficult to achieve so-called "controlled conditions" in studying social or behavioral phenomena.

Research is needed to understand whether and how alternative residential and land use patterns impact traffic fatalities as well as environmental meas-ures such as air pollution. More generally, Frumkin (2002: 13) argues that studies are needed to understand how urban or suburban design affects the "walkability" of neighborhoods, and what incentives need to be put in place through public policy to affect changes in behavior that lead to greater mobility and thus health. Another health-related aspect is that recovery from stress is apparently more rapid among individuals experiencing natural envi-ronments. One study cited by Frumkin (2002) found that recovering patients who could view greenery (tree clusters) from their hospital windows in place of building walls not only remained in the hospital for shorter periods after their operations but also required fewer sedatives. In another study, Frumkin (2001) argues that "contact with nature" benefits not only physical but also mental well being.

As noted in the introduction, there is also growing interest in the relation-ship among traffic congestion, mental stress and workplace performance (Hennessy 2003). Outside the workplace, traffic-related stress has been linked to violence in soccer moms, for example (Squires 2002: 1). However, whether land use patterns and gridlock are the primary causes of such behav-ior and health outcomes, or one of many complex causes, is an unanswered question.

Conclusion

The subject of land use is complex. While sprawl has been blamed for many societal ills, causes and effects for most of these relationships are far from clear. Individual decisions that are perfectly rational taken one at a time can have aggregate consequences that are less-than-desirable, leading to social traps. Tackling sprawl in general may be ineffective if the true goal is to address a particular problem, such as urban poverty, inequality, obesity or congestion, and it is important to be explicit about the problem to be addressed if policy tools selected are to be effective.

A clearer understanding is also needed of the actual benefits derived from sprawl and suburban lifestyles. Aside from the fact that households are clearly voting with their dollars when making home purchase decisions – although some observers contend that homebuyers have no alternatives to sprawling subdivisions – relatively little is known about the perceived and actual benefits and costs associated with suburban or urban lifestyles (see also Gordon and Richardson 2000).

For virtually all of the hypothesized relationships discussed here, better and more systematic measurement at the level of all United States counties and sub-counties is likely to yield a substantial payoff. The existence of most of these relationships has not been established unequivocally. For example, Katz and Bradley (1999: 3) write that nobody is "duping" homeowners into buying houses in low-density, bucolic sub-divisions with excellent public schools. Nevertheless, they continue, public policies tend to enhance the attraction as well as the affordability of suburbia relative to inner cities. However, the General Accounting Office finds that the effect of federal spending on urban sprawl is "unclear" (US General Accounting Office 1999). To our knowledge, no one is presently analyzing these relationships in a systematic and comprehensive manner across the United States or in other countries. In the United States, county-level data available from the Census, Centers for Disease Control and the Environmental Protection Agency are an excellent starting point for such an analysis.

Notes

1 Brian Lego and Ozgur Tunceli provided research assistance but the author is solely responsible for the content of this chapter. The chapter has also benefited from the literature compilations contained in Rupasingha and Goetz 2001.
2 *Business Week* on October 22, 2001 published a special report on the question, "The Future of New York – will it remain the preeminent global and financial capital?" The *New York Times* on January 29, 2002 featured an article with the title, "Seeking Safety, Manhattan Firms are Scattering."
3 http://mobility.tamu.edu/ums/study/larger_urban_areas.stm. There are notable exceptions, with some smaller metros averaging delays much longer than ten hours per capita. Per capita numbers are calculated using the entire population of a metro area, not only drivers.
4 Data are from the NAHB's web-site, www.nahb.com, accessed January 21, 2001.

5 We measure social capital at the level of counties using the density of membership associations and non-profit organizations as well as participation in the civic activities of voting and responding to the national Census.

6 Ironically, as Freeman (2001) points out (*ibid.*), sociologists such as Wirth (1938) also in part blamed elevated urban density for the decline of *Gemeinschaft* [community], allowing *Gesellschaft* [society] to emerge instead as a means of organizing society today.

7 "Suburban rise hurts Catholic schools – traditionally Catholic schools were built in urban areas," CNN.com/Education, 01/17/2002. "Catholic officials [in Philadelphia] blame the declines [in enrollment] on the fact that white, working class Catholic families have moved to the suburbs. The trend began as early as the 1960s, but has become more noticeable in recent years, school officials suggested."

8 The second and third paragraphs of this section draw heavily from Jackson and Kochtitzky (2001).

Part III

Data and empirical issues

11 Spatial analysis and applied land use research

Kathleen P. Bell

Introduction

By simplifying the measurement of spatial relationships, geographic information systems (GIS) and remote sensing (RS) technologies are changing the
ways in which researchers describe, visualize and model the use of land
resources. Coupled with advances in data collection and management, computing and statistics, GIS and RS technologies are stimulating innovative
treatments of space in applied land use research. Researchers have long
recognized the relevance of space to the study of land use issues (e.g., Alonso
1964; Anas 1987; Hotelling 1929; von Thunen 1826). However, descriptive
and statistical analyses of the spatial aspects of land resources were constrained
historically by a lack of spatial data and analysis tools.[1] Prior to these recent
technological developments, the measurement of spatial relationships such as
proximity and adjacency, the representation of spatial regions such as neighborhoods and landscapes, and the evaluation of spatial networks such as road
and river systems, which are easily measured using current tools, were difficult tasks.

The spatial aspects of land necessitate the treatment of space in applied
land use research. Two spatial aspects of land are notable. First, land is immo-
bile, making its location an important attribute from both consumptive and
production perspectives. Studies of land use issues inevitably center on
describing location, a characteristic that is often measured in terms of relative
proximity to other activities and one that varies over time. For example, the
return to a land parcel in residential use may depend on its proximity to
transportation networks, schools, employment centers, shopping opportunities, parks and recreation areas. A given land parcel's proximity to these
items may change over time as new facilities and roads are constructed or as
facilities or park areas are shut down. Second, land resources provide a variety
of service flows. Some depend solely on the attributes of a specific parcel,
while others depend on the attributes of a suite of land parcels or a landscape.
Therefore, a given land parcel often produces a set of private service flows to
its owners and a set of public service flows to owners of surrounding parcels,
and it contributes to a broader set of public service flows as part of a mosaic

of lands. The production and consumption of these public and private service flows also depend on relative proximity and they vary over time. For instance, one agricultural land parcel may provide direct production benefits to its owner, produce open space benefits to the community in which it is located, and serve as habitat for a variety of wildlife species. Because of the influence of immobility and location on the value of land resources and the production and consumption of their service flows, space is essential to applied land use research.

This chapter stresses the significance of the relationship between spatial analysis tools and applied land use research. Land use applications of spatial analysis tools are introduced, and attention is given to both the challenges and benefits of using these tools. Emphasis is given to a set of research issues that arise when conducting spatial analysis, including choices of temporal and spatial scale, definition of units of analysis, representations of human behavior as a spatial process, and measurement of landscape and other spatial variables. Discussions of these issues may also be found in Anselin (2002) and Bailey and Gatrell (1995). The development of economic models of land use decisions, land use patterns, and land-based externalities poses a variety of novel and, in some cases, formidable empirical hurdles. Although attention is given to the challenges of working with spatial data, the objective of the chapter is not to discourage researchers from using such data. Instead, its intent is to raise awareness of these empirical issues and to highlight the benefits of using spatial analysis tools. For the purposes of this chapter, spatial analysis is defined as research that employs spatial data. Spatial analysis often begins with two basic realizations: data have a spatial configuration and absolute and relative locations of data matter.

This chapter is divided into two sections. The first section presents a discussion of empirical issues directly related to spatial data; the second section provides an introduction to spatial analysis of land resources. Both sections emphasize how economic models of land use issues may be revised to take advantage of new data and computing resources and to account for spatial dependence.

Using spatial data

Buffeted by the rise of geographic information systems and remote sensing technologies, many spatial data sources are available to study land use issues and conflicts.[2] Pertinent discussions of spatial data may be found in Bell and Irwin (2002) and Nelson and Geoghegan (2002), which respectively provide reviews of micro- and macro-scale data sources for the study of land use issues. Relevant resources include data on land use and land cover as well as data summarizing biophysical, social, and economic aspects of landscapes. The first sub-section of this chapter offers an overview of spatial data resources. New and improved data management and analysis tools enable researchers to consider a range of spatial relationships. As is the case when using any type of data for empirical research, numerous decisions are required to conduct applied research. The final sub-sections provide an overview of issues related to the choice of spatial scale, temporal scale and scope of analysis.

Data resources

In some instances, GIS, RS, and other spatial analysis tools have advanced the development of new data resources. Consider the availability of parcel-scale GIS data, showing ownership boundaries and describing features of land parcels such as land area, assessed value, sales price and attributes of structural improvements. As local government agencies employ GIS technology to streamline tasks related to tax assessment, zoning, permitting and the provision of emergency services, parcel-level data are increasingly being made available to the public.[3] A second example is RS data covering multiple time periods, which allow historical assessments of land use change over large areas. Aerial and satellite images are a valuable source of land use data because they record data uniformly over large areas and at multiple points in times. Classified or interpreted data based on these images are increasingly becoming available to the public. For example, the digital orthophotograph quadrangles (DOQs) produced by the US Geological Survey (USGS) for the entire country facilitate a rich description of the landscape. Access to RS data has improved in recent years because of improved public access via federal agencies, lower costs and technical advances in data storage and viewing. A final example involves the use of global positioning systems (GPS). The flexibility, ease, and low cost of using hand-held GPS units to create new spatial data sources are remarkable. GPS has incredible potential to influence collection of data related to land use issues and is quickly becoming an integral part of field research.

In other instances, spatial analysis tools have elevated the utility of older data sets by facilitating the recognition of spatial relationships. Consider the US Census of Population and Housing. This decennial data set is widely used by researchers to describe levels of population and housing, and changes in these stocks over time. The sampling frame permits data to be summarized at a variety of spatial scales, ranging from large areas such as states, counties and metropolitan areas, to small areas such as municipalities, tracts and blocks. Recently available boundary files stored in GIS format expedite measurement of bordering units and proximity among units and aggregation from smaller to larger areas.[4] Prior to the existence of these boundary files, these basic spatial relationships were cumbersome to represent using standard statistical or spreadsheet packages.

A review of the applied land use literature indicates researchers are using a variety of data to study the use and management of land resources. Parcel-level data appeal to empirical researchers because the parcel directly corresponds with the decision unit in models of land use decisions. A second advantage of these data is the ability to describe the history of a parcel or a set of parcels based on the tax and assessment records. When modeling land conversion decisions, these data permit the researcher to describe fully the nature of the land conversion – original land use, ultimate land use and timing of change. Unfortunately, these data are not available in a spatially explicit format for all areas, and the quality of these data are not consistent across areas, which complicates regional analyses. Moreover, sample sizes can quickly grow large, complicating data management and econometric analysis. Studies of land conversion (e.g., Bockstael 1996; Bockstael and Bell 1997; Hite *et al.* 2003; Irwin *et al.* 2003) and land-related externalities such as open space (Irwin 2002) and hog farms (Palmquist *et al.* 2002) have made effective use of parcel-level data.

Small area census data such as those collected at block, block group and tract levels offer an alternative means to study land use issues. Advantages of the US Census of Housing and Population data extend from their availability over space and time and their low cost. Disadvantages include changing boundaries and explanatory variables as well as the indirect measurement of land use. Boundaries, particularly for smaller areas, may change over time. In addition, questions and response categories have changed over time, limiting the validity of comparisons over extended time periods. Moreover, if researchers employ these data to describe land use change, caution is necessary because the correspondence between changes in population and housing units and changes in land use may be tenuous. Researchers have used these data to make inferences on changes in land use based on changes in population and housing units (e.g., Fulton *et al.* 2001) and to describe neighborhoods in socioeconomic terms.

Plot-level sampling data are the basis of several data resources provided by the US Department of Agriculture on land use and land cover. Although confidentiality requirements often prevent the direct use of plot-level data by researchers, these resources can be used to describe changes in land use and land cover. The National Resources Inventory (NRI) data and Forest Inventory Analysis (FIA) data, which are based on plot samples, offer useful descriptions of the landscape and are available for the entire United States. Examples of applied land use research using these data sources include Skaggs and Ghosh (1999) and Kline and Alig (1999).

Remotely sensed data are available at a variety of spatial scales and geographic extents. Higher resolution RS data (e.g., 30 and 15 meter resolution) such as the US Geological Survey's Thematic Mapper and Enhanced Thematic Mapper products provide a useful description of land cover in the United States. These products are based on Landsat satellite imagery. SPOT (Systeme Pour L'Observation de la Terre) images are another useful source of higher resolution RS data. Other products such as the lower resolution (e.g., 1 km resolution) USGS Global Land Cover Characterization and AVHRR (Advanced Very High Resolution Radiometer) data are designed to describe global changes in land cover. Chen (1998) provides an annotated guide of RS data sources for social scientists, which include a variety of products designed and collected by NOAA, NASA, and USGS. An advantage of these data is the ability to track changes in land cover over time in a consistent manner across broad areas. In addition, the uniformity of the data collection unit (e.g., cells) simplifies analysis of these data. Many spatial analysis software packages offer powerful tools to analyze raster data. Disadvantages of these data stem from the classification algorithms used to interpret the images as well as the attributes of the landscape that are detectable from images. In some cases, the description of human use of land resources is limited. In addition, use of macro-scale data may complicate the ability to link macro outcomes with individual behavior and limit the treatment of heterogeneity within the cells. Lastly, because of the arbitrariness of the cell boundaries, combining land cover data with socioeconomic and biophysical data often requires manipulation or aggregation of these data. As the resolution of RS data increases, many of these shortcomings will no longer be relevant. Examples of economic applications of RS data include Wear and Bolstad (1998), Nelson *et al.* (2001) and Cropper *et al.* (2001).

Spatial scale

When studying a land use issue, the choice of spatial scale is paramount. A primary influence on this choice is the decision unit or market being modeled. Is it a study of individual land use decisions in the city of Bangor, Maine? Or is it an analysis of deforestation trends in the southeastern region of the United States? A secondary, important influence on the choice of spatial scale is data availability. The great range of spatial scales used in applied land use research mirrors the extensive range of subjects falling under the auspices of land use research. Contrast the spatial scale adopted by researchers studying the global implications of climate change on forest land cover with that adopted by researchers studying the regional effects of the Conservation Reserve Program in the United States on agricultural land use, the efficacy of tax incentives at affecting firm location decisions, or the impacts of air pollution on surrounding property values. Different phenomena manifest themselves at fundamentally different spatial scales. Hence, the choice of spatial scale can dramatically influence the empirical results, a finding that inspires consideration of issues related to the modifiable areal unit problem and ecological fallacy (Anselin 2002). The modifiable areal unit problem refers to the sensitivity of modeling results to scaling of data over space and to the use of various spatial zones to organize spatial data. Ecological fallacy problems arise where relationships observed in groups (e.g., one macro spatial scale) may not necessarily hold for individuals (e.g., another micro spatial scale).

When conducting land use research, two fundamental decisions extend from the choice of spatial scale. First, researchers must select the spatial scale at which land is to be characterized. For example, Miller and Plantinga (1999) and Plantinga *et al.* (2002) examine land use decisions using county-level data on the shares of land in different uses. In contrast, researchers employing satellite imagery to examine land use patterns employ land cover data collected at a variety of resolutions. For example, Wear and Bolstad (1998) use 1 acre resolution; Nelson *et al.* (2001) 0.25 km grid cells; and Cropper *et al.* (2002) use 100 m² resolution. Researchers using parcel-level data demonstrate the utility of yet another spatial scale of data for the study of land use issues (Hite *et al.* 2003; Irwin *et al.* 2003). Second, researchers must decide what spatial unit will serve as the organizational unit for the model – the spatial scale or the dependent variable. In some cases, the first decision will coincide with the second. In other instances, land use data will be aggregated to match the spatial scale of other explanatory variables. For example, remotely sensed data could be aggregated to match a political spatial unit such as a parcel, municipality or county.

Attention and care are needed when organizing spatial data and combining data across different scales. First, measurement errors in both data attributes and specification of locations are commonly found when scrutinizing spatial data. For example, measurement errors are introduced when points are used to represent polygon or line features. Using points to represent polygon features such as lakes, where the point is the centroid of the lake, introduces measurement error when distance to the lake is measured. Similarly, classification algorithms used to interpret satellite data or aerial photographs may induce errors. As is the case with all types of data, researchers should begin their analysis with a careful review of their data. A useful reference when using GIS data is the metadata file, which describes the properties of data in detail. Second, most spatial analyses require the marrying of data from different sources. Differences in data formats (e.g., vector or raster) and coordinate systems/projections (e.g., Universal Transverse Mercator or State Plane) are noteworthy. These differences can complicate the management of spatial data, and although GIS software offers methods to resolve such discrepancies, researchers are encouraged to be careful when converting data from one scale, format, or coordinate system to another. Although some software packages allow for data stored using different coordinate systems to be viewed without conversion, the choice of a single coordinate system/projection is highly recommended when conducting analysis. Different coordinate systems and projections are designed to maintain the accuracy of specific features (e.g., distance or area or shape) at distinct scales. An unfortunate choice of coordinate system/projection can bias results. Third, edge effects are anticipated when using spatial data. Sensitivity to boundary areas is important, especially when using polygon data. If the polygons are based on arbitrary cell boundaries, the description of the attributes of these polygons may result in measurement error and biased estimates of spatial influences. Examining the sensitivity of results to different assumptions of spatial scale is a worthwhile endeavor when conducting applied land use research.

Temporal scale

The choice of temporal scale is also central to an empirical land use study. For example, the researcher must select the range over which change in land uses is defined – days, months or years. Researchers often explain land use and land cover changes over discrete sets of years. In many cases this reflects the objective of the analysis as well as data availability. The extent to which these researchers account for the ordering of such changes often varies with choice of estimation method. For example, conventional discrete choice models usually treat any conversion of land equally using a binary code to distinguish change areas from other areas (Bockstael 1996; Bockstael and Bell 1997; Cropper *et al.* 2001; Nelson *et al.* 2001). Hazard models directly represent the order of land use-related events and permit a richer treatment of time-varying explanatory variables (Hite *et al.* 2003; Irwin and Bockstael 2002; Irwin *et al.* 2003). In other cases, such as when researchers are examining the location decisions of firms, farmers or households, land use data at only one point in time are required.

Similar choices are necessary when describing a land use-driven externality such as health risks posed by Superfund sites (Kiel 1995; Smith and Desvousges 1986), amenities provided by open space lands (Irwin 2002), and disamenities from hog farms (Palmquist *et al.* 1997). In this case, the choice of temporal scale may coincide with the researcher's assumption of the timing of external impacts. The sensitivity of the empirical results to various timing assumptions is often explored as part of the empirical analysis. Novel extensions of these issues arise when considering external impacts that are jointly defined over time and space.

Analogous to spatial scale, data availability may drive the choice of temporal scale. For example, building permit data are collected by the US Census Bureau on a monthly and annual basis. In contrast, RS data and parcel-level data contain information regarding land use that is measured on a daily basis. Because annual measurements are a common temporal unit for the collection of socioeconomic data, researchers often aggregate data to match this temporal scale.

Many land use and land cover change models are developed with input from social and ecological scientists (Bockstael *et al.* 1995; Bockstael 1996). Multidisciplinary research projects require consideration of the temporal aspects of human and biophysical processes, many of which operate on vastly different time scales. This task poses interesting challenges necessitating the transfer of information across models of human and ecological systems.

Scope

Scope is defined here as a category of choices that bound empirical research. In setting the boundaries of an empirical study, researchers make several important decisions. This sub-section discusses three challenges that may arise in the study of land use issues when deciding whether or not to use land use or land cover data, how to define the extent of the study area, and if and how policy variables may be incorporated into the analysis.

The distinction between land use and land cover is significant. Social scientists often pose hypotheses concerning how humans specifically use lands. Use may include activities taking place on the land and the intensity at which other inputs are combined with the land to produce marketable goods or other service flows. In contrast, cover refers to the biophysical characteristics of the land, distinguishing various classes of vegetation as well as impervious surfaces. Consider a parcel of land in a rural area of Maine. This parcel could easily be in a residential land use and forest land cover. Recognition of the distinction between use and cover is paramount when using RS data. Methods devoted to interpreting images from RS data sources have focused traditionally on biophysical attributes (cover) instead of use attributes. The increasing availability and accessibility of RS data are likely to draw attention to the distinction between land use and land cover. In turn, as social scientists employ these data more, innovative combinations of data sources have emerged to characterize both land cover and use (Rindfuss and Stern 1998).

Economists often demarcate study areas to correspond with or respect market boundaries. The extent of land or housing markets is an empirical issue that has been addressed in the hedonic property and urban economics literatures (Palmquist 1991). When studying land use issues and conflicts, multiple boundaries are relevant. For example, political economic boundaries such as state, county and municipal boundaries may demarcate regulatory constraints and provision of public services. In contrast, biophysical attributes may demarcate ecological and watershed boundaries. As alluded to in the discussion of temporal scale, multidisciplinary research on land cover and land use change provides examples of useful methods for the consideration of overlapping boundaries (Bockstael *et al.* 1995).

The myriad policies that influence the use of land and emergence of conflicts are an intriguing aspect of land use research. Policies that have a direct impact include zoning, building and site design regulations, comprehensive plans, and land preservation or protection programs. Other relevant policies include agricultural and forest management policies, property tax programs, and transportation planning regulations. Moreover, public and private infrastructure decisions such as the maintenance and construction of roads or commuter rail lines, the location of and access to public sewer and water, and the accessibility to services such as high speed Internet connections or digital cable influence returns to land and therefore land use (see Barnard 2004, chapter 4 this volume). Ignoring the effects of policies is likely to erode the quality of land use research. Yet the inclusion of policies in an analysis may be an arduous task. In some cases, the challenge is related to converting information on zoning and other restrictions into a spatially explicit format. In other instances, difficulties arise when making inferences about endogenous and exogenous provision of infrastructure and other public services.

Finally, the unit of analysis affects the extent to which policies may be considered. When using micro-scale data, there is often greater flexibility in terms of integrating policies into the analysis. In contrast, more macro-scale data may prevent the incorporation of policy variables, especially in instances where there is a spatial mismatch between the scale at which land use is measured and that at which policies are implemented. For example, zoning requirements affect individual parcels. Employment of county-level data on land use inhibits the degree to which a researcher may meaningfully incorporate zoning into their analysis.

Spatial analysis

In the previous section, emphasis was given to empirical issues related to spatial data. In this section, the discussion turns to applications of these data. In some cases, the employment of spatial data necessitates a fundamental change in perspective that may result in an entirely new model. In other cases, the employment of spatial data simply results in additional explanatory variables. The extent of these changes is often dictated by the extent to which relative locations of data matter.

Throughout this chapter, references have been made to the rising availability of spatial data. An analogous statement can be made about spatial analysis and visualization tools. Many spatial analysis tasks are built directly into GIS and RS software. For example, some GIS software packages offer extensions dedicated to statistical tasks (e.g., ESRI's Geostatistical Analyst Extension for ArcGIS Desktop). In addition, several statistical packages such as SpaceStat, Matlab, GeoDa, S+ and SAS include routines for analyzing GIS data and interfacing with GIS software.

An extensive review of spatial analysis is beyond the scope of this chapter. Refer to Anselin (2002) and Bateman *et al.* (2003) for more comprehensive discussions of spatial analysis and applied economics. The creation of spatial variables, the definition of testable hypotheses of spatial behavioral processes and the application of spatial econometric tests and models are examples of spatial analysis relevant to the study of land use issues. Brief discussions of these issues follow.

Measurement and definition of spatial variables

As alluded to previously, spatial analysis is often concerned with the study of relative locations of data. The measurement and definition of spatial variables to represent proximity, neighborhoods and regions are central to applied land use research. All of these measures hinge on perceptions of nearness. Proximity is typically defined in terms of distance. In contrast, neighborhoods or regions are often defined in terms of both area and distance.

Proximity is often used to describe location. The returns to land in various uses may depend on factors such as access to central business districts (CBDs), processing facilities, transportation routes, coastal amenities or park lands. Proximity to a specific site may also influence the external impacts, both positive and negative, of land-based activities. In practice, there are many decisions to make when measuring proximity. Proximity is often measured in terms of access and therefore is represented as a function of distance. For example, distance can be measured "as the crow flies" or along a road or water network and can be expressed in a variety of units (e.g., meters or hours). Moreover, it is often not clear how best to measure this distance. Consider access to a central business district. Should the distance be measured from the centroid of a land parcel to the centroid of a CBD or from the border of the land parcel to the border of the CBD? In addition, should this proximity variable be a weighted average of distances to various CBDs or be measured using distance to the nearest CBD? Should proximity be measured in discrete (0, 1) or continuous units? These are empirical questions and draw attention to the somewhat arbitrary derivation of spatial variables.

The motivation for describing neighborhoods and regions is similar to that of proximity. Interactions among neighbors are often responsible for spatial dependencies or correlations. A region or neighborhood is a useful way to limit the spatial extent of interactions that matter. For example, returns to land may be influenced by characteristics of surrounding land parcels, attributes of the broader neighborhood, or the quality of local schools. Measurement of these spatial variables requires the definition of surrounding land parcels, the broader neighborhood, or school districts. In some instances, such as the case with school districts, definitions are clear. In other situations, the boundaries or extent of these spatial relationships are less clear.

A second example involves habitat assessment. Quality of habitat for a given species is contingent on the distribution and characteristics of lands in a region. In this case, the definition of the region requires consideration of the behavior and needs of the relevant species. A final example involves the transmission of external impacts. Externalities often vary with regional (or neighborhood) characteristics. For example, the land cover of an area may influence the spread of a certain pollutant from a given source and, in turn, affect the extent to which surrounding properties are impacted. Variables describing spatial relationships delineated using areas or zones are measured based on definitions of neighborhoods or regions. Because neighborhoods bound influences over space, the concept of neighbors is also crucial to spatial econometric applications. Similar to the case of proximity, there are no steadfast rules for defining these measures of relative location.

Area and distance can be used to define neighborhoods or regions, as can edges or borders. For example, landscape attributes are often measured as descriptive statistics calculated for a designated area around a feature such as the centroid of a parcel (e.g., the percent of land in different uses within a specified radius). The designated area becomes a proxy for region or neighborhood and is referred to as a buffer when conducting spatial analysis. In some cases, political borders such as those of municipalities will demarcate regions. In these instances, the definition of neighborhoods or regions is sim-plified by overlaying different spatial data layers. In other cases, neighbor-hoods or regions will be defined as entities that border a unit (e.g., neighboring counties or states). When using raster data, neighborhood analy-sis functions define neighborhoods as groups of cells based on specifications of neighborhood shape, width, and height.

A more formal representation of neighbors involves the specification of a spatial weight matrix. This N by N matrix specifies the spatial relationship among each of N observations and other observations. The matrix posits a hypothesized structure of spatial dependence within the sample. There are two basic types of spatial weight matrices: distance decay and contiguity. Dis-tance decay weight matrices assume that the strength of dependence is a function of the distance between two observations. Typically, the relationship imposed is a negative one, such that near things are considered neighbors. Contiguity weight matrices are often applied to raster data and polygon data, observations that fill the surface. Contiguity weight matrices assign neighbors based on the sharing of a common edge or common vertex. Neighbors may all be treated similarly (e.g., 0 or 1) or an ordering of neighbors may be imposed such that the intensity of dependence over space is specified. Spatial weight matrices are used to calculate spatially weighted explanatory variables and to represent the dependence among residuals in a spatial error model or dependent variables in a spatial lag model (Anselin 2002).

Spatial processes

Relative proximity is also central to thinking about the modification of behavioral models to incorporate space. Haining (1990) distinguishes four types of spatial processes: diffusion, exchange and transfer, interaction, and dispersal or spread. His classification of processes is a useful way of thinking spatially about the use and management of land resources. For example, a dif-fusion model centers on the adoption or acquisition of an item by a fixed population. A relevant example may be the entry of parcels into an agricul-tural conservation easement program. Exchange and transfer processes encompass spatial spillovers and regional competition. Examining the respon-siveness of neighboring counties to changes in property tax rate structures is a land use related example of such a process. Interaction refers to events that are dependent over space. For example, interaction is implied if the probab-ility of conversion of parcel *j* from undeveloped to residential use is a func-tion of the probability that parcel *k* is similarly converted. Dispersal or spread processes involve monitoring the spread of a population. The migration of population within a given area would be a dispersal process.

Spatial econometrics

Spatial econometrics, which focuses on econometric models estimated using spatial data, has emerged as an area of research in recent years (see Anselin 1988 and 2002 for a review of this literature). Spatial dependence and spatial heterogeneity are important spatial econometric issues. Spatial dependence arises when observations in space are functionally related. Spatial heterogeneity arises when the behavior being modeled is not stable over space. Spatial econometric techniques build on techniques developed for time-series research. However, there are important differences between time and space that complicate the direct transfer of methods. Time is one-dimensional and renders a clear ordering of data, where past years influence current and future years. In contrast, spatial effects are two-dimensional and multidirectional. Location offers no neat ordering of data. Although these differences do not affect the structure of the models, they do influence the estimation process as well as the properties of the estimators.

Spatial dependency is either due to structural dependencies or spatially autocorrelated error terms. A structural dependence often manifests itself through the dependent variable. For example, the likelihood that a conservation easement is applied to a specific land parcel may depend on whether or not neighboring parcels have conservation easements. Similarly, the adoption of a specific best management practice by a farmer may depend on whether or not neighboring farmers have adopted this technology. In both these cases, the structural dependence may be linked with the flow of information over space and time. Spatially correlated residuals are associated with omitted variables, which are correlated over space, and measurement errors, which result from spatial data units. The consequences of ignoring spatial dependence vary with the nature of the dependence. Omitting a spatial relationship among the observations on the dependent variable (when present) and estimating the model using ordinary least squares results in biased and inefficient estimates. Alternatively, if only the error terms of the model are spatially correlated, ordinary least squares produces unbiased but inefficient estimates. In the case of discrete choice models, the consequences are severe in both cases (Anselin 2002; Fleming 2002; LeSage 2000).

Spatial heterogeneity arises when the behavior being modeled is not stable over space. To accommodate such instability, models are adjusted to permit functional forms and estimated parameters that vary over space. For example, a hedonic model of land values in a watershed could be adjusted to allow for parameters that varied by town or neighborhood. Conventional varying parameter methods can be employed to incorporate spatial heterogeneity (Anselin 1988). Because spatial heterogeneity can be accommodated using established methods, much attention has been devoted to improving methods for the treatment of spatial dependence.

Structural or substantive dependence arises in the case of interactions or interdependencies across space. For example, the conversion of land parcels may illustrate spatial dependence if the individual conversions are strategic and influenced by the decisions of others. In contrast, spatial dependence among the errors is often due to omitted variables, which are themselves spatially correlated. For example, the return to land in residential use may depend on neighborhood attributes, some of which are unobserved to the researcher and are therefore omitted from empirical models of housing values. Measurement error is also a cause of spatially correlated residuals. When there is a mismatch between the spatial boundaries of observations and the boundaries of the spatial process, residuals can become correlated over space. For example, the measurement of socioeconomic data at the county level may result in spatial dependence of the error terms since county boundaries may be an arbitrary delineation of the spatial process that generates the socioeconomic values.

Spatial autocorrelation (originating with Whittle 1954, and Cliff and Ord 1973) is conventionally represented as a spatial autoregressive process. Analogous to time series applications, this approach represents dependence in space in a lag form using a weight matrix to impose much of the structure. The spatial weight matrix is an N by N matrix whose elements posit the extent of dependence between each observation in the sample. Spatial lags may be applied to the dependent variable indicating structural spatial dependence (a spatial lag model) or to the residuals in cases where spatially autocorrelated disturbances (a spatial error model) are expected. While first-order autoregressive structures are most common among spatial models, higher orders are feasible, as are alternative forms of representing the spatial dependence (e.g., moving average).

In practice, when estimating a spatial autoregressive model, the nuisance parameter is estimated in conjunction with the other parameters of the model, while the spatial weight matrix is specified a priori. Because the spatial weight matrices are N by N, they cannot be estimated. Much of the structure of the dependence is imposed when selecting the spatial weight matrices and deciding who is considered a neighbor over space. Maximum likelihood, generalized method of moment, and Bayesian approaches have been employed successfully to estimate models correcting for spatial dependence. Methods correcting for spatial dependence have proven more challenging to implement for a discrete choice than for continuous models.

Conclusion

Whether modeling human decisions regarding how lands are used, human preferences for land attributes, or externalities transmitted over lands, the recognition of spatial relationships is integral to the study of land resources. Recent technological advances have spurred increased access to spatial data and analysis tools and removed analytical constraints on the visualization and representation of spatial relationships. In turn, these resources have stimulated innovative and exciting applied land use research.

There are challenges and rewards to using spatial data. Researchers are cautioned to pay attention to the limitations of data and the pitfalls of canned software routines and encouraged to think spatially. There is a need for further research on many of the issues highlighted in this chapter. Lastly, there is a growing obligation to learn from researchers from other fields, within and outside economics, focused on spatial analysis (Anselin 1988; Anselin and Florax 1995; Anselin 2001; Fotheringham and Rogerson 1994; Fotheringham *et al.* 2000; Fujita *et al.* 1999; Haining 1990; Krugman 1995; Lawson 2001).

Notes

1 A second, important constraint involves the tractability of optimization problems involving complex treatments of space. A detailed discussion of this constraint is beyond the scope of this chapter. Interested readers should refer to the development of monocentric and polycentric models of urban land use.
2 Useful online guides to GIS and remotely sensed land cover data may be accessed at http://www.geography.com and http://edc.usgs.gov/doc/edchome/world/wdcguide.html.
3 Maryland's MdProperty View data is a notable example of such data. Refer to the MdProperty View web site at: http://www.op.state.md.us/data/mdview.htm.
4 Boundary files for US Bureau of the Census geographic units are accessible at http://landview.census.gov/geo/www/cob/.

12 Public preferences for farmland attributes in conservation easement programs[1]

Robert W. Paterson, Kevin J. Boyle,
Mary C. Ahearn,[2] Anna Alberini, John C. Bergstrom,
Lawrence W. Libby and Michael P. Welsh

Introduction and background

Preservation of open and green space land has become a prominent issue across the US. Over the past five years, many state and local initiatives to curb sprawling development have been put to the vote on statewide and local ballots. Programs to acquire or donate scenic easements to open and green space land are in place in all 50 states (American Farmland Trust 1997; Daniels 1999; Wiebe *et al.* 1996). While many of these programs are targeted at open and green space in general, farmland is an important source of open and green space. Of the nearly two billion acres of private land in the US, half is in agriculture (range, crop and pasture land) (Vesterby *et al.* 1994).

The Farmland Protection Policy Act of 1981 required federal agencies to conduct reviews for the purpose of "minimizing the extent to which federal programs contribute to unnecessary and irreversible conversion of farmland to nonagricultural uses" (7 USC. Sec. 4201b). The Farms for the Future program in the 1990 farm bill authorized a pilot program of subsidized loans to state and local governments to purchase conservation easements on farmland. This was superseded by the Federal Agricultural Improvement Act of 1996 (FAIR) that authorized up to $35 million in matching funds for state and local farmland protection programs. Maintaining farmland has the direct impact of protecting open land from being converted to other uses that do not provide the same sets of amenities. In 2002, the act was amended in the Farm Security and Rural Investment Act to establish the Farm and Ranch Land Protection Program (FRPP). The conservation easement program is open to cooperating state and local governments, Indian tribes and certain nongovernmental organizations. For fiscal year 2004, up to $84 million was made available for the FRPP.

Agricultural policies also affect the quality of farmland as open and green space. For example, the Conservation Reserve Program takes land out of agricultural production for ten years while maintaining the land as open or green space that is planted to grasses or trees. This program affects water quality by retiring highly erodible soils and creating more grassland habitat for wildlife.

Open and green space amenities (hereafter, just amenities) of farmland are a classic joint production example where the joint product is a public good (Bromley and Hodge 1990). While farmers receive compensation for the products they produce, there is no market to compensate them for the quantity and quality of amenities they provide. Public views of scenic vistas provided by farms are nonrival and nonexcludable in consumption. There is also the tragedy of the commons that arises as urban sprawl encroaches upon farmland; each new resident contributes to a diminishment of the amenities. These market failures appear to be a motivating factor behind public efforts to protect farmland amenities.

Several studies have employed contingent valuation techniques to estimate the value of farmland amenities. For example, in early research, Halstead (1984) estimated the value of agricultural land preservation in western Massachusetts. Bergstrom *et al.* (1985) estimated values for amenity benefits of prime agricultural land in Greenville County, South Carolina. Similarly, Beasley *et al.* (1986) estimated willingness-to-pay (WTP) to prevent residential and commercial development of agricultural lands in the Matanuska-Susitna valleys of south central Alaska. More recently, Bowker and Didychuk (1994) estimated the value of farmland preservation in three counties in New Brunswick, Canada. Rosenberger and Walsh (1997) estimated WTP to protect ranchland in the Yampa River Valley of Colorado and Krieger (1999) estimated WTP for farmland protection in three counties around Chicago.

Each of these studies generally examined how WTP varied with the extent of preserved land and respondent characteristics. Other studies have examined individuals' motivations for farmland preservation. For example, Fursueth (1987) found that public support for farmland protection in a North Carolina county was motivated by desire to protect food supply, preserve open spaces and preserve heritage. Similarly, motivations described in Krieger (1999) included slowing development and protecting food supply, family farms and rural quality. In a study of Rhode Island residents, Kline and Wichelns (1998) examined how motivations such as protecting environmental resources, scenic quality, food supply and farming lifestyles influenced preferences for preservation of different types of farmland and open space using a contingent ranking format.

While studies such as these have estimated the value of farmland protection programs and identified motivations in specific regions or for specific types of farmland, they do not provide insight into how preferences vary by region of the country, nor do they adequately identify the attributes of farmland most desirable to the public. This information is crucial to the design of agricultural and other policies so that they do not diminish amenities provided by farmland.

In the research reported in this chapter, a series of focus groups was conducted in five states to begin to develop an understanding of the public's view of the role of agriculture in the provision of amenities and the characteristics of farmland that the public prefers in the context of a protection program. The results of several choice exercises that provide information about preferences for specific farmland attributes and their role in a desirable protection program are described.

Focus group administration

Four focus groups each were held in five states: Ohio, Georgia, Colorado, Oregon and Maine.[3] Two groups were held per evening on successive evenings at commercial facilities that recruited participants, provided the focus group room with an adjacent viewing room behind a one-way mirror, and audio- and videotaped the groups. A professional moderator led the focus groups.

Facilitators were instructed to recruit enough participants to ensure that each group consisted of 10 to 12 people. We also asked the facilitators to undertake random recruitment of participants and to not draw participants from an established panel of people they maintain to staff focus groups, i.e., we did not want "professional" focus group participants. The facilitators attempted to recruit two urban groups, one suburban group and one rural. While protection of farmland as open and green space is physically a rural issue, any program to protect farmland as open and green space will require broad public support. Thus, it was important to develop an understanding of the perspectives of people who live in urban and suburban areas. Any general population survey, at the state or national level, would be primarily composed of urban and suburban residents.

Focus group sizes ranged from 7 to 12 persons, with an average of 10. These numbers of participants are clearly insufficient to test for differences in results between groups. However, the aggregate results from each set of groups is useful in initiating the development of a general picture of what characteristics of farmland people do and do not care about in the provision of farmland amenities.

Data collected and analysis procedures

In the first two sets of groups, exercises focused on identifying terminology and language associated with farmland amenities, as well as important farmland attributes. Subsequent groups concentrated on learning about how individuals compare and tradeoff these attributes.

The first set of focus groups was held in Ohio and an open format was used. Respondents were asked by the moderator to explain what the term "open space" meant to them and to identify attributes of desirable and undesirable farms. The last set of focus groups was held in Maine with a structured format in which respondents were given a survey instrument to complete and were debriefed by the moderator after completing the survey. We report selected results from the major exercises administered in each set of focus groups. These exercises are summarized in Table 12.1.

In Georgia, participants were presented with color photographs of

Table 12.1 Primary participant exercises conducted in focus groups across states

State	Exercises			
	Group 1	Group 2	Group 3	Group 4
Ohio	General discussion			
Georgia	Rated 30 photographs		Rated a subset of 10 photos	
Colorado	Rated five sets of four photographs and answered one conjoint question		Answered one conjoint question[a]	
Oregon	NA[b]		Answered three conjoint questions	
Maine	Answered five conjoint questions			

Notes
a The photograph rating exercises were not conducted in groups 3 and 4.
b On the first night (groups 1 and 2) we experimented with a design of the conjoint question where respondents saw all levels of all attributes. This proved to be too complex a task and therefore only the results of the second night (groups 3 and 4) were used in the estimation reported in this chapter.

farmland scenes from around the state. Examples of these photographs are shown in Figure 12.1a and 12.1b. The intent was to obtain a more precise idea of what attributes of farmland participants liked and disliked. The two groups on the first night evaluated 30 pictures while the groups on the second night evaluated only 10 of these photographs. The number of photographs was reduced the second night because respondents seemed to tire when evaluating 30 scenes and more time for discussion was desired. Participants were asked to rate the scenes on a 10-point Likert scale that ranged from 1 (very undesirable) to 10 (very desirable).

In Colorado, participants were asked to evaluate sets of scenes. In Georgia the evaluations of attributes, such as the presence of livestock, depended on the context of the picture(s) where they occurred. In Colorado, participants were presented with sets of four scenes. For example, one set portrayed beef cattle grazing in a harvested grain field with trees in the background, in a feedlot, on open range, and grazing a harvested alfalfa field in the mountains. This was done for different types of livestock confinement facilities, different types of farm building scenes, different types of field operations, and different types of crops being grown. As in Georgia, we had respondents rate each of the scenes in the pictures, but on a three-point scale of "like," "dislike" and "neither like nor dislike."

Participants' evaluations of the scenes in Georgia and Colorado were analyzed using an ordered-probit model. This framework is appropriate given the discrete, ordinal nature of the responses. Explanatory variables were a set of binary variables developed to describe the farmland characteristics collectively portrayed in the photographs.[4] Two members of the study team independently reviewed the photographs and coded the explanatory variables.

(a)

(b)

Figure 12.1 Examples of livestock and crop photographs shown during Georgia focus groups.

When disagreements arose in the coding, a third member of the team reviewed the specific photographs to break the deadlock.

Participants in Colorado, Oregon and Maine were asked to answer conjoint questions. The purpose of the conjoint question was to identify how participants evaluated protecting farmland as open and green space with different farm characteristics. The conjoint questions presented two farmland protection programs (A and B) that differed in terms of selected farm characteristics (Figure 12.2). Participants were first asked to choose between

1   Suppose you had to vote between two conservation easement programs, Program A and Program B. These programs differ in terms of the attributes of the farms that would receive priority in the bidding process, the number of acres in the program and the cost to you. We understand that you might not like either program and you will get a chance later to let us know if you would prefer doing nothing. However, please tell us which of the two programs you would support if you had to choose between Program A and Program B. *(Please check one box in the last row)*

	Program A: *Gives priority to farms with:*	**Program B:** *Gives priority to farms with:*
Livestock	*Not considered*	*Not considered*
Crops	*Vegetables*	*Berries*
Water	*Streams and ponds*	*Not considered*
Size	*Not considered*	*Medium - 100-260 acres*
Area of Maine	*Southern Maine*	*Not considered*
Ownership	*Not considered*	*Corporate - not family*
Location in towns containing	*Four or fewer operating farms*	*Five or more operating farms*
Soil quality	*High quality soil*	*Not considered*
Acres with easements	*80,000 acres*	*120,000 acres*
One-time cost to your household	*$75*	*$100*
Check the box for the program you would prefer	☐	☐

2   Suppose you could vote between Program A, Program B and doing nothing. How would you choose? *(Circle one number)*

     1   I would vote for Program A
     2   I would vote for Program B
     3   I would vote to do nothing

Figure 12.2 Example of conjoint questions used in the Colorado, Oregon and Maine focus groups.

Program A and Program B, and then were asked to choose between Programs A and B and Do Nothing (maintain the status quo), as in a voting situation.

As shown in Figure 12.2, the first column in the questions listed the attributes and the second and third columns listed the levels of these attributes for Programs A and B. Attribute levels were randomly assigned with the condition that the levels had to vary for at least one attribute between Programs A and B. As will be shown later, the attributes and attribute levels varied from state to state. These changes occurred as we attempted to address concerns discussed by participants.

The choices in the conjoint questions dealt with purchasing conservation easements on farmland. Farmland with the specified levels of the attributes in the programs would receive priority in the purchases of the easements. All attributes, except the total number of acres of easements and cost, also had a level of no targeting (or not specified). The total acres of conservation easements and household cost attributes are not specific to farmland characteristics, but are key program attributes. The acres protected were fixed in Colorado (1 million) and varied in Oregon and Maine. The same cost amounts were used in Colorado and Oregon, but were increased in Maine due to a lack of price sensitivity in the Colorado and Oregon responses.

As shown in Table 12.1, the number of conjoint questions answered by participants varied across states. In Colorado, participants in each group answered one conjoint question. In Oregon, participants in the last two groups answered three conjoint questions. In Maine, participants in each group answered five conjoint questions. The choices between Programs A and B and Do Nothing (responses to the second question in Figure 12.2) are analyzed using multinomial logit models. Explanatory variables are the levels of the attributes. Each attribute level is coded as a binary variable, and the omitted categories are the conditions when the attribute levels are "not specified."[5]

Given the small sample sizes, we investigate the effects of the attributes by entering one set of attribute variables in the models at a time. All models, however, include the cost attribute and alternative-specific constants for Programs A and B. Thus for the Maine example in Figure 12.2, nine equations were estimated. The equation for livestock, for example, contains four binary variables for each of the attribute levels used in the design. Again due to the small sample sizes, we investigated the significance of attributes up to the 20 percent level. Specifics of these analyses are explained in the respective result subsections below.

Focus group results

Ohio

On the first evening participants were asked what the term "open space" meant to them. While professionals who deal in land use issues on a daily basis have a general consensus of what this term means, the interpretations of focus group participants included more than undeveloped land (for example, large foyers in buildings). Those who thought of undeveloped land were more likely to think of public land than private land. Thus, in talking to a lay audience, open space is not a particularly useful term, especially in the context of farmland. On the second night, we used the term "rural landscape" and this term appeared to be more likely to encourage people to think of undeveloped rural land and farms. We also investigated the term "countryside," which many people associated with small towns. To get away from potentially loaded terminology, we simply discussed preserving farmland and queried participants about characteristics of protected farmland they find desirable and undesirable for the focus groups held in other states.

The desirable attributes of farmland noted by more than five participants, in descending order of the number of respondents who cited them, are food supply, livestock, work ethic, openness (not crowded), crops in fields and not contributing to pollution. The undesirable attributes cited by more than five respondents, again in descending order of the number of times cited, are odor, sensitive to weather (production), and poor access to modern conveniences; the last two attributes were cited primarily by the urban groups. The odor issue appeared to arise mainly from a large egg farm located in the area from which focus group participants were recruited.

When asked if open space or rural landscapes should be preserved, participants indicated that preservation is an important but not urgent issue. People had difficulty understanding the concept of "purchasing development rights" and tended to reject any payment vehicle that involved increasing taxes. In the remainder of the focus groups we worked on refining the definition of "purchasing conservation easements" and this terminology seemed to work fairly well in the final set of focus groups that was held in Maine.

Georgia

The explanatory variables developed to identify the farmland characteristics portrayed in the photographs are presented in Table 12.2. The first four variables describe the physical landscape portrayed in the scenes. The omitted category for *Popen* and *Ptrees* represents scenes that are neither predominantly fields nor predominantly woods. The second set of variables describes the farm structures and implements portrayed in the scenes. *Oldbuildings* are typically barns that are not obviously in current use by farmers. *Livestock* simply indicates whether stock is present in the photograph. The crop variables represent the types of crops being grown in the scenes. *Rows* indicate scenes where crops are grown in rows, and *Horticulture* designates rows that are horticulture and not field crops, such as corn and tobacco.

In both Ohio and Georgia, respondents indicated that the orderly nature of rows was very desirable. The last four variables break field crops into four categories, with the omitted category being scenes with abandoned fields or where we could not identify what type of crop was being grown. While the focus group discussions revealed that respondents often could not identify the types of crops that were being grown in the scenes, it was obvious that they found some crop scenes more desirable than others. Thus, *RowCrops, Grain and Hay* represent what we refer to as informed coding, where we investigate crop effects even though we know participants cannot identify the crops.

Estimates from three equations are reported (Table 12.2). The first equation presents estimates using responses from all participants for the ten scenes evaluated by all respondents. This smaller number of photographs did not contain all of the variables portrayed in Table 12.2. In addition, some variables were perfectly correlated. Thus, we present estimates for a parsimonious set of variables. The second and third equations use the responses for the groups on the second night that evaluated 30 scenes. The second equation did not use our "informed" coding of crops – only *Row* and *Horticulture*. The third equation removes the *Row* variable and uses the variables that designate specific crops.

In the first model, six of nine variables are significant at the 10 percent level. Participants like farm homes, water and crops grown in rows. It is interesting that land that was primarily fields or had horticultural crops had significantly lower ratings. It is not surprising that land where timber was recently harvested is undesirable. Another interesting feature is that the presence of livestock did not significantly affect ratings of the scenes.

In the second model, with 30 scenes and naive coding of crops, 14 of 16 variables are significant. Three variables that were insignificant in the 10-scene model become significant. Participants like farm landscapes that were primarily trees, had topography, farmsteads, livestock and crops grown in rows. *Oldbuildings, Silos, Equipment, Horticulture*, and scenes with harvested crops or timber each have negative effects on ratings. The lack of significance for *Water* may be the result of water being present in only two photographs. One was a wetland scene that some interpreted as flooding and the other was a small farm pond in a pasture for watering livestock. In addition, respondents appeared to believe that there were ponds in other scenes, but they were not visible from the perspective of the photographs.

In the third model, with 30 scenes and informed coding of crops, 13 of 19 variables are significant. Here *Water, Outbuildings, Silos* and *Livestock* are no longer significant. Three of the four crop variables are significant and have positive effects on ratings. In addition, the coefficient on *Horticulture* changes sign.

Several general insights arise from these results. Land with a substantial portion in trees is preferred to land that is largely fields. Topography is desirable, farm buildings are important, dormant equipment is undesirable, harvested crops and timber are undesirable, various crops are desirable, and the presence of livestock does not appear to have a significant effect. This suggests attributes that would be important in a program to protect farmland as open and green space. Buildings are an important attribute of the farm and

Table 12.2 Ordered probit analysis of scene ratings for Georgia

Dependent variable is scene rating	Coefficients (standard errors)		
	All groups/ ten pictures	First two groups/ 30 pictures	
	Naive coding of crops	Naive coding of crops	Informed coding
Popen	−1.235**[a]	−0.282*	−0.288*
(= 1 if the scene is primarily fields)	(0.423)	(0.147)	(0.152)
Ptrees	−	0.958**	0.552**
(= 1 if the scene is primarily trees)	−	(0.189)	(0.197)
Topogy	0.765	0.603**	0.912**
(= 1 if the land has topography, 0 otherwise)	(0.500)	(0.196)	(0.301)
Water	0.672**	−0.0724	0.468
(= 1 if farm has a pond present, 0 otherwise)	(0.300)	(0.245)	(0.308)
Home	1.084**	1.042**	1.115**
(= 1 if a residence present, 0 otherwise)	(0.394)	(0.205)	(0.200)
Buildings	−	1.096**	0.636**
(= 1 if farm buildings present, 0 otherwise)	−	(0.192)	(0.242)
Oldbuildings	−	−0.653**	−0.183
(= 1 if old farm buildings present, 0 otherwise)	−	(0.224)	(0.308)
Silos	−	−0.864**	−0.292
(= 1 if silos present, 0 otherwise)	−	(0.375)	(0.450)
Equipment	−	−0.868**	−0.781**
(= 1 if farm equipment present, 0 otherwise)	−	(0.149)	(0.155)
Irrigation	−	0.586**	0.508**
(= 1 if irrigation equipment present, 0 otherwise)	−	(0.181)	(0.180)
Fence	−	0.0893	0.404
(= 1 if fences present, 0 otherwise)	−	(0.207)	(0.338)
Livestock	0.371	0.464**	0.105
(= 1 if livestock present, 0 otherwise)	(0.515)	(0.237)	(0.476)
Rows	0.729**	0.803**	−
(= 1 if crops growing in rows, 0 otherwise)	(0.329)	(0.148)	−
Hort	−0.707*	−0.581**	0.329*
(= 1 if horticultural crops, 0 otherwise)	(0.374)	(0.158)	(0.175)
Harvested	−0.422	−0.466**	−1.766**
(= 1 if fields with harvested crops, 0 otherwise)	(0.296)	(0.162)	(0.405)
Timber	−3.775**	−4.252**	−4.008**
(= 1 if timber harvesting, 0 otherwise)	(0.518)	(0.390)	(0.400)
RowCrops	−	−	1.066**
(= 1 if row crops present, 0 otherwise)	−	−	(0.173)
Grain	−	−	2.030**
(= 1 if grain field present, 0 otherwise)	−	−	(0.499)
Hay	−	−	0.645**
(= 1 if hay field present, 0 otherwise)	−	−	(0.178)
Pasture	−	−	0.127
(= 1 if pasture present, 0 otherwise)	−	−	(0.434)
Constant	3.519**	2.127**	1.980**
	(0.576)	(0.167)	(0.178)

Notes
a Significant at the * = 10 percent, ** = 5 percent level.
Sample sizes: All groups/ten pictures N = 430, first two groups N = 687.

crops appear to be more desired than livestock operations. In addition, aspects of the land that are independent of the farming operation also matter.

Colorado

The variables and coding differed from those used in Georgia to represent unique aspects of agricultural lands in Colorado (Table 12.3). For example, trees are sparse in eastern Colorado, but increase in density as one moves into the foothills. Mountains are the primary type of topography. We also added photographs with ongoing farming activities, which were not present in the Georgia photographs, and a variable for growing crops, which distinguished between green landscapes and plowed fields.

Eight of the 14 variables are significant in explaining respondents' ratings

Table 12.3 Ordered probit analysis of scene ratings for Colorado

Dependent variable is scene rating	Coefficients (standard errors)
Trees	0.890**[a]
(= 1 if trees present, 0 otherwise)	(0.377)
Mountains	−0.0489
(= 1 if mountains present, 0 otherwise)	(0.306)
Tradbuilding	1.078**
(= 1 if traditional farm buildings present, 0 otherwise)	(0.328)
Modbuilding	0.0197
(= 1 if modern farm buildings present, 0 otherwise)	(0.507)
Elevator	1.430**
(= 1 if grain elevators present, 0 otherwise)	(0.556)
Equipment	0.806*
(= 1 if farm equipment present, 0 otherwise)	(0.452)
Pivots	1.163*
(= 1 if central pivot irrigation present, 0 otherwise)	(0.674)
Livestock	−0.391
(= 1 if livestock present, 0 otherwise)	(0.329)
Confinement	−0.301
(= 1 if livestock in confinement present, 0 otherwise)	(0.540)
RowCrops	−0.161
(= 1 if row crops present, 0 otherwise)	(0.530)
Grain	−1.109**
(= 1 if grain field present, 0 otherwise)	(0.479)
Grow	0.198
(= 1 if crops growing, 0 otherwise)	(0.464)
Harvesting	1.080*
(= 1 if active harvesting present, 0 otherwise)	(0.574)
Plowed	−0.877**
(= 1 if fields are plowed, 0 otherwise)	(0.328)
Constant	0.632*
	(0.332)

Notes
a Significant at the * = 10 percent, ** = 5 percent level.
N = 364.

of the pictures (Table 12.3). *Trees, Tradbuildings, Equipment, Elevator, Pivots* and *Harvesting* all lead to higher ratings. *Grain* and *Plowed* both led to lower ratings, which suggests that participants did not like large, open fields without other features. This dislike of large, open landscapes is similar to what we found in Georgia. While farm buildings in active use were not characterized in Georgia, the results here suggest the type of building matters; traditional buildings (typically wood) contribute positively to ratings, while modern buildings (typically steel) do not have an effect. Equipment had a negative effect in Georgia, and the positive effect in Colorado may be due to it being portrayed in active use versus just being stored. The change of sign for harvest between Georgia and Colorado appears to be due to the fact that the Georgia scenes were harvested fields, while the Colorado scenes were of ongoing grain and hay harvesting activities.

Respondents often appeared to use the pictures to seek clues as to whether the scene represented a small, family farm. In addition, participants tried to evaluate the quality of the soil, the quality of the farming operation, and the quality of the photographs themselves. Thus, while pictures were initially helpful in identifying important farmland attributes, they were providing unintended cues to respondents. In proceeding to the conjoint questions we decided to focus on verbal descriptions of attributes that would not be accompanied by pictures.

Based on the results from the scene-rating exercise in Georgia the following attributes of farmland were considered for use in the conjoint question for Colorado: location of the land, type of farm structures, water on the land, farm/ranch size, ownership, livestock and types of crops (Table 12.4). We also added the geographic location of the farm, the size of the farm in acres and the ownership of the farm. Location in Colorado is highly correlated with the extent of trees and topography. Participants in both previous focus groups mentioned in general discussions that farm size and ownership were important.

While participants indicated that location was important in the verbal discussions, none of the levels of this attribute were significant (Table 12.5). We did find that participants liked traditional, wooden buildings and disliked modern, steel buildings. In addition, farms from 250 to 1,000 acres, no livestock, and hay fields were significant and made respondents more likely to choose the alternatives in which they were contained. Corporate ownership was negative and significant. These results support the general findings from the evaluations of pictures and the verbal comments of participants. *Cost* was never significant, which suggests that the highest price point of $50 was not sufficient to choke respondents out of the market for protecting farmland amenities.

Oregon

Best management practices (BMPs) were added as an attribute because participants had indicated concern for pollution from farm chemicals and

Table 12.4 Explanatory variables used in conjoint analysis for Colorado

Attributes	Attribute levels	Variable names
Location	Not specified	
	Eastern plains	*Plains*
	Front range	*Frange*
	Mountain valleys	*Mvalleys*
Water	Not specified	
	None	*NoWater*
	Irrigation ponds for wildlife	*Ponds*
	Stream buffers for wildlife	*Streams*
Buildings	Not specified	
	None	*NoBuildings*
	Traditional, wooden	*Tradbuildings*
	Modern, steel	*Modbuildings*
Farm/ranch size	Not specified	
	<250 acres	<250 acres
	250–1,000 acres	250–1,000 acres
	>2,000 acres	2,000+ acres
Ownership	Not specified	
	Family	*Family*
	Corporation	*Corporate*
Livestock	Not specified	
	None	*NoLivestock*
	Grazing	*Grazing*
	Feedlots	*Feedlot*
Crops	Not specified	
	None	*NoCrops*
	Hay	*Hay*
	Row crops	*Row*
	Grains	*Grain*
	Mix of crops	*Mix*
Program cost	One-time cost to household	*Cost*
	($1, 5, 10, 20, 30, 40 or 50)	

other residues and because there are government programs to encourage adoption of BMPs (Table 12.6). In addition, while the program size was fixed in Colorado, it was varied in Oregon.

Farmland protection as open land was important in all three designated regions of the state (Table 12.7), but verbal discussions indicated different reasons behind each region. Respondents said the *Coast* because there is so little farmland, the *Valley* because it is threatened by sprawling development and *Eastern* because it is an important part of the local economy. Farms with small to medium acreage are significant and make participants more likely to support protection, while confinement livestock has the opposite effect. Targeting ownership was undesirable to participants. In discussions, participants

Table 12.5 Results of multinomial logit analysis of program voting: Colorado

Dependent variable: choice (A, B, or Do Nothing)	Location	Water	Buildings	Size
Program A constant	-1.686**[a] (0.854)	-1.251* (0.736)	-1.225* (0.733)	-1.634** (0.793)
Program B constant	-1.523* (0.861)	-1.064† (0.725)	-0.940† (0.708)	-1.745* (1.002)
Cost	-0.001 (0.016)	-0.002 (0.017)	0.011 (0.017)	0.007 (0.017)
Plains	0.821 (0.917)			
Frange	0.471 (0.998)			
Mtvalleys	1.010 (0.854)			
NoWater		_[b]		
Ponds		0.116 (0.731)		
Streams		0.476 (0.725)		
Nobuildings			-0.443 (0.748)	
Tradbuildings			1.287† (0.840)	
Modbuildings			-1.673† (1.155)	
<250 acres				0.232 (1.036)
250–1,000 acres				1.316† (0.907)
2,000+ acres				0.555 (0.857)

Dependent variable: choice (A, B, or Do Nothing)	Ownership	Livestock	Crops
Program A constant	-0.620 (0.702)	-1.122† (0.729)	-1.734* (1.024)
Program B constant	-0.611 (0.708)	-1.298† (0.839)	-0.246 (1.057)
Cost	0.003 (0.016)	-0.006 (0.018)	0.006 (0.019)
Family	0.060 (0.691)		
Corporate	-1.657* (0.888)		
Nolivestock		1.218† (0.869)	
Grazing		-0.141 (0.896)	
Feedlot		0.042 (1.002)	
Nocrops			-1.394 (1.340)
Hay			2.650** (1.111)
Row			-0.039 (1.123)
Grain			-1.238 (1.204)
Mix			-1.788 (1.422)

Notes
a Significant at the † = 20 percent, ★ = 10 percent, ★★ = 5 percent level.   b This parameter could not be estimated due to lack of variation.

Table 12.6 Explanatory variables used in conjoint analysis for Oregon

Attributes	Attribute levels	Variable names
Location	Not specified	
	Coastal	*Coast*
	Willamette Valley	*Valley*
	Central/eastern	*Eastern*
Water	Not specified	
	With ponds or streams	*Water*
Farm/ranch size	Not specified	
	<50 acres	<50 acres
	50–1,000 acres	50–1,000 acres
	>1,000 acres	1,000+ acres
Ownership	Not specified	
	Family	*Family*
	Corporation	*Corporate*
Livestock and crops	Not specified	
	Feedlots	*Feedlot*
	Orchards and nurseries	*Horticulture*
Management	Not specified	
	Best management practices	*BMPs*
Program size	0.5 million acres protected	*Omitted category*
	1.0 million acres protected	1.0 million
	1.5 million acres protected	1.5 million
Program cost	One-time cost to household	*Cost*
	($1, 5, 10, 20, 30, 40 or 50)	

indicated they want open land regardless of the location and ownership, and some felt that corporate ownership would lead to larger areas of contiguous open land. The total acreage with conservation easements was significant. In contrast to the Colorado results, *Cost* is negative in all but one equation and is significant in one equation.

Maine

In Maine, an attribute for soil quality and the number of farms in a town was added to the focus group (Table 12.8). Soil quality may be an important attribute because farmland preservation programs have historically used this as the single most important criterion. Participants in prior focus groups listed soil quality as an attribute and high quality soils for farming in Maine are quite limited. Participants in prior groups were also concerned about the number of farms located in an area. They felt that a small number would preclude a farmer from expanding if needed and they may not have anyone to sell the farm to when they retire. Given the general insignificance of *Cost* in Colorado and Oregon, the magnitudes were increased.

Table 12.7 Results of multinomial logit analysis of program voting: Oregon

Dependent variable: choice (A, B, or Do Nothing)	Location	Water	Size	Ownership	Livestock/crops	Management	Program size
Program A constant	−2.148★★[a] (0.962)	−0.628 (0.703)	−0.572 (0.682)	0.542 (0.564)	0.014 (0.521)	−0.280 (0.550)	−0.624 (0.574)
Program B constant	−2.451★★ (0.950)	−1.020† (0.692)	−1.149† (0.871)	0.084 (0.572)	−0.323 (0.550)	−0.829† (0.638)	−1.321★★ (0.653)
Cost	0.002 (0.015)	−0.015 (0.014)	−0.018 (0.014)	−0.011 (0.147)	−0.015 (0.014)	−0.017 (0.014)	−0.022† (0.014)
Coast	1.841★★ (0.903)	—	—	—	—	—	—
Valley	2.260★ (0.891)	—	—	—	—	—	—
Eastern	1.819★ (0.967)	—	—	—	—	—	—
Water	—	0.695 (0.614)	—	—	—	—	—
<50 acres	—	—	1.349★ (0.729)	—	—	—	—
50–1,000 acres	—	—	1.055† (0.827)	—	—	—	—
1,000+ acres	—	—	−0.287 (0.933)	—	—	—	—
Family	—	—	—	−0.940† (0.620)	—	—	—
Corporate	—	—	—	−1.010† (0.648)	—	—	—
Feedlot	—	—	—	—	−0.894† (0.641)	—	—
Horticulture	—	—	—	—	0.233 (0.511)	—	—
BMPs	—	—	—	—	—	0.434 (0.528)	—
1.0 million	—	—	—	—	—	—	1.324★★ (0.628)
1.5 million	—	—	—	—	—	—	0.966† (0.621)

Notes
a Significant at the † = 20 percent, ★ = 10 percent, ★★ = 5 percent level.
N = 48, standard errors in parentheses.

Table 12.8 Explanatory variables used in conjoint analysis for Maine

Attributes	Attribute levels	Variable names
Location	Not specified	
	Southern	*Southern*
	Central	*Central*
	Northern	*Northern*
Water	Not specified	
	With ponds or streams	*Water*
Farm size	Not specified	
	<100 acres	*<100 acres*
	100–260 acres	*100–260 acres*
	>260 acres	*>260 acres*
Ownership	Not specified	
	Family part-time	*P-T family*
	Family full-time	*F-T family*
	Corporation	*Corporate*
Livestock	Not specified	
	Beef	*Beef*
	Dairy	*Dairy*
	Poultry	*Poultry*
	Sheep	*Sheep*
Crops	Not specified	
	Berries	*Berries*
	Greenhouse	*Greenhouse*
	Vegetables	*Vegetables*
	Orchards	*Orchards*
Soil quality	Not specified	
	High soil quality	*High quality*
Number of farms in town	Not specified	
	More than five	*Five or more*
	Less than or equal to four	*Four or fewer*
Program size	80,000 acres protected	*Omitted category*
	100,000 acres protected	100,000
	120,000 acres protected	120,000
Program cost	One-time cost to household ($10, 25, 50, 75, 100)	*Cost*

Location within the state did not have a significant effect (Table 12.9). Streams and ponds had a positive and significant effect. Target farm size had a significant, positive effect for farms larger than 260 acres. Corporate ownership resulted in a protection program being less likely to be selected and family farms had a significant, positive effect. Farms with *Poultry* or *Sheep* resulted in a protection program being less likely to be selected. This result for *Poultry* is not surprising given the controversy surrounding a single, large

Table 12.9 Results of multinomial logit analysis of program voting: Maine

Dependent variable: choice (A, B, or Do Nothing)	Location	Water	Size	Ownership	Livestock
Program A constant	0.569**[a] (0.311)	0.398† (0.263)	0.403† (0.313)	0.494* (0.292)	0.722** (0.279)
Program B constant	0.411† (0.295)	0.215 (0.267)	0.280 (0.299)	0.450† (0.308)	0.567** (0.278)
Cost	−0.003 (0.003)	−0.005† (0.330)	−0.003 (0.003)	−0.006* (0.004)	−0.003 (0.003)
Southern location	0.395 (0.326)	–	–	–	–
Central	−0.035 (0.298)	–	–	–	–
Northern	−0.342 (0.311)	–	–	–	–
Water	–	0.461** (0.229)	–	–	–
<100 acres	–	–	−0.156 (0.335)	–	–
100–260 acres	–	–	0.186 (0.276)	–	–
>260 acres	–	–	0.430† (0.314)	–	–
P-T family (ownership)	–	–	–	0.755** (0.341)	–
F-T family	–	–	–	0.610** (0.307)	–
Corporate	–	–	–	−0.740** (0.360)	–
Beef (livestock)	–	–	–	–	−0.238 (0.347)
Dairy	–	–	–	–	−0.016 (0.271)
Poultry	–	–	–	–	−0.479† (0.349)
Sheep	–	–	–	–	−0.558† (0.402)

Dependent variable: choice (A, B, or Do Nothing)	Crops	Soil quality	Number of farms	Program size
Program A constant	0.223 (0.380)	0.483* (0.265)	0.740** (0.280)	0.661** (0.273)
Program B constant	0.119 (0.366)	0.359† (0.254)	0.548** (0.255)	0.469* (0.256)
Cost	−0.003 (0.003)	−0.004 (0.003)	−0.004 (0.329)	−0.004 (0.334)
Berries (crops)	0.347 (0.378)	–	–	–
Greenhouse	0.522† (0.367)	–	–	–
Vegetables	0.272 (0.393)	–	–	–
Orchards	0.340 (0.407)	–	–	–
High quality (soils)	–	0.207 (0.216)	–	–
Five or more (farms per town)	–	–	−0.256 (0.275)	–
Four or fewer	–	–	−0.289 (0.265)	–
100,000 acres protected	–	–	–	0.131 (0.262)
120,000	–	–	–	−0.333 (0.286)

Notes

a Significant at the † = 20 percent, ★ = 10 percent, ★★ = 5 percent level.   N = 179, standard errors in parentheses.

facility in the state that has been well publicized by the local media. Targeting of greenhouse crops increased the probability that a protection program would be selected. The number of farms present in a town did not appear to influence program choice. We found that *Cost* was negative in all equations, though only significant in two of the six.

Discussion

Some general insights and trends arise from the focus group results reported in this chapter. From the initial focus group and discussions in subsequent focus groups, terms like "open space," which are quite familiar to us as professionals, have very different meaning to the public. In addition, focus group participants found the idea of purchasing conservation easements a very odd concept and had difficulty understanding how someone could simply sell the right to a specific use of their land. Thus, when conducting surveys of the public on land use, or doing any type of public education related to land use, it is important to carefully consider and explain the terminology used.

The evaluations of photographs of agricultural scenes present several interesting insights (Table 12.10). While there are inherent differences in farmland and farming activities in Georgia and Colorado, the statistical analyses of the scene ratings indicate some commonality and differences in focus group participant preferences. For example, participants in both locations appear to dislike large, open landscapes and the seasonal effects of harvested or plowed

Table 12.10 Summary of statistical analyses of ratings of farm scenes (variable signs in parentheses)

	Georgia (30 picture model)	*Colorado*
Landscape	Primarily open (−) Primarily trees (+) Topography (+)	Trees present (+) Mountains (+)
Farmstead	Residences (+)	Traditional buildings (+)
Farm equipment	Stored equipment (−)	Farm equipment (+) Grain elevator (+)
Farm operation	Irrigation (+) Harvested fields (−) Harvested timber (−)	Center pivot irrigation (+) Field activities (+) Plowed fields (−)
Crops	Horticulture (+) Row crops (+) Grain (+) Hay (+)	Grain (−)
Livestock	NS[a]	NS

Note
a NS indicates that the coefficients on all attribute levels were not significant.

fields. Similarly, the results suggest that livestock is not a factor in either location. While crops seem to be important in Georgia, they were insignificant or negative (grains) factors in Colorado.

The results of the conjoint exercises similarly highlight the importance of specific attributes and regional variation (Table 12.11). These results indicate that farm ownership and size are important. Other attributes such as water, crops and livestock may be more or less important depending on the region.

The number of acres protected, while fixed in Colorado, was not significant in Oregon and Maine. This variable is crucial to any program to purchase conservation easements and deserves further consideration in future analyses. This is particularly true given the concern about the ability of contingent valuation studies to detect marginal values for the scope of a program (National Oceanographic and Atmospheric Administration 1993). The scope of any program to purchase conservation easements can be defined as the total number of acres for which easements are purchased. Several studies have shown that acreage preserved is a positive determinant of WTP for protection programs (Bergstrom *et al.* 1985; Bowker and Didychuck 1994; Rosenberger and Walsh 1997). The cost of the program to participants' households, while generally negative for all models, as expected, was only statistically significant in selected models in Oregon and Maine. This variable would be expected to be significant in a study with a larger sample size.

Table 12.11 Summary of conjoint findings regarding significant attribute levels (variable signs in parentheses)

	Colorado	Oregon	Maine
Farm location	NS[a]	All (+)	NS
Water	NS	Ponds/streams (+)	Ponds/streams (+)
Number of farms	X[b]	X	NS
Buildings	Traditional, wood (+) Modern, metal (−)	X	X
Farm size	250–1,000 acres (+)	<50 acres (+)	>260 acres (+)
Farm ownership	Corporate (−)	Family (−) Corporate (−)	Family, part time (+) Family, full time (+) Corporate (−)
Best management practices	X	NS	X
Soil quality	X	X	NS
Crops	Hay (+)	NS	Greenhouses (+)
Livestock	None (+)	Confinement (−)	Poultry (−) Sheep (−)
Total acres protected	X	NS	NS
Household cost	All NS 3 of 7 (−)	3 of 6 significant All (−)	2 of 6 significant All (−)

Notes
a NS indicated that the coefficients on all attribute levels were not significant.
b X indicates the attribute was not considered for the particular state.

Concluding comments

The results of the focus groups reported in this chapter clearly indicate that specific farmland attributes and the different mix of amenities provided influence over individuals' preferences for farmland preservation. The results indicate that perceptions of farmland amenities and preferences for farmland protection are influenced by attributes such as the physical location of the farm, the type of farm and the farming practices used, all of which are directly and indirectly influenced by state and federal agricultural policies. Thus, it is important to consider these attributes when targeting efforts and funds to farmland amenity protection policies and programs. These attributes should also be considered in future research designed to estimate economic values for farmland amenities.

Notes

1 This research was supported by USDA/NRI grant CSREES 99-35403-8658, the University of Maine Agricultural and Forest Experiment Station, the Swank Professorship at Ohio State University and the University of Georgia.
2 The views expressed here are those of the author, and not necessarily those of the Economic Research Service or the US Department of Agriculture.
3 These states were chosen because they were home to the researchers on the team, and because they represent a variety of agricultural settings.
4 We attempted to estimate the equations using random effects as the data contain multiple responses (10 or 30) from each respondent. Random effects were identified for the analysis for all participants based on the evaluations of 10 scenes, but this specification would not converge for the two models based on the 30 scenes for the Georgia data. In the latter models we have more responses per respondent than we do respondents and the opposite holds for the first model, which may explain this difference in convergence. We also tried including variables to represent each of the four groups and the coefficients on these variables were not significant and are not reported. We did not find significant random effects for the Colorado data.
5 Due to small sample sizes we did not investigate random effects or group effects in the analyses of the conjoint data.

13 Value conflict and land use planning

An example at the rural–urban interface

Max J. Pfeffer, Linda P. Wagenet,
John Sydenstricker-Neto and Catherine Meola

Introduction

Land use policy is a central component of environmental management, but efforts to regulate land use in the United States often clash with the strongly valued right to own property without restrictions. While most people support both property rights and environmental protection, advocates of one or the other have increasingly come into conflict during the past two decades. In the face of this opposition, a practical problem in land use policy and environmental management more generally has been to find acceptable compromises.

This chapter presents a case study of an environmental conflict in which land use policy was a central component. In attempting to meet the requirements of the Safe Drinking Water Act, New York City (NYC) attempted to implement a watershed management plan that included land use restrictions and the acquisition of hydrologically sensitive, privately held lands. NYC's water supply system harvests water in rural watersheds, some of which are more than one hundred miles away. The city's watershed management efforts aroused strong protests from residents of the rural watersheds that led to lawsuits against NYC by the watershed communities. NYC and the rural towns eventually reached a negotiated settlement that included land use regulations, a land acquisition program and several forms of compensation paid by NYC to the watershed communities.

In this chapter, we characterize the opposition between property rights and environmental protection advocates and present the NYC watershed controversy as an example of such conflict. The chapter examines both the sources of this conflict and the agreement that resolved it. We then conclude with a discussion of the factors contributing to the compromise reached between NYC and the watershed communities and the broader lessons that can be drawn from this case study.

Environmental value spheres

Growing concern for environmental protection led to the enactment of major legislation in recent decades. Environmental policies sought to protect a variety of common environmental goods, and the elaboration of the expanding array of regulations challenged a range of specific interests and social institutions. Of particular concern in recent years have been conflicts between environmental regulation and the prerogatives of the private sector. This controversy pits values associated with the protection of common environmental goods (e.g., high quality water) against those related to protecting the private interests of landowners.

This opposition represents competition between distinct value spheres.[1] Two value spheres are directly related to human use of the environment. The oldest, and long the most pervasive value sphere in North American culture, is defined by the private appropriation and exploitation of natural resources. Central to this value sphere is private property and its creation, accumulation and protection. The other is characterized by an overarching concern with the protection of natural resources in the interest of maintaining ecological integrity (Murphy 1994). The latter value sphere emphasizes that the common interests of the ecosystem must take precedence over private property interests. This ecological value sphere is relatively young, having emerged in the United States in reaction to consequences thought to be associated with actions guided by the private property sphere.

The connection between the private property value sphere and the environment is best exemplified by the history of land use in the United States. Among the most important incentives offered to Europeans to resettle North America in the eighteenth and nineteenth centuries was the opportunity to acquire landed property. In fact, one of the most important tensions between colonists and the British was the government's unwillingness to permit settlement in the frontiers beyond its colonial territory. This policy favored landowners who speculated on increasing land values in the context of limited supply and strong demand created by a growing population. Under these circumstances, landowners engaged in land use practices that yielded short-term profits at the expense of soil conservation (Cochrane 1979). The depletion of soils is one of the earliest examples of the negative environmental consequences associated with the private property sphere.

After the American Revolution, the lure of landownership continued to attract settlers to the frontier. The exploration and mapping of the frontier, as well as the development of transportation and communication infrastructures served to both assure and accelerate settlement across the continent during the nineteenth century. As settlement across this vast expanse proceeded, natural resources seemed infinite, and their private appropriation and exploitation was unquestioned. This orientation began to be challenged with the closing of the frontier around the turn of the century. Concerns about the depletion of the natural resource base began to be voiced by people associated with a growing conservation movement (Nash 1967; Shabecoff 1993). Conservationists attempted to condition the private property value sphere by advocating the "wise use" of natural resources.[2]

Conservationists operated within the private property value sphere, but they drew greater attention to the finite supply of natural resources. This accentuated concern with natural resources opened the door to considerations of their inherent value. While transcendentalist thinkers of the nineteenth century like Emerson and Thoreau had conceived of nature as having inherent value independent of market considerations, such views did not attract a large following until the early twentieth century after attention had been drawn to the need to conserve the natural resource base. With the popularization of transcendentalist views by Muir, a preservationist movement developed. Nature, the preservationists argued, had value in itself and civilization could survive and flourish only if such value was preserved. This position established the preservation of natural resources as an end in itself, excluding at least a portion of the natural resource base from appropriation as private property (Bergstrom 2004, chapter 6 this volume; Nash 1967; Shabecoff 1993).

Nash (1967) argues that the passage of the Wilderness Act in 1964 represented the coming of age of modern environmentalism. The sociological significance of this legislation was that it made a portion of the nation's natural resource base unavailable for extraction. It did so by emphasizing the intrinsic value of wilderness areas over their use or market value. Because of their inherent value, it was argued, the preservation of wilderness areas took precedence over individual interests, as well as the particularistic interests of the human species. This view did not exclude the possibility of humans benefiting from nature. Rather, it emphasized the importance of wilderness areas as shared environmental goods, i.e., goods that are enjoyed only in combination with others on a basis of commonly accepted meaning. The shared meaning attributed to these goods is what makes them valuable (E. Anderson 1993). In this sense, wilderness and, some would argue, all of nature, are social artifacts (Cronon 1991). The social recognition of these goods as valuable also creates a collective sense of responsibility for their care (E. Anderson 1993).

As such, the Wilderness Act symbolized the emergence of an independent ecological value sphere with its own values, norms and obligations. This value sphere defined a realm of activities concerned with environmental protection in the public interest. Public concern about the environment was aroused with the publication of *Silent Spring* in 1962 (Carson 1962), and organizers of the first Earth Day in 1970 emphasized individual responsibility and encouraged widespread public participation in environmental protection (Shabecoff 1993). In the 1970s, the US Congress enacted a variety of major environmental protection laws, e.g., the Clean Air Act (1970), Clean Water Act (1972), Marine Protection and Sanctuaries Act (1972), Safe Drinking Water Act (1974), Resource Conservation and Recovery Act (1976) and

Toxic Substances and Control Act (1976) (Rosenbaum 1991). These legislative actions represented a significant expansion of the ecological value sphere.

Many of the efforts to address the large-scale consequences of private actions took the form of preemptive federal and state environmental regulations that eroded private and local control over land use (Nolon 1993; Popper 1992). Such regulations often ran counter to deeply held values about the independence of private property holders. Nevertheless, environmentalists provided strong and continuing support for land use control. The more inclusive definition of wetlands in 1989 under the Clean Water Act and the designation of the northern spotted owl as a threatened species in 1990 under the Endangered Species Act counted as highly visible examples of political conflict over land use restrictions imposed by federal environmental legislation: limits on the conversion of wetlands to alternative uses in the former case and restricted logging of old-growth forests in the latter (Shabecoff 1993). While highly visible, these examples of environmental regulations restricting land use are hardly exceptional. Such constraints often result in conflicts between the ecological and private property value spheres.

A clear example of the conflict is the property rights movement that has blossomed in recent years. Leaders of Alliance for America, an umbrella property rights group, estimated that over six hundred local property rights groups had been formed nationwide (Ingersoll 1995; Schneider 1995). During the 1990s, bills to protect property rights were introduced in more than forty state legislatures. Thirteen states passed such laws (Tibbets 1995). Environmental laws (and environmentalists) were the main target of the property rights advocates. The leader of one group in Washington State articulated this position, "We're aligned against classic or orthodox environmentalists. We want to rely on markets, not demand-and-comply government, to reach environmental objectives" (Lewis 1992: 10).

Property rights advocates reasserted the particularistic interests of landowners over shared environmental goods. An attorney involved in property rights litigation characterized the objective of the movement as follows: "It has traditionally been understood that property is yours to use under certain limitations. But now property advocates believe they should be reimbursed if they can't use land in an unlimited way" (Tibbets 1995: 5). They object to environmental laws and land use planning more generally, when the laws require property owners to provide for the public good as a condition for using their land. Such restrictions, they claim, amount to a taking of property without compensation, and, as such, violate the Fifth Amendment of the US Constitution. The reassertion of property rights against demands for the protection of shared environmental goods has become a central activity associated with the property rights value sphere.

In the 1990s several successful Supreme Court challenges were mounted against land use restrictions imposed by states.[3] Having experienced success in the courts, property rights advocates went on to pursue a national political agenda. In 1994, the newly elected Republican 104th Congress eagerly accommodated the property rights movement and its opposition to environmental regulation, including a call in the Contract with America to compensate landowners for losses in the value of their property of more than a specified proportion resulting from environmental regulation (Fisher 1995; Schneider 1995). Some members of Congress aggressively pursued this agenda, unsuccessfully introducing "takings" amendments into every environmental law considered to have a chance of passing. Although none of the takings amendments passed, their introduction was instrumental in delaying the re-authorization of the Endangered Species Act, the Clean Water Act, and the Safe Drinking Water Act. Specific property rights bills were also introduced in the House of Representatives and the Senate, but failed (Tibbetts 1995).

One reason property rights legislation failed to pass was that compensation of property holders for diminished property value would be prohibitively expensive, interfering substantially with efforts to balance the federal budget (Fisher 1995). Republican members of Congress also began to refrain from aggressive attacks on environmental regulations for reasons that are of direct interest here. A substantial majority of voters, Republican, Democrat and Independent, were opposed to the Republican Party's environmental policy proposals. Pollsters found that a majority of Republicans did not trust their party to protect the environment. Only one third of the public said they would vote to re-elect representatives who voted for a Republican-sponsored bill to cut the US Environmental Protection Agency (EPA) budget by one third (Cushman 1996).

The Republican predicament reflects contradictions emerging from two key value spheres involved in human use of the environment: one concerned with ecological preservation for the general good, and the other emphasizing particularistic interests associated with the private appropriation and exploitation of natural resources. When these value spheres relate to common objects (e.g., land), each may value those objects differently and the value spheres therefore conflict with one another. Hence, identifying opportunities for a workable compromise becomes a matter of practical significance. Our case study is an example of an attempt to forge such a compromise.

Data and methods

The data for this analysis were gathered as part of a longitudinal case study of a conflict between NYC and rural towns in the watersheds where the city collects its drinking water. This controversy erupted in 1989 when NYC announced plans to impose new land use regulations in the watersheds (National Research Council 2000; Pfeffer and Wagenet 1999; Platt *et al.* 2000). We began collecting data for this study in 1994 and ended our data collection efforts in 1998 after NYC and the watershed towns reached an agreement regarding management of the watersheds. We provide more details about this controversy and the agreement below. In this analysis, we combined qualitative and quantitative data to offer an account of key elements of this controversy and its resolution. The analysis that follows relied on several sources and types of data.

Qualitative data were collected in several ways: interviews with key informants, attendance at public meetings, and monitoring watershed community newspapers. Key informants were identified via a snowball method of successive contacts with informants. We attended a wide range of public meetings organized in response to both an Environmental Impact Statement prepared by NYC and the Memorandum of Agreement signed between NYC and the watershed communities. We selected a sample of public hearings dealing with these documents to cover a wide geographic area of the watershed and a diverse set of communities. We subscribed to newspapers serving six communities located throughout the watershed. We monitored these newspapers from 1994 through 1998 for articles about watershed management issues. The articles we identified were clipped and catalogued.

We also conducted a panel study of residents in twelve watershed towns. Of the sixty towns in the NYC watershed, only fourteen are entirely within the watershed, and eleven have no more than 10 percent of their population within it (New York City Department of Environmental Protection 1993). We drew our sample from a subset of twelve towns with at least 70 percent of their population residing within the watershed. These study sites were spatially dispersed across the 1,900 square mile watershed area.

We selected households randomly from published telephone listings in each community. According to the 1990 Census of Population and Housing, 96 percent of all households in the study sites had telephones. Within these households, we randomly chose respondents by asking for the person, age 18 or older, who last had a birthday. That person was then interviewed or, if not available, contacted later. Interviews were typically about 20 minutes long. Four hundred and twenty-nine respondents participated in four annual survey waves, between 1994 and 1997.

Finally, we also collected data throughout the 60 NYC watershed communities and in NYC's five boroughs in spring 1998 via telephone interviews of individuals living in households randomly selected by random digit dialing. Overall about 70 percent of the contacts resulted in completed interviews. We asked individuals answering the call for the person in their household age 18 and older who last had a birthday, and then asked to interview that person. The 1,008 and 1,578 interviews in the NYC watershed and NYC respectively averaged about 20 minutes each.

A case study in value conflict at the rural–urban interface

Efforts to protect NYC's drinking water supply provide an example of conflict between the private property and ecological value spheres. At issue

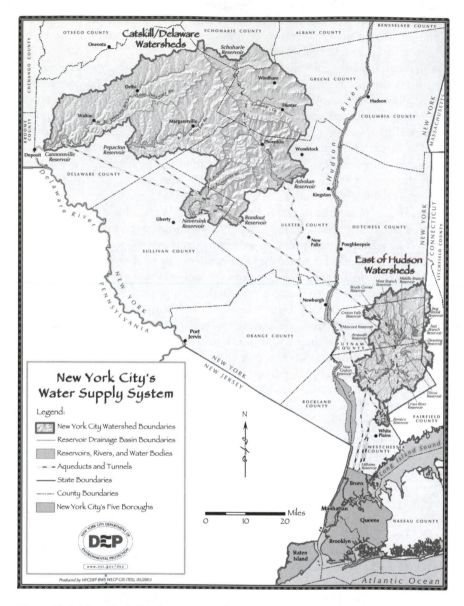

Figure 13.1 New York City's water supply system.

are land use regulations to protect the quality of the city's drinking water. NYC collects its drinking water in upstate watersheds covering about 1,900 square miles in eight counties. This water is collected in a 19-reservoir system connected by tunnels and aqueducts that transports water to NYC almost exclusively by means of gravity. Some of the reservoirs are more than 125 miles distant from the city. This system provides drinking water to more than nine million city residents from a watershed inhabited by about 235,000 residents living in about 60 communities (National Research Council 1999, 2000).

In 1986, Congress amended the Safe Drinking Water Act, raising water quality standards. To enforce this legislation, the EPA in 1989 issued the Surface Water Treatment Rule that required communities relying on surface sources to filter their drinking water. This rule had tremendous fiscal implications for NYC. About 90 percent of its drinking water coming from the Catskill and Delaware portions of the supply system was (and continues to be) unfiltered. Estimates of construction costs for such filtration facilities ranged up to $6 billion with annual operating expenses estimated to be more than $300 million (National Research Council 2000; New York City Department of Environmental Protection 1993; Paden and Shen 1995). The EPA ruling did, however, provide the city with the possibility of avoiding filtration. To avoid filtration, NYC would, among other things, have to develop a watershed protection program to reduce the risks of waterborne diseases like *cryptosporidiosis* and *giardiasis* (US General Accounting Office 1994; New York State Water Resources Institute 1994).

In the attempt to meet this requirement, NYC developed plans for more stringent watershed regulations and for the acquisition of privately owned watershed land. These plans posed a number of potential direct and indirect threats to property values in the watershed. First, updating the watershed rules and regulations, initially adopted in 1953, might reduce property value by making land unavailable or unsuitable for development. For example, some land would become unavailable for development under the revised rules and regulations which called for: (1) maintenance of buffer zones around watercourses and reservoirs thus restricting the construction of roads, parking lots and storage facilities for hazardous substances and waste, and (2) restrictions on the siting and construction of sewerage and service connections (New York City Department of Environmental Protection 1993). Even more extreme impacts on the availability and value of private property were posed by NYC's plans to acquire watershed land. Under the most extreme scenario, NYC suggested an extensive land purchase program under which "all developable waste land in the entire watershed could be protected from further development by direct acquisition or conservation easements" (New York City Department of Environmental Protection 1993: 246). The city estimated that it would need to spend about $2.7 billion to purchase land or easements on about 240,000 acres of vacant land in the watersheds. Because NYC would own this land for the purpose of buffering its reservoirs, this would prevent private development of unused land in the watershed (New York City Department of Environmental Protection 1993; Pfeffer and Wagenet 1999). In responding to NYC's Draft Environmental Impact Statement, the Coalition of Watershed Towns (CWT) concluded:

> The City has hidden from discussion ... its short-term and long-term land acquisition programs which it is already beginning to implement. The total program would involve the acquisition of approximately half of the developable land ... The net result is that the watershed will suffer unmitigated impacts of both the regulatory program and a land acquisition program.
>
> (Coalition of Watershed Towns 1993: 78)

Animosity between NYC and watershed communities came to a head in late 1993 when NYC filed a state application for a water supply permit that included plans to acquire 80,000 acres in the watershed and submitted to EPA a Long-Term Watershed Protection and Filtration Avoidance Program for the Catskill/Delaware System. Uncertainty over NYC's intent to use eminent domain to gain control of the land and the perception that NYC was shifting the costs of watershed protection to upstate communities resulted in the deterioration of relations between NYC and upstate communities.

The following comments by watershed residents characterize the local opposition to land acquisition and land use regulations:

> The land acquisition conditions are absurd; absurd on the grounds that no sound reasoning has yet been shown for the need to grab 80,000 acres by 1999.
>
> (Sodoma 1994)

> The City's target of 80,000 acres to be purchased was "pulled out of a hat." I heard that someone asked how much land does the city now own, and then said, let's double it.
>
> (Gitter 1994)

> The acquisition issue, and [the NYC Department of Environmental Protection Commissioner's] ... refusal to flatly rule out the use of eminent domain to purchase environmentally sensitive land, remain a major sticking point.
>
> (Galusha 1994)

Concerns about the violation of property rights were a significant basis for opposition to the NYC land acquisition plan, and those who owned property expected to be regulated were more likely to be opposed. Figure 13.2 shows towns in our panel study sorted by the proportion of respondents who had property within 100 feet of a water body. Both the proportion of residents who felt land acquisition was unnecessary and who favored suing NYC to stop land acquisition were highly correlated with the proportion who had land within 100 feet of a water body (Pearson correlations = 0.56 and 0.71, respectively, $p < 0.05$).

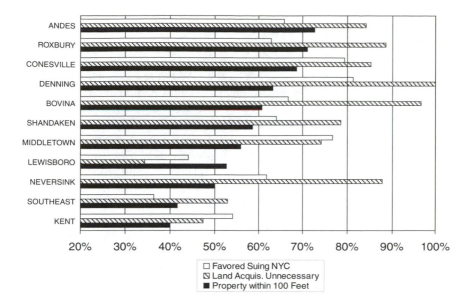

Figure 13.2 Percent of respondents who had property within 100 feet of a water body, felt land acquisition was unnecessary, and favored suing NYC to stop land acquisition, by town.

The tensions peaked when the Coalition of Watershed Towns (CWT), representing about 30 watershed communities, filed suit to prevent NYC from implementing its filtration avoidance plans. The CWT cited economic burdens on watershed residents resulting from restrictions placed on the use of privately owned land. It claimed that NYC would benefit almost exclusively from environmental measures in the countryside to protect drinking water supplies (Pfeffer and Wagenet 1999).

Watershed residents claimed that efforts to protect surface water quality imposed unreasonable costs on property owners directly, and indirectly on all watershed residents by reducing economic growth and associated economic opportunities. In the words of New York State Senator Charles Cook, who represented watershed residents west of the Hudson River, "They (NYC) don't want to pay for filtration, so they'll make the countryside pay in the form of regulations." The costs, according to the Senator, were borne by watershed residents in the form of impaired viability and growth of small businesses, as well as the erosion of real estate values (Cook 1994). Many watershed residents considered the imposition of these costs unjust. One watershed resident expressed this sentiment: "It's not right! The regulations are OK, but they have to pay. Pay us for what you need. It's simple" (Stave 1998: 223).

Resolution

The CWT lawsuit led to an impasse in efforts to reach a compromise between the city and the watershed towns about a watershed management plan. In April 1995, New York State Governor George Pataki intervened by facilitating negotiations involving NYC, the CWT, the EPA, selected county governments, and an *ad hoc* environmental coalition. In January 1997, the parties signed a Memorandum of Agreement (MOA) establishing a comprehensive watershed protection plan. Under the terms of the agreement, the EPA would permit NYC to avoid filtration for a limited period, the city would invest up to $1.2 billion to protect its water over 15 years, the updated watershed rules and regulations would be implemented and enforced, and the city would allocate $250 million for the purchase of environmentally sensitive land (National Research Council 2000; Pfeffer and Wagenet 1999; Platt *et al.* 2000).

The Land Acquisition Program was a cornerstone of the MOA, because it addressed the hot button property issue in conflicts between the rural towns and NYC. The agreement allowed NYC to acquire land in the form of fee title in real property or conservation easements on real property. But under the terms of the MOA, NYC would not exercise eminent domain to acquire fee title or conservation easements for the purposes of watershed protection. The program was voluntary, operating under a willing buyer/willing seller principle. Furthermore, the agreement provided that all land acquisition take place with the knowledge, review and consultation of affected towns and villages so that NYC would be aware of and take into consideration local interests, such as tax revenues. For example, under the MOA NYC would pay taxes in accordance with the assessed value of the properties acquired and agreed not to challenge the initial assessed value of the parcels purchased, provided certain conditions were met.

The Land Acquisition Program was a targeted approach to land acquisition (see Table 13.1). This targeted approach to land acquisition was to maximize water quality protection while also providing reasonable opportunities for growth in and around existing population centers. One watershed newspaper characterized the MOA as follows: "The landmark agreement seems to have something for everyone" (Oberlag 1995: 1).

Discussion

What insights does this case study of land use conflict and its resolution offer about the opposition between the property rights and environmental movements? After the signing of the MOA, we surveyed more than 1,000 residents of rural communities in the NYC watershed. When asked whether they supported the environmental, property rights, or both movements, only one in ten said they supported both.[4] This finding suggests that the individuals interviewed saw the alternatives as distinct from one another, much like the

Table 13.1 Land acquisition program goals and accomplishments

Priority area	Definition	Solicitation goals	Acquired (2002)
		Acres	
1A	Subbasins within 60-day travel time to the distribution system that are near intakes	61,750 (1A and 1B combined)	4,100
1B	Subbasins with 60-day travel time to the distribution system that are not intakes		9,933
2	Subbasins with terminal reservoir basins that are not within priority areas 1A and 1B	42,300	6,484
3	Subbasins with identified water quality problems that are not in priority areas 1A, 1B and 2	96,000	7,624
4	All remaining subbasins in non-terminal reservoir basins	155,000	6,375
	Total	355,050	34,516

value spheres outlined above. These value spheres, we claim, represented distinct and often irreconcilable realms of values, norms, and obligations.

Panel 1 of Figure 13.3 offers additional evidence of value differences between supporters of the property rights and environmental movements. About three fourths of the property rights supporters agreed that the government should pay property owners for the lost value of land resulting from environmental regulations restricting land use, compared with just one half of environmental movement supporters. There were no differences, however, when we asked respondents if they thought NYC should pay the rural towns for protecting the city's drinking water supply. In other words, there were clear differences between adherents of the two movements when the issue of government compensation was posed as a general response to a loss of property value, but there were no differences of opinion regarding compensation of the rural towns for the environmental service of protecting water quality. In fact, opinion was strongly in favor of NYC compensating the towns – four fifths of both groups favored such compensation.

These results become more intriguing when we consider findings from the parallel survey of more than 1,500 NYC residents. Panel 2 of Figure 13.3 shows the same pattern for NYC as for the watershed towns: distinct differences on the abstract question of whether the government should pay, but little difference on whether NYC should pay the towns. The similarity between these two populations suggests these populations may share common values that lead supporters of distinct political positions to hold such similar views about the desirability of NYC compensating the watershed towns for protecting the water supply.

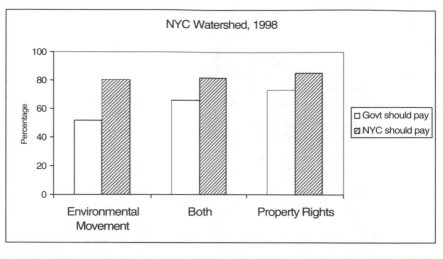

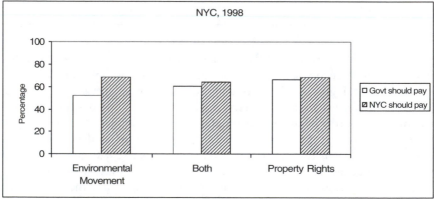

Figure 13.3 Proportion who support government compensation by political orientation (source: Survey of 1,008 and 1,578 residents of the New York City
watershed and New York City, respectively).

Figure 13.4 shows that there is strong support across the board for the principle of equality of opportunity. More than 80 percent of both watershed and
NYC residents considered equality of opportunity very important, and the
differences between supporters of the property rights and environmental
movements were relatively small (6 and 4 percent, respectively). In contrast,
there were more marked differences between the supporters of these movements in the proportion who considered both the right to own property
without restrictions and environmental protection very important. In the most
striking contrast, only two thirds of the property rights supporters in the NYC
watershed considered environmental protection very important compared
with 95 percent of environmental movement backers – a 30 percent spread.

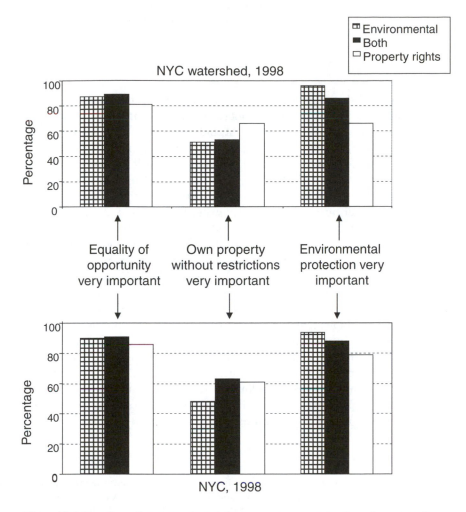

Figure 13.4 Equality of opportunity, right to own property and environmental protection very important by support for property rights movement,
environmental movement or both (source: Surveys of 1,008 and 1,578
residents of the New York City watershed and New York City, respectively).

These findings suggest that equality of opportunity is a core value that is
widely shared and a common ground around which people with very different values and political orientations may unite. Equality also is associated with
justice and fairness. Concerns about fairness were certainly important in the
watershed, as indicated in the quotations cited above. What is interesting is
that differences between political orientations also disappeared in NYC when
we asked about compensation of the watershed towns for protecting water

quality. It appears that the common concern for fairness and equality in protecting the environment transcends political orientations as well as the rural–urban divide.

Conclusion

We have argued that a growing number of environmental goods are valued in different ways by distinct value spheres with different values, norms and obligations. In particular, the ecological and private property value spheres conflict over land use. On the one hand, the private property sphere asserts the prerogatives of landowners to appropriate and exploit land for personal benefits. On the other hand, the ecological value sphere emphasizes limits on private behavior. Attempts to regulate land use to maintain the common good of high water quality in the NYC watershed illustrate the content and scope of such conflict.

This value conflict represents a practical problem for policy makers. When ecological and private property interests are mutually exclusive, what is the basis for achieving support for and consensus about land use policy? The results presented here indicate land use policy can garner widespread support if it addresses equity issues by compensating private property owners for losses incurred in the implementation of policies protecting common environmental goods or for environmental services rendered (e.g., protecting water quality). These findings highlight the importance of equity in questions of environmental and natural resource management, and indicate that environmental justice concerns are not limited to poor communities in urban centers, but also apply to rural communities in their relations with urban centers (Getches and Pellow 2002; Pfeffer *et al.* 2001a, 2001b).

Notes

1 We assume that these value spheres are "distinct realms" (Murphy 1994) of activity that have their own inherent dignity, and in which certain values, norms and obligations are imminent (Brubaker 1984: 69). Value spheres are logically coherent sets of values (Brubaker 1984). Because different value spheres develop an internal logic independent of one another, they often imply conflicting norms and obligations (Weber 1946). Over time, the inner logic of particular value spheres has solidified to more comprehensively guide environmental actions on the basis of inter-connected values, norms, and obligations (Murphy 1994: 39; Weber 1978).
2 Wise use is most commonly associated with forest management, its objective being to assure maximum yields on a sustained basis (Hays 1991).
3 A key legal question posed by these Supreme Court challenges was, "How much latitude does government have in requiring the dedication of private property for public use" (Franzen 1994)? In one case, with widespread implications for environmental and land use planning (*Lucas versus South Carolina Coastal Council*), the plaintiff claimed his property was unconstitutionally taken when the Coastal Council implemented the 1988 Beachfront Management Act drawing setback lines along the coast to protect the beachfront from erosion. Lucas was thus prevented from building the permanent structures he had planned to sell as part of a business

plan. State courts ruled against Lucas, but he appealed to the US Supreme Court which in 1992 ruled in his favor. Based on this decision, any regulation that had the effect of taking all economic value could be vulnerable to challenge (Lewis 1992). In another significant Supreme Court decision, *Dolan versus City of Tigard, Oregon*, the court ruled that the city could not force Dolan, a plumbing store operator, to donate 10 percent of his land for construction of a bicycle path in exchange for a building permit. The court held that a rough proportionality must exist between land use restrictions and the actual impacts of the proposed development. Furthermore, and most importantly, the court placed the burden of proof on the government, thus making it more difficult to implement environmental and land use regulations (Ingersoll 1995; Rehnquist 1994).

4 About 30 percent supported the property rights movement and 60 percent favored the environmental movement.

14 The impacts of land use on nearby property values

Estimates from a hedonic house price model[1]

Richard C. Ready and Charles W. Abdalla

Introduction

Increased attention is being focused throughout the Northeast US on how land use is changing over time. Concerns over urban "sprawl," with its patchy, diffuse pattern of development, include the loads placed on the transportation infrastructure, the costs of delivering local services, the impacts on natural systems, and the effects on the aesthetic and cultural value of the landscape. As residential development occurs in rural areas, traditional as well as more modern and larger-scale agriculture can become located in close proximity to residences, leading in some cases to conflict over land uses and property rights. Local authorities responsible for managing growth need information on the relative desirability of alternative land use patterns. Property values provide one way to measure community members' preferences for land use patterns, as revealed through markets.

This chapter reports on a study designed to estimate the impact of neighboring land use on residential property values. Land use issues addressed included both open space (versus developed uses) and land uses that may be seen as locally undesirable due to perceived or actual disamenities. Potential local disamenities included: landfills, airports, mushroom production, large-scale animal production, sewage treatment plants and high-traffic roads.

The above goal was accomplished in two phases. First, a geographic information systems (GIS) database on land use and residential property values was developed for Berks County in southeastern Pennsylvania, a region characterized by highly productive agricultural land but also by continuing development pressure and a rapid rate of farmland loss. Second, a hedonic house price function was estimated to explain variation in the sales price of single-family residential properties. Explanatory variables included: structural characteristics of the properties, factors that vary spatially by local government, measures of proximity to employment centers, measures of surrounding land use, and proximity to potential local disamenities. Based on the estimated hedonic house price function, the marginal impacts of surrounding land use and local disamenities on residential property values were calculated.

Previous research

Many papers have used hedonic pricing models to analyze the effects of open space and/or local disamenities on residential property values. However, results from these papers are mixed due to different kinds of open space considered, differences in the specification of the open space variables, and differences across study regions. The study closest to this one in purpose and method is that by Irwin (2002).

In a hedonic pricing analysis of residential properties in Maryland, Irwin measures the proportion of area within 400 meters of each house in different land uses. Irwin finds that compared to residential, commercial or industrial uses, open space located within 400 meters of a residential property has a positive impact on that property's price, indicating that open space is a positive amenity for nearby residents. Further, pasture and cropland generate higher amenity benefits to nearby residences than forested open space. Finally, both permanent conservation through easements and public ownership increase the positive impact that open space has on neighboring residential prices.

In addition to open space, we investigate the impact on nearby residential property values of several different types of potentially undesirable facilities and land uses. These include sewage treatment plants, landfills, high-traffic roads, airport runways, mushroom production facilities and large-scale animal production facilities. Particular attention is paid to the potential local disamenity associated with animal production, as this is a current controversial issue in many regions of the United States.

Few hedonic price studies have been conducted that specifically address the amenity impact of animal production on residential property values. Abeles–Allison and Connor (1990), in a study of property values near large hog operations in Michigan, found that house values decreased by $1.74 for each additional hog within a 2 kilometer radius of the house. They did not find significant impacts outside of 2 kilometers. One limitation of the Michigan study is that it only included eight hog operations that had received multiple odor complaints. Property value impacts from these eight operations might well be greater than those from other operations that did not receive complaints.

Palmquist *et al.* (1997) measured the impact on residential property values of hog production in the coastal plain of North Carolina, where some of the largest animal production facilities in the nation are located. For each residential property, the total amount of hog manure produced within one half mile, within one mile, and within two miles was determined. They found that house price was negatively affected by the concentration of hogs near the house, and that the negative impact on house price from a single hog operation could be as large as 8.4 percent.

This study builds on previous research in several ways. The Michigan study assumed that the negative impact from a livestock operation on house prices increased proportionally with the number of livestock located near the house. The North Carolina study assumed that the impact from hog production was tied to the total tons of manure generated within each ring around the house. One issue this research addressed is the relationship between the impact of animal production on house price and the scale of animal production near the house. Second, the Michigan and the North Carolina studies are both restricted to hog operations. This study includes poultry, swine, and beef and dairy operations. Finally, the Michigan and North Carolina studies investigated the impact of animal production on house price in isolation. This study estimates the impacts from several potential local disamenities simultaneously, as well as potential effects from open space versus developed land use.

The study area: Berks County

Berks County occupies an area (864 square miles) between Philadelphia and Harrisburg in southeastern Pennsylvania. Farming remains a very important sector in the county amidst a suburbanizing countryside and a diversifying economy. Currently, about 40 percent of the county's land is devoted to agriculture. An additional 34 percent is in other, mostly forested, open space uses. As of 1997, Berks County had 221,511 acres in farmland, 187,645 acres in crop production, and 1,586 farms yielding total farm sales of almost $248 million. It ranked third in Pennsylvania in number of farms, cash receipts from agriculture products, layers, swine, corn grain, soybeans and apples. It ranked fourth statewide in dairy, broilers, cattle and calves, peaches, nursery and greenhouse crops (includes mushrooms) and barley. Animal agriculture is significant to Berks County's agriculture. Fifty-two percent of the market value of agricultural products sold is livestock. In addition, 35 percent of the market value is nursery and greenhouse, including mushrooms. Mushrooms are the largest market value crop grown (US Department of Agriculture 1997b).

More recent growth patterns reflect suburban sprawl outward from Reading as well as development in rural land beyond suburban areas, leading to increasing conflicts between rural residents and agriculture production over issues such as odor, flies, chemical use and farm traffic. To reduce rural–urban conflict and increase the viability of the county's agricultural industry, Berks County has developed a suite of land use management tools to encourage landowners and municipalities to protect farming and related industries. The "Purchase of Agriculture Conservation Easements" and development of "Effective Agriculture Preservation Zoning" are the two approaches that are viewed as providing the agricultural resource base needed for future production. In its 1991 county comprehensive plan, the county set the goal of preserving 200,000 acres of farmland through these two programs. Specifically, the county desired to preserve large contiguous areas (minimum of 500 acres) with existing agricultural productivity. In addition, the Planning Commission initiated an Agricultural Zoning Incentive Program in 1997 to encourage municipal adoption of effective agricultural zoning (Myers and Auchenbach 2002).

Data and methods

The hedonic house price function was estimated using 8,090 residential properties that were sold between 1998 and 2002. To focus on the rural–urban fringe, houses located in the city of Reading and New Morgan Borough were excluded from the analysis. Data on house sales and character- istics were obtained from a county-wide parcel map maintained by the Berks County Office of Assessment. For each house in the analysis, information was collected on the sale price of the house, the size of the house, the lot size, the number of bedrooms, the number of bathrooms, whether the house had a basement, whether some of the finished area in the house was located in an attic, the exterior façade of the house, whether the house had central air con- ditioning, the physical condition of the house, the year of construction, the year sold and whether the house had public water and/or public sewer. Nominal sale prices were inflated to 2002 dollars. The dependent variable used was the natural log of the sale price.

A county-wide land use map was constructed based on the parcel map. Categories of land use were open space, residential, commercial, and indus- trial. For each house included in the analysis, the amounts of land in each land use within 400 meters of the house and within 1,600 meters of the house were measured. Within the category of residential use five sub- categories were defined: small-lot single family (less than 0.2 acres); medium- lot single family (0.2 to 0.5 acres); large-lot single family (0.5 to 1.5 acres); very large-lot single family (over 1.5 acres); and non-single family residential, which includes row homes, duplexes and townhouses. Within the category of open space, the amount of open space that is in crop, pasture or grass cover (as opposed to forested or open water), the amount of publicly owned open space, the amount of open space that is currently vacant but zoned for developed use, and the amount of open space covered by conservation ease- ments were measured.

The locations of potential disamenities were determined and mapped. There are four landfills located in Berks County, one regional airport, 27 sewage treatment plants (not counting plants located in the City of Reading), 74 properties that have been used for mushroom production, and 71 large- scale animal production operations, defined here as an operation with more than 200 animal equivalent units (AEUs), as defined for each species by the Pennsylvania Nutrient Management Act (Act 6 of 1993) (Beegle 1997).

For each property, the proximity of the house to potential local dis- amenities was measured. For landfills, mushroom production facilities and high-traffic roads, the distance to the closest landfill, facility or road was measured. For the regional airport, the distance to a line extending two miles from either end of the main runway was measured, to approximate airplane

approach and takeoff paths. For sewage treatment plants and animal production facilities, the distance to each plant or facility was measured.

For each potential local disamenity, an index of proximity was constructed.
These indices have the property that the impact on house price decreases as
the distance from the house to the local disamenity increases, reaching 0 at a
defined distance. For sewage treatment plants and animal production facilities,
the indices have the additional property that each plant or facility can impact
house price independently of other plants or facilities. Other databases used in
the analysis included information on elevation and slope, soils, location of
streams, zoning, school district, and commuting distance to the regional
employment centers of Reading, Allentown and Philadelphia.

The hedonic house price function was estimated using an instrumental
variables approach, similar to that used by Irwin (2002). The instrumental
variables approach is used to avoid potential bias in the estimation due to a
form of relatedness, termed endogeneity, between land use and house prices.

Results of statistical analysis of residential property values

Regression results – house characteristics

Complete regression results are presented in Ready and Abdalla (2003). The
variables included in the estimated hedonic house price function accounted
for about 87 percent of the variation in house price. All of the coefficients for
the structural characteristics of the house were statistically significant different
from zero, and of the expected sign. The following characteristics are associated with higher house price: more square feet, more bathrooms, more bedrooms, existence of a basement, a brick, stone or masonry exterior, central air
conditioning, better physical condition, and newer construction. For a given
size, a house was worth less if some of its finished area was in an attic. Houses
located in school districts with higher average standardized test scores had
higher sale prices.

Houses on more sloped lots were worth less. Elevation in and of itself did
not influence house price, but elevation relative to the surrounding terrain
did. Houses that sat above the surrounding terrain were worth more than
those that sat below the surrounding terrain. Public water service increased
house value, but public sewer service did not. The high correlation between
these two features made it more difficult to distinguish their individual
effects. House prices did not increase as fast as inflation during the study
period (real prices declined over time). Shorter commuting distance to Allentown and Philadelphia was associated with higher house prices, but shorter
distance to Reading was not seen as a positive amenity. Zoning had little
impact on house price.

Of particular interest are the results related to lot size. The relationship
between house price and lot size is shown in Figure 14.1. The price of a

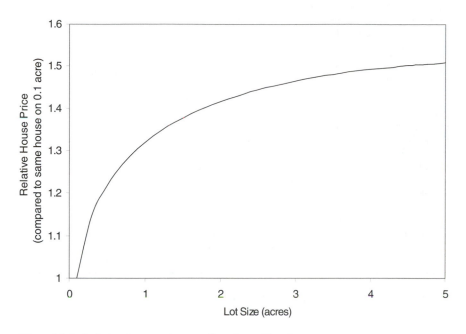

Figure 14.1 Relative house price as a function of lot size.

house built on a 0.1 acre lot is normalized to equal 1.0. Figure 14.1 shows how the house price will increase as the lot size increases. So, for example, a house built on a 1 acre lot will cost 32 percent more than the same house built on a 0.1 acre lot. The marginal impact of additional lot size decreases, however, so that a house built on a 5 acre lot is worth only a little bit more than a house built on a 3 acre lot. This relationship can help inform developers and planners when considering density of a new residential development.

Regression results: surrounding land use

Table 14.1 summarizes the impact that neighboring land use has on house price. All impacts are measured relative to industrial use. In other words, for every acre of land within 400 meters of the house that is in forested, privately owned open space, the house's price is 0.276 percent higher than it would have been if that acre of land had been in industrial use instead. The significance level states the degree of confidence that the number listed is actually different from zero, and not simply the result of sampling error.

Within 400 meters of the house, the land use with the largest positive amenity impact is forested, publicly owned open space. However, forested, privately owned open space has a similarly high amenity value, and the difference between the two is not statistically significant. Open space in

Table 14.1 Marginal impacts of land use on house price

Distance from house land use type	Within 400 meters		400 to 1,600 meters	
	% impact on house price	Signif. level	% impact on house price	Signif. level
Privately-owned forested open space	0.276	★★ᵃ	−0.008	★★
Publicly-owned forested open space	0.281	★★	0.0123	★★
Privately-owned grass, pasture and crops	0.2373	★★	0.000562	ns
Eased, privately-owned grass, pasture and crops	0.162	★★	0.011	★★
Vacant privately-owned open space	−0.091	ns	−0.002	ns
Single family residential, small lot	0.0284	ns	0.0087	★★
Single family residential, medium lot	0.1927	★★	0.0032	ns
Single family residential, large lot	0.2405	★★	0.0293	★★
Single family residential, very large lot	0.2143	★★	0.0305	★★
Other (non-single family) residential	0.0383	ns	0.013	★
Commercial	0.1089	ns	0.0328	★★

Note
a Statistically significant at the ★ = 10 percent, ★★ = 5 percent level; ns = not statistically significant.

grass, pasture, and crops is less valued than forested open space, but again the difference is not statistically significant. Eased open space is less valued than noneased open space, and here the difference is statistically significant. Vacant open space is the least valued, and has in fact a more negative impact on land values than industrial land.

Medium-, large-, and very large-lot residential development has a positive impact on house price, relative to industrial use. Differences among these three groups are not statistically significant. Small-lot residential use and non-single family residential use have lower amenity value than larger-lot residential, and are not statistically distinguishable from industrial use. Commercial land use within 400 meters of the house has a more positive impact than small-lot and non-single family residential, but the difference between commercial use and industrial use is not statistically significant.

As already noted, all of the house price impacts listed in Table 14.1 are calculated relative to industrial use. The impact of a change in land use from one non-industrial use to another non-industrial use can be calculated by taking the difference in the values listed in Table 14.1. So, for example, conversion of one acre of privately owned open space with grass, pasture or crop cover to small-lot single family residential would decrease nearby house values by 0.2089 percent (the difference between 0.2373 and 0.0284). This net impact is statistically significant at the 5 percent level.

Other differences are statistically significant as well. The amenity impact of privately owned, forested open space is significantly higher than for industrial use, commercial use, small- and medium-lot single family residential use and non-single family residential use. The amenity impact of privately owned grass, pasture and cropland is significantly larger than that for small-lot single family residential, non-single family residential, commercial and industrial land. The amenity impact of eased, privately owned grass, pasture and cropland is significantly larger than that for small-lot single family residential, non-single family residential and industrial land.

To summarize, within 400 meters of a house, the surrounding land use that has the highest amenity impact is open space. Whether that open space is forested or in grass, pasture or crops does not matter much. Whether that open space is publicly or privately owned does not matter much. If the open space is eased, it has a smaller positive impact on house price. Among developed land uses, the neighboring land use with the most positive amenity impact is medium- or larger-lot single family residential. The land uses with the least positive impact on house price are small-lot residential, non-single family residential, commercial, industrial and vacant land.

Moving farther from the house, the picture changes somewhat. Amenity impacts of land uses between 400 and 1,600 meters from the house are generally an order of magnitude smaller than those for land use within 400 meters. This makes sense not only because the land use is located farther from the house, and is therefore less noticeable to the occupants, but also because one acre of land represents a smaller proportion of the total located at that distance.

Still, land use between 400 and 1,600 meters from the house does impact house price. At that distance, the land use with the most positive impact on house price is commercial, closely followed by large- and very large-lot residential. Of open space uses, only eased or publicly owned open space has a significant positive impact on price relative to industrial use. Grass, pasture and crops have a significantly more positive impact than forested open space, but the difference is small.

Comparing land uses between 400 and 1,600 meters from the house, while open space uses are significantly less attractive than commercial or large- or very large-lot single family residential use, eased or publicly owned open space is significantly higher valued than industrial land. However, estimated amenity impacts for land uses located farther than 400 meters from the house should be interpreted with caution. Land use within 400 meters from the house is highly correlated with land use outside 400 meters, making statistical inference difficult.

To summarize, the ideally situated house would be immediately surrounded by open space, with commercial properties (stores and offices) located 400 to 1,600 meters away. While open space with conservation easements is viewed less positively than open space without such easements if the parcel is located within 400 meters of the house, such easements are perceived as a positive amenity if the parcel is located between 400 and 1,600 meters from the house.

Regression results: potential local disamenities

Of potential local disamenities, landfills, high-traffic roads, the regional airport, mushroom production, and large-scale animal production facilities (over 200 animal equivalent units or AEUs) all have statistically significant negative impacts on nearby house prices. No significant impact was found for sewage treatment plants.

Landfills had the largest negative impact on house price. Investigation of the spatial limit of the disamenity impact showed that the impact of landfills on house price extended to 3,200 meters from the house, but not farther. The impact a landfill has on nearby house prices is shown in Table 14.2. Mushroom production and the regional airport had much smaller impacts on house prices. For these two local disamenities, the impact extended up to 1,600 meters from the house. Proximity to high-traffic roads (greater than 10,000 vehicles per day) had a small negative impact on house prices that extended only 100 meters.

Three questions were considered in estimating the potential local disamenity impact from animal production. First, is the disamenity impact from an animal production facility proportional to the number of animals at the facility? Second, does the disamenity impact depend only on the closest facility, or does it depend on farther facilities as well? Finally, how far from a facility does the price effect of the disamenity impact extend?

To address the first question, two different proximity indices were constructed – one based on the number of unique production facilities located close to the house, the other based on the number of AEUs housed in those facilities. A facility is defined as a cluster of buildings located within 400 meters of each other. Based on analysis of both indices, the building cluster-based index was better at statistically explaining house price variation than the AEU-based index.

Next, the question of whether only the closest building cluster generates house price impacts was addressed. The building cluster index was divided into two parts – one containing information only on the closest building cluster, the other containing information on all other building clusters located within 1,600 meters of the house. In a hedonic regression that includes both of these indices, the estimated coefficients on both indices were negative, and not significantly different from each other, indicating that all building clusters within 1,600 meters have an impact on house price.

Table 14.2 House price impacts by distance from the house (%)

Distance from the house	500 m	800 m	1200 m	2,400 m
Landfill	−12.4	−6.9	−3.8	−0.8
Airport runway	−0.3	−0.2	−0.1	−
Mushroom production	−0.8	−0.4	−0.1	−
Animal production	−6.4	−4.1	−1.6	−

The spatial extent of the disamenity impact from large-scale animal production was then investigated. A model was estimated that included two indices, one including all building clusters within 1,600 meters of the house, the other including all building clusters located between 1,600 and 3,200 meters from the house. The estimated coefficient on the first index is negative and statistically significant, but the coefficient on the second index is not, indicating that the disamenity impact from animal production does not extend past 1,600 meters. Similarly, Palmquist *et al.* (1997) found that hog operations located between 0.5 and 1 mile from the house had a statistically significant negative impact on house price, but that operations between 1 and 2 miles from the house did not.

The best index for measuring the disamenity impact of large-scale animal operations therefore includes all building clusters within 1,600 meters of the house but does not include information on the number of AEUs at those facilities. Table 14.2 shows the impact of an animal production facility (one building cluster) on the sale price of a nearby house. An outer limit to the impact of 1,600 meters is imposed, so the impact from animal production facilities is assumed to be zero past that point. Because very few houses are located within 500 meters of a building cluster, the model cannot reliably predict impacts for such distances. While it is reasonable to assume that the impact of an animal production facility on a house located less than 500 meters away would be no less than 6.4 percent, the data needed to measure how much greater it might be are not available.

To further investigate whether the scale of the operation at a building cluster influences its disamenity impact, building clusters were divided into three groups: medium (200 to 300 AEUs), large (300 to 600 AEUs) and very large (more than 600 AEUs). Of the 71 facilities identified in Berks County, 32 fall into the medium size category, 30 fall into the large category, and 9 fall into the very large category. No information is available on the location of smaller operations (less than 200 AEUs). A house price function was estimated that modeled the impact of each size class separately. That estimation showed that the medium-sized facilities, considered by themselves, have a significantly negative impact on nearby house prices. The estimated impacts of large and very large facilities were negative, but were not statistically significant, likely because a limited number of such facilities exist in Berks County. However, pairwise comparison among the three size classes showed no statistically significant differences at the 5 percent confidence level.

A similar approach was used to investigate whether the impact of an animal production facility on nearby house prices depended on the species of the animals housed at the facility. The impact was found to be highest for poultry, intermediate for hogs, and lowest for dairy and beef cattle. However, the differences among species were not statistically significant at the 5 percent confidence level.

To investigate whether managerial care influences the house price impact from an animal production facility, facilities located on farms that have a detailed conservation plan on file with the conservation district were compared to facilities located on farms without such plans. Whether a farm has a conservation plan is an admittedly imperfect indicator of the amount of care the operator takes in managing the operation to minimize off-farm impacts. The property value impact of facilities located on farms without conservation plans was larger than the impact of facilities located on farms with conservation plans, but the difference was not statistically significant.

Because differences among facilities related to size, species, or presence of a conservation plan were not statistically significant, a model that does not distinguish among facilities was used to calculate the amenity impacts listed in Table 14.2. Those estimated impacts apply to all facilities larger than 200 AEUs.

Proximity of housing and animals

The total impact that an animal production operation has on residential property values depends on the location of residences relative to the operation. There are no setback requirements when constructing animal barns, though manure handling facilities must be located at least 100–300 feet from property boundaries, depending on slope. In this section, the housing density near animal facilities was measured and compared to the average density in rural parts of Berks County.

The following analysis was performed for the 60 animal building clusters located at least 1,600 meters from the county's border. For each building cluster, the number of single family houses located within 400 meters, within 800 meters and within 1,600 meters was determined. The average numbers of houses are given in Table 14.3.

For comparison purposes, 60 random points were selected in the county. These were located on parcels that were in privately owned open space use and that were at least 5 acres in size. These are the types of parcels on which animal operations are likely to be located. Table 14.3 shows that the actual animal facilities tend to be located in areas that have few houses. The number of houses located within 400 meters and within 800 meters of actual animal facilities is about one quarter of that which would be expected if these facilities were located randomly in the landscape.

Part of the reason why there are fewer houses near animal facilities than would otherwise be expected may be due to the effect of agricultural zoning

Table 14.3 Number of houses located near animal facilities

Distance	Animal facilities	Randomly chosen points
400 m	2.6	16.8
800 m	16.7	60.3
1,600 m	105.9	238.2

and Agricultural Security Areas (ASAs). ASAs are locally designated areas where farmers are given extra protection from nuisance suits and from eminent domain takings. Fifty-nine of the 71 animal production facilities (83.1 percent) are located in ASAs. In contrast, of the privately owned open space parcels of at least 5 acres in size, only 37.6 percent of the land (by area) is located within ASAs.

It is also interesting to look at the relationship between agricultural conservation easements (ACEs) and location of animal production. Twenty-two of the 71 animal production facilities are located on farms with ACEs. In contrast, of the privately owned open space parcels of 5 acres or more, only 8.8 percent (by area) are under ACEs. We conclude that animal production facilities have a tendency to locate on farms with ACEs (or conversely, that farms with ACEs are more likely to have animal production facilities).

Illustrative calculations of the impact of potential local disamenities on property values

The total impact that a potential local disamenity has on residential property values depends on the location of the residences relative to the local disamenity, and on the value that the residences would have absent the local disamenity. In this section, the total impact of a landfill, the regional airport, and an animal production facility on neighboring residential property values are calculated. The numbers presented here are illustrations, and should not be interpreted as averages. The information on the location of mushroom production facilities is not specific enough to allow a similar calculation for mushroom production.

The landfill in Exeter Township is chosen to serve as an illustrative example. For each house located within 3,200 meters of the landfill, the percent decrease in house price due to the landfill's presence was calculated. This percent price decrease was then multiplied by the total assessed value of the house, to give the dollar impact on house price due to the landfill. Assessed values were used because recent sale prices are not available for all properties. Because there were few house sales observations in the hedonic price analysis where the house was located less than 500 meters from a landfill, the predicted house price impacts are less reliable for such houses. To be conservative for residences located very close to the landfill, the percent impact on house price is set equal to the impact on a house located 500 meters from the landfill.

For the 1,561 residences located within 1,600 meters of the landfill, the average house price impact from the landfill is $3,937 (all values are in 2002 dollars). For the 1,781 houses located between 1,600 and 3,200 meters away from the landfill, the average house price impact is $1,132. The average impact on all 3,342 houses is $2,442, for a total impact on all houses within 3,200 meters of $8,162,000, which represents 2.6 percent of the assessed value of those properties.

The disamenity impact from the regional airport extended 1,600 meters from a line extending two miles from either end of the main runway. There are 1,246 single family houses located within 800 meters of the flight path, and a total of 4,647 single family houses located within 1,600 meters. Of these, however, 2,391 are located within the city of Reading. Because the hedonic price function was estimated only for residences outside the city of Reading, it should not be used to calculate property value impacts within the city.

For each of the remaining 2,256 single family residences located outside of the city of Reading and within 1,600 meters of the runway or flight path, the impact on property value was calculated. For consistency with the analysis on landfills and animal production facilities, houses located within 500 meters of the runway and flight path are treated as if they were located exactly 500 meters away. The average house price impact from the airport was $104, and the total impact on the 2,256 residences was $235,000, which is 0.1 percent of the assessed value of those 2,256 houses. However, this is a partial estimate of the total impact of the airport, as it only counts the impacts on houses located outside of the city of Reading.

We chose an animal production facility for analysis that is close to the average in terms of its location relative to houses, with 119 houses located within 1,600 meters and 17 houses located within 800 meters. For each house, the percent decrease in price due to the animal production facility is calculated, and this is multiplied by the house's assessed value. No houses were located within 500 meters of this animal production facility.

For this illustrative case, the average house price impact due to the animal production facility is a decrease in value of $1,803. The total impact on all 119 houses is $215,000, which is 1.7 percent of the total assessed value of the 119 houses. This total is intended as an illustration, and should not be viewed as an average value for all animal facilities. The impact from any given facility will depend on the number of houses near the facility, the location of those houses relative to the facility, and the value of those houses.

It should be noted that the estimates of the impact on property values of open space or potential local disamenities do not include amenity or disamenity impacts that are not tied to house location. For example, price differentials for houses located in areas with more open space would not capture aesthetic benefits of the open space experienced by commuters or tourists who travel through the region. Similarly, house price impacts from an animal production facility would not capture any negative impact on downstream water quality.

Conclusions and future directions

Key findings of this research

The conclusions from this research include the following:

- Surrounding land uses do impact the sales prices of nearby parcels. In Berks County, we found both nearby land uses and proximity to potential local disamenities impact the sale prices of single family houses.
- Within 400 meters of a house, open space is the most desirable surrounding land use, followed by larger-lot residential use. Commercial, industrial, and small-lot single family and multifamily residential uses are less desirable. One implication is that conversion of open space to commercial, industrial, small-lot single family residential, or multifamily residential will have a negative impact on house prices within 400 meters.
- Within 400 meters, privately owned open space with conservation easements has a less positive impact on house price than privately owned open space without easements. Purchasing a conservation easement may not in itself drive neighboring house prices down. Rather, it may be that conservation easements tend to be associated with a certain type of open space (actively farmed, productive farmland) that is less desirable as a near neighbor. Consistent with this explanation is the finding that open space within 400 meters that is covered in grass, pasture or crops has a lower amenity value than forested open space, though the difference in estimated amenity values is not quite statistically significant.
- Open space that is zoned for residential, commercial or industrial use, but that has not yet been built, has a significantly lower amenity value than medium- or larger-lot residential use, and is not significantly different from industrial land. This may be a short-term decrease in house price, reflecting the uncertainty and disruption that accompany new construction.
- Between 400 and 1,600 meters from a house, commercial is the most attractive land use, followed by larger-lot residential, and then open space. Of open space uses, grass, crops and pasture are preferred to forested open space and eased open space is preferred to uneased open space, both results opposite to the results for open space within 400 meters of the house. Outside 400 meters, publicly owned open space is preferred to privately owned, uneased open space. Summing up, the ideal house can be characterized as being immediately surrounded by forested open space, but with commercial uses (offices and shopping) located within one mile of the house. At all distances, small-lot and multifamily residential use is less attractive than larger-lot residential development.
- The statistical analysis was able to measure impacts on house prices from

potential local disamenities. Among the potential local disamenities investigated, landfills and large-scale animal production facilities had the largest negative impact on house prices. Mushroom production and the airport had smaller negative impacts. High-traffic roads had a small negative effect that extended only a short distance from the road. No statistically significant impact could be identified for sewage treatment plants.

- Large-scale animal production facilities have a significant negative impact on house prices within 1,600 meters, but the impact does not extend farther than 1,600 meters. Facilities with between 200 and 300 AEUs are large enough to have a negative impact on neighboring house prices. However, firm conclusions cannot be made about whether the negative impact varies by species of animal, size of operation, or the operator's level of environmental care, as indicated by the existence of a detailed conservation plan.

- Single family residences tend not to be located near large-scale animal production facilities. It is not known whether this is the result of decisions made by animal producers to locate in areas with fewer houses, by decisions made by developers not to build homes near animal facilities, or whether each group is locating on land with different attributes, resulting in a natural separation. It could not be determined whether this separation is a result of policy measures such as Agricultural Security Areas or Effective Agricultural Zoning. However it has occurred, this separation tends to mitigate the impact that animal production facilities have on property values.

- The total impacts of one landfill, the airport, and one animal production facility on nearby house prices were calculated as illustrations. The total impact of a landfill on the value of 3,342 properties located within 3,200 meters was calculated to be $8,162,000, or 2.6 percent of the assessed value of the affected properties (in 2002 dollars). The impact of the regional airport on 2,256 properties located within 1,600 meters of the runway and flight path was calculated to be $235,000, or 0.1 percent of the assessed value of the affected properties. The total impact of an animal production facility on 119 properties located within 1,600 meters was calculated to be $215,000, or 1.7 percent of the assessed value of those properties (all impacts are measured in 2002 dollars). These estimates capture only those impacts that fall on residents who live near the facilities. They do not include costs of impacts that occur farther from such facilities, such as impacts on downstream water quality, or positive or negative amenity impacts on tourists or commuters who travel past such facilities. These calculations are illustrative, but should not be viewed as averages for similar facilities. The total impact from a given facility like these will depend on the number of houses located near the facility, the distance between the facility and the houses, and the market value the houses would otherwise have.

Strengths and limitations of the research

The study area chosen, Berks County, was well suited for this study. First, Berks County has well-developed GIS data resources, and local officials and their staff were very helpful during the study. Second, Berks County has a high proportion of open space that is in ASAs and a high proportion enrolled in ACEs, and these lands are spread throughout the county. This is important because it allows us to identify the impact of these lands on house prices independent of other factors that vary spatially. Third, it was possible to map all animal production facilities larger than 200 AEUs in Berks County – a task that might be somewhat more difficult in another county.

At the same time, performing the analysis in only one county has its limitations. Berks County is still fairly endowed with open space. It may be that the amenity value of open space near a house will be larger in a county where open space is scarcer. Restricting the analysis to only one county limited the number of animal operations included in the house price regression analysis. Extending this research approach to other counties will increase the amount of data, allowing more precise estimation of the house price regression, and will allow a determination of the degree to which the relationships found in Berks County exist in other regions.

When expanding the study area, it would be particularly useful to include counties where open space is scarcer, and where animal production is located closer to residential areas. It is quite possible that the amenity value of open space will be higher in areas where open space is more scarce, and that the marginal impact of eased open space will be positive, as it was found to be in Maryland by Irwin (2002).

More observations on house/animal interactions will also allow better measurement of the relative impacts of different scales of animal operation, and different species. To the extent that operation-specific information can be collected without violating the privacy rights of the operators, that information could be also used to help explain variation in the disamenity impacts from animal production. Similarly, more detailed information on mushroom production facilities would allow a more refined analysis of their impact on house prices.

Finally, until more research is conducted in more counties, care should be taken in applying the results from this study outside of Berks County. At this time, we have no a priori expectations about whether the impact of animal production facilities on house prices will be the same, larger or smaller in other counties.

Note

1 This research was supported by The Northeast Regional Center for Rural Development (NERCRD), under Internal Agreement No. 2093-TPSU-USDA-0496, and by Citizens for Pennsylvania's Future (PennFuture), under Grant in Aid No. 62114. The authors are grateful for support and assistance from Dr. Timothy

Kelsey, Dr. Rick Day, Stewart Bruce and Yanguo Wang; for local knowledge of agricultural production provided by Clyde Myers, Donald Reinert, Mena Hautau, and Dr. David Beyer; for invaluable help in assembling data sets from Martin Moyers and Bill Kochan; and for the guidance and help provided by the Project Local Advisory Group, Clyde Myers, Judith Schwank, Glenn Knoblauch, Duane Rashlich, Tami Hildebrand, Kenneth Grimes, and Robert Behling. The authors are also grateful to four anonymous reviewers for their comments and suggestions. The authors assume all responsibility for all statements and conclusions.

Part IV

A closer look at solutions to land use problems and conflicts

15 Agri-environmental complementarities

Challenges and opportunities in an old world

Ian Hodge

Conflict and complementarity

Most analysis of land uses assumes that there is a conflicting relationship between the production of alternative outputs: given a defined set of resources, an increase in the output of one product can only be achieved by a reduction in production of another. This is represented in the simple production possibility frontier, showing a tradeoff between alternative products. However, in some cases an increase in production of one output can be associated with an increase in production of another. Such products are said to be complementary.

While there are indeed commonly conflicts among alternative claims over the use of land, as is demonstrated in many chapters in this book, this is not always the case. In some instances, the production of different sets of outputs can be complementary. In this chapter, we argue that agricultural land use in an "old world" context can offer one such example. In these circumstances, public support for certain agricultural activities can be the efficient solution and not a distortion to trade. But the specific circumstances and the particular policy approaches adopted require careful definition.

Agriculture and environment in an "old world"

We think of the old world represented particularly by countries in Europe and Japan in rather loose terms as areas where land has been in continuous human use with the application of relatively constant technology over periods of several hundreds or even thousands of years.[1] This is not to say that land in other parts of the world has not been in some sort of continuous use. Rather, the point is that in the old world, the land has been used in a similar way, relatively intensively and more or less continuously over this very long period of time. In contrast in the "new world," typified by the United States and Australasia, European settlement has brought in a different technology and an approach to agricultural production that has made a significant break in the continuity of land use. B. Green comments:

It is the gradual development of farming over millennia that has permitted the largely spontaneous colonization of cultural landscapes by
indigenous species recruited from naturally open habitats such as dunes,
cliffs, wetlands and woodland glades grazed by wild animals ... The
familiarity to the European of cultural landscapes composed of aggrega-
tions of these semi-natural managed ecosystems should not obscure the
fact that such landscapes are virtually absent from those parts of the world
where Western human intervention is more recent. Even in seemingly
comparable and superficially similar parts of eastern North America,
forest clearance and farming have resulted not in species-rich semi-
natural ecosystems of native species but in species-poor examples of
meadow and pasture dominated by common European grasses and herbs
... None of these [new world] countries has anything comparable to our
[European] semi-natural heaths and downs.

(Green 2002: 183–184)

Over long periods of continuous use, patterns of habitats and ecosystems have
co-evolved with human activities. Particular species colonize particular niche
habitats that are associated with particular human activities. For instance, the
pattern of grazing intensity and the annual cycle in the management of
upland pastures over long periods of time have created selective pressures
favoring certain associations of wild plant and animal species. Over time these
have developed into characteristic habitats and landscapes. Wetland farming
systems with managed water levels and drainage ditches offer a variety of
habitats dependent on the continuity and intensity of the agricultural management practiced. Migratory birds visiting the area in the winter rely on the
ability to feed in wet pastures. The wet ditches are suited to a variety of
insect and plant species not found elsewhere in the local environment. Even
in more intensively cultivated lowland areas, associations exist among arable
weeds, other plants and wildlife species, such as small mammals. Traditional
buildings can also be part of the human or wildlife interaction. For instance,
owls nesting or bats roosting in traditionally constructed buildings can be
integrated into the local ecosystem, without alternative niches in the
"natural" environment. The interactions and interdependencies between
species within these systems are complex, often with links at the microbial
level, and largely remain unclear.

Typically, the "traditional" landscape reflects a mixed farming system associated with some degree of subsistence production or a pattern of extensive
grazing. For whatever reason, this tends to create patterns of landscape,
habitat and biodiversity that are appreciated and valued by the local population. This traditional rural environment is thus a product of a specific
pattern of agricultural use. But often land uses are associated with particular
patterns of community activities and institutions, such as communal grazing
of upland pastures, local ceremonies, or craft industries based on locally produced raw materials. Thus, the landscape can be associated more intimately

with the local culture and may be referred to as a cultural landscape. It may even be that it is a long-term association between landscape and community that has itself generated some degree of emotional attachment. There appears to be a preference for a particular type of man–made landscape in England that is represented in both art and literature (Lowenthal and Prince 1965), and this might explain the variations in preferences between different countries.

However, this traditional environment can be threatened, either by techno–logical change and agricultural intensification, or by excessive extensification or land abandonment. Figure 15.1 suggests a stylized relationship between the level of agricultural output generated within a particular area of land and the level of environmental quality. This then takes the form of a production possi–bility frontier,[2] over some range of which there is a complementary relation–ship between the alternative outputs. Environmental quality is represented by some composite bundle of non-commodity outputs associated with the land, as reflected in the provision of countryside goods,[3] such as biodiversity, land–scape, amenity, access for informal recreation, and so on.[4] Some characteriza–tions of the multifunctionality of agriculture (see for instance Organization for Economic Cooperation and Development 2001a) would include other values

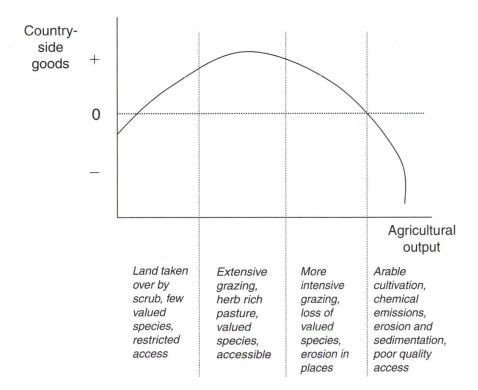

Figure 15.1 Agricultural and environmental production opportunities.

such as food security, rural employment and community development, but here we concentrate on agri-environmental relationships.

The figure suggests that as agricultural production increases there is an increase in the standard of environmental quality; i.e., that the outputs are complementary. In the absence of agricultural management, the land is taken over by scrub and common "weed" species. It will be inaccessible for recreation and visually unattractive.[5] Increased agricultural production intensity brings with it a higher degree of land management. This is often characterized by extensive livestock grazing systems with some arable production, perhaps in small fields surrounded by hedges originally significant for the control of animal movement. Not all areas are well suited for agricultural use, such as wet or rocky areas, and these less intensively used areas provide space for wildlife. But as the intensity of agricultural production increases further, the space for wildlife is lost and the agricultural activity has a more direct damaging impact on the landscape through water pollution, soil erosion and the loss of space and food for wildlife species. It is possible that at the highest intensities both environmental quality and agricultural output declines (in a form of negative complementarity), such as where high rates of soil erosion cause yield loss and off-site environmental damage.

The horizontal line drawn at "0" identifies the reference level of environmental quality and thus of property rights (Hodge 1989). Landholders are expected to achieve this environmental standard. An act that allows environmental quality to fall below this line would be regarded as pollution and "the polluter pays" principle should apply. On the other hand, acts to raise the environmental quality above the standard would be regarded as beyond the requirements of landownership, with the implication that the "provider gets" principle would apply (Organization for Economic Cooperation and Development 1999). Landholders can expect to receive a payment for the provision of such environmental goods.

Agricultural change and environmental quality

The modernization of agriculture, especially through the period since World War II, has been associated with major changes in the type of technology that has been adopted in agriculture. The substitution of machinery for labor, the increasing specialization of farms on a smaller range of enterprises, often involving a shift from mixed farming systems to predominantly arable or livestock, the reliance on artificial fertilizers and pesticides, the increasing scale of operation and the intensification of land use, especially at the extensive margin, have all had consequences for the environment. Hedgerows have been removed as they have lost their function in the management of livestock and interfere with the operation of modern machinery. Ponds and wetlands have been drained and rough pastures have been "improved." Even the increased effectiveness of modern methods in excluding pest species has the effect of removing the food supply for a range of birds and other wildlife.

The process of modernization has been accelerated by the public support provided for agriculture following World War II. This was primarily a response to public concerns for food security but it was also anticipated that agricultural support would benefit the rural economy indirectly and, indeed, the rural environment. Experience prior to World War II had been one of agricultural neglect and land abandonment. The environmental concern had been that land use was too extensive rather than too intensive in the terms of Figure 15.1.

One way of describing the different impacts of price support looks at the impacts at intensive and extensive margins. Figure 15.2 shows economic rent on the vertical axis and ranks land by its quality on the horizontal axis. Economic rent is the residual that remains to the farmer after all costs have been paid, i.e., it is the net income. Land quality is simply measured in terms of the capacity of the land to generate an income. The best quality land generates the highest rent. This declines from the origin as the quality decreases.

AA represents the rent line in the absence of any government price support, while BB represents the higher rent levels achieved with support. The diagram suggests expansion of the margin in two ways.

First, there is an outward expansion of the intensive margin. A higher output price raises the value of the marginal product of inputs and so stimulates higher levels of input use. This causes a shift in the intensive margin, providing an incentive for the application of more inputs per unit area across all of the land that is in production. This then tends to be associated with increased rates of emissions of chemicals into the wider environment reflecting the higher levels of output in Figure 15.1.

The other effect is shown by the outward shift of the extensive margin, reflecting the lower levels of agricultural output in Figure 15.1. Land will be

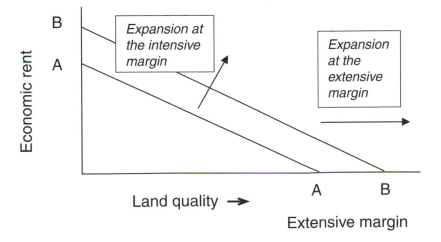

Figure 15.2 Economic rent and the intensive and extensive margins.

brought into production up to the point where it can generate an economic rent. The poorest quality land will thus be left unused. As the price support shifts the rent curve, there will be an outward movement of the extensive margin and some of the poorer land will be brought into production. This "poorer" quality land applies to marginal farming regions, particularly in the uplands, although in the UK practically all land is in some form of agricultural use, albeit at low levels of intensity. The better quality land tends to be in the valleys with soil quality and productivity decreasing at higher altitudes. An increase in agricultural profitability creates an incentive for poorer quality land to be brought into production in the higher altitudes. Thus, traditionally we might have observed arable farming moving up and down the hill and the marginal quality land moved in an out of production with varying levels of output prices. But the poorer quality areas can also be thought of as applying to marginal areas within farms, such as to the edges or inaccessible corners of fields, wet areas with drainage problems or land under hedges or covered with trees.

There is a tendency then for the higher levels of intensity in the more productive areas to be associated with the competitive relationship between agricultural production and countryside goods and the less intensive areas to be associated with the complementary relationship. But this is not straightforward to the extent that some areas remain at the extensive margin even within the more productive regions.

Publicness and its consequences

The presence of complementary production relationships is not in itself a justification for government intervention. However, many of the countryside goods associated with agricultural production have some degree of public good characteristics. Public goods are defined in terms of their excludability and rivalness (or depletability). Agri-environmental benefits tend to be non-rival in that the availability of the good for consumption by one person is not decreased by consumption by another. They also tend to be non-excludable in that once provided, it is not possible to exclude people from enjoying their consumption. A typical example here would be an attractive landscape. In practice, most rural amenities have these characteristics to some degree, but they are rarely "pure" public goods. Non-rivalry occurs over some range of use levels. Public access to the countryside can be enjoyed by substantial numbers of people without affecting each others' enjoyment, but at some point congestion arises such that the quality of the recreation experience is reduced. Landscape can in principle be rendered excludable by setting up and enforcing boundaries around an area, but in practice the cost of so doing would exceed the revenue that might be obtained from the undertaking. Thus publicness often results from the high transaction costs of exclusion.

One particular problem is that both demand and supply sides have non-point characteristics. Many people may have some interest in environmental enhancement and many land holders have the potential to alter their land uses in order to provide the benefits that they would value. But each individual has relatively limited interest in any particular piece of land. The overall environmental impact often depends on the coordination of land uses across a significant area and such changes will provide relatively small benefits to a large number of people. There is thus a problem of excluding non-payers from enjoying the benefits once the good is provided and of coordinating the actions of the land holders.

In practice, the degree of publicness varies between different aspects of environmental quality, ranging perhaps between a small garden, where exclusion is possible at relatively low cost and where benefits are readily depleted by congestion, and the existence values associated with the protection of spectacular scenery or rare emblematic species, where the knowledge that such items exist is the source of value. In this context, benefits are essentially non-excludable and non-rival. Most agri-environmental benefits lie somewhere between these two extremes.

The public good character of the countryside goods means that there is generally no market for them and hence no market price. The optimal allocation between two outputs on a production possibility frontier is generally identified with respect to the products' relative prices. However, in these circumstances, the optimal provision can be represented by the inclusion of a community indifference curve, such as in Figure 15.3.

The policy problem then is to identify and promote the optimal mix of countryside goods and agricultural output. But, given that the non-commodity outputs have public good characteristics, we may ask why they have traditionally been produced at all.

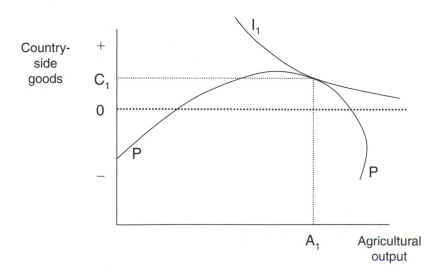

Figure 15.3 Production opportunities for countryside goods and agricultural output.

There are various elements to an answer with different influences over different time periods. Perhaps the simplest might be that the available technology happened to provide the desired outcome. There is probably some merit in this argument. Given the levels of technology available historically, certain types of location have been best suited to certain types of production. And it has been the continuity of production practices over long periods of time that has been important in developing the valued landscapes and habitats.

A second sort of argument is that there has been more deliberate control over landscape and habitat than is generally appreciated. In the second half of the nineteenth century in the UK a significant proportion of the agricultural area was owned in very large estates. The owners of these estates placed considerable emphasis on the quality of the landscape as a setting for their country houses and on the use of the estate for recreational purposes, especially for hunting and shooting. They influenced the management of the land accordingly. The decline of these large estates during the twentieth century has preceded a more general decline in the quality of the rural landscape.

A third factor is the influence of agricultural policy. In the period following World War II, support for the output prices received by farmers under UK agricultural policy and then under the Common Agricultural Policy has had a significant impact.

The position is illustrated in Figure 15.4, which juxtaposes a supply and demand diagram for agricultural products with the production possibility frontier from Figure 15.3. This suggests possible levels of agricultural price, WP, the world price and SP, a level at which domestic prices are supported. The support policy raises the price received by farmers from the world market price (WP) to the support price (SP). In the figure, SP leads to production at A_2 and provision of countryside goods at C_2, below the optimal level of provision.

However, the world market price would not necessarily deliver the desired environmental quality either. In Figure 15.4, the world market price would lead to a level of agricultural management that would be insufficient to generate the optimal environmental quality. At the world price level (WP) the level of domestic production falls to A_3 and an even lower level of countryside good provision at C_3. The implication is that the price should be set somewhere between the world market price and the support level. The figure suggests that there is potentially a level of price at SP_s at which the level of agricultural production, A_1, generates the optimal level of countryside goods (C_1).

However, the support provided for agriculture by raising the output price is a particularly blunt instrument. There are of course familiar costs of supporting agricultural prices above the world level, including the loss of consumer surplus to consumers, the budgetary costs to government, the excessive use of resources within agriculture and the impact on international trade. Several of these might in principle be elaborated within the same figure following Josling (1969), but they are not included for simplicity. And in

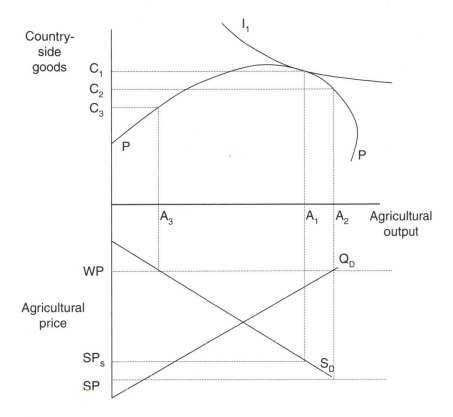

Figure 15.4 Production opportunities and the agricultural product market.

practice, there are many different agricultural output prices and different returns to farming in different localities. We need to adopt a more considered approach towards agri–environmental policy.

Thus, while the diagrams do illustrate some basic arguments, they embody many simplifying assumptions that may lead us to simplistic policy conclusions. First, the relationship between agricultural production and countryside goods provision is not necessarily fixed. It will often be possible to adopt different agricultural methods and systems to deliver different environmental qualities for a given intensity of agricultural production. Second, different localities have quite different agricultural production capabilities and environmental characteristics and hence different relationships between agriculture and the environment. These points suggest that control over the profitability of agriculture through a manipulation of agricultural prices may not be the best approach to agri–environmental policy. This will depend on various factors.

One immediate issue is whether there is a fixed relationship between countryside goods and agricultural production, i.e., whether it is possible to shift the curve in Figure 15.1. With joint products, the proportions in which the products are produced may be fixed, such as could be the case with grain and straw or sheep, meat and wool. Where the proportions are fixed, there is in effect only one product and so costs may not be separately estimated (e.g., Stigler 1966). Where the joint products may be produced in variable proportions, it is generally possible to assign a marginal cost to the production of each of the products. However, this is not possible where there are several products, and although this is attempted in various ways in practical contexts, such an allocation must be arbitrary (Stigler 1966: 165).

Joint product relationships lead to interrelationships between markets. Where there is jointness between agricultural production and countryside goods, a policy to promote countryside goods will have an impact on the production from agriculture and vice versa. Thus it is possible to use support for agricultural production in order to promote the production of jointly produced countryside goods.

In practice, some degree of flexibility between products is generally possible. Thus, for example, the variety of wheat can be altered to produce different proportions of grain and straw or the breed of sheep can be altered to produce different proportions (and qualities) of meat or wool.

There is in fact a bundle of different countryside goods that have differing degrees of jointness with the agricultural production. The maintenance of a traditionally constructed stone barn or planting and managing an area of woodland might have little necessary relationship with the level of agricultural production. They are unlikely to be significantly promoted by a higher agricultural output price.

On the other hand, the production of characteristic grazed upland pastures is probably inescapably linked to the production of sheep. While in principle it might be possible to mow the grass mechanically this would be very difficult in rocky upland locations and the manure produced by the sheep provides a necessary element of the ecosystem that supports the characteristic mix of species in an upland landscape. But it remains necessary to promote the desired level of grazing intensity. Experience suggests that policy payments directly linked to the numbers of livestock kept can, in some contexts, lead to overgrazing and environmental damage while leaving other areas with insufficient grazing intensity. The implication is that the optimal payment per head of livestock may need to be different in different locations (English Nature 2001). This would clearly present practical problems for the operation of policy.

Approaches to agri–environmental policy

Public policy toward the rural environment thus presents a significant challenge.

- A variety of environmental impacts are associated with alternative types of agriculture. Some of the impacts are positive and others are negative.

They are associated not simply with the intensity of production, but also with the type of system that is used.

- The impacts arise from diffuse sources. Environmental quality is influenced by actions that take place across the land's surface and impact on human welfare through a variety of pathways.
- The impacts are generally difficult to measure and quantify in any units. Thus, for instance, landscape quality depends on the number and composition of various landscape attributes that are subject to control by land managers, such as trees, hedges or stone walls, as well as on the general topography that cannot be so controlled. It may also depend on its historical and cultural associations.
- There is asymmetry of information. The landholder has better information than the regulator about the costs and returns to alternative land uses, but may be less well informed about the environmental implications of her actions.
- The value of the environmental impacts varies spatially with respect to both supply and demand conditions. The same agricultural operations will have different implications in different locations due both to the local environmental characteristics and to human preferences.
- Efforts to deliver particular environmental impacts may only be effective in the long term and the outcome of efforts taken on an individual farm may depend substantially on external factors outside of the farmer's control and on the actions of neighbouring farmers.

The promotion of particular environmental outcomes depends on the creation of some sort of linkage between those who value the countryside goods and those whose land management decisions can supply them. As in other areas of resource allocation, the aim is to match demand and supply. Figure 15.5 sets out schematically the possible relationships.

From among the possible variety of policy instruments, we can identify four broad classes of approaches toward the provision of countryside goods: general agricultural support, environmental contracts, linked markets and policy by intermediary.

The selection of a policy instrument and its implications

A number of criteria may be applied in evaluating alternative policy approaches. Vatn (2002) analyzes policies in terms of their precision and their transaction costs. Vatn defines a precise solution as being reached when the standard conditions for optimality are met in the production of the good (i.e., marginal cost equals marginal gain) and thus precision represents the closeness to optimality. Transaction costs are the costs involved in establishing and running a policy: collecting information, formulating contracts and monitoring and enforcing them. These are incurred both by government and by the

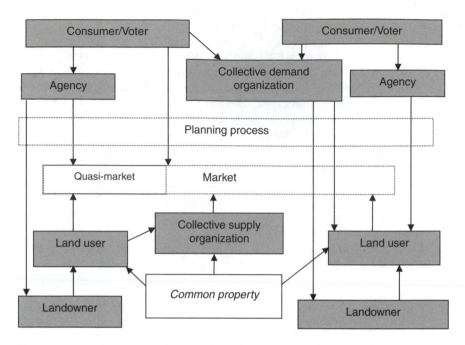

Figure 15.5 An institutional framework for the provision of countryside goods.

private actors who are affected by the policy. Thus policies have both public and private transaction costs.

There is generally a tradeoff between precision and transaction costs. With more information and more detailed contracts, governments can implement policies for land uses that deliver a more valuable package of countryside goods prescribing the least cost method of provision. This will take account of both supply considerations, in terms of the capacity for local areas to supply countryside goods using alternative means of provision, and demand considerations, taking account of the demand within that local situation, given the size, location and preferences of the affected population. But the acquisition of such information is expensive and in practice the information available to government is always imperfect, and it is particularly affected both by the degree of spatial heterogeneity in supply and demand conditions and by the incentives that decision makers face to hide information and actions.

This suggests a somewhat static view. In practice, the optimal approaches to the provision of countryside goods change over time. New information and techniques can respond to changing preferences and reduce costs. As a further criterion we also consider the dynamic incentives within a system for land management decisions to seek out opportunities for the provision of countryside goods and methods by which production costs might be reduced.

We also consider a fourth criterion: leverage. The free-rider problem means that, given their public goods characteristics, countryside goods are likely to be underprovided. In practice, government has tended to intervene either through support for agriculture or through the introduction of specific agri-environmental policies. But other approaches are possible that promote more market and private sector approaches through the demand for country-side goods, either through linked markets or through intermediate non-profit organizations. These alternative approaches have the advantage that they can shift the burden of countryside provision onto the beneficiaries who value them. They can bring in resources for their provision at lower opportunity cost. They can reduce the role of the public sector and so avoid some of the economic distortions associated with taxation and the problems associated with government bureaucracy. Leverage relates to the extent to which the countryside goods delivery mechanism draws in resources and information from members of the public who place a particular value on their provision, through market payments or voluntary contributions.

Agricultural support

One option for countryside goods provision is to provide general agricultural support. This is an implication of the simple diagrammatic exposition in Figure 15.4. Support may be provided by raising output prices received by farmers; as already noted, however, this is likely to be a very blunt policy approach with a variety of undesirable consequences. Indeed, in the absence of some sort of restraint it may be a cause of environmental damage. More plausibly, a policy might operate by means of area payments associated with desirable land uses, probably within areas characterized by a particular topography. Farmers will then make production decisions on the basis of the market price received for their agricultural output.

A policy of this sort still affects production, but the implication is that some level of production is necessary in order to maintain the desired provision of the countryside goods. However, the precision of the policy is likely to be relatively low in that payments will not prescribe specific land management approaches or reflect specific local circumstances. But the transaction costs of the policy will also be relatively low as standard payments are made to farmers on the basis of simple criteria. Assuming that it is possible to observe land uses, enforcement should also be relatively straightforward. There are limited incentives for land use decision makers to respond to new opportunities for the provision of countryside goods. There is effectively no leverage as this is a standard government payment made directly to the farmer.

Environmental contracts

In practice, agri-environment policies have relied heavily on various forms of environmental contract and they have now been the subject of considerable research (e.g., Buller *et al.* 2000; Centre for Rural Economics Research 2002; Hanley *et al.* 1999; Moxey *et al.* 1999; Whitby 2000). Typically, these involve an environmental contract between a government agency and an individual farmer under which the farmer agrees to manage the land in a specific way in return for an annual payment. The schemes are voluntary and usually available to all farmers within specifically designated areas. They often require farmers to adopt more "traditional" agricultural systems defined in terms of livestock stocking densities, use of chemicals and pesticides, the timing of certain operations (such as mowing grass), and the maintenance of hedges, walls and buildings.

This arrangement in principle facilitates a high degree of precision in that contracts can be differentiated down to the individual farm level to implement land uses that reflect the very local supply and demand conditions. But this does also involve high transaction costs. While this approach represents a significant innovation in policy terms and is as yet relatively underdeveloped, there are a variety of quite fundamental limits to the general approach.

These limits are generally associated with problems of information. Government agencies do not have good information about public preferences at the local level and the emphasis has tended to be backward-looking, on the protection and re-creation of "traditional landscapes" despite the fact that such landscapes were the product of historic patterns of prices, technologies and institutions and may not represent the most appropriate solutions in today's or tomorrow's circumstances. At the same time, land managers have better information than government agencies about their costs and their actions. This presents problems of adverse selection and moral hazard. The government agency cannot know exactly what costs individual farmers face in meeting contract conditions and thus how much they should be paid in compensation. In practice, farmers with the lowest costs, who are likely to make the least contribution to the provision of countryside goods, will be most likely to participate in voluntary schemes. Farmers will also have an incentive to default on aspects of the contract that incur a net cost and that may not be readily observable by the government agency.

The prescriptive role of a government agency means that there are few incentives for producers themselves to act entrepreneurially or to seek out methods of reducing costs, especially in individually negotiated contracts. The nature of the contracts may limit the incentives and opportunities for cooperation between landholders, such as in coordination over water level management. Again, there is no leverage. Funds have to be raised through taxation. In practice, many landholders are already willing to forego income in order to maintain a certain standard of environmental management. The payment of compensation may drive out this positive behavior and encourage efforts to exploit the potential gains from asymmetric information.

Linked markets

Markets for countryside goods are missing primarily because of high transaction costs. This means that the costs of providing a good that can be marketed are high relative to the level of income that can be generated from its sale. Generally there are two ways in which markets might be developed in order to address this problem. The first is to concentrate on developing a market for a joint product and the second is to seek to establish a market for the environmental good itself. At the same time two types of intervention might be taken, generally but not always by government. The first is to reduce transaction costs, especially by providing information not otherwise available. This might provide potential consumers with some degree of assurance about the product or enable potential suppliers to exclude non-payers. The second means is to establish new forms of property right. This identifies the four categories shown in Table 15.1, illustrating possible examples.

When consumers purchase a product, they acquire a variety of attributes. It is possible that certain attributes of particular products have a high degree of jointness with the provision of countryside goods. But it may be that in many circumstances the consumer cannot recognize whether or not the product offered for sale does or does not have these attributes. Organic products offer an illustration, although the same principles would apply to niche products. We assume that the production of organic products has a more positive impact on the environment than does the production of a conventional product. It is not possible for a consumer to determine by visual inspection whether or not a product is organic and the transaction costs would rule out any possibility of the consumer seeking out information about the particular production processes of individual products available from the supermarket. However, it is possible for a licensing authority to provide the consumer with assurance that the product does indeed have this particular attribute, of being organic. In response, consumers will be willing to pay a premium for it. Consumers may purchase the product because they believe that it is of better taste or lower risk to health, but the creation of a market for organic products can have beneficial impacts on the environment.[6]

Further, consumers who appreciate the quality of the environment may be willing to pay a premium for a product if they believe that in doing so they are helping to improve environmental quality. Given that the environmental

Table 15.1 Linked markets for the provision of countryside goods

	Providing information/ reducing transaction costs	*Establishing new property rights*
Joint product	Organic standard	Right to operate tourist enterprise
Environmental commodity	Private park or co-ordinated bridleway	Conservation easement/covenant

improvement is unlikely to benefit them personally, they are in effect paying for the provision of a public good. This then raises the problem of free-riding, but the evidence of consumers' willingness to pay a premium for environmentally friendly products and to make donations to environmental charities indicates that not all consumers' free-ride perfectly. By providing information alongside the product, consumers inclined to make a contribution towards the costs of providing countryside goods can be given an opportunity to do so. Again, organic or niche products offer an example.

Circumstances in which the creation of a property right can lead to the creation of a market for a joint product are less obvious. One example might be where a decision maker who has control over environmental quality is given a right to operate an activity that would benefit financially on account of a higher standard of environmental quality. Thus, a reallocation of property rights would effectively internalize an external benefit. Thus, for instance, the owner of a river and adjoining land might be given the right to operate a tourist enterprise that provides accommodation for anglers and other visitors to the area. The attractiveness of the area to the visitors, and hence the profitability of the tourist enterprise, will depend on local environmental quality such that it may be worth investing more into the maintenance of the local environment. Where the enterprise is separately owned the incentive will be absent.[7]

Similar sorts of issues arise in the context of the creation of a market for an environmental commodity directly. The provision of information, effectively the reduction of transaction costs, can make possible new market opportunities. One illustration arises when the information facilitates the coordination of behavior amongst potential suppliers. Individually, landowners may not have sufficient land area to offer recreational opportunities to charge potential visitors, but if a group of landowners coordinate their behavior they may be able to do so collectively. Farmers in some areas of England have worked together to provide bridleways across their farms. Riders pay for a license to have access to this network. Thus a new market commodity has been created that was otherwise not present. There is perhaps no necessary role for government in promoting this provision, although in practice government agencies do often have a role in promoting models of what is possible and in bringing prospective suppliers together.

The final category is where individual property rights relating to environmental quality are separated out from conventional bundles of ownership rights. The most familiar example is where the right to develop land is acquired separately from other land rights by an individual, or more often an organization, that is prepared to pay to prevent the development from taking place. Legislation exists in the United States under which non-profit organizations can hold conservation easements. Thus, these organizations can act to protect the quality of the local environment by buying such easements from local landowners. Similar opportunities exist in the United Kingdom but the conditions are more restrictive. Covenants can only be held by local authorities or by the National Trust, or else covenants may be made by agreement between adjoining landowners under common law. In principle, easements or covenants might relate to a range of land management actions that have wider implications for local environmental quality, such as the removal of trees and hedges, the use of chemicals or the management of water.

Policy by intermediary

A number of private sector organizations have objectives that match quite closely those of the state. This is clearly the case for most charities and includes a variety of conservation bodies, several of which have the provision of conservation goods by means of direct management of land among their objectives. Such organizations are referred to as Conservation, Amenity and Recreation Trusts (CARTs) (Dwyer and Hodge 1996). These are non-profit-making organizations with the aim of generating wide public benefit through nature conservation and environmental improvement, provision of amenity and opportunities for public recreation and conservation of landscape heritage.

While agri-environmental policy involves agreements with existing owners, the CART model implies some change in the character of property owners. An alternative approach is therefore for the state to promote the actions of organizations that have similar objectives in common with those of the state. This may be done in terms of grants for the purchase of land, contributions toward labor costs and the tax relief generally available to non-profit organizations.

The achievement of conservation goals can often require detailed information both about the ecology of the habitat being managed and about the agricultural system that is operated within it. Under some circumstances, guidelines for management can provide sufficient information for a farmer without a detailed understanding of the ecosystem involved. However, under other circumstances, for instance where habitat is being recreated or where a rare habitat is being protected against external pressures, a more proactive form of environmental management may be necessary. This would involve a more regular monitoring of the ecosystem and review of the appropriate management responses. This may require a range of skills that are not always available to the particular landholders who happen to be owners of the relevant conservation sites and may be difficult to write into contractual agreements.

Where such an organization owns land that is being managed for landscape or wildlife conservation, it will be the residual claimant. As such, it will seek to maximize the value to it of the residual that is left after all costs have been paid. In this case, the value will include the non-monetary value of the conservation goods. The conservation organization will have an incentive to seek out least-cost ways of generating and protecting the conservation values under its particular circumstances. It will be prepared to tradeoff costs against conservation gains. In this, the implied price of conservation goods may not be different from that implied in government actions. Therefore, such organizations will tend to act entrepreneurially, seeking new products and new methods of achieving conservation goals and responding to changes in relative prices and technology. This suggests that the conservation organization will require less detailed monitoring than a conventional landholder and that in the longer term it would be likely to develop more cost-effective methods of conservation management.

Conservation organizations may also be more flexible and less bureaucratic than many government agencies given their generally smaller size and the lack of democratic accountability. They may be able to respond more rapidly to opportunities that arise, such as in purchasing significant conservation sites when they become available on the market.[8] Such organizations often specialize in particular types of conservation, such as the protection of birds, or may focus their efforts within a particular area. In this way, although they may be relatively small organizations, they can build up a level of expertise within their own particular speciality. But at the same time, their activities are likely to be guided by the institutional and financial environment created by government.

Comparative evaluation of approaches

This suggests four broad classes of approach toward the provision of countryside goods. The variations in approach that are available within these classes means that care should be taken in seeking to provide any comparative evaluation at this scale. However, some general observations may be made about their strengths, limits and relevance. A simple characterization is offered in Table 15.2 against the criteria suggested earlier. The table also suggests their potential applicability and gives a possible illustration. No individual approach would seem to dominate any other. This suggests that they may each have some potential role, given the variety of circumstances under which countryside goods provision may be desired.

There are without doubt also ways in which these general approaches may be applied that are not appropriate. Thus, general support for agriculture, especially by means of artificial increases in agricultural product prices, will lead to a variety of distortions and may damage rather than enhance environmental quality. But under certain circumstances, it does seem possible that certain forms of support can be effective. See Vatn (2002) for an analysis of this issue. While governments are involved in supporting the linked markets and the policy by intermediary approaches, there has been much less research on their operation and effectiveness, and apparently none on the comparative performance of these different classes in practice.

Table 15.2 Comparative performance of classes of instruments for the provision of countryside goods

	Agricultural support	Environmental contracts	Linked markets	Policy by intermediary
Precision	Low	High	Low to medium	High
Transaction costs				
public	Low	High	Low	Medium
private	Low	High	Low	Possibly high
Dynamic incentives	Low	Low	High	High
Leverage	Low	Low	High	High
Potential applicability	High degree of jointness in homogenous environment not threatened by production intensity	Specialist identification of environmental values; weak jointness; high publicness	High jointness between food "quality" and provision of countryside goods; low publicness	Charismatic species and recreational value; low publicness
Illustration	General support for agriculture in mountain areas	Specialist contracts for conservation of rare species	Organic farming providing general environmental enhancement	Conservation of attractive species and historic sites

Conclusion

The solution to the problems of the provision of countryside goods is as complex as the variety of goods and of local environmental and human circumstances. Mixes of instruments will inevitably be required. At the same time, we cannot anticipate a separate policy instrument for every individual good or service. The transaction costs of such an approach would be excessive and so there will be considerable crudeness in the ways in which policies are implemented in practice. Economic analysis of first best solutions will provide some, but limited, indications of what can work in practice. The other factors of dynamic incentives, transaction costs and leverage will also be important.

These policies will inevitably have some impact on levels of agricultural production, and hence some impact on international trade. But this impact on production and trade should not be assumed to be a "distortion." The level of prices and patterns of trade that would happen to arise under conditions of "free trade," generally taken to be represented by the outcome where all agricultural policies have been removed, should not necessarily be taken as the benchmark against which to assess "distortion." The complementary relationship between agricultural production and the provision of countryside goods must imply that the support of the latter tends to increase the production of the former. Thus the internalization of the values associated with countryside goods cannot be entirely production neutral. The introduction of "good" policies for the provision of countryside goods may then be seen as having a trade-correcting effect. These are policies that have high precision, low transaction costs, incentives to respond to demand and to lower production costs, and strong leverage. Some general rules have been suggested (e.g., Ervin 1999) but much remains to be done to specify how these different approaches can be integrated into coherent rural environmental policy.

Notes

1 Recent excavations at Heathrow Airport, west of London, have found evidence of continuous agricultural use over thousands of years. Farming began during the Neolithic period (4,000 BC–2,400 BC) when forests were gradually cleared and crops were planted and gathered communally. Pollen found from hedges used as field boundaries showed that people were creating fields with boundaries from around 2,000 BC, during the early Bronze Age.
2 Strictly, in this and the figures that follow, this is not the conventional textbook production possibility frontier in that extra resources will be introduced in order to increase the volume of agricultural output.
3 Following Vatn (2002) the concept of a "good" here also includes what might often be described as a "service."
4 In principle this bundle is comprised of a mix of positive and negative services, each potentially with a different relationship with the level of agricultural production so that the figure represents the net value at any particular level of production intensity.
5 It might be argued that this is a short-term phenomenon in that over a longer period of time there will be a process of ecological succession that will deliver a landscape of higher environmental quality. However, whether such an alternative landscape would be equally valued and how long it might take to develop in practice remains controversial. There have, for instance, been suggestions in the UK that certain areas might be left to regenerate without significant human management but that has not as yet been taken up (Adams 2003).
6 This is essentially the same as the complementary relationship between production and countryside goods discussed earlier except that the rules relating to the production methods used for organic products do more to ensure that the complementarity is maintained.
7 In fact, in the absence of transaction costs we would expect separate owners to coordinate their behavior and so the distinction between the transaction costs and property rights arguments is somewhat artificial.
8 In fact, under some circumstances the opposite may be true and government agencies make an initial purchase while a private organization sets about fundraising.

16 Multifunctionality, land use and agricultural policy

David Abler

The primary function of agriculture is to supply food, fiber and industrial products. However, agriculture can also be a source of several public goods and externalities. Rural and urban populations often value agricultural land as open space and as a source of landscape amenities. Agricultural land is frequently a habitat for wildlife species, and the agricultural sector can contribute to the economic viability of many rural areas and to food security. On the other hand, conversion of forest and wetlands to agricultural production can damage ecosystems. Agricultural nutrients, pesticides, pathogens, salts, and eroded soils are leading causes of water quality problems in many countries. Water used for irrigation in agriculture is water unavailable to non-agricultural sectors or ecosystems. There is concern about the negative effects of livestock production on animal welfare. On both the positive and negative side, agriculture can be both a sink for and a source of greenhouse gases.

The term multifunctionality refers to the fact that an activity can have multiple outputs and therefore may contribute to several objectives at once. As applied to agriculture, the term first came into use in the late 1990s in the European Union for, it is often argued, protectionist reasons (Bohman *et al.* 1999; Swinbank 2001). Some governments have attempted to justify agricultural price and income support programs and trade restrictions as a means of preserving the multifunctional attributes of their countries' agriculture. This has led to frictions among member governments at the World Trade Organization negotiations and in the Organization for Economic Cooperation and Development (OECD).

The objective of this chapter is to examine the effectiveness and efficiency of agricultural price and income support policies in promoting landscape and open space amenities as well as other multifunctional attributes of agriculture. After reviewing multifunctional attributes often attributed to agriculture, this chapter addresses the question of jointness between production of agricultural products and the production of multifunctional attributes. It then addresses the comparative costs of traditional price and income support policies versus policies focused more directly on multifunctional attributes, particularly policy-related transaction costs.

Multifunctional attributes of agriculture

Agriculture globally is a source of a number of public goods and externalities (Abler 2001a, 2001b; Blandford *et al.* 2003; Organization for Economic Cooperation and Development 2001a, 2001b, 2003b; Shortle *et al.* 2001). Table 16.1 lists public goods that are often mentioned as multifunctional attributes of agriculture, along with several negative externalities identified in the literature.

Agriculture is a major user of land in most countries, and rural landscapes are often defined by agricultural structures, cropping patterns, the presence of livestock, and the presence of wildlife in agricultural areas. Agricultural structures often identified as important include barns, stonewalls, hedges, roads, ponds, irrigation canals and watercourses surrounding agricultural fields to capture runoff. Crops generate a much different landscape than pastureland, and different crops can generate much different landscapes (e.g., soybeans versus sunflowers). Related to landscape amenities are open space amenities. Farmland, forests, wetlands, parks, wildlife refuges, golf courses, undeveloped vacant lots and even cemeteries fall into the general category of open space. There is concern in many areas about conversion of agricultural land to urban uses and agricultural land abandonment, and how the loss of agricultural land might change the character of rural landscapes.

Landscape and open space amenities are perhaps the most frequently mentioned multifunctional attributes for agriculture. In a basic sense, they refer to use and non-use values derived from open areas and landscapes. They include utility derived from recreational activities in open areas (hunting, fishing, camping, swimming, hiking, bird watching, etc.), which are public goods insofar as these activities are not subject to exclusion or congestion effects. These terms are sometimes used in a broad sense to encompass several of the other public goods listed in Table 16.1 (e.g., Hellerstein *et al.* 2002). Open areas may have more than one use. For example, farmland may be used by hunters in the fall or winter after crops have been harvested. For those living near rural landscapes or other open space, non-use values can include enjoyment derived from scenic views and the satisfaction of living in an uncongested area. Both those living in rural areas and those in cities may value rural

Table 16.1 Public goods and negative externalities from agriculture

Public goods	*Negative externalities*
Landscape and open space amenities	Eutrophication
Cultural heritage	Sedimentation and turbidity
Rural economic viability	Drinking water contamination
Domestic food security	Odors from livestock operations
Prevention of natural hazards	Animal welfare
Groundwater resource recharge	Irrigation – overuse, salinization
Preservation of biodiversity	Loss of biodiversity
Greenhouse gas sinks	Greenhouse gas emissions

landscapes as a habitat for wildlife. There may also be beneficial externalities that do not rise to the level of a pure public good – for example, open space may increase property values on adjacent parcels of land (Geoghegan *et al.* 2003; Ready and Abdalla 2004, chapter 14 this volume).

With respect to cultural heritage, farmers and others in rural areas are often viewed as preservers of cultural values that have been lost in urban areas. For many people, agriculture also provides a link to the past when their ancestors lived on farms. Cultural heritage values may depend in part on traditional agricultural structures such as barns, stonewalls and hedges, which evoke a sense of tradition and security (Auer 1989). However, as George (1997) cautions, public opinions about farming tend to be nostalgic and do not reflect the reality in rural areas today. Technological, economic, and social changes have had profound impacts in both urban and rural areas. Nevertheless, the preservation of cultural heritage is often cited as one multifunctional attribute of agriculture.

The economic viability of rural areas is a concern in most developed countries. Rapid technological progress in agriculture over the last century has made it possible for a small percentage of the labor force to produce ample food supplies at prices that are significantly lower, in inflation-adjusted terms, than they were 50 or 100 years ago. Rural populations in many regions of the United States and other countries have fallen significantly in recent decades. However, whether the economic viability of rural areas is in fact a public good is open to debate. The question is essentially whether rural areas have an economic value above and beyond their value added in the goods and services they produce. One economic argument sometimes made is that market distortions can cause the social opportunity cost of labor in rural areas to be lower than market wage rates, so that calculations of the economic contribution of rural areas based on market wages understate that contribution. As Horbulyk (2001) emphasizes, however, economists view employment as a social cost, not a social benefit. From an economic perspective, employment gives rise to social benefits only in proportion to the value of goods and services produced by workers.

It is also sometimes argued that maintaining rural populations is important because there are economies of scale associated with public services, social services and infrastructure supportive of economic development. The small size of most rural communities prevents them from taking advantage of these economies of scale (Green 1997). This argument appears to have some merit. However, one must acknowledge that these same economies of scale are present in neighborhoods and communities in urban areas. Urban population growth permits urban areas to take greater advantage of such economies of scale.

Food security is often defined as regular access (either through production or purchasing power) to enough food for a healthy and productive life. However, when used in the context of multifunctionality, food security has usually been defined in terms of national security, i.e., access to a sufficient amount of food in national or international crises. The argument is that domestic food production can help insure against disruptions in imports caused by war, blockades or other international events.

In terms of natural hazards prevention, irrigated rice production in Japan and South Korea is sometimes cited as a form of flood prevention, because irrigated paddy fields can store water during the rainy season. In this respect irrigated paddy fields serve one of the functions often ascribed to wetlands. In mountainous countries, agricultural vegetation on hillsides and alpine pastures is sometimes mentioned as a form of protection against landslides and avalanches. With respect to groundwater resources, seepage from irrigation systems has been cited as a mechanism for groundwater resource recharge. On the other hand, irrigation in many areas suffers from overuse of scarce water, salinization, and waterlogging.

Agricultural production can have profound impacts on biodiversity, both for better and for worse (van Dijk 2001). Agriculture replaces a natural ecosystem – which might be a forest, prairie, desert, wetlands, coastal area or some other system, depending on the location – with a human-managed ecosystem. Species of flora and fauna that have a comparative advantage under the natural ecosystem will decline or become extinct in that area, while species that have a comparative advantage under the human-managed ecosystem will prosper. Similarly, agriculture can be both a sink and a source for greenhouse gases (Intergovernmental Panel on Climate Change 2001).

Other negative externalities from agricultural production include eutrophication of surface waters from excess nutrients in fertilizers and animal wastes, sedimentation and turbidity in surface waters due to soil erosion, drinking water contaminated from pesticides, fertilizers and animal wastes, odors from livestock, and – to many people – problems of animal welfare, particularly in intensive livestock operations (Blandford *et al.* 2003; Shortle *et al.* 2001).

In any analysis of agricultural/environmental policy and multifunctionality, it is essential to consider not only public goods and beneficial externalities associated with agriculture but also negative externalities. Some proponents of multifunctionality have emphasized only public goods and beneficial externalities while downplaying negative externalities (Abler 2001b). Failure to consider both positive and negative external effects can lead to erroneous policy conclusions. Policies adopted to promote public goods could worsen, or at least fail to improve, negative externalities. Results in Peterson *et al.* (2002) illustrate this point using a simulation model with two externalities (landscape amenities, human health costs from agricultural chemicals) and two policies (land subsidy/tax, chemical tax).

The question of jointness

The most important issue on the production side of multifunctionality concerns the nature and degree of jointness between the production of crop and livestock products, on the one hand, and production of multifunctional attributes, on the other hand (Organization for Economic Cooperation and Development 2001a). If there were no jointness, multifunctional attributes could be provided independently of agricultural commodities and there would be no case for agricultural price and income support programs as a mechanism for promoting multifunctionality.

In general, jointness can arise due to either technical interdependencies in production or economic interdependencies (Burrell 2001; Organization for Economic Cooperation and Development 2001a). Technical interdependencies refer to inherent features of the production process governed by biological, chemical, and physical relationships. Economic interdependencies refer to linkages created by non-allocable inputs or linkages created by allocable fixed or quasi-fixed inputs. A non-allocable input contributes to multiple outputs simultaneously, so that it is non-rival for one output when used to produce another. For example, a combine may be used to harvest one crop during the summer and another during the fall. If a non-allocable input is used in the production of an agricultural commodity and also in the production of a public good, a change in the commodity output will lead to a change in the non-allocable input and in turn the supply of the public good. An allocable fixed or quasi-fixed input is available to a producer in a fixed amount or along an upward-sloping supply curve, so that a change in one output leads to a change in the amount of the input allocated to that output, and in turn the amount of the input remaining for other outputs. If different commodities are associated with different levels of public goods, then reallocation of fixed or quasi-fixed inputs among these products will alter the supply of public goods from agriculture.

Technical interdependencies

The case for technical interdependencies in agriculture is strongest for negative externalities. Problems such as soil erosion, nutrient runoff and leaching, and methane from livestock manure are all governed by biophysical processes, although they can be mitigated using alternative production or abatement technologies. The case for technical interdependencies for the public goods listed in Table 16.1 is much weaker. One could argue that flood prevention and groundwater resource recharge are inherent features of irrigated agricultural production, at least in some areas. However, technical linkages with production could be weakened or broken because they depend on cropland being irrigated and not on the amount of a crop harvested, or even (within the class of irrigated crops) on the choice of crop itself. Replacing agricultural land with wetlands would also be an option for flood control. Similarly, planting vegetation on hillsides without harvesting anything, or reforestation of hillsides, are options for avalanche and landslide protection.

Landscape and open space amenities are not technically linked to commodity production *per se* but rather to land use practices and agricultural structures (Abler 2001b). Strictly speaking, it would not be necessary to harvest any crops or produce any livestock products at all in order to derive landscape and open space amenities from cropland and pastureland. More generally, crop and livestock yields could increase or decrease significantly without any change in landscape and open space amenities. A farm field with low yields is no less "open" than a field with high yields. Survey results in Krieger (1999) indicate that respondents value open space primarily in order to protect wildlife habitat (64 percent of respondents), slow and control development (53 percent), and preserve rural quality (53 percent). Only 5 percent of respondents mentioned ensuring future food supplies as a reason for protecting open space. It would also be possible to conserve traditional agricultural structures – which often serve to remind people of agriculture – even if they no longer have any agricultural value.

Due in part to a desire to preserve open space, most US states and many local governments have adopted measures designed to preserve agricultural land from development (American Farmland Trust 1997). These measures include agricultural protection zoning, conservation easements that give farmers tax benefits or cash payments in exchange for agreeing to keep their land in agriculture, and differential assessment policies that tax agricultural land at a lower rate than non-agricultural land. However, all of these measures are targeted at agricultural land, not agricultural production. Agricultural production enters the picture only insofar as it affects the magnitude of tax benefits or cash payments that must be offered under conservation easement programs in order to induce farmers to keep their land in agriculture, and here the effect is negative. Farmers with highly productive land do not need as large a tax benefit or cash payment to voluntarily induce them to keep their land in agriculture as do farmers with less productive land, other things being equal.

Economic interdependencies

The case for economic interdependencies for the public goods in Table 16.1 is stronger than the case for technical interdependencies. In the production of landscape and open space amenities, agricultural land and structures are essentially non-allocable inputs that contribute to commodity production and can also contribute to these public goods. By the same token, agricultural land can simultaneously contribute to commodity production and the prevention of natural hazards, though as noted above this is not a case of technical interdependence. Agricultural land, traditional structures, and farm household labor may also contribute to the preservation of cultural heritage. Of course, comparing one agricultural commodity versus another, farm household labor, land and structures are usually allocable and usually behave like fixed or quasi-fixed inputs.

Jointness between public goods and agricultural land and structures does not necessarily imply jointness between public goods and agricultural output. Econometric evidence indicates that the elasticity of supply of land to agriculture as a whole is very low, and elasticities of supply to individual crops and livestock products are also relatively low (Abler 2001c; Salhofer 2001). At the same time, elasticities of substitution between land and purchased inputs, particularly fertilizer, are relatively high (Abler 2001c and Salhofer 2001). The result is that changes in agricultural output are accomplished primarily through changes in purchased inputs rather than changes in land. Indeed, agricultural output has grown in virtually all US states since 1960, and grown substantially in many states, in spite of a decline in agricultural land in every single state (Ball *et al.* 2001).

Structural changes in agriculture in recent years appear to have reduced landscape and open space amenities generated by agriculture. Growth in intensive livestock operations has led to concerns in many communities about surface water and groundwater pollution from animal wastes and about odors, especially from hog operations (McBride and Key 2003; National Research Council 2003). A 1998 survey of farmers in urbanizing areas of Pennsylvania by Larson *et al.* (2001) found that 44 percent had received complaints in the past few years about agricultural practices, particularly odors. A 2001 US nationwide survey by Esseks and Kraft (2002) found significant support for farmland protection among urban and suburban respondents, but also significant concern among these respondents about contamination of drinking water from pesticides and livestock manure. These findings suggest that landscape and open space amenities in urban and suburban areas are reduced by the presence of nearby intensive livestock operations. Changes in agricultural technology have also reduced landscape amenities generated by agriculture. Mechanization, increases in farm size and changes in crop varieties have led to growth in monoculture and a decline in landscape diversity in many areas (Abler 2001b). As a result, what is now perceived as a "traditional" landscape may in fact have looked quite different 30 or 40 years ago. Within a given area, a broad mix of agricultural land uses and other types of open space appears to generate more amenities compared to a single land use (Kline and Wichelns 1998).

One question that arises in regard to agricultural price and income support programs is whether land would remain in agriculture following a decrease in production of agricultural commodities or a decrease in commodity prices. A study of farmland conversion in the Mid-Atlantic region by Lynch and Carpenter (2003) yielded inconsistent results for 1978–1997 on the role of farm prices and costs in farmland conversion. Population density had a positive and significant impact on conversion. Hardie *et al.* (2001) found that farmland prices in the Mid-Atlantic region were determined primarily by nonfarm factors such as average household income and population density, rather than farm-related factors such as net farm returns. Parks and Quimio (1996) found that farmland conversion to developed uses in New Jersey is driven primarily by capital gains from selling land to developers, and that net farm income has no statistically significant impact on conversion. The reason for this finding is that the capital gains from selling farmland to developers are so large in most cases that moderate changes in farm income do not make a difference in the decision to sell. This suggests that policies targeted at increasing farm income might have little impact on farmland preservation, at least in relatively urbanized states such as New Jersey.

Parks and Schorr (1997) found that the US Conservation Reserve Program (CRP) is not an effective mechanism for preserving open space in metropolitan counties in the northeastern United States, where open space tends to be scarce. The CRP helps offset the agricultural opportunity costs of the conservation practices that farmers must adopt, but payment rates are far too low to offset the opportunity costs of not converting agricultural land to developed uses. On the other hand, Parks and Schorr found that the CRP was effective in keeping land in agriculture in nonmetropolitan counties in the northeastern United States, where the opportunity cost of agricultural land is much lower and open space is generally more abundant. Larson *et al.* (2001) found that policies designed to preserve farmland were successful in arresting farmland conversion in Pennsylvania between 1988 and 1998, but only provided that urbanization pressures were not too strong. Farmers in rapidly urbanizing areas tended to reduce their farmland between 1988 and 1998 in spite of farmland protection policies.

In the European Union, there are concerns that significant cuts in agricultural price supports could lead to widespread agricultural land abandonment or conversion to urban uses (Burrell 2001; Dobbs and Pretty 2001). The presumption would appear to be that while the elasticity of supply of land to agriculture is currently low, the land supply curve has a more elastic portion that would become evident as cuts in agricultural prices shifted the demand for land inward. The experiment has not been run so we do not know whether this presumption is correct. Following a sudden and near-complete end to agricultural subsidies in the 1980s, New Zealand experienced only a slight decline in agricultural land as marginal lands were converted to forestry or reverted to native bush, and a diversification of commodities produced on agricultural land (Federated Farmers of New Zealand 2002; Rae *et al.* 2003). The degree to which the New Zealand experience is relevant to the EU or United States is unknown.

Proponents of food security as a multifunctional attribute claim that agricultural production is linked to food security because current production helps ensure that a sufficient quantity of land will be available for domestic production, should a crisis disrupt imports (Abler 2001b). However, the same events that would impair access to imported food would probably also impair access to imported agricultural inputs used in domestic production (Organization for Economic Cooperation and Development 2001a). Critical inputs that are largely imported by many countries include fertilizers, pesticides, seeds, oil, machinery, machinery parts and livestock feed. In addition, food security does not necessarily imply a continuation of current land usage patterns. Allowing for cutbacks in food consumption toward survival levels and substitution among foods produced and consumed could significantly reduce land usage below current levels (Brunstad *et al.* 2001). Public stockholding of agricultural commodities is also an option for ensuring the availability of food during a crisis (Organization for Economic Cooperation and Development 2001a).

Among the public goods listed in Table 16.1, the case for economic interdependencies with agricultural production is weakest for rural economic viability. Agriculture in developed countries is a small percentage of the rural economy, and is becoming smaller. Farms currently account for only 5 percent of the rural US population (US Census Bureau 2002), and farm income accounts for only 4 percent of total personal income in nonmetropolitan US counties (Kassel and Carlin 2000). Even among US farm households, only 12 percent of household income comes from farming (Gunderson *et al.* 2000). The majority of household income among farm households comes from off-farm wages and salaries and off-farm business income.

The rural nonfarm share of the US population has been relatively constant since 1900 in spite of a major decrease in farming's share of this population (Gale 2000). If agriculture had been a linchpin of the rural economy, the rural nonfarm share of the population should have declined as a result of decline in the farm share of the population. Even in the short run, adverse conditions in agriculture need not threaten the economic health of rural areas provided that other conditions are favorable. For example, the unemployment rate in rural areas of the United States declined substantially in the second half of the 1990s, as rural areas joined in the US economic boom at the time. This occurred even as agricultural prices were falling significantly (Gale 2000). Agriculture's contribution to the economic viability of rural areas in the European Union is also small (Hofreither 2002).

Income and employment growth in most rural areas of the United States has been driven by other sectors in recent decades, particularly the service sector. The service sector was the largest source of new employment for nonmetropolitan counties during 1991–1996, accounting for about one third of employment growth (Gale and Kilkenny 2000). The retail trade accounted for another 20 percent of employment growth. By contrast, agriculture accounted for about 3 percent. Beyers (2000) found that the trade and service sectors accounted for 87 percent of employment growth in the rural South during 1985–1995. The most rapidly growing industries were health services, retailing, and business and professional services. Rural development strategies based on increasing agricultural production will have little value because the success or failure of agriculture has little direct effect on the rural US economy (Cosby 1997).

Policy-related transaction costs and multifunctionality

Transaction costs have been defined broadly as the "the economic equivalent of friction in physical systems" (Williamson 1985: 19). Within this broad definition, transaction costs include all costs of acquiring information, making decisions, reaching agreements, and administering agreements once reached. Although transaction costs have usually been applied to private decision making, they are increasingly being applied to governmental decisions (e.g., Carpentier *et al.* 1998; Falconer *et al.* 2001; Falconer and Whitby 1999; McCann and Easter 2000; Vatn 2002). The Organization for Economic Cooperation and Development (2001c) gives the example of a targeted direct payment to farmers, in which case there are costs to the government of designing the policy, obtaining legislative and executive approval, establishing criteria for which types of farms or farm regions are eligible to receive payments, establishing criteria for what eligible farmers must do to obtain payments, determining payment levels, disbursing payments, monitoring and auditing payments, and evaluating policy outcomes. To these transaction costs should be added the costs to farmers of learning about the policy, deciding whether to apply for payments, the application process, depositing payments, and complying with audits and other reporting requirements. When disputes arise, there may also be costs of arbitration or litigation that should be counted as part of transaction costs.

Policy-related transaction costs are important to multifunctionality for two reasons. First, it may be possible to economize on transaction costs by using one policy instrument to achieve multiple objectives. Tinbergen's (1952) well-known maxim that at least as many policy instruments are required as there are policy objectives need not hold in a world with policy-related transaction costs. Agriculture has a wide variety of multifunctional attributes and it may or may not be efficient to have a separate policy for each of them. Second, different policy instruments can carry different transaction costs. Vatn (2002) argues that the transaction costs of targeted agri-environmental policies may be so high that agricultural price and income support policies, including policies that restrict international trade, may be the most efficient option for promoting multifunctional attributes. On the other hand, in a model with no transaction costs, trade barriers never lead to a social optimum, even in the presence of multifunctionality (Paarlberg *et al.* 2002).

Estimates of administrative costs for agricultural programs suggest significant differences across programs. Administrative costs are available from public budgets; estimates of other types of transaction costs are more difficult to derive and tend to be rare. Traditional price and income support programs carry administrative costs that generally lie between 1 percent and 5 percent of total program costs to the government (Falconer and Whitby 1999; Vatn 2002). By contrast, administrative costs for agri-environmental programs in the US and Europe range from about 5 percent of total government costs to nearly 50 percent (Falconer *et al.* 2001; Falconer and Whitby 1999; McCann and Easter 2000; Vatn 2002). It is relatively easy to transfer funds to farmers based on acreage or production, but more difficult to ensure that environmental or land management conditions are followed in return (Falconer and Whitby 1999).

In the United States, agri-environmental programs include the Conservation Reserve Program (CRP), Wetlands Reserve Program (WRP), Environmental Quality Incentive Program (EQIP), conservation compliance requirements for farm commodity programs and Federal, state and local farmland preservation programs (Hellerstein *et al.* 2002; Ribaudo 2001). In the European Union, there are hundreds of agri-environmental programs at various levels of government. These programs are generally voluntary and generally compensate farmers for following certain management practices (Gatto and Merlo 1999; Hanley 2001). The majority have more than one objective, with the most common being the reduction of negative externalities from agriculture, wildlife conservation and landscape conservation (Gatto and Merlo 1999).

One reason why agri-environmental programs carry relatively high administrative costs may be that most of these programs have been relatively small in scale to date, covering fewer farms than the number covered by price and income support programs. This means that fixed administrative costs for agri-environmental programs (costs independent of the number of farms covered) are relatively large when expressed on a per farm basis. In their study of administrative costs for Environmentally Sensitive Areas (ESAs) in the United Kingdom, Falconer *et al.* (2001) found economies of scale with respect to the number of agreements made with farmers in any one ESA. They also found significant learning-by-doing effects, with administrative costs falling as the number of years of experience in managing agreements increased.

Targeted agri-environmental programs can have the advantage of incurring transaction costs for only those farms where public goods or negative externalities are most important (Organization for Economic Cooperation and Development 2003b). There is significant spatial variability in agricultural landscapes, the economic contribution of agriculture to rural areas, natural hazards, biodiversity and nonpoint agricultural pollution (Abler 2001b). Agricultural price and income support programs incur transaction costs for all farms producing commodities covered by the programs, regardless of whether or not they are located in areas where multifunctional attributes are important. Carpentier *et al.* (1998) found that targeting nitrogen runoff performance standards toward farms most responsible for runoff would increase transaction costs per farm covered under the standards but reduce total transaction costs because fewer farms would be covered. They also found that targeting would reduce total program costs (transaction costs plus compliance costs).

Related to this is the potential for geographic mismatches between farm program benefits and multifunctional attributes. US farm program benefits are geographically concentrated in the Corn Belt and Great Plains (Gunderson *et al.* 2000), where open space is abundant. In the Mid-Atlantic and Northeast, where there are significant concerns about loss of agricultural land to housing and urban uses, farm program benefits are comparatively small. Similar geographic mismatches occur in the European Union (Hofreither 2002; Potter 2002).

Any comparison between farm price and income support programs and targeted agri-environmental programs must also consider efficiency losses in agricultural markets created by farm programs and deadweight losses associated with tax collection for programs that involve significant government spending (Organization for Economic Cooperation and Development 2003b). Agricultural price and income support programs in developed countries carry high consumer and taxpayer costs. Total support to agriculture in OECD countries was $318 billion in 2002, or about 1.2 percent of gross domestic product (Organization for Economic Cooperation and Development 2003a). OECD also estimates that prices received by OECD farmers in 2002 were nearly one third (31 percent) higher on average than those on world markets (Organization for Economic Cooperation and Development 2003a).

The transaction cost issue is mainly applicable to public goods positively associated with land, structures, or other agricultural inputs. For dealing with negative externalities, there are unlikely to be any transaction cost savings with price and income support programs because these programs generally worsen negative externalities. Price and income support programs have been widely identified as a contributor to nonpoint agricultural pollution through effects on the scale of production, input usage, and farm structure (Organization for Economic Cooperation and Development 1998; Shortle *et al.* 2001). These programs tend to encourage farmers to produce on environmentally sensitive lands and make more intensive use of environmentally harmful inputs (fertilizers, pesticides, irrigation water and fossil fuels). Agricultural policies that increase livestock production also imply an increase in livestock wastes. One might think that supply controls such as production quotas or acreage restrictions would be environmentally beneficial because they reduce output, but this need not be the case. Acreage restrictions may lead to substitution of environmentally harmful inputs such as fertilizers and pesticides for land. The rents created by output quotas and acreage restrictions may encourage resources to remain in agriculture that would otherwise exit.

Agricultural policies targeted at land are a somewhat different case than policies targeted at commodity outputs. Payments based on land area encourage the supply of agricultural land and perhaps the supply of public goods associated with land, albeit to a limited degree because the elasticity of supply of agricultural land is low (Abler 2001c; Salhofer 2001). Land payments can also encourage extensification of agriculture in which land is substituted for environmentally harmful inputs (fertilizers, pesticides, irrigation water). Compared to other forms of agricultural price and income support, payments based on land area carry lower social costs and lead to fewer distortions in international trade (Dewbre *et al.* 2001). Payments requiring the planting of specific crops are more inefficient and trade distorting than payments made irrespective of which crops are grown, but these differences are small compared to the differences between land payments and other forms of agricultural support (Dewbre *et al.* 2001).

Conclusion

This chapter raises serious doubts about the effectiveness and efficiency of agricultural price and income support policies in promoting landscape and open space amenities or other multifunctional attributes of agriculture. Public goods associated with agriculture are not joint with commodity production *per se* but rather with land use practices and agricultural structures such as barns. The elasticity of supply of land to agriculture is currently low, with the result that changes in agricultural commodity outputs are accomplished primarily through changes in purchased inputs rather than changes in land. On the other hand, negative externalities associated with agriculture are joint with production to at least some degree. Negative externalities have worsened significantly in several countries in recent decades as the intensity of agricultural production has increased. More research is needed on how the supply of land to agriculture might respond to the large decreases in output prices that elimination of farm price and income support policies in many countries would entail.

In terms of efficiency, agricultural price and income support programs carry high consumer and taxpayer costs and encourage socially costly negative externalities. However, they may economize on policy-related transaction costs compared to more complicated agri-environmental policies. It is relatively easy to transfer funds to farmers based on acreage or production, but more difficult to ensure that environmental or land management conditions are followed in return. More research is needed on estimating policy-related transaction costs, especially types of transaction costs other than administrative costs. More research is also needed on whether policy-related transaction costs for agri-environmental programs could be reduced through selective targeting of farms subject to the programs. In addition, research is needed on whether any savings in transaction costs achieved by using agricultural price and income support programs would be sufficient to outweigh the large social costs of these programs due to market distortions and negative externalities.

17 Sprawl

Contemporary land use planning's paradigm

Mark B. Lapping

It has passed into the mythology of the field of rural sociology that when asked to define rural sociology, a wise wag responded, in some futility, that rural sociology is what rural sociologists do (Friedland 2002). Given that the practice of urban and regional planning is diverse and ever-changing it might be argued – with some degree of veracity – that if asked the same question planners might very well respond in much of the same manner: planning is what planners do. Yet there has always been a core to planning and this has been its overriding concern for land, how it is used, by whom, and to what ends. Land, in nearly all of its manifestations, remains the essence of planning; this has not changed over the centuries nor does it appear to differ from one cultural milieu to another. By no means is this to suggest that all planners are land use planners in the contemporary sense of the term. That is not the case. However, the larger point is that planners tend to think about and work with the problems of space as a central organizing principle.

Perhaps not coincidentally land is also one of the very few local assets that cities, towns and villages actually can control. Land markets and land values, as Henry George understood many years ago, are shaped by the timing and placement of public infrastructure investments, such as roads and water and sewage service. The rules of land settlement and land development are subject to the processes, policies and products that planners develop and administer. The extent and quality of local services and amenities are closely tied to the valuation of land and the way this is determined and assessed. And how a community functions, its legibility within the larger pattern of region and nation, as well as its very social and economic fabric and texture, are also subject to the strategies and decisions that planners help make and deploy. Planning and land are inseparable from one another in the contemporary community context.

With land, then, as the organizing principle, several themes in contemporary planning practice, each related to sprawl in one way or another, suggest both the centrality of land to community planning as well as its multi-dimensionality and multifunctionality as the "room and situation" of planning (Hite 1979).

Sprawl is currently one of the core paradigms through which land use and planning discourse is organized and understood. By its very nature the notion of sprawl brings with it a degree of conceptual unity and clarity to land use problems by seeing things as a whole and deeply interrelated. Sprawl affects rural areas, suburbs, and cities at one and the same time and solutions must be crafted that address the manifestations of sprawl across the entirety of the American landscape.

Sprawl control antecedents

The emergence of the anti-sprawl/smart growth/New Urbanism movement constitutes one of the more exciting developments in contemporary American planning. This loose coalition is growing and generating useful information as well as developing imaginative strategies and approaches to development and growth containment. Founded upon a critique of current development patterns and their consequences, as well as the policies and subsidies that foster them – ones that continue to threaten the integrity, quality and sustainability of cities, suburbs and the countryside – the attack on sprawl has important antecedents in past planning practice. In a sense, the movement to contain and reverse sprawl is old wines in new bottles, at least to a degree.

Perhaps the most recent precedent is that of the growth management and "critical areas" initiatives of the 1960s–1970s, themselves part of the larger "quiet revolution" in land use, as Bosselman and Callies (1973) described it. These approaches tended to focus on the identification and protection of areas of unique environmental quality and the necessity to manage growth in ways that would not overwhelm such places and regions, or, as in the case of Vermont, an entire state (Sanford and Lapping 2004). During the quiet revolution in almost every situation local planning regimes were found to be inadequate in addressing the problems of growth management and environmental protection. In some instances the argument for institutional reform was based upon the perceived inability of existing organizational and planning systems to deal effectively with dynamic ecosystem change and threats to long-term ecological sustainability. In other cases local parochialism and a pro-growth ideology – often described as the "growth machine" (Logan and Molotch 1987; Molotch 1976; Pfeffer and Lapping 1994) – were blamed for a myriad of problems that prevented the careful and aggressive review of growth-inducing proposals. And in still other situations local governments and their planning authorities were perceived as simply outmatched and under-resourced when confronted with projects of a regional scale and impact. In almost every case extra-local interest groups, sometimes elites that saw planning as a mechanism to preserve their traditional patterns of ownership and resource use, successfully argued for new planning systems and regimes that would more adequately control and manage growth (Heiman 1988). The result was that such big places very often ended up with big plans and new bureaucracies for land use governance.

An older antecedent of today's anti-sprawl/smart growth/New Urbanism movement can be located in the British "Garden City" movement at the turn of the twentieth century, identified very largely with the efforts of Ebenezer Howard. He sought to rein in the development of London so that it would not spill into the countryside. He wanted to do this through the creation of certain growth controls, such as a massive greenbelt surrounding the city, and the establishment of new towns to absorb population and industry – which in many contemporary cases has resulted in little more than edge cities which foster yet more sprawl. Howard's Garden City sought to understand and to utilize technology in community design to create both vital cities and a thriving countryside, each in harmony with the other. Howard's foremost American interlocutors, the Regional Planning Association of America (RPAA) – Lewis Mumford, Clarence S. Stein, Catherine Bauer, Benton MacKaye and Henry Wright – saw the problem of unrestrained urbanization and growth in a manner consistent with many of today's "smart growth" advocates. As Stein wrote then, the key question was: "How can we live happily, safely and graciously in the motor age?" (Stein n.d.: 92, quoted in Lapping 1977). In a very real sense the contemporary anti-sprawl/smart growth/New Urbanism coalition asks much the same question while focusing on sprawl, the destruction of urban, suburban and village cores, and the piecemeal erosion of working rural landscapes (Lapping 1982).

At approximately the same time as the RPAA was working on regional plans for New York State and other jurisdictions, designing highways like the Taconic, which straddles the New York–Connecticut border country, and other housing projects, the seminal work of Howard Odum at the University of North Carolina at Chapel Hill was bringing renewed attention to the problem of rural community disintegration and regional backwardness, especially in the American South.

Odum and his colleagues, labeled the "Regionalists," advanced a progressive line of argument that attempted to understand in a more nuanced and robust way the nature of rural decay, dependency and poverty. As Freidman and Weaver (1980: 35) have observed, the regionalists "wanted to fend off the attack of northern industrialists and metropolitan culture on southern rural values; they wanted to alleviate agrarian poverty and racism" (also see Dorman 1993; Singal 1982). Odum and other reformers advocated land reforms to break the hold of tenancy and to favor small and family-owned farms, both black and white, a transformation in southern agriculture away from export and cash cropping systems, like "King Cotton" and peanuts, toward a more diversified food production model, the introduction of critically important physical infrastructure into rural places, the provision of new rural credit systems and other financial institutions, the conservation of marginal lands and forests, and the establishment of a broad system of co-operatives, amongst other programs and policies (Odum 1934). For our purposes here Odum's greatest contribution was in recognizing the integrity of rural places and rural people. He demanded that policy makers not take rural people for granted and that their problems were national in scope and required national attention so that individual rural regions might no longer be relegated to the periphery. Too many advocates of sprawl-busting fail to see what Odum so well understood. The anti-sprawl coalition sees rural areas that are witnessing sprawl as landscapes largely devoid of established communities, existing resource utilization patterns, and social and political arrangement. Nothing could be farther from the truth, then or now.

Together these antecedents bequeathed to today's movement several key insights. Among these are: a renewed focus on the problem of human scale in urban and regional development; an appreciation for the role that working rural landscape and green spaces play in terms of the containment of growth and sprawl; the critical nature of the land/transportation interface; an understanding of the pivotal role which the automobile – and the infrastructure and subsidy systems that have grown up to serve it – continue to play in fostering sprawl and the lack of alternative transportation modalities in community design; and how closely the Garden City notion conforms to the ideals of the New Urbanism movement (Rees 2004). As Robert Fishman has observed, "the Garden City is the locus classicus of the New Urbanist idea of the planned community that combines work and residence, housing for a wide range of incomes, and a town center with well-defined civic space – all at a walking scale, with easy access to parkland" (Fishman 1998: 128).

Together the contemporary movement and its antecedents have refocused attention on cities and the rural–urban fringes of such cities, perhaps the most contested landscape in America.

Forest fragmentation and parcelization

Approximately one of every three acres in the US is forest-covered and a large number of nonmetropolitan counties across the nation are defined by the USDA as being forestry-dependent for their economic base. States in northern New England and the Upper Midwest, as well as in the Pacific Northwest and the deep South, are among those where the forest resource provides livelihood and lifestyles to many. Planners, like many others, conceive forests as synonymous with wildlands in that they are seen as largely inaccessible rural areas where few people and fewer communities are located and the land is controlled either by large multinational corporations or governmental agencies at both the federal and state levels. This generalization overlooks the reality that many of the nation's expanding metropolitan regions also contain significant amounts of forest land, though here ownerships tend to be small and private in nature. While some of these areas can be rather substantial in size and contain the watersheds for major cities, such as the Catskills area for New York City (Pfeffer and Wagenet 1999), most are modest-to-small in the amount of acreage under ownership and are seldom managed for commercial production (Thompson and Jones 1981). Here the primary rationale for ownership is related to residential or recreational uses and habitat protection and aesthetics. Still numerous wood products firms exist in these areas and they are often the economic backbone of communities in the rural–urban fringe where largely unchecked sprawl continues to bring these places into the expanding metropolitan orbit and commuter-shed.

One of the land use results of sprawl is the piecemeal fragmentation and parcelization of the American forest. While very largely a manifestation of development pressures on exurban and suburban forests, fragmentation and parcelization also occur in more rural areas, especially those with a concentration of second homes and high amenity tourism-based economies (Egan and Luloff 2000; Rickenbach and Gobster 2003). Yet, the problem is primarily one of sprawl-induced land use change in the rural–urban fringe and sprawl is the fundamental change agent at work upon the landscape. Fragmentation occurs when large, contiguous pieces of forest are subdivided into a number of smaller parcels as new roads systems, private and public, make such lands accessible. This pattern of development generates a substantial number of environmental problems, such as the decrease in habitat and species diversity, increased surface runoff, flooding, and soil erosion, greater levels of air and water pollution, and the loss of many native plants and other vegetation. To this list we may now add sprawl's negative impact upon public health as a number of studies indicate that the rapid spread of lyme disease in suburban areas throughout the country is closely linked to the increase in forest fragmentation and parcelization (Society of American Foresters 2003). Curiously, in a recently published analysis of the environmental problems generated by sprawl, the loss of forestland is not specifically mentioned, while the loss of agricultural land is – though the externalities associated with forest fragmentation and parcelization are enumerated (Johnson 2001). Not only is the environmental integrity of forestland compromised by sprawl-induced changes in the landscape, but so are management practices, which speak to the long-term health and sustainability of the forest itself. Utilizing much of the best statistical analysis and data from ownership studies, Sampson and DeCoster predict that by 2010 some 150 million acres of forestland will be held in parcels of 100 acres or smaller, with the average individual ownership being 17 acres in total. While a considerable amount of this land will be in rural areas, much of it will be in what constitutes today's rural–urban fringe. What is most disconcerting to forest managers is the likelihood that the owners of these parcels will continue to be "less likely than their predecessors to participate in standard public forestry programs, largely because they see forestry as irrelevant to their landowning objectives and immediate concern" (Sampson and DeCoster 2000: 4). Hull and his colleagues go so far as to argue that "the rapidly increasing number of new owners of small parcels has the potential to change how forestry is practiced and understood" (Hull *et al.* 2004: 14).

The problems generated by fragmentation and parcelization, triggered as they are by sprawl and growth in the rural–urban fringe, have not gone unnoticed. In 2000 the US Forest Service's Urban Forestry Center in Portsmouth, NH, held a conference on the problem, that led to the publication of *Forest Fragmentation and Urbanization: Effects on Forests*, wherein all of the New England states presented the latest data on the magnitude and scale, as well as the causes and implications, of fragmentation. The data for this study were generated at the state level and this tended to mask local and community-level impacts. The problems generated by fragmentation and parcelization are far from unique to the Northeast. Indeed, a recent newspaper article outlined another US Forest Service study on these problems as they relate to the southeastern region of the country (Seelye 2001). And it would seem that every summer brings with it the travails of lives and property lost to forest fires in the Intermountain West where parcelization has substantially increased the number of homes and other facilities sited in arid forest fire-prone areas.

A case study indicates the degree to which sprawl-induced fragmentation and parcelization can affect local economies and society. In a recently released study, The Brookings Institution's Center for Urban and Metropolitan Policy listed the Portland, Maine region as one of the nation's most rapidly urbanizing areas (Fulton *et al.* 2001). Its pattern of development is typified by a high degree of sprawl, leap-frog land development, automobile dependency with an attendant lack of mass transportation options, a growing absence of affordable housing, and poor coordination of land use controls across the region.

Like many communities throughout this growing region, many outlying towns are coming within the commuter-shed of Portland. Moreover, both because of the lack of affordable housing in the city's inner suburbs, as well as in the city itself, those who seek reasonably priced housing range farther and farther from the urban core in search of lots and housing units that they can afford. A number of these outlying communities, whose traditional economic bases were tied to farming, forest products, small business and crafts, have become host to an ever growing number of commuters. The separation of work from residence has increased and sprawl has brought new housing, some service-industry employment, and a sustained level of land development and land use change. Parcelization and fragmentation of the forest is one of the consequences of this new geography. A 2002 newspaper article appearing in the *Maine Sunday Telegram* described what was occurring in the region's forests as "Threats to Timberland" (Bell 2002). The author of the article discussed how sprawl and the rapid suburbanization in the rural–urban fringe of Portland were threatening the very survival of forest products firms in the area. A case in point was Limington Lumber of Baldwin, Maine – located from 32 miles west of Portland – which was losing its high-quality eastern pine, the firm's mainstay, to parcelization. This particular business is the town of Baldwin's single largest employer and many of its employees are key to maintaining the town's civic culture in that they serve as volunteers for the local fire department, participate in local school activities, sit on town council, and serve the community in many other ways. Additionally, the firm and its workforce are generators of significant multipliers in the local and regional economies through their purchases and savings. Because of the loss of white pine timber the firm is now forced to roam ever farther from its home base to secure its needed raw product and its owner is worried about the long-term viability of his firm because local, high-quality eastern pine is becoming less available in stands that can be commercially harvested.

Another local firm, also dependent upon white pine – LaValley Lumber – grew so concerned about its future access to timber that it simply gave up and sold its 7,000 acres in southern Maine to a liquidator who subsequently logged the land and then subdivided most of it for house lots. To some extent this is akin to the type of liquidation sales witnessed through eastern and northern Maine. As the noted Maine forest economist Lloyd Irland has indicated, "the essence of liquidation is not stripping [the land]; it is parcel fragmentation" (Irland 2001: 7).

In these two cases, as well as in others, sprawl has been the impetus for forest fragmentation and parcelization. While the environmental and public health implications of these land use changes are profound, so are the community-level impacts. Hither-to-fore rural communities are rapidly changing into full-fledged suburbs and the local economic bases of these communities are changing from being resource-based into ones that reflect a transformation into bedroom communities where only the service sector is growing. Good jobs with benefits are being lost and are replaced by lower paying ones, often without an accompanying portfolio of benefits. And the social capital existing in the community is also eroding as the separation between work and residence becomes that much greater.

Brownfields redevelopment

The redevelopment of abandoned, contaminated and vacant properties is one of the mainstays of contemporary urban planning and policy, as Nancey Green Leigh has noted in a thoughtful paper. Of the various approaches to redevelopment none are as ubiquitous, so she has observed, as programs to clean up and restore brownfields. As she writes: "adopted by 48 states, brownfield voluntary cleanup programs are perhaps the most widespread of these approaches. While these programs vary in their overall effectiveness, they can be a successful tool for encouraging the redevelopment of con-taminated sites" (Leigh 2003: 7). Some of the most aggressive programs of this type are found in Pennsylvania, Michigan, Massachusetts and especially in New Jersey. All such programs aim to direct development onto brown-fields and away from greenfields, thus helping to promote a smart growth agenda.

Unlike vacant fields, brownfields are harmed lands and, by definition, "land and structures that are known to be contaminated or perceived to be contaminated that are underutilized or not used" (Greenberg et al. 2001a: 130). Remnants of America's great industrial and manufacturing age, there are literally hundreds of thousands of brownfield sites across the country. Most such sites are located in urban areas, especially the industrial zones and districts of older cities. However, they are also found in the mature suburbs surrounding these cities and even in small towns across the American land-scape (Greenberg *et al.* 2001b).

Slavesen, writing in the mid 1990s, noted that in addition to the 1,250 brownfield sites on the "national priority sites list" of the Environmental Protection Agency (EPA), there were perhaps as many as another 40,000 contaminated industrial and commercial sites located across the American landscape (Slavesen 1993). This number did not include the several million underground storage tanks for petroleum and hazardous wastes that the EPA estimates are leaking into underground water resources and the soil (Evans 1988). Even if these estimates are deemed excessive, it is still abundantly clear that an enormous amount of land in US cities is tied up in brownfields. Simons has estimated that between 5 to 10 percent of all urban land in the United States may be classified as brownfields with higher concentrations in the "rust belt" of the Northeast and the Midwest (Simons 1998). These lands pose significant environmental and public health problems, lead to further deterioration of other sites in proximity to them, and fail to generate revenue for hard-pressed and fiscally constrained cities and towns. They do not repre-sent a reservoir of new urban opportunity unless these sites are remediated and rehabilitated. If successfully renovated, these lands constitute the single largest pool of undeveloped urban land in the nation. As such they represent a unique opportunity for the purposes of urban economic development, new and potentially affordable housing, and urban open space.

Federal policy sought to address the problem of brownfields redevelop-ment through the 1980 Superfund program. Unfortunately, the program actually proved to be a disincentive for site rehabilitation because it left current and past landowners entirely liable for the consequences of any hazards on their lands (Yount and Meyer 1994). Over time and with the real-ization that the Superfund program was not working, policy evolved and led to implementation of EPA's Comprehensive Environmental Response Com-pensation Liability Information System. The latter provided a substantial number of communities throughout the country with funding to undertake studies and the remediation of specific sites (Van Horn *et al.* 2000). Import-antly, the outlay of these funds was initially targeted to many of the most economically distressed communities in the country and thus the sites so enu-merated have come to represent genuine opportunities for many of our most desperate communities (Solitare and Greenberg 2002).

This program addressed the single greatest obstacle – that of liability – standing in the way of brownfields redevelopment. As Greenberg and his col-leagues have noted, "these actions led States like New Jersey to change their liability laws so that new owners and lenders were not threatened with the responsibility for cleaning up contamination they had nothing to do with" (Greenberg *et al.* 2001a: 135). In Pennsylvania, as another example, this change in federal law led that state to adopt its own Land Recycling Act that, according to one analyst, "has returned 1,350 once-polluted properties to productive use across the Commonwealth, creating or saving about 300,000 jobs" (Hylton 2003: 1).

Not all brownfield sites can or should be redeveloped. Some sites exist in locations that are not economically viable in terms of transportation, infrastructure, accessibility or other factors. Others are odd-shaped or so small that their highest and best use might not be as the location of rateables but rather as pocket parks or in some other open space uses – which can still add enormous value to a community. And then some sites are so polluted and dangerous that renovation is too costly, even under the very best of circumstances. One must add to this the fact that the thorough evaluation of a brownfield site, together with the cost of rehabilitation, may simply be prohibitive for either or both the private and public sectors. A survey of over 100 sites in New Jersey carried out by the National Center for Neighborhood and Brownfields Redevelopment at Rutgers University, found that approximately one half of the sites identified could not be developed for one reason or another (Lowrie *et al.* 2002).

While most communities seek to renovate such sites for economic development purposes, the need for housing, especially affordable housing, is so intense that many see brownfields as prime locations for new residential development and growth. Using such sites for housing raises some substantial issues, however. Greenberg (2002), perhaps the nation's most authoritative student of the brownfields issue, notes three reasons why housing on such sites is desirable. These are: brownfields constitute a ready supply of available land for public purposes; brownfields may be the only supply of buildable land in a community; and building housing on such sites not only addresses an important environmental problem but also improves communities by halting the physical decay of neighborhoods and areas. To this he also lists a number of drawbacks to housing development. These include: developers' reluctance to absorb the full costs of rehabilitation; concerns over the reliability of site clean-ups and site rehabilitation; and the on-going threat of toxic-tort legal cases. On balance he makes the argument that communities and developers should build housing on such sites but that prudence, collaboration between the public and private sectors, tax policies that reward risk-taking and substantial citizen participation in the redevelopment process are essential to creating any successful project (Greenberg 2002).

The social costs of not rehabilitating brownfield sites for new development are substantial. As Page and Rabinowitz point out,

> there are serious problems of unemployment and poverty concentrated in the same urban areas that contain contaminated sites. These sites attract a large set of interrelated socioeconomic problems. On the other hand, these sites are often located in the midst of a trained workforce, transportation services, utilities, and other infrastructures that support redevelopment.
>
> (Page and Rabinowitz 1994: 361)

The case has been made by many that an aggressive program of brownfield rehabilitation and redevelopment, facilitated by subsidies, partnerships between the public and private sectors, tax policy reform and liability limitations, will aid in the control of sprawl. By freeing up significant numbers of properties for redevelopment, so the logic goes, growth will refocus itself back into central cities and mature suburbs rather than in the rural–urban fringe (Greenberg *et al.* 2001a). The opposite is just as likely to be the case, however. It has been argued that if smart growth strategies and anti-sprawl measures take hold across the country, only then will the rehabilitation of urban sites become feasible and attractive. This ought not to be a "chicken or egg" policy debate, however. Rather, the real answer is to pursue both approaches simultaneously and in tandem as part-and-parcel of an integrated policy thrust that deploys resources and strategies to control sprawl and doing what is necessary to spur the rehabilitation and redevelopment of brownfields. Only then will society realize a safer and healthier environment, the protection of open space and working rural landscapes, new productive land uses in older urban centers, and a reduction in the social costs that reflect the current situation of sprawl into the countryside and areas of urban decay and blight.

Exurban places

Traditionally planners have paid little attention to rural areas. With its chronic poverty and out-migration, poor quality housing and inadequate infrastructure, and a lack of educational and other human services, rural areas were often considered peripheral to national development and hence were subject to neglect, except for some important large-scale regional economic development efforts, such as the Tennessee Valley Authority (TVA) and the Appalachian Regional Commission (Lapping 2004). This neglect was easily rationalized in a profession with a strong urban bias. In truth, agriculture and resource-based industries have always been critically important to national economic growth and development and these sectors have long kept the nation's trade imbalance at least in sight.

With the growth of interest in farmland preservation and the rise of the environmental movement in the 1970s and 1980s, things began to change and the attention of many planners came to focus on rural and even wildlands problems. Often the impetus for this change lay in new patterns of urban consumption, as in the cases of the growth in tourism and recreation, wilderness and habitat preservation, and second-home development. In other instances urbanites came to appreciate that the environmental integrity of rural areas plays an increasingly important role in the overall quality of life of cities through the provision of relatively cheap, abundant and reliable foods, clean water from rural watersheds, and sinks for the sequestration of carbon dioxide and other greenhouse gases (Wolff and Carter 2002). The anti-sprawl movement has continued this trend by focusing considerable attention on the preservation of working rural landscapes – the greenfields – which continue to be threatened by the lack of effective growth management programs and urban redevelopment, poor regional cooperation among governments, and the lack of plan coordination. Additionally, the anti-sprawl movement has been a catalyst for a "new regionalism" that sees cities, suburbs and the countryside as inseparable and highly connected.

As positive a development as this is, it would be a mistake to see rural problems as all being of one type, as some do. Indeed, the preservation of farmland may well be a rural–urban fringe issue with economic viability constituting a far greater concern for farmers in large agricultural regions and "deep" rural places. Right-to-farm problems, endemic in communities where sprawl and development have come into conflict with commercial agriculture, are also essentially a rural–urban fringe issue (Lapping and Leutweiler 1988; Lapping *et al.* 1985). And while long-term economic viability continues to be a genuine problem and concern in all places where farming is a significant economic activity, metropolitan agriculture is substantially idiosyncratic and different from agriculture in well-established farming regions. So are the problems it faces (Pfeffer and Lapping 1995).

If the preservation of greenfields, and especially farmland, is the single most apparent and visible way that the anti-sprawl coalition understands and conceptualizes rural land issues, it is not the only case wherein the impact of sprawl on rural lands is significant and substantial. Increasingly, attention is coming to be focused on the rather large rural places facing the seemingly inexorable tide of sprawl.

The Pocono Mountains region of northeastern Pennsylvania, as an example, has witnessed stunning rates of growth and development over the past decade or so. Long known as a resort area, a honeymoon haven, and more recently as a second-home area, the region is increasingly the site of sprawling housing developments, mini-malls and scattered small commercial and industrial sites. Development has been triggered by the search for affordable housing and a "place in the country." This has led large numbers of people who work in the New York City metropolitan region to settle in the area, even in the face of a two-hour commute each way. Developers in the Poconos extol the serenity and peace-and-quiet of the area, especially in contrast to life in New York and Philadelphia. One developer routinely distributes thousands of videos that feature shootings, gang warfare, drug use and such – all purported urban vices – throughout the larger region to make its point that life in the Poconos is better for "the kids" (Birkback 2001). Led by the Brandywine Conservancy and local leadership, including several developers, a plan to deal with sprawl in the region has been devised. The plan lays out a strategy that will employ the transfer of development rights (TDR) technique to preserve rural lands, and local townships will be encouraged to reduce lot size requirements and provide appropriate infrastructure and services so that developers can build on less land, thus stemming some of the pressure that encourages sprawling (Applegate 2002).

A similar but older attempt at curbing sprawl has been in evidence in the Pinelands of southern New Jersey through a unique federal/state/local partnership to protect the unique aquifer that underlies the region, while allowing controlled growth and development (Mason 2004). Local governments, the states and residents of the large Sterling Forest Preserve, on the border of New Jersey and New York, as well as the Highlands region of northwestern New Jersey, are likewise seeking to control growth and avoid sprawl development while not forcing landowners to relinquish their fundamental property rights.

Conclusion

The previous cases suggest that sprawl has, to some large degree, refocused the attention of planners and policy makers on the region as the appropriate scale for analysis and new policy initiatives. Demand for land for those seeking affordable housing and rural amenities are the catalysts for forest fragmentation. Brownfields will be renovated and redeveloped to provide cities and older suburbs with new land when the costs of sprawl development – social, environmental, political and otherwise – on greenfields becomes prohibitive. And exurban places will receive greater levels of protection as it becomes apparent that the integrity of these places, and the communities and people within them, are crucial to the cities and suburbs that they surround. Too many presently see these large rural areas near cities, often the exurban portion of metropolitan areas, as something of a "tabula rasa," a landscape essentially devoid of people and communities, wealth-creating activities, and the environmental resources crucial to maintaining everyday life and to sustaining the future. Perhaps sprawl-busting will usher in the long hoped-for reform of the fragmented system of governance that typifies most of the country's metropolitan regions.

As this short essay suggests, the anti-sprawl/smart growth/New Urbanism movement that has become such a defining element of the planning landscape, is not really about a new set of problems. The subtext of sprawl has really been with us for a considerable period of time. It has a long legacy in the history of planning, one that continues to serve us well by understanding the point that land and how it is used remain the *axias mundi* of so many of our problems and debates.

18 The smart growth approach to urban land use

Implications for farmland protection

Alvin D. Sokolow

What is not to like about smart growth? It was a felicitous choice in the 1990s to coin this metaphor,[1] an expression that has brought much public visibility to efforts to change the ways in which urbanization occurs in the United States. (Are there any alternatives? Who could support "dumb" growth?) The metaphor may be new, but the specific techniques it encompasses – compact growth, urban density and in-fill, neighborhood improvement, open space protection, etc. – have long been in the planning and journalistic lexicon. However, they lacked the resonance of urgency and popular use until governors, mayors, a vice president, and other public figures began to promote the smart growth idea in the last few years.

What is new about the concept is how it brings together the multiple limitations that characterize American urban land use planning (or the lack thereof) of the past 50 years and the multiple policy methods for changing these conditions. The smart growth literature highlights the interdependencies of both problems and solutions. Some of these penetrate geographical borders, especially the connections between inner city and older suburb deterioration, and the fragmentation of rural landscapes, including agricultural land. As many writers in the smart growth vein highlight, urban neighborhood problems generate rural area problems (EcoCity Cleveland 1996; Orfield 1997; Smart Growth America 2001). Other interdependencies are more functional, linking physical, social and economic concerns. At the heart of all of this is the issue of land use efficiency – or the difference between low–density sprawl and high–density compact development.

This chapter contains both synthesis and specific analysis. We first summarize the conventional wisdom about sprawl and the smart growth prescriptions for dealing with inefficient land use patterns, paying particular attention to issues of implementation. We then turn to the role of farmland protection in the smart growth agenda, emphasizing the mix of compensatory and regulatory policies.

The sprawl problem

While the country has experienced extraordinary population growth in the decades since World War II, the central issue in much of the smart growth literature is not the numbers of persons added but how they are located on the land (Calthorpe and Fulton 2001: 67; Chen 2000: 88). One way of measuring the smart growth dimensions of urban development is to track the efficiency with which rural lands are turned into houses and other urban uses – the consumption of land in relation to persons housed. Such efficiencies have decreased greatly in the past 50 years, in terms both of development densities and the location of new urban uses. Put simply, sprawl is shorthand for referring to relatively low urban densities and a less compact and more scattered placement of new residences, stores, and factories. The following are striking illustrations of decreasing efficiencies (see also Barnard 2004, chapter 4 this volume):

- Population density in the nation's urbanized areas in 1950–2000 dropped from 8.4 to 4.1 persons per acre (Heimlich and Anderson 2001: 19).
- Of all new homes built in 1994–1997, nonfarm homes (most on sites of one acre or larger) constructed in rural areas consumed 80 percent of all built-on acreage, while urban homes (generally on much smaller sites) took up 15 percent and farm homes 5 percent of total acreage (Heimlich and Anderson 2001: 14).
- For a number of metro areas in the past few decades, the percentage increases in land devoted to urban use have far exceeded the percentage increases in population. For example, land used for housing in the Chicago metro area increased by 46 percent in 1970–1990, while the region's population grew by only 4 percent (Sorensen and Esseks 1998: 2). Even more startling, residential development in the five county region around Cleveland between 1980–2010 is expected to occupy 30 percent more land while the region's population *decreases* by about 3 percent (EcoCity Cleveland 1996: 9).

As an example of how a large population can be accommodated on a relatively small amount of land with better planning, the EcoCity report notes that all 2.1 million residents of the Cleveland region could fit into the borders of just the central county, if the reasonable density of 4,900 persons per square mile (7.6 persons or less than two houses per acre) found in the suburban city of Shaker Heights were applied to all five counties in the region (EcoCity Cleveland 1996: 9).

Outmigration combined with homeowner preferences is the major force behind these inefficient land use patterns. People leave inner-city neighborhoods and older suburbs for larger homesites in rural areas, lowering residential densities and steadily pushing out development in particular metro regions. These shifts in turn produce a variety of physical, social and economic problems, demonstrating the sprawl–related connections between the depopulation of urban neighborhoods and the fragmentation of rural landscapes. A short list of such problems, culled from a number of sources, includes traffic congestion, urban neighborhood deterioration, limited housing choices for low- and moderate-income families, water and air pollution in the countryside, and the loss of farmland and other rural spaces. A number of studies document the various fiscal, social and environmental costs that are generated by sprawl (Clarion Associates 2000; Sorensen and Esseks 1998; Wassmer 2001). Included are tax subsidies to serve residential development in fringe areas, increased traffic congestion and longer home–job commutes, increased response times for emergency services, environmental deterioration, and higher housing costs.

Smart growth prescriptions

Considering the broad and loose nature of the concept, there is no standard definition of smart growth as a set of prescriptions for urban growth. But different definitions have in common the use of multiple strategies targeted on cities, suburbs, and rural areas:

> Smart growth principles favor investing in central cities and older suburbs, supporting mass transit and pedestrian friendly development, and encouraging mixed use development while conserving open space, rural amenities, and environmentally sensitive resources.
>
> (Heimlich and Anderson 2001: 56)

> We define smart growth as growth that protects open space, revitalizes neighborhoods, makes housing more affordable, and improves community quality of life.
>
> (Smart Growth America 2001: 1)

> Smart growth is intelligent, well-planned development that channels growth into existing areas, provides public transportation options, and preserves farmland and open space.
>
> (Sierra Club 2000: 2)

Table 18.1 lists some of the numerous specific strategies included in the smart growth concept, as culled from the several sources consulted for this chapter. They represent three different dimensions in terms of scale and process. First and most local in scale, there are the design and other strategies that focus on the livability of individual urban neighborhoods. Second, there are policies and tools that affect whole communities or cut across community boundaries and deal with the specifics of planning and land use regulation, transportation, housing and open space preservation. Third and most explicitly regional in nature, there are strategies oriented to the regional processes of intercommunity cooperation and resource sharing.

Table 18.1 A short list of smart growth strategies by geographical scope

Neighborhood design	Growth management
Narrow streets	Designated growth areas
Minimal building setbacks	Designated open space preserve areas
Rear garages	Urban growth boundaries
Energy efficient buildings	Urban in-fill
Mixed use zoning and building codes	High-density development
Pedestrian-oriented streets	Brownfield redevelopment
Access to public transit	Integrate transportation investment and
Attractive public spaces	land use planning
Affordable housing options	Jobs–housing proximity
	Reuse of old industrial and commercial
Regional processes	parcels
Interjurisdictional cooperation	Impact fees for new development
Tax sharing and redistribution	Limit public improvements in rural areas –
Shift public resources from outer areas	roads, water, sewers, etc.
to urban neighborhoods and inner	
suburbs	

Source: Author's review of smart growth literature.

Neighborhood design

Frequently identified with the New Urbanism school of urban planning, these strategies in large part are a reaction to the layout and auto dependence of traditional suburbs. They seek to create close-knit and compact neighborhoods with a sense of "community" and where residents can interact in a pedestrian and environmentally friendly manner. The emphasis is on sidewalks, narrow streets, traffic slowing, attractive public spaces, town centers, mixed-use neighborhoods, housing diversity, jobs near residences, and local connections to public transit. Even the design of individual homesites is included in this approach, with such features as narrow lots, minimal building setbacks, rear-facing garages, and residential energy efficiency.

As a formal set of principles, the New Urbanism originated at the 1991 Ahwahnee (Yosemite) conference of planners and environmentalists. Bill Fulton, a California-based editor and journalist who writes widely about urban planning matters, also traces the origins of these principles – sometimes described as "neotraditional" – to the City Beautiful and Garden City movements of the early twentieth century that sought to integrate open space with urban development (Fulton 1996).

To critics, some of these design prescriptions are on the picturesque side and lead to artificial neighborhoods, a misguided effort to recreate the look and feel of small-town America of 80–100 years ago (Duany 2000). Neighborhood design strategies, however, have an important role in the overall smart growth agenda in conjunction with other, geographically broader strategies. This point is made in a recent report of the Sierra Club that identifies examples of exemplary and poor urban planning in each of the 50 states. At least one example of a well-designed project, a new town in Idaho, is found wanting in smart growth principles because of its massive scale, location in a river bed some miles from the closest urban area, and lack of access to public transportation and jobs (Sierra Club 2000: 13).

Growth management and related policies

Beyond the neighborhood scale, smart growth strategies emphasize the public policies that control land use patterns and the character of communities. The central goal is to explicitly direct new urban growth to certain areas and away from other areas (Gurwitt 1998). The two interrelated parts of this goal are to: (1) add residential and other kinds of development to older urban areas, to help revitalize neighborhoods and downtowns and take advantage of existing public infrastructure; and (2) preserve the rural landscape – farmland, natural resource lands and other rural spaces – and thus limit sprawl and avoid higher public sector costs. This approach depends largely on how local governments use their powers to regulate and spend on land use and development, in the extent to which they make use of such techniques as comprehensive planning, zoning, growth boundaries, urban in-fill, density requirements and requiring new development to pay its full costs for public infrastructure through impact and connection fees.

The smart growth menu also includes a range of other strategies related to and affected by land use policies, especially access to public transportation, the supply of affordable housing, and the distribution of employment opportunities. As well as dealing with physical land patterns, these policies address the social and economic inequities that exist in a region because of how urban development has occurred over time (EcoCity Cleveland 1996). Communities and neighborhoods in most metro regions vary widely in levels of poverty and affluence, crime, housing conditions, quality of public services and public revenue base. Sprawl and inequity are closely related, according to the authors of *The Regional City*. "On a regional level, sprawl exacerbates inequity and growing inequity, in turn, begets more sprawl" (Calthorpe and Fulton 2001: 11).

Regional processes

An essential part of the smart growth agenda is the promotion of regional cooperation and solutions. Interconnected problems that cut across local boundaries demand interconnected and geographically comprehensive answers, an elementary observation made by numerous commentators over the years. As presented by smart growth advocates, the regional approach contains two sets of strategies. One is seemingly mild and inoffensive, the other is ridden with controversy.

First is the obvious call for greater cooperation and coordination among the separate communities of a region – hardly a new concept. Regions in the United States, especially those classified as metro because of dense urban cores, have a long and complex history of efforts to overcome the fragmentation created by community boundaries and local government fiefdoms. Metro government has been promoted for particular regions since the 1930s, and after World War II received a boost from Federal government through planning grants and from state governments in enabling legislation. While weak planning agencies and councils of government were easily created, proposals for more comprehensive and powerful metro governments were rejected by voters in all but a few regions, notably Miami, Nashville and Indianapolis. Still, limited forms of regional government exist in virtually all metro areas – usually special authorities or districts that provide single functions that clearly are beyond the capacity of individual local governments, such as sewage disposal, water supply, airports, community colleges and regional parks. But the key regulatory functions, especially control over growth and land use, and basic services like police and fire protection, are still jealously handled by individual municipal and county governments.

Creating new layers of government is not part of the smart growth agenda, which instead appears to emphasize less ambitious and more voluntary forms of regional cooperation that make use of existing institutions and political leadership (Calthorpe and Fulton 2001: 61–62; Heimlich and Anderson 2001: 57; Katz and Bradley 1999). Included are multi-jurisdictional planning efforts among adjacent communities, transportation coordination and informal intergovernmental forums to deliberate about particular issues.

Much more controversial are the second set of regional strategies, proposals to establish the sharing of property or sales tax revenues among separate local governments. They have important redistributive consequences and they impinge on local revenue authority and discretion. Calthorpe and Fulton see interjurisdictional tax sharing as essential to creating a truly regional framework for joint activity by reducing large gaps in community tax bases, compensating for the imbalance in housing and jobs, reducing the local incentive to make land use policies according to their revenue consequences, reducing the negative externalities of urban growth and stimulating other modes of cooperation.

> The tax system is set up on the assumption that each jurisdiction is self-contained, requiring – and having – its own healthy mix of housing, stores, offices, factories, and other land uses. In this ideal situation, each jurisdiction would receive a healthy balance of tax revenues needed to support the community.
>
> But in the typical region, things don't work this way. Housing, shopping, and labor markets operate at a larger level – usually a 10–30 mile radius – that almost always transcends municipal boundaries. Thus, the activities that generate tax revenue – and the social and economic need

for public revenues – have little geographical relation to the distribution of those taxes among local governments that provide the public services.

(Calthorpe and Fulton 2001: 84)

The model for tax sharing is the arrangement in the Minneapolis–St Paul region in Minnesota, where under state legislation the cities and counties of the multi-county area since the 1970s have shared according to population a part of the annual increase in local property taxes. As a result, tax revenue ratios between the richest and poorest jurisdictions have dropped from 50:1 to 12:1 (Orfield 1997: 86). Although widely touted in planning and urban policy circles, the Twin Cities model or any other systematic sharing arrangement has not been adopted elsewhere. Less comprehensive plans, however, sometimes are voluntarily negotiated by local governments in particular areas, often in connection with the costs or revenue shifts of municipal annexations or development projects.

Implementation: obstacles and achievements

As is often noted, the "devil is in the detail." The detail in the case of the smart growth agenda involves the translation into practice of the numerous, well thought-out ideas for changing established patterns of urban growth in the United States. Because it requires major adjustments in longstanding institutional and personal behavior, implementing the full scope of smart growth strategies, or even a few of them, is a much more difficult task than the development of these ideas in the first place.

One inherent obstacle is the decentralized nature of the planning and urban growth management process in the United States. There are thousands of community-level decision points in the nation, represented by the governing boards and planning bodies of cities, counties and towns, where authority is exercised over urban growth matters. Many are conservative in nature and unwilling to revise existing practices, especially if this means the use of regulatory powers. And many local decision makers may not be convinced or even aware of the seriousness of the land use problem that the smart growth agenda takes for granted. Invoking the principle of local control is often the rationale local government officials use to resist policy and organizational change, as suggested above in the discussion about the difficulty of getting communities to share tax revenues in a region.

The prospects of achieving more compact and dense development in existing urban areas suggest another obstacle. Are large numbers of American homebuyers ready to accept smaller single-family homesites in compact neighborhoods? Since World War II, the housing preferences for families who can afford to choose have been for large lots in suburban communities or the rural countryside – one of the major driving forces of sprawl. Up to now, builders and local governments have been only too pleased to accommodate these preferences. Some smart growth advocates suggest that these trends are reversible, with attractive development, neighborhood amenities and reduced transportation costs. The key step is to get home builders and local governments to offer alternatives to conventional suburban housing (Calthorpe and Fulton 2001: 272–273; Chen 2000: 87; EcoCity Cleveland 1996: 5; Sierra Club 2000: 6).

In fact, change is ongoing regarding how particular communities and regions handle urban growth – although not as widespread nor as comprehensive as called for by the smart growth agenda. Increasingly, communities in suburban and rural areas experience a great deal of political ferment around growth issues, often producing election upsets and shifts in policy. The demands for change in existing land use policies are more likely to come from outside than inside local government, from business leaders interested in more predictable and rational land use decisions (Calthorpe and Fulton 2001: 62) and from homeowner–environmental coalitions with slow growth desires. Many communities throughout the nation have reputations for policy innovations in this area, including programs to require new urban development to pay its full costs for infrastructure, urban growth boundaries, affordable housing requirements, and building codes that address energy efficiency.

Two substantial signs of local innovations are the inventory of exemplary 1990s urban development projects in each state reported by the Sierra Club (2000) and the growing support for spending on open space protection and other smart growth measures by voters in recent elections in many communities (Smart Growth America 2001: 2).

Other sources of innovation in urban growth policy are external to the community, particularly the actions of certain state governments. As is the pattern among local governments, the distribution of significant policy changes is very uneven, with a few states leading the field in recent decades with new programs while most have been inactive. Since local governments owe their existence and powers to state constitutions and legislation, state governments can impose mandates of various kinds on the local agencies. But the states can also provide fiscal and other incentives for cities and counties, establish a planning vision for an entire state or particular regions, and change the programs of state agencies such as road departments that affect local land use patterns. All of these types of actions have been employed at the state level to redirect local policies. State governments in Maryland, Oregon, Washington, New Jersey and Florida are most often cited as having adopted smart growth-type policies, starting with Oregon's legislation in 1973 that required cities to adopt urban growth boundaries and counties to establish protective zoning for agricultural and forest lands (Calthorpe and Fulton 2001: 185–192; Heimlich and Anderson 2001: 56–57; Ndubisi and Dyer 1992; Thompson 2001: 6). Most recently, Maryland's Smart Growth and Neighborhood Conservation program, enacted in 1997, directs state infrastructure spending into existing urban areas. Under the Rural Legacy initiative, state funds are also devoted to conservation of farm and other open space lands (Calthorpe and Fulton 2001: 189–190).

Farmland and smart growth

Where does farmland fit in the smart growth agenda? Protecting farmland and directing urban growth elsewhere within a region obviously is one of the strategies for cutting back on sprawl and increasing land use efficiency. Thompson's recent essay on the sustainability of agriculture in urban regions succinctly makes the case for linking farmland to regional land use and urban neighborhood concerns:

> Farmland contributes to smart growth and the livability of our communities. Farms and farmland are valued as scenic landscapes and a part of our heritage. They demand fewer services and, therefore, cost taxpayers less than sprawling subdivisions. If protected as part of the "green infrastructure" around metropolitan areas, they can help guide suburban growth and promote urban revitalization.
>
> (Thompson 2001: 2)

Most other commentators in the smart growth genre, however, are much less explicit about the specific role of farmland in regional growth patterns. In most accounts farmland is barely mentioned, and then as merely another form of open or green space along with habitat and other rural lands. Little attention is paid to the character of farmland as a working landscape with economic as well as scenic value, and hence quite distinctive and requiring different kinds of protective measures than other rural lands valued for their natural resource attributes. The productivity of farmland as a source of food, jobs and other economic activity could give smart growth advocates another important reason besides open and green space considerations for protecting large parts of the rural landscape in the face of extensive urbanization.

In fact, much of American agriculture is found in the midst or on the fringes of heavily urbanized areas, a condition termed "urban influenced" by United States Department of Agriculture (USDA) researchers and agricultural economists (Heimlich and Anderson 2001: 5). This is both an asset and a liability for farming in such situations. On the one hand, close proximity to urban populations gives farmers direct access to large markets and sources of off-farm income. On the other hand, urban neighbors often create problems for commercial agricultural operations, reducing productivity and raising costs because of vandalism, pilferage of farm products, safety issues with chemical use, traffic on rural roads, and complaints about farm operations. Of course, the negative impacts run in both directions in agricultural–urban edge locations, with farm operations creating dust, chemical spray, noise and other problems for urban neighbors. Given the increasingly industrial nature of farming and the nonfarm roots of growing numbers of rural residents, commercial agricultural and adjacent residences in current times are essentially incompatible land uses.

Reducing or preventing these land use incompatibilities is an overlooked objective, but it clearly fits the smart growth agenda. To the view of farmland as serving the broader regional agenda, it adds a reverse emphasis on farmland and agricultural operations as a resource to be protected by other smart growth policies and tools (Thompson 2001: 2). So any strategies that lead to more efficient and compact land use – including attractive urban neighbor-hoods, higher development densities and in-fill, and redirecting infrastructure to existing built-up areas – get at the urban sources of population pressures on farmland. A critical part of this equation is to recognize two kinds of resi-dential growth or other forms of urbanization that encroach on agriculture (Heimlich and Anderson 2001: 17–18). One proceeds incrementally from existing urban cores and the other produces a more scattered pattern of homes in a rural area. The first is likely to involve relatively compact subdivi-sions with high densities, and the second is likely to consistent of small resi-dential clusters or isolated homes on large lots. While incremental urbanization typically houses larger populations, scattered growth is a less effi-cient use of land and one that fragments the agricultural landscape. While the first type of development produces relatively solid agricultural edges, the second creates numerous small exposures between residences and farming and thus presents more extensive risks and problems for agriculture in a given area. Many communities still regard scattered rural residences as a benign use of the countryside that blends with agriculture, because of the small popula-tions involved, large lots, and semi-agricultural appearance of raising a few animals and growing some vegetables.

One clear advantage in being associated with the smart growth agenda is the greater visibility and public support this gives to efforts to protect farmland. In effect, advocates of farmland protection are able to piggyback their cause on top of the broader movement to combat sprawl, drawing support from urbanites, environmentalists and business leaders. Funding for easement programs and other farmland protection techniques benefits from this association, since farmland has been included in the open space and conservation measures on state and local ballots approved by voters in recent years. However, as Thompson notes, spending on farmland projects generally constitutes very small shares of these programs that place much more emphasis on habitat, recreational and water conservation purposes (Thompson 2001: 6).

Friendly and not so friendly policies in farmland protection

The smart growth argument, with its interconnections among multiple strat-egies, offers at least indirectly a lesson or two for the farmland protection area. To the extent that it concentrates on urban and regional planning and land use techniques for redirecting urban development, the smart growth agenda strongly supports regulatory as well as more voluntary policies. Limit-ing new development to designated urban areas while preserving large chunks of rural land, higher development densities, strict zoning, and urban growth boundaries all restrict options for landowners, developers and home-buyers.

By contrast, the most popular and widely discussed techniques for farm-land protection are largely voluntary and compensatory in nature. They provide fiscal and other incentives for keeping farms in production and holding off urban conversion and programs for supporting agricultural opera-tions impacted by urbanization. Among these landowner-friendly tools are preferential property taxation for farmland, compensating landowners for giving up their development rights and accepting perpetual easements, participation in agricultural districts, right-to-farm laws, and protection from municipal improvement fees. Because they offer economic and other benefits and make few demands on landowners, thus avoiding the conflicts of prop-erty rights concerns, these measures are much more politically palatable in agricultural and other circles than the regulations of zoning, growth bound-aries, and other development restrictions. Spending public funds to save agri-cultural land or declaring farming a protected species are more easily accomplished in US communities, even those with popular anti-tax senti-ments, than trying to restrict landowner options.

Yet the friendly policies are essentially responses to current issues and largely ignore the urban roots of the farmland problem. That problem has two dimensions: (1) urban conversion of farmland, and (2) the edge circum-stances of urban-impacted farm operations. Policies like districts, right-to-farm ordinances and preferential property taxation are useful and probably effective in responding to existing edge issues, by telling urban neighbors about the value of local agriculture and supporting in other ways the viability of impacted farming. But they do little to head off the arrival of new residents and the inefficient land uses that harm agriculture. They do not reduce the rate or direction of farmland conversion nor do they seek to lower the future intensity of edge issues. To accomplish these objectives means using planning and regulatory policies to influence the location and density of urban growth and prevent development in agricultural areas.

Following up on this distinction, Table 18.2 lists a number of farmland protection policies and tools as either reactive or proactive in emphasis, focused either on protecting agriculture in current situations or looking to direct the future pattern of urban growth. Reactive policies largely include voluntary and compensatory measures; proactive policies are primarily plan-ning and regulatory tools.

Effective farmland protection, as Thompson (2001: 7–8) and others have argued, requires both kinds of policies. This is evident in the burgeoning use of agricultural easements to remove the development possibilities from farm-land. Easement programs work best when combined with land use planning and regulation, so that parcels under easement are strategically located to protect larger blocks of farmland and influence the direction of urban growth. Without such policy connections, easement programs have limited

Table 18.2 Reactive and proactive policies for farmland protection

Reactive policies (mostly voluntary and compensatory)	Proactive policies (mostly planning and regulatory)
Preferential taxation for farmland	Comprehensive general plans
Right-to-farm ordinances	Agricultural zoning
Agricultural districts	Limit rural residential development
Exclude farmland from municipal improvement fee	Designated urban growth areas Review agricultural impacts of proposed
Agricultural buffers	development projects
Cluster zoning	Urban growth boundaries
Mediation for edge conflicts	Municipal boundary controls
Perpetual easements on farmland[a]	Higher development density
	Urban in-fill
	Perpetual easements on farmland[a]

Source: Sokolow (2002).

Note

a Easements are proactive or reactive, depending on whether or not they are linked with land use planning and regulations.

geographical impact as their parcels are easily isolated and flanked by future urban growth.

The important lesson for farmland protection efforts derived from this review of the smart growth field is that the job of achieving more efficient land use and conserving land resources requires multiple and integrated policies.

Conclusion

Introduced in the 1990s, the smart growth concept generated a new public interest in local and regional growth management strategies in the United States. The popular phrase, "smart growth," signaled a new sense of urgency for dealing with sprawl – inefficient urbanization – by highlighting multiple policy solutions and techniques. The solutions are highly interdependent, linking distinct geographical areas (inner cities, older suburbs, newer suburbs, remote rural areas) in given regions. They also link a range of physical, social and economic concerns. The prescriptions include neighborhood design innovations, preservation of rural landscapes, access to public transportation, and revenue sharing and other forms of regional collaboration.

Despite the seeming popularity of these strategies, their implementation is slowed by the decentralized character of urban growth management and the strong preferences of homebuyers for homes on large lots in the countryside. Some state governments have tackled the problem by providing fiscal and other incentives for smart growth actions at the local levels.

Protecting farmland is an accepted smart growth strategy that fits the intention to reduce residential sprawl. But the value of farmland as a working landscape composed of active agricultural operations, as compared to its more generic benefits as another form of open space, is generally overlooked. A central distinction in farmland protection efforts is between land use regulatory controls and the more landowner-friendly measures of voluntary participation in compensatory programs. Farmland protection and its contribution to the smart growth agenda are enhanced by combining both approaches.

Note

1 The invention of the "smart growth" term is attributed to Governor Parris Glendening of Maryland to describe his legislative proposal in 1997 for a new state growth management program (Calthorpe and Fulton 2001: 189).

19 Protecting farmland

Why do we do it? How do we do it? Can we do it better?

Lori Lynch

Protecting farmland

Many Americans consider the loss of farmland, especially in the coastal states, to be one of the most significant land use problems. Since 1950, the nation and the Mid-Atlantic region in particular have seen substantial reductions in farmland acreage (Gardner 2002).[1] From 1950 to 1997, the United States experienced a 20 percent decrease in the amount of land in farms; the six states of the Mid-Atlantic region (Delaware, Maryland, New Jersey, New York, Pennsylvania and Virginia) experienced a 50 percent decrease (Figure 19.1). Between 1949 and 1974, the loss in the Mid-Atlantic region averaged

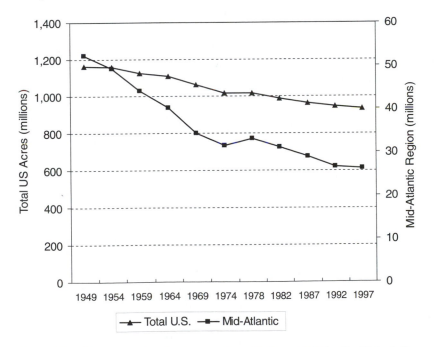

Figure 19.1 Changes in farmland acres from 1949 to 1997 in the United States and Mid-Atlantic regions (source: Carpenter and Lynch 2002).

800,000 acres per year. Concern about the loss of farmland resulted in the advocacy, beginning in the mid 1950s, of farmland protection programs to control the loss. As a result of these programs and for other reasons as well, the rate of farmland conversion to other uses has decreased.

Even though the rate of loss in the Mid-Atlantic region has decreased since the early 1970s, the Maryland Office of Planning predicts that if current trends continue, 500,000 more acres of farms, forests and other open space in the region will be converted to development over the next 25 years (*Bay Journal* 1997). Population growth and an increasingly high land consumptive development pattern are two culprits of this on-going conversion. In the Washington, DC metropolitan area, for example, the rate at which land is being consumed exceeds the population growth rate by almost 2.5 times. Growth is expected to consume more land for developed uses over the next 20 years than all the land used for development purposes in the Chesapeake watershed over the past 200 years (Chesapeake Bay Foundation 2000, 2002). Similar predictions are being made for other regions such as California, Florida and the Northeast. If society wishes to protect farmland, additional action from already implemented programs may be necessary. Policy intervention can encompass two approaches – to protect farmland from conversion and/or to redirect the desirability of development to non-rural areas. This chapter provides an overview of some of the issues regarding farmland protection.

The chapter begins by asking whether society should attempt to retain farmland. If society determines that it will benefit from farmland retention, then it needs to determine why farmland is being lost. Some factors affecting farmland loss are explored. Given these factors, what would a farmland preservation strategy have to prioritize? A range of mechanisms that can be used to prevent farmland conversion are presented. An evaluation of these techniques' effectiveness in achieving certain goals is provided. Other germane issues, such as how much land should be retained to preserve a viable agricultural sector, who will be able to buy preserved farms in the future, and how preservation itself may be changing the farmland protection equation, are discussed. Conclusions follow.

Should farmland be retained?

Although loss of farmland is of concern to many, policy makers need to consider whether farmland retention is a goal that should be pursued. The US population is increasing, and people have to live somewhere. Moreover, technological advances in agriculture have increased per acre yields, requiring less farmland for food and fiber production. Thus, it is logical for economists to ask: "What is the market failure in the conversion of this farmland?" If conversion occurs because people are willing to pay more for land for residential and commercial structures than a farmer can earn by growing a crop on it, then it would appear that the optimal outcome is conversion.

However, a region, state or nation could decide to retain farmland if it will improve society's welfare.[2] In some cases, people may be willing to pay more to retain land as farmland for amenity and environmental reasons, rather than allow the market to prevail and have the land be developed for non-farm purposes. In addition, policy interventions such as transportation policies, educational policies, banking regulations and crime prevention or lack thereof all affect development patterns and may contribute to sub-optimal levels of farmland being retained in farming. In order for people to be able to express a willingness to prevent conversion, however, a market or policy intervention is needed. Programs for farmland retention could be designed to address the market failure that results in a level of farmland that, from society's perspective, is sub-optimal (see also Hodge 2004, chapter 15 this volume).

What are the reasons given to justify farmland preservation? Citizens advocate the preservation of farmland for food security, local economic reasons and amenity value. Gardner (1977) proposed that four benefits can be derived from the protection of productive agricultural land: (1) local and national food security, (2) employment in the agricultural industry, (3) efficient development of urban and rural land, and (4) protection of rural and environmental amenities. Farmland preservation programs have sought to preserve a productive land base for the agricultural economy, to preserve the amenity values of open space and rural character, to slow suburban sprawl, to provide wildlife habitat, and to provide an opportunity for groundwater recharge in areas where suburban development is occurring (Bromley and Hodge 1990; Fischel 1985; Gardner 1977; McConnell 1989; Wolfram 1981). A recent national analysis of legislation enabling states to form preservation programs has identified five categories of goals: development patterns, food security, a healthy viable local economy, environmental services and protection of rural amenities (Hellerstein *et al.* 2002). States tended to indicate food security, environmental services and protection of rural amenities as goals more frequently than they did planned development patterns and a healthy local economy. Maryland, for example, developed a purchase of development rights program to preserve agricultural land and woodlands as sources of agricultural products, to control urban expansion and to protect open-space land (Maryland Agricultural Land Preservation Foundation 2001).

The goal of preserving farmland has widespread support among the public, according to contingent valuation studies on the values of preserving land (Beasley *et al.* 1986; Bergstrom *et al.* 1985; Drake 1992; Foster *et al.* 1982; Halstead 1984; Pruckner 1995). Public choice research on the voting outcomes also indicates public support (Kline and Wichelns 1994; McLeod *et al.* 1999). In 1998, US voters approved 72 percent of the 240 ballot measures designed to preserve parks, open space, farmland and other amenities, resulting in more than $7.5 billion in additional state and local spending (Myers 1999). According to Land Trust Alliance data, US voters have continued to pass numerous similar ballot initiatives: in 2002, $5.7 billion in conservation funding was authorized; in 2001, $1.7 billion; and in 2000, $7.5 billion. The American Planning Association and American Institute of Certified Planners (2000) found that 67 percent of those surveyed considered preserving farmland and open space a priority. When asked about preferences regarding farmland preservation goals, citizens indicated that protection of groundwater and wildlife habitat and preservation of natural places were the preferred objectives (Kline and Wichelns 1996a). Given this type of endorsement for preservation programs, farmland preservation appears to be a desired goal by the public and the public is willing to pay to achieve this goal.

Why is farmland being lost?

Given the assumption, then, that society's welfare will be improved by preserving farmland, one would want to ensure that any program or policy introduced actually does retain farmland. To do so, one must first try to understand the forces that result in its conversion. These forces include demand for land for housing and commercial development that raises the price of land for these uses much higher than for agricultural uses, speculation in the land market, decreasing relative returns from agriculture in urbanizing areas, difficulties with non-farm neighbors and inability of farm families to diversify their income sources with off-farm employment in some areas.

Since 1950, the population of the United States has increased by 137 million people (90.6 percent), with a large percentage of this change occurring in states on either coast. The increase in population in the Mid-Atlantic states alone is 17.5 million (48.4 percent). Population growth increases the demand for land for housing and commercial purposes. Lynch and Carpenter (2003) found that as population increases in a county, the rate of farmland loss also increases. The difference in rates was striking between metropolitan and non-metropolitan counties. For Mid-Atlantic counties that have been metropolitan areas since the 1950s, Carpenter and Lynch (2002) found that the average annual rate of farmland loss was 2.04 percent compared to rural counties with an average loss rate of 1.32 percent. In addition, low-density housing development and sprawl are very land-intensive development strategies and increase demand for farm and forest land. Weller and Edwards (2001) found that between 1973 and 1997, Maryland converted 371,348 acres of forest and agricultural land to developed land uses, approximately two thirds of which became low-density residential development (Weller and Edwards 2001). They attribute the conversion to the increase in Maryland's median income, the exodus from the inner suburbs (due to "push" factors such as crime, undesirable school quality, and decreasing quality of housing stock), and the high land-intensive (low-density) development patterns.

In addition to making it attractive to farmers to sell their land due to higher prices, the increased demand for land on the urban fringe is pricing farmland out of the reach of existing farmers wishing to expand their operations and new farmers desiring to start a farm. Barnard (2000) finds that urban influences affect about 17 percent of the nation's agricultural land. Two thirds of the value of farm parcels in urban–influenced zones is attributed to urban proximity ($1,240 of the $1,880 per acre average). Hardie *et al.* (2001) found that a $1,000 increase in median housing value increased the value of farmland by $27.50 per acre. This encourages speculators to purchase the appreciating land.

While problematic in many ways, proximity to urban areas can also present opportunities to farmers. If farmers adapt to and take advantage of these prospects, they can be successful. Defining adaptive farms in metropolitan counties as those with high-value products of $500 sales per acre, Heimlich and Barnard (1992) found that more than 66 percent of household income for these farms was from farming. This type of farm had an average net farm income of more than twice the income of traditional farms in metropolitan and non-metropolitan areas. Lockeretz (1989) found that farmers in metropolitan areas enjoyed a higher standard of living than US farmers as a whole, which he attributed to off-farm income and the proximity of employment opportunities. Although metropolitan counties have higher rates of farmland loss, farmers do not appear to be idling land but to possibly be selling lower-quality land for development. Thus, although population growth and closeness to metropolitan areas can increase farmland loss, it is not inevitable if farmers adapt to the changes and take advantage of the proximity of markets or find off-farm employment opportunities.

While population growth and increasing land prices can explain why much of the farmland is being converted, it does not explain all farmland conversion. Of the 266 counties in the six Mid-Atlantic states examined over the last 50 years, out of the 1,330 county/decade combinations, 418 (31 percent) lost agricultural land even when the population was not increasing (Figure 19.2) (Lynch and Carpenter 2003). They also found that as the unemployment rate in a county increases, the rate of farmland loss also increases. Thus, in areas with limited development opportunities (low or negative population growth) and limited off-farm income opportunities, farmers may be idling or abandoning their land or letting the farmland revert to forest. The overall health of the local economy thus impacts the viability of the farm sector. Incorporating agriculture into the local economic development strategies may help develop a strong local economy and decrease the rate of farmland conversion in rural areas.

Spillover effects on land conversion, and overcoming the impermanence syndrome

While adapting to surrounding urbanization is important, the pattern of previous land conversion can result in lower profits on remaining farmland, as spillover effects from non-farm neighbors can decrease the relative net returns for producers. The closeness of non-farm neighbors can result in objections to odor, dust, noise, farm waste disposal and the timing of agricultural activities.[3] These can result in farmers altering their farm practices to those

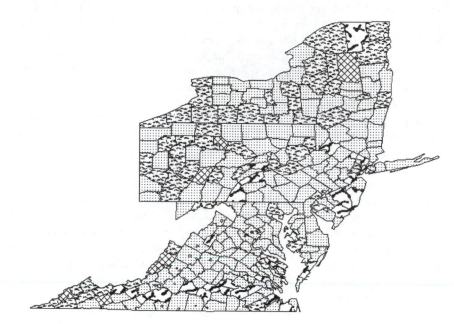

Legend

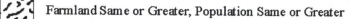 Lost Farmland, Population Same or Greater

 Farmland Same or Greater, Population Same or Greater

 Lost Farmland, Lost Population

 Farmland Same or Greater, Lost Population

Figure 19.2 Changes in farmland and population between 1987 and 1997.

that are less cost-effective or can escalate and result in formal nuisance complaints and lawsuits. The fragmentation of farmland across the landscape led Pfeffer and Lapping to suggest that,

> Without strict zoning regulations farmland often becomes parcelized as entire farms or parts of farms are sold to developers. This parcelization of farmlands leads to a "checkerboard" distribution of farmlands, i.e. many noncontiguous fields. Farming such scattered plots is problematic. Under these conditions, consolidation of land holdings to achieve efficient scales of operation is nearly impossible.
>
> (Pfeffer and Lapping 1995: 85)

These spillover effects may reduce net returns, but just as importantly they cause uncertainty about the long-run profitability of the farm. Given this uncertainty, farmers might decide to invest less money in the farm or to stop learning about new technologies that might increase their yields or decrease their costs. In addition, on a more macro level, if there are fewer farmers left to support the input and output sectors, an area might see the loss of its farm support businesses, increasing the costs of operating the farm (Lynch and Carpenter 2003; Pfeffer and Lapping 1995). The overall effect of these two phenomena is a decrease in the profitability of the farm and another shift in the relative attractiveness of selling the farm. In some sense, the uncertainty creates an "impermanence syndrome" and becomes a self-fulfilling prophecy.

To overcome this impermanence syndrome and maximize society's gains, any farmland protection policy would have to decrease farmers' uncertainty about the future profitability of farming in the region, decrease the obstacles to productive farming created by non-farm neighbors, increase or maintain investment activities to ensure profitability, eliminate or decrease the "speculative" value that might have individuals buying farmland for investment purposes rather than farm production and slow or end housing development in the farming area. Farmers may be more optimistic about the long-run profitability of farming if a sufficiently large number of acres have been preserved permanently in their area, if these acres have been preserved in contiguous blocks in order to decrease potential nuisance problems, and if the land preserved is being used intensively and profitably for an agricultural purpose – i.e., not as a hobby farm – and is thereby patronizing the local agricultural support sector.

Mechanisms to retain farmland

How have different jurisdictions implemented programs to retain farmland? In 1956, Maryland enacted the first state preferential tax assessment program, assessing the value of the land at its profitability in an agricultural use to reduce property taxes on land in agricultural use. Southampton, New York, created the first local purchase of development rights (strips the right to build housing on the land in exchange for a cash payment) program in 1972, followed by New York's Suffolk County in 1974. Maryland and Massachusetts each introduced state purchase of agricultural conservation easement/purchase of development rights (PACE/PDR) programs in 1977. From these beginnings, states and counties have employed a variety of policy mechanisms to slow or stop farmland conversion, including exclusive agricultural and low-density zoning, preferential property tax rates based on agricultural value, PACE/PDR programs and transfer of development rights (TDR) programs (Duncan 1984; Lynch and Horowitz 1998; Mulkey and Clouser 1987; Parks and Quimio 1996; Rose 1984).

Yet more options exist to protect farmland from conversion. Duke and Lynch (2003) classify farmland preservation techniques into four different types – regulatory, incentive-based, participatory and hybrid. Classification depends on the way in which the agricultural land market is affected. Regulatory techniques define the property rights in the agricultural land market. Some examples include agricultural protection or use zoning, right-to-farm laws, growth boundaries and state executive orders. Incentive-based techniques change the relative returns for different decisions and often make it more costly for landowners to make land use decisions that are not desired by society. They may provide additional options for landowners or make it less costly to use land in a way that satisfies societal goals. Incentive-based techniques differ from regulatory techniques in that they do not alter the institutional structure of markets; they simply alter relative prices within markets. These types of techniques could include use-value, differential, or preferential assessment for property tax reasons, impact fees and exactions, purchase of agricultural conservation easement or purchase of development rights programs, or a charitable tax deduction for a conservation easement. When the state itself enters the market as a demander or supplier of land, Duke and Lynch (2003) classify the tool used as a participatory preservation technique. The state can exercise or refuse to use its eminent domain power in a way to ensure agricultural land preservation, can sell under a fee-simple format or conduct a fee-simple purchase, and can purchase a right of first refusal from farmland owners. Hybrid techniques combine the characteristics of two of the preceding types of techniques. Hybrids include transfer of development rights programs and agricultural districts. A list of current and possible techniques is presented by type in Table 19.1.

While there is a multitude of different approaches to retain farmland, some programs have found more favor than others. All 50 states now have some version of preferential taxation for agricultural land.[4] More than 110 governmental entities have implemented transfer of development rights and purchase of development rights or purchase of agricultural conservation easements programs to permanently preserve farmland (American Farmland Trust 2001a, 2001b, 2001c). As of February 2001, at least 20 states had agricultural land preservation programs and have preserved 806,300 acres, while local governments have preserved 190,839, for a total of nearly one million acres in preserved status. Spending in both state and local programs to purchase this acreage was $1.743 billion (American Farmland Trust 2001a, 2001b). To date, the per capita cost has ranged from $0.25 in North Carolina to $78.36 in Delaware. Twenty-four states permit agricultural zoning. Six states have implemented growth management statutes that address farmland conversion (American Farmland Trust 1997). Sixteen states have agricultural district laws with a variety of incentives to encourage farmers to participate.

Table 19.1 Comparative evaluation of farmland preservation techniques by 15 factors

Technique	Financing[a]	Right holder[b]	Duration[c]	Persistence[d]	Maximize acres[e]	Conversion prevented[e]	Maximize productive farms[e]
Regulatory							
Growth boundaries	S	P	Pm	Fl	+	+	+
State executive orders	TB	P	Pm	Ps	+	+	+
Growth management	S	P	Pm	Fl	+	+	+
Agricultural protection zoning	S	P	Tm	Fl	+	+	+
Cluster zoning	S	P	Tm	Fl	+	+	+
Right-to-farm laws	S	P	Pm	Fl	+	−	+
Incentive based							
PDR/PACE	TB	L	Pm	Ps	+	−	++
Exactions	S	P	Tm	Fl	0	−	+−
Mortgage assistance	TB	L	Tm	Ps	+	0	0
Leasing ACE	TB	L	Tm	Fl	+	+	0
Tontine	S/TB	L	Tm	Ps	+	0	+
Circuit breaker tax	TR	−	Tm	Ps	+	+	++
Capital gains reduction	TR	L	Pm	Ps	+	+	++
Installment payments	−	L	Pm	Ps	+	+	++
Bargain sales	TB/TR	L	Pm	Ps	+	+	++
Recapture taxes	S	P	Tm	Ps	+	+	++
Transfer tax	S	P	Tm	Ps	+	+	++
Revolving funds	TB	L	Tm	Ps	+	+	++
State income tax forgiveness	TR	L	Pm	Ps	+	+	++
Charitable deductions	TR	L	Pm	Ps	0	0	++
Programs – viability of agriculture	TB	N	Tm	Fl	+	− −	++
Participatory							
Land banks	TB	L	Pm	Ps	−	0	0
Eminent domain	TB	L	Pm	Ps	−	0	0
Rights of first refusal	TB	L	Pm	Ps	−	++	+

continued

Table 19.1 Continued

Technique	Financing[a]	Right holder[b]	Duration[c]	Persistence[d]	Maximize acres[e]	Conversion prevented[e]	Maximize productive farms[e]
Hybrid							
Eminent domain/ROFR	TB	L	Pm	Ps	–	++	+
Pension plan PACE	TB	L	Pm	Ps	++	–	–
Point systems	TB	L	Pm		0	++	++
TDR	S	L	Pm	Fl	+	– –	– –
MDR	S	L	Pm	Fl	++	– –	– –
Agricultural districts	S	L	Tm[a]	Fl	+	+	+

Technique	Maximize critical mass[e]	Agricultural landowner[f]	General public tax-payers[f]	Environmentalist[f]	Developers[f]	Forest industry[f]	Simplicity of implementation[g]	Attract non-participants[h]
Regulatory								
Growth boundaries	+	– –	+	+	– –	+	–	++
State executive orders	+	– –	+	+	– –	0	–	++
Growth management	+	– –	+	+	– –	+	–	++
Agricultural protection zoning	+	–	+	+	– –	+	–	++
Cluster zoning	0	0	0/+	0/+	–	0	0	++
Right-to-farm laws	+	+	+	–	–	0	+	–
Incentive based								
PDR/PACE	+	+	+	0	–	+	+	– –
Exactions	0	– –	++	+	– –	0	0	+
Mortgage assistance	+	+	+	+	+	+	+	0
Leasing ACE	++	+	+	+	–	+	+	+
Tontine	++	0	+	+	0	+	0	+
Circuit breaker tax	+	0	+	+	0	+	–	0
Capital gains reduction	+	+	+	+	–	+	+	++
Installment payments	+	+	+	+	0	+	+	++

Technique	a	b	c	d	e	f	g	h
Bargain sales	+	+	+	+	+	0	+	++
Recapture taxes	+	−	−	+	+	−	+	0
Transfer tax	+	−	−	+	+	−	+	0
Revolving funds	+	+	+	+	+	0	+	+
State income tax forgiveness	+	+	+	+	+	−	++	++
Charitable deductions	+	+	+	0	+	−	0	+
Programs – viability of agriculture	+	+	0	−	−	0	0	−
Participatory								
Land banks	+	0	−	++	++	−	?	++
Eminent domain	++	−	−	++	++	−	?	++
Rights of first refusal	+	0	0	0	0	−	?	++
Hybrid								
Eminent domain/ROFR	+	−	+	0	0	−	?	++
Pension plan/PACE	0	++	−	−	+	−	+	++
Point systems	++	+	+	+	+	−	0	++
TDR	++	+	+	−	0	−	0	+
MDR	−−	−	0	−	0	−	0	+
Agricultural districts	+	+	0	0	0	0	+	0

Source: Duke and Lynch (2003).

Notes

a Beyond the costs of administration, what is the source of the financing for this technique? TB = general tax revenues and bonds; TR = tax reducing; S = self-funding or private funding by affected parties (right holders are compensated by non-right holders).

b Implied holder of rights to develop at intensities above prevailing agricultural uses: L = agricultural landowner; P = public; N = none specified.

c How long is the preservation intended to last? Pm = permanent; Tm = temporary.

d The credibility of persistence. How easy is it to redefine rights, for example, through variances? Ps = persistent; Fl = flexible.

e The goals of farmland preservation. For these four goals, does the technique promote one goal much more (++), more (+), less (−), or much less (−−) effectively than the average (0) novel technique. If unclear, then (?).

f Acceptance of technique by interest groups. For each group, will the technique tend to have high (++), somewhat high (+), somewhat low (−), or low (−−) acceptance than the average (0) novel technique. If unclear, then (?).

g Simplicity of implementation. Some techniques will tend to be much easier (++), easier (+), harder (−), or much harder (−−) than the average (0) novel technique to implement. If unclear, then (?).

h Does the program have an ability to attract (or force) those not participating in existing farmland preservation efforts? Unusual ability (++), some ability (+), little ability (−), or very low ability (−−) than the average (0) novel technique to implement. If unclear, then (?).

What should be the goals?

Can the goals set and programs implemented counteract the factors that affect farmland conversion? As mentioned above, farmland preservation programs have set a variety of objectives (Hellerstein *et al.* 2002; Maryland Agricultural Land Preservation Foundation 2001). To evaluate whether these large over-arching goals are being achieved, one must determine what specific criteria might be used to evaluate them. Lynch and Musser (2001) take the overall goals of ensuring the survival of the agricultural economy by preserving productive and profitable farmland, retaining open and green space and limiting sprawl development (dealing with the population growth in a way that does not consume farmland at an excessive rate), and collapse it into four goals that can be assessed using parcel characteristics of preserved parcels. These four goals are to maximize the number of acres preserved, to preserve productive farms, to preserve farms most threatened by development and to preserve large blocks of land. A large number of acres may be needed to ensure the viability of support industries in the area. Productive farms are defined as large farms with prime soils that are being used for crops rather than as forest or pasture. Farms most threatened by development must be preserved soon or they will be lost forever. Contiguity is desirable to ensure that farmers can use the most profitable farming techniques and can move their equipment between parcels without complaints from non-farm neighbors. Table 19.1 also presents how well the myriad of techniques achieve these goals.

How effective are the techniques at preserving farmland?

Table 19.1 provides an assessment of many creative approaches to preserving farmland. However, since many of these techniques have not yet been implemented, no empirical evaluation of their effectiveness has been made. A few of the more popular techniques have received some attention from researchers interested in their effectiveness. Their research results are presented below.

Duke and Lynch (2003) evaluate 15 factors of farmland preservation techniques to aid in the selection of the optimal policy for a given set of goals (Table 19.1). These include an evaluation of how the technique is financed – whether by tax revenues, a reduction in taxes collected, or a decrease in the landowner's land value; of who has the right to develop or to set the intensity of development on agricultural land – the agricultural landowner, the general public, or a non-specified agent; and of how long farmers and the general public would expect the preservation to last – permanently or temporarily. Another factor is the credibility of a technique's persistence, or continuation after its enactment – i.e., will there be flexibility in the future regarding the land use decision or will it be difficult to undo? Will a variance from the county board suffice to undo the decision?

While overall these techniques strive to protect a strong agricultural sector and to preserve open space, in order to assess a particular technique one must be aware of more specific goals. Using the four more specific goals outlined by Lynch and Musser (2001) and mentioned above, Duke and Lynch (2003) evaluate each technique on the basis of how well it promotes the goal – from "very well" to "not very well." They also evaluate each technique on its degree of acceptability to the different stakeholder groups: agricultural landowners, taxpayers, environmentalists and developers. The degree of difficulty of implementing these different preservation tools is also assessed. Given that a program will not be effective if agricultural landowners do not participate, they also determine whether landowners will be attracted (or forced) to participate.

Development rights programs

As mentioned above, PDR and TDR programs were among the first preservation mechanisms used and have been used by 110 governmental entities. Whether through a TDR or PDR/PACE program, the sale of development rights results in an easement attached to the title of the land restricting the current and all future owners from converting the parcel to a residential, commercial, or industrial use. These easement restrictions have been upheld in court (Danskin 2000). These programs result in permanent preservation in the sense that once an easement is in place, that farmland will never be converted to a developed use. However, in most cases, "negative" easements are used – i.e., easements spelling out what a landowner cannot do rather than what he or she must do. In addition, some of the programs have an "escape" clause under which the landowner can purchase the development rights back at their present day value if he or she can prove that agriculture is no longer profitable in the area. There is really no guarantee, then, that the land will be actively farmed in the future.

Lynch and Musser (2001) evaluated the effectiveness of different types of development rights programs in four counties in Maryland. They focused on comparing the characteristics of the parcels chosen to be preserved given the preservation program's goals, and evaluated the tradeoffs among goals given the institutional structure of each program. Their analysis identified the type of program most effective in achieving particular goals (such as maximum number of acres preserved) and the type most effective in trading off among these goals (e.g., contiguous parcels versus productive farms). They found high levels of technical and cost efficiency, indicating that the TDR and PDR programs have made tradeoffs in a logical way between the various characteristics and the easement costs of the preserved parcels. The MALPF program is a PDR program that uses a bidding system to determine the price of the easement. Its efficiency ranged between the PDR programs that did not discount the easement price paid and the TDR program. The transfer of development rights program was found to be less efficient in preserving parcels with desired characteristics than the county-level PDR or state-level PDR programs (Figure 19.3). The TDR programs studied had based their allocation strategies primarily on acreage rather than on other parcel characteristics such as prime soils or proximity to urban areas. Given that these acreage-based programs have not been found efficient, governmental entities developing TDR programs could consider setting up the assignment of TDR rights using other characteristics such as prime soils or a combination of characteristics.

Number of acres, percent of prime soil and percent of cropland had the most influence on efficiency, whereas variables indicating how threatened a parcel might be by possible conversion and how close it was to another preserved block were not found to be important criteria to the programs. Landowners of parcels closer to urban centers could have chosen not to participate in the preservation programs, or the purchase price of the easement for these farms could have been too high to select this type of parcel for preservation. The analysis concludes that the programs have not been successful in enrolling threatened or contiguous parcels.

A concern expressed by many administrators and private citizens is whether farmland preservation programs are inducing the participation of those farms that would actually contribute to the survival of the agricultural economy. They think that the programs attract hobby farms rather than working farms. In a study of agricultural landowners, Lynch and Lovell (2003) found that while three quarters of the survey respondents earn more than 75 percent of their income from non-farm sources, those with a

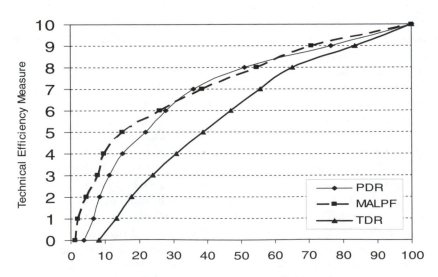

Figure 19.3 Cumulative distribution of technical efficiency by program (source: Lynch and Musser 2001).

higher percentage of farm earnings are more likely to join a preservation program, as are those who have a child who plans to take over the farm. In addition, the more acreage a farm has, the more likely it is to participate. It appears that working farms are therefore actually more likely to enroll in the programs.

While PDR/PACE programs can attain the goals of farmland preservation more efficiently than TDR programs, they have a major limitation. They tend to be financed by taxes and bonds and thus often operate under tight budget constraints. Despite Maryland's successful state PDR program, under which 186,000 farmland acres have been preserved, 371,000 farmland acres have been converted to another (usually residential or commercial) use since the program's inception. Thus, only half as much agricultural land was preserved as the amount that was converted. More land could have been preserved if the program had a higher budget allocation and a waiting list remains to date. Maryland has spent $232.8 million to date, which is estimated to be $43.96 per Maryland resident (American Farmland Trust 2001a, 2001b). A recent Maryland Agricultural Land Preservation Foundation (MALPF) Taskforce report concluded that the program needs more funding ($1 billion over the next 20 years) and more targeting of its resources.

In addition, in Maryland, the state land preservation funding, the county funding used to match the state contributions, and the county preservation programs funding are all generated at least in part by the agricultural transfer tax. This agricultural transfer tax is assessed when farmland leaves an agricultural use for a residential, commercial, or industrial use. Through simple calculations for three counties, one can determine that preservation of one acre of land at the average easement price per county using the agricultural transfer tax as the sole funding mechanism would mean converting $64,080 worth of farmland in Calvert County, $31,067 in Carroll County and $124,933 in Howard County. Using the 1997 value of land and buildings per acre of $3,584 in Calvert County, $3,694 in Carroll County and $5,518 in Howard County, Lynch and Lovell (2002) determine that the conversion of almost 17.9 farmland acres in Calvert, 8.4 acres in Carroll and 22.6 acres in Howard would be needed to finance the preservation of one acre in each of those counties. Nickerson and Lynch (2001) found that the actual sales price for unpreserved farmland sold between 1994 and 1997 was $8,998. However, even when this higher market price per acre is used in the calculations, each county would still need to convert many acres – 7.1 in Calvert, 3.5 acres in Carroll and 13.9 in Howard – to finance the preservation of just one acre.

Given the cost of PDR programs, some jurisdictions have decided to use TDR programs. In TDR programs, a government entity assigns marketable permits to landowners based on their right to build on the agricultural land. These permits can be sold in a private transaction to a second party, such as a developer, who then uses the permits to increase density in a planned growth or receiving area. These programs use little government money, and preservation of agricultural land is only constrained by the demand for increased density in growth areas. Fifty jurisdictions have TDR ordinances on the books; however, few of these have been very successful. Three programs have actually been revoked since their implementation. Twenty-two programs have protected no agricultural land, 15 programs have protected more than 100 acres of farmland and only eight programs have protected more than 1,000 acres of farmland (American Farmland Trust 2001c). Even when a TDR program has been successful in preserving agricultural land, many remain skeptical about whether the program is achieving its goals. For example, in Montgomery County, Maryland, the TDR program has protected more agricultural land (over 40,000 acres) than any other TDR program. However, the county still permits one house to be built on approximately every 25 acres in the TDR sending area. Critics suggest that this results in low-density development which negatively impacts on agricultural productivity, rendering the preservation of acreage less effective in terms of sustaining a viable agricultural economy.

TDR programs may also have different distributional consequences than PDR programs. Taxpayers fund PDR purchases through a variety of different taxes. In contrast, developers pay for TDRs and may pass on the cost to purchasers of new houses. In addition, the neighbors in the receiving areas who experience higher density may perceive that their quality of life has diminished. Oftentimes these distributional consequences are not explicitly considered in decisions about which program to initiate.

Preferential property tax valuation

Given its longevity (the first program was implemented in 1956) and its widespread adoption, preferential or use-value taxation has been analyzed more frequently. Most of the research has found that these programs slow the rate of farmland conversion but do not preserve land in the long run. Heimlich and Anderson (2001), for example, find that preferential property taxation does not provide a strong incentive for conserving farmland. One reason is that use-valuation reduces the holding costs for land speculators, developers and hobby farmers who may not actively farm the land. In most cases, the transfer taxes applied when the land leaves farming and used to recoup some of the property tax are low enough to have little or no impact on the decision to convert the land. By changing the relative costs of converting, preferential assessment can slow the conversion, but by itself will not permanently retain farmland. Similar conclusions were found by Gardner (1994) and Lynch and Carpenter (2003). Lynch and Carpenter found that Mid-Atlantic counties with preferential taxation programs had an annual rate of farmland conversion of 0.821 percent compared to a rate of 1.58 percent for counties without a program. Blewett and Lane (1988) also found that use-value taxation slows down the pace of conversion but does not stop land from being converted. Parks and Quimio (1996) found that preferential taxation programs may not be enough to stop farmland conversion in urbanizing areas. They cite non-agricultural considerations such as capital gains and interest rates as stronger factors in landowner decision making than the incentives provided by decreased property taxes. Anderson (1993) and Anderson and Bunch (1989) found that property tax credits in Michigan's circuit-breaker programs are partially capitalized into the land value but that the programs do not stop the conversion of land to an urban or suburban use. Chicoine *et al.* (1982) found that landowners' wealth increased under use-value assessments as reduced property taxes were capitalized into the farm price. They concluded that differential property taxes brought relief to both the landowners and the farm operators at the urban fringe. However, they found cash flow conditions on the farms that suggested the need to liquidate some assets such as land to ensure their continued operation.

Agricultural protection zoning

Agricultural protection zoning (APZ) is a regulatory approach that redefines property rights. The technique has been used to ensure that contiguity is preserved in an agricultural area. Officials hope this will sustain a higher relative agricultural value for the land and decrease spillover impacts. However, APZ is often difficult to implement as agricultural landowners perceive that the limitations imposed on their permitted uses will decrease their land value. This may not always be the case. Henneberry and Barrows (1990) found that exclusive agricultural zoning can increase or decrease the price of land parcels depending on their location. Higher prices were found for large agriculturally zoned parcels located far from the nearest urban area. Conversely, parcels close to the city that were zoned for agriculture had lower prices per acre. Esseks and Long (2001) found that local agricultural zoning can be an effective policy for protecting financially productive farmland from "premature" development. However, Esseks and Long qualified their results by suggesting that zoning will be implemented only if farmland owners believe they have the political power to change it in the future, if land has acceptable agricultural financial returns and if the landowners perceive that it will benefit them in some way (such as reducing nuisance complaints). While some jurisdictions, such as Berks County in Pennsylvania, will purchase easements only in areas with agricultural zoning, most jurisdictions with TDR and PDR programs do not restrict participation to those farms within areas with restrictive zoning, even though many jurisdictions perceive this may be the only method of ensuring ongoing profitable farming. For example, the MALPF Taskforce (Maryland Agricultural Land Preservation Taskforce 2001) concludes that if areas to be preserved are not insulated from development through zoning and land use management, then the result of the PDR program and the tax money expended to purchase easements might be privately owned, inaccessible open and green space surrounded by large-lot residential development.

Some have suggested that APZ signals local support and continued profitability of the agricultural sectors. Policy efforts to increase agricultural profitability or to signal support for the agricultural sector could impact landowners' willingness to participate in preservation programs. Recent research suggests that both the profitability of agriculture and non-consumptive values affect the decision to enroll one's land in a preservation program (Lynch and Lovell 2003). The decision of a farmer's child to continue farming (a factor that increases the probability that a farm will be preserved) may also be determined by the expectations for future farming profitability and again would suggest that investment in agricultural profitability (including APZ) could be worthwhile. Whether agricultural zoning provides the appropriate signal to farm families is an empirical issue.

How much preserved agricultural land is enough?

State and local governments have enacted programs designed to retain farmland, and significant resources have been expended toward this goal – $1.7 billion in direct payments alone (American Farmland Trust 2001a, 2001b). However, little work has been done to determine how much land an area needs to preserve to retain a viable agricultural community. Loss of farmland may result in fewer farmers to purchase inputs and less output to sell to the local agricultural support and processing businesses. If this decreases the profitability of these support businesses, they might decide to exit the area. If that occurs the remaining farmers will have to go farther for their supplies or markets and/or pay higher prices to the remaining support businesses. Thus, government entities want to retain enough agricultural land (a critical mass) to ensure that the support sectors do not exit the area.

Focusing on agriculture commodities grown in the Philadelphia–New York–Boston corridor, Dhillon and Derr (1974) estimated a critical mass threshold for dairy (24,600 cows and 74,000 acres of cropland), egg production (1.25 million hens) and fresh market vegetable production (10,000 acres). Given the technological changes since the early 1970s, these numbers may not be appropriate measures for today, but they do provide an indicator of what a county or region might want to consider. Daniels and Lapping (2001) on their expert judgment proposed that a county has to retain a critical mass of at least 100,000 acres, $50 million in agricultural sales, and/or 20,000 acres of preserved farmland to ensure the continued viability of the farm sector. Analyzing at what level of harvested cropland acres the rate of farmland loss accelerated, Lynch and Carpenter (2003) estimated a critical mass threshold of 189,240 farmland acres per county for six Mid-Atlantic states for the period 1949 to 1997. They qualified this definition, however, because few of the counties in their study area exceeded this number of farmland acreage. In addition, no evidence of a critical mass of agricultural acreage was found for the later period between 1978 and 1997. They concluded that while certain sectors or commodities might be doomed once an area loses a certain number of acres, farmers could shift to alternative crops or technologies to overcome the loss of the local input suppliers or processors.

Who will buy (take over) the farms when current owners retire?

In addition to how much land is enough, one must consider that someone needs to take over the land from the aging farm community. Will young farmers be able to purchase land as the current agricultural landowners retire? Theoretically, one would expect that any parcel prohibited from further residential, commercial, and industrial development would be less expensive with one of the remaining uses, agriculture, and thus possibly within the reach of new farmers. In fact, lowering the cost of farmland so that it is affordable to young farmers as older farmers retire is one of the expressed purposes of many farmland preservation programs (Gale 1993). However, limited evidence exists that easement restrictions of PDR and TDR programs actually decrease the price of agricultural land as expected. Blakely (1991) did find that a Washington State PDR program lowered the sales price of preserved farmland compared to that of unpreserved farmland. However, the market price of preserved farmland was still much higher than the current agricultural rental value would have predicted. Vitaliano and Hill (1994) found that participation in New York's agricultural district program did not result in lower prices for participating farmland than for non-participating farmland. Nickerson and Lynch (2001) found that while preserved parcels' per acre prices were lower on average than unpreserved farmland's prices, there was little statistical evidence that once all parcel characteristics were taken into account then the easement restriction lowered the price for preserved farmland. Chicoine *et al.* (1982) found that the reduced property taxes due to use-value assessment increased the price of the farmland near urbanizing areas. They suggest that this increase in land values creates barriers for new farmers trying to enter the land market. Thus, to ensure the continuation of agriculture in an area, some provisions or assistance may be needed to ensure that a new generation of farmers can purchase the agricultural land.

A further complication for preservation programs is that preserved agricultural land appears to increase the residential value of parcels adjacent to it (Geoghegan 2002; Geoghegan *et al.* 2003; Irwin and Bockstael 2001; Irwin 2002). As preserving land increases the desirability of living in a rural area and increases the value of the land surrounding the preserved parcel, increased development in these areas or at the very least a higher cost of preserving the remaining farmland is often the resulting irony.

Conclusion

Many Americans consider the loss of farmland to be one of our most significant land use problems for a variety of reasons. In part, this is due to the
increasingly high land consumptive pattern of development (low density and
sprawl) and the visibility of the farmland loss to many citizens. Some of the
farmland lost earlier (1950 to 1974) may have converted back to forest. The
public's perception of that loss of farmland may be quite different from the
current loss. Given that the conversion of farmland particularly to low-
density residential housing can impact the profitability of farming, decrease
the rural character, affect other amenity values and impact wildlife habitat and
groundwater recharge, some type of policy intervention is needed to ensure
that an optimal level of farmland is retained to overcome these negative
externalities. Evidence exists that society is willing to support farmland
preservation as well as open space and wildlife habitat retentions through
taxes and other types of mechanisms.

Farmland loss is caused in part from population increases. As the number
of people in an area increase, so does the demand for land. Land price
increases and landowners are motivated to sell out. However, most farmers
cannot afford to buy land at these higher prices and cannot expand their
operations; new farmers cannot begin an operation. Developing programs
that assist or subsidize new or existing farmers to buy land may be needed to
sustain the agricultural sector. As important as the population growth is the
rate of land consumption per person. The low-density development and
urban sprawl consumes farmland at a much higher rate per person. Areas that
attempt to retain farmland through low-density zoning may find this
approach backfires.

Low farm income is another factor in farmland conversion. Low incomes
encourage agricultural landowners to cash out and take the money for developing their land. Low farm income can be due in part to the fragmentation
of the farming area and the spill-over effects from non-farm neighbors. Programs or zoning policies that advocate exclusive or contiguous agricultural
sectors may be needed to ensure that farmers can continue to use the most
profitable farming techniques. A stagnant local economy may also be driving
farmland loss in less urban areas with little or no population growth. Many
farm families are diversifying their income sources with one or more
members of the household working off the farm. If few employment
opportunities exist in the local area, this could convince the family to sell the
property, to idle it, or to permit it to revert to forest. Incorporating agriculture into local economic development plans may help to overcome these
trends. Farmers in both rural and urban areas need to take advantage of
opportunities to increase household income. Farmers need to adapt to the
changing conditions to ensure profitability. Counties can adopt strategies or
hire agricultural development officers to assist with increasing profitability
and adaptation.

If the goal of the land preservation program is retention of an agricultural economy, not just preservation of open and green space, then the programs must seek to decrease uncertainty about future profitability, decrease the obstacles to using the most profitable farming techniques, motivate continued investment in the farm infrastructure and in the owner's knowledge base, eliminate or decrease the speculative value of the land and eliminate or decrease the fragmentation of the farm areas. Farmers may be more optimistic about the long-run profitability of farming if a sufficiently large number of acres have been preserved permanently in their area, if these acres have been preserved in contiguous blocks in order to decrease potential nuisance problems, and if the land preserved is being used intensively and profitably for an agricultural purpose – i.e., not as a hobby farm – and is thereby patronizing the local agricultural support sector.

Four different types of mechanisms can be used to achieve these objectives: regulatory, incentive-based, participatory and hybrid techniques. The financing, the implications for who owns the property rights, the persistence, the credibility, the ability to achieve a range of goals and the acceptability to stakeholders vary widely among the many techniques.

Few of the many possible techniques have been used widely. Three techniques have been employed most frequently. These include PDR and TDR programs, which restrict the rights of the land in exchange for a cash payment, use-value or preferential assessment, which reduces agricultural landowners' property tax and agricultural protection zoning, which limits the acceptable land use to agriculture in varying degrees. PDR programs have been evaluated and found to be efficient in achieving many of the objectives outlined above. However, the programs are expensive. Several authors suggested a higher degree of funding and targeting could make them even more effective. TDR programs were not found to be as effective as PDR programs. However, the TDR programs studied had based their allocation strategies primarily on acreage rather than on other parcel characteristics such as prime soils or proximity to urban areas. Given that these acreage-based programs have not been found efficient, governmental entities developing TDR programs could consider setting up the assignment of TDR rights using other characteristics to ensure more efficient tradeoffs between characteristics. TDR programs are less expensive to government entities but do have distributional consequences on residents in the receiving areas. And to date even where implemented, the TDR programs have not been used as widely.

Use value assessment was found to be effective in slowing the rate of farmland conversion but does not permanently preserve the land. To slow the rate of loss further, programs could increase the transfer or recapture taxes used to recoup some of the tax savings from these use-value programs and make the relative benefits of leaving agriculture even lower. Use-value taxation, though, can increase the farmland price, making it more difficult for younger farmers to purchase. Agricultural protection zoning can increase or decrease the land value. While difficult to implement because of the possibility it will decrease the land value, landowners may find it acceptable if they think they can reverse the zoning in the future. Thus, while it may increase profitability and decrease nuisance complaints in the short run, APZ may not provide permanent protection of farmland unless accompanied by funding from additional programs.

Several questions remain unanswered about farmland preservation. First, how much farmland is optimal to preserve from society's perspective? This encompasses how much the general public is willing to pay for the amenities provided and how much is needed to sustain a viable agricultural economy. No clear-cut rules exist on this issue. In addition, if these programs are not decreasing land value following the easement and/or zoning restrictions, how will young farmers be able to purchase the land from retiring farmland owners? Concerns about the next generation of farmers remain. To complicate this issue, recent research indicates that proximity to preserved farmland may increase the value of adjacent parcels. This will increase the cost of preservation and increase the value of farmland to the point where few operators can afford it.

Notes

1 Total farmland increased by nearly 100 million acres between 1900 and 2000 (Gardner 2002), peaking in 1950.
2 This assumes that society is willing to assert dominance over an individual landowner's right to do whatever he or she wants with the land.
3 Larson *et al.* (2001) found that 40 percent of survey respondents had received some complaints about their farming practices in the previous five years.
4 There is some debate about whether or not the Michigan circuit-breaker program should be considered preferential taxation.

20 What would an ideal Federal rural land use policy look like?

Thomas Johnson

Introduction

This chapter reflects on what the essential features of an ideal Federal and state land use policy would look like. It starts by defining what is meant by a good or ideal policy, and ideal land use policy in particular. Next, we enumerate several services provided by rural land. Together, these principles of good policy and the list of services provided by land are used to describe the essential characteristics of ideal Federal and state land use policies.

A review of current guides to policy making (Hamilton 2003; Munger 2000; State of Queensland 2003; United Kingdom Cabinet Office 2003) does not reveal any widely accepted criteria for good land use policy, as it does for other policies such as tax policy (American Institute of Chartered Public Accountants 2001; National Conference of State Legislatures 2001), but there are many suggested principles, too many to fully acknowledge here. A synthesis of these guides to policy making leads to the nine following proposed principles. Good land use policy should:

1 Be effective. It should do what it is intended to do. This, in turn, requires an explicit articulation of the policy's goals, objectives and performance measures.
2 Be efficient. It should achieve its goals at minimum cost, broadly defined.
3 Be equitable. Stakeholders must feel that the policy is good for everyone, and that those who benefit bear their fair share of costs.
4 Be strategic. It should be forward looking and lead to long-run goals. It should be sustainable.
5 Be flexible and robust. It should be possible to adapt the policy to different local conditions, and to adjust it over time as conditions change.
6 Involve stakeholders. Those impacted by the policy should understand it and influence its implementation.
7 Involve all agencies. It should be "joined-up," that is, it should avoid the silo-effect in which different agencies fail to coordinate their efforts.

8   Be evidence-based. The policy should reflect the experience of other policy makers; it should rely on research, experts and knowledgeable stakeholders.
9   Be constantly evaluated and adjusted if necessary.

These principles help us assess the efficacy and likely success of a policy. They do not, however, identify the ideal characteristic of a land use policy. To do this we need to identify what the policy is intended to do (i.e., its goals).

Goals of land use policy

Land is a fundamental element in quality of life. As argued by Bergstrom (this volume) and Hodge (this volume), even as land has become less important as a factor in the production of food and natural resource commodities, it has become more important from other perspectives such as providing environmental, recreational and cultural services. The overall goal of rural land use policy then must be to yield the highest stream of services possible over time at minimal cost. As discussed in other chapters in this volume, rural land today provides the nation with food, fiber and other natural resources; environmental services such as clean air and water, wildlife habitats, ecosystems and carbon sinks to reduce greenhouse gases; outdoor recreation; scenic vistas; historical sites; industrial, commercial, military and governmental space; and housing. In order to produce this stream of services, land use policy should have five contributory objectives. It should:

1   Contribute to safe and abundant food supplies, fiber and the provision of most natural resource commodities.
2   Contribute to the economic growth and development of communities, regions and the nation.
3   Protect the environment, including water, air and wildlife habitat.
4   Protect unique or rare natural and historical amenities and encourage the production of man-made amenities such as scenic countryside and recreational opportunities.
5   Provide for optimal residential choice for consumers.

In our system of public and private landownership, the market is key to the optimal allocation of land uses.[1] But, as demonstrated by Hodge (2004, chapter 15 this volume), markets will allocate land efficiently between alternative uses, and between public and private uses only when each transaction and each land use change reflects opportunity costs. Thus, a "perfect" market would be able to achieve goals 1, 2 and 5 if these were the only goals. However, market failure will likely prevent the optimal achievement of goals 3 and 4 (because they involve public goods). In addition, reasonable arguments can be made that due to irreversibilities and the interrelationships between economic growth, the environment and natural, historical and man-made amenities, goals 1, 2 and 5 are in fact difficult, if not impossible, to achieve.

Thus, a rationale exists for public intervention to improve allocation of resources. In our Federal system, primary responsibility for land use resides at the local level, but all three levels of government – Federal, state, and local – influence land use through policy. Often these policies are not labeled as land use policy but they nevertheless have significant influence over the allocation of land uses. This chapter focuses on Federal and state policy.

Federal policy

Land use policy is primarily the domain of local governments, which are usually granted this policy domain by state governments. Some states restrict the responsibility of local governments more than other states. In addition, some states have home rule while others do not. The Federal government has very little direct authority over land use, but if we consider the important determinants of land use – economic growth, transportation systems, quality of public services, demand for agricultural products, natural amenities, tax policy, environmental policy, forestry policy, national parks and others – we see that the Federal government actually has a significant indirect influence on rural land use. If one adds to this the potential role of Federal rural development and regional policies – policies that largely do not exist but that would clearly influence land use – the role of the Federal government could be even greater.

Thus, the ideal land use policy would coordinate many of its other policies and focus them on directly creating incentives that lead to better land use, and indirectly guiding states and local governments toward more optimal land use policies. It would be a "joined-up" or "horizontal" policy. Such a cross-cutting policy has much in common with the often debated rural policy, and in fact a rural agency might be an appropriate home for a national land use policy.

Direct land use policy on Federal lands

The US Federal government is directly responsible for land use in the case of Federally owned land. Most Federally owned lands are located in the western states. The Federal western lands policy directly affects land use on 262 million acres. This direct policy indirectly affects many more acres of land adjacent to public lands. The mission of the Bureau of Land Management is to "sustain the health, diversity and productivity of the public lands for the use and enjoyment of present and future generations" (Bureau of Land Management 2003). The Bureau's goals in its current strategic plan are six-fold:

1   Provide opportunities for environmentally responsible recreation.
2   Provide opportunities for environmentally responsible commercial activities.

3   Preserve natural and cultural heritage resources.
4   Reduce threats to public health, safety and property.
5   Provide land, resource and title information.
6   Provide economic and technical assistance.

The US Forest Service is responsible for 191 million acres of forest and grass lands. Its mission is to "sustain the health, diversity, and productivity of the nation's forests and grasslands to meet the needs of present and future generations" (USD Department of Agriculture, Forest Service 2003). It has the following four goals:

1   Promote ecosystem health and conservation.
2   Provide a variety of uses, values, products, and services for present and future generations.
3   Develop and use the best scientific information available to deliver technical and community assistance.
4   Ensure the acquisition and use of an appropriate corporate infrastructure.[2]

The goals of both agencies closely resemble the overall goals of land policy in general, and they make up an important part of overall Federal land use policy. In addition, the National Park Service manages a large amount of public land, especially in Alaska. The desirability of these policies depends on how effectively, efficiently and equitably they are executed, and how well they are coordinated with other policies. An assessment of these existing policies is beyond the scope of this chapter.

Food and agricultural policy

The official statement of US food and agricultural policy does not list any goals. It does, however, state that the challenge to policy is to manage change and to modernize American agriculture. US agricultural policy has increased the productivity of all inputs in agriculture, reduced uncertainty, and made food safer and more abundant. At the same time it has encouraged larger and more concentrated farms, monoculture and regional specialization in agricultural production. This has contributed to safe and abundant agricultural products and to national economic growth, but it has harmed the economies of some communities and regions, degraded the environment, and done nothing to protect natural amenities.

Ultimately, the amount of agricultural land converted to non-agricultural uses depends on the relative returns to agricultural and non-agricultural uses (as indicated by their relative market prices). The net impact of agricultural policy on agricultural land values is unclear. By themselves, subsidies to agriculture increase land values for agricultural uses, but to the extent that subsidies lead to over-production they reduce commodity prices, increase variable input prices and thus reduce land values. Other agricultural policies are designed to reduce production. The set-aside programs provide subsidies in return for reduced production of targeted agricultural commodities. An example is the Conservation Reserve Program, which encourages the long-term idling of millions of acres of farmland. Analysts generally agree that this has increased the flow of environmental and recreational services from agricultural land.

An ideal agricultural policy would not only raise returns to agricultural uses of land (which would make it more competitive with other uses on the margin), but it would also reward landowners for producing a broader array of goods and services. From a social welfare perspective, it would have the effect of encouraging higher valued overall production on agricultural land. This valuation would include all the services produced by the land, including the environmental amenities and benefits mentioned earlier. In the process, it would raise farm income, support rural communities and reduce the gap between agricultural and non-agricultural land values.

Environmental policy

Federal environmental policy has five goals (US Environmental Protection Agency 2003). These are to:

1   Protect and improve the air so it is healthy to breathe and free of levels of pollutants that harm human health or the environment.
2   Ensure that drinking water is safe. Restore and maintain oceans, watersheds and their aquatic ecosystems to protect human health, support economic and recreational activities and provide healthy habitat for fish, plants and wildlife.
3   Preserve and restore the land by reducing and controlling risks posed by releases of harmful substances; promoting waste diversion, recycling and innovative waste management practices; and cleaning up contaminated properties to levels appropriate for their beneficial reuse.
4   Protect, sustain or restore the health of people, communities and ecosystems using integrated and comprehensive approaches and partnerships.
5   Improve environmental performance through compliance with environmental requirements, preventing pollution and promoting environmental stewardship. Protect human health and the environment by encouraging innovation, and providing incentives for governments, businesses and the public that promote environmental stewardship.

Much of current environmental policy is remedial, especially from the perspective of land use. The policy involves the correction of environmental problems rather than the protection of the environment. And while land use is a critical factor in the quality of air and water, the location and nature of waste, and the health of communities and ecosystems, the goals are silent on this issue.

An environmental land use policy would identify those services from land that are of national significance, such as air quality, reduced acid rain, reduced greenhouse gases, protection of endangered species and waste management. Then programs would proactively promote the production of these services through such means as incentives and the creation of new markets.

As an example, consider the siting of large-scale confined animal feeding operations (CAFOs). Local governments are left with little guidance, incentives, or tools to deal with the location of CAFOs. Clearly, there are locations where these operations would have minimal impacts on air and water quality. At present the operations are located where local resistance to them is minimal and where regulation is scant. Similarly, solid waste, state prisons, power transmission lines, gravel pits, new transportation rights-of-way and other varieties of locally undesirable land uses (LULUs) tend to be located where the narrow costs of land, legal fees, lobbying costs and negotiated settlements are minimized. It is unlikely that these are close to the full costs of the sitings. Because of asymmetric information, high transaction costs involved in organizing opposition and the existence of smaller rural jurisdictions,[3] these sitings tend to disproportionately occur in poorer, more rural locations. This practice undoubtedly minimizes some costs, but far from all costs, and it leads to issues of environmental injustice and redistributions of income. Furthermore, and perhaps ironically, the siting process is often inefficient, leading to lengthy delays in investments and unnecessary costs to both those proposing and those opposing the sitings.

A good policy in this case would lead to the creation of efficient markets for otherwise external costs of locally undesirable land uses. This would require state and possibly Federal action because uniform regulations are necessary for this to work effectively. Consider confined animal feeding operations again. Research has shown that the odors from CAFOs depress property values in an area 3 to 5 miles around the farm itself (Hamed *et al.* 1999). A market for "odorshed" rights would require investors in CAFOs to acquire the odorshed rights from landowners in a prescribed radius of the facility.[4] This would favor the location of these facilities in the least objectionable locations, compensate those who are adversely affected by the siting, and provide incentives to reduce the environmental impacts of the CAFOs.

Transportation policy

The goals of Federal transportation policy are to (US Department of Transportation 2003):

1　Promote public health and safety by working toward the elimination of transportation-related deaths and injuries.
2　Shape an accessible, affordable, reliable transportation system for all people, goods and regions.
3　Support a transportation system that sustains the nation's economic growth.

4   Protect and enhance communities and the natural environment affected by transportation.
5   Ensure the security of the transportation system for the movement of people and goods, and support homeland security objectives.

Since much of our nation's transportation policy is the responsibility of state and local governments, Federal policy focuses on interstate connectivity, financing, technology development, education, research and information dissemination. In these capacities, Federal transportation policy plays a limited but significant role in land use. The interstate highway program, for instance, has had an enormous impact on local and regional land use, land values and economies. The allocation of transportation trust fund disbursements to highways, transit and trails affects our settlement patterns and land use. Support for inland waterways affects the profitability of agriculture and industry and indirectly affects land use. Airports, passenger rail and rail freight policies all affect land use as well.

Sound Federal land use policy would be based on a solid understanding of the full social costs and benefits of alternative transportation designs. It is quite likely that such a policy would include transportation financing programs that encourage reinvestment in existing cities and communities, and research programs that focus more on efficiencies in mass transit and freight.

Coordination of Federal land use policy

It should be clear that Federal policy is an important element in our overall land use milieu. It should also be clear that this policy is comprised of many policies and programs that are potentially uncoordinated. There are numerous examples of policies that work at cross purposes with each other – policies that promote greenfield development while others promote brownfield development, policies that subsidize use of scarce water, on the one hand, and discourage agricultural production, on the other.

How might the many policies, and agencies involved in policies, that directly or indirectly affect land use be coordinated? In Canada and Europe, important policies receive horizontal or intergovernmental review. In Canada, coordination of sustainable development policies is achieved through two horizontal institutions – the Deputy Minister Sustainable Development Coordinating Committee, and the Interdepartmental Network on Sustainable Development Strategies. In the rural development arena, Canada has an "Interdepartmental Working Group on Rural" that coordinates a wide array of policies. The working group employs a process called the Rural Lens, which is used to assess all policies from a rural perspective. In Europe, all European Union policy changes are reviewed by the Social and Economic Committee, and by the Committee of the Regions. These are examples of institutionalized processes that could be created in the United States to ensure greater coordination between Federal agencies and policy making.

State policies

Since state governments generally determine the responsibilities and powers of their local governments, one of the more critical roles that states play in land use is in enabling, and providing incentives for, local governments to adopt programs that benefit the state. States will benefit from local policies that (1) contribute to the economic growth and development of communities, regions and the state; (2) protect the state's environment; (3) protect unique or rare natural and historical amenities and encourage the production of man-made amenities such as scenic countryside and recreational opportunities; and (4) provide for optimal residential choice for state residents. Good state-level land use policy will enable, encourage and guide cities, counties and townships to adopt and use the kinds of tools outlined in other chapters of this volume. In general this will involve cost-sharing of programs with significant spillover effects beyond local boundaries, the encouragement of intergovernmental cooperation, judicious use of the taxing authority (more about this below) and focused infrastructure investments in areas where development and redevelopment have the highest net social benefits.

Local government tax structure is a critical determinant of land use (Pagano 2003). Reliance on sales taxes encourages development of commercial outlets, especially those that are believed to attract nonresident shoppers (usually these are near transportation routes on the edges of cities). The goal of placing the tax burden on nonresidents encourages vigorous competition among local governments, which in turn leads to sprawl (Center on Urban and Metropolitan Policy 2002). Differential sales taxes affect the location of commercial outlets. Sales tax exemptions for Internet and certain mail order businesses disadvantage "brick and mortar" businesses.

Heavy reliance on property taxes induces local governments to stress intensive land development. Higher real property taxes increase the cost of landownership while better local public services increase the benefits of landownership. Differentials in property tax assessments by land use (agricultural use value assessment, for example) affect land values, conversion rates and the spatial distribution of land use. In turn, these impacts affect local government revenues, expenditures and tax rates.

Local income taxes encourage local governments to compete for higher-income jobs. Residential developments and public services are stressed in economic development programs.

Development (or impact) fees influence the spatial distribution and level of new development. Optimal tax policy can increase property values, and ultimately reduce *ad valorem* tax rates. On the other hand, the revenues generated from development fees can increase the quality of public services and thus the rate of economic growth. Recent research supports the notion that impact fees can have a positive effect on economic development (Nelson and Moody 2003). Finally, good state land use policy will reduce the competition among local governments for retail sales and other types of predatory practices.

Conclusion

This chapter has sampled only some of the Federal and state policies and programs influencing land use in this country. Each of these policies and programs shapes the incentives faced by consumers, investors and local governments and influences their land use decision and policies.

The Federal government has a responsibility to influence land use for the ultimate benefit of the nation and to adjudicate interstate rivalries in the interest of all Americans. The Federal government also is a major actor in land use directly, as owner of hundreds of millions of acres. The goals of these direct policies are relatively easy to assess. But the Federal government also influences land use indirectly through its agricultural, environmental, transportation and other policies. The impact of these policies on land use are much more difficult to discern, but it is clear that they are significant and uncoordinated, if not contradictory.

Similarly, state governments have a responsibility to influence land use for the ultimate benefit of their residents and to adjudicate rivalries among localities. States have a particularly important role in creating the constraints and incentives faced by local governments since it is these local governments that have the most direct impact on private land use.

This multi-level, multi-sectoral, land use policy system in the United States leads to frequent conflict and stalemate. Many of the consequences are all but irreversible, and diminish present and future quality of life for large numbers of people. Good land use policy requires coordination among these levels and sectors and gives careful attention to the nine principles of good land use policy.

Notes

1 An optimal allocation is one that contributes to that combination of public and private goods and services that maximizes social welfare. Social welfare is a function of individual utility functions.
2 Goal 4 is essentially related to internal operations of the Service, including fiscal management and accountability, human resource development, information systems.
3 Solid waste facilities, nuclear power generators and prisons often locate in a geographically smaller as well as more sparsely populated jurisdiction where a relatively small inducement by the proponent of the project to the local government can significantly reduce the taxes to all tax payers in the jurisdiction. This creates an inter-jurisdictional externality borne by neighboring jurisdictions.
4 Alternatively, the property rights assignment could be reversed, which would require landowners to acquire odorshed rights from each of their neighbors to prevent these neighbors from siting CAFOs within their odorshed. This however would create a common property, with its inherent free-rider problem.

21 Future research needs for rational land use decisions

Stephan J. Goetz, James S. Shortle and John C. Bergstrom

Land use and how and where people live are complex subjects at the center of a growing debate over the efficiency and equity of contemporary land use decisions and patterns. Choices deemed sensible for individuals, households and businesses can have less than desirable consequences when viewed from the perspective of a community. In this sense, Schmid writes that:

> As long as we praise individualism and selfish maximization, we will get the world as we now see it – a collection of local boosters and real estate rent collectors ... [along with a] hurried, harried, congested, polluted lifestyle ... We are caught in a grand prisoner's dilemma where the dominant choice is a trap.
>
> (Schmid 2003: 717)

The challenge is to identify and implement reforms and innovations in property rights, the provision and pricing of public services, tax policies, land use planning, and other collective institutions that society uses to directly and indirectly control land use in order to bring about land use patterns that are socially preferred. This is a tall order. It requires understanding what types of land use are socially preferred. It also requires identifying and evaluating potential reforms and innovations to arrive at specific actions that will be effective, efficient, fair and not overly restrictive of freedom of choice. The irreversible nature of many current land use decisions and patterns has added a sense of urgency to this challenge. However, there is no consensus regarding how and to what degree land should be managed in different local areas, regions and nations. Additionally, little is known about the values that individuals – and society in general – assign to different land uses and landscapes.

Increases in human populations mean that more homes (and retail stores) have to be built to accommodate that growth. Land use discussions about housing development and urban sprawl usually ignore the fact that individuals would be worse off if they were prevented from moving into the new subdivisions developing around metro areas. These opportunity costs associated with restricting consumer housing and lifestyle choices must be considered in discussions of land use planning and development.

One result of doing nothing is continuation of current land use trends. These include the rising costs of traffic congestion and various health concerns associated with urban lifestyles based on sprawl, including exposure to environmental pollution and poor physical fitness. Individual communities will continue to have difficulty balancing the needs of newcomers with those of long-time residents. In addition, fragile ecosystems will be further fragmented or completely lost, threatening or endangering certain species. Farmland and green space will continue to disappear at rapid rates, resulting in the loss of both commodity and amenity values.

Four long-term research priority areas

Four critical research questions need to be addressed to facilitate rational problem solving and decision making related to land use problems and conflicts.

1 What are society's objectives for how land is used?

Precise definition and measurement are needed of what society in general, and different groups in particular, value about land ("values spheres") and the various services provided by a piece of land or landscapes. What is the willingness to pay for particular private and public commodities and services provided by land and landscapes? What are the public objectives for rural land conservation and development and – in a political economy context – whose preferences are counted under which circumstances? How are current public sentiments toward rural land use related to interest groups or sociodemographic characteristics? Again, some information is available from selected local areas and regions, but more systematic and multidisciplinary studies are needed on national scales. In addition, the public's desires for land use must be communicated more effectively.

Research results will drive the development of a new framework for public policy education on land use issues and decision making. The framework will serve several purposes and allow a number of objectives to be accomplished. It must be able to (a) distinguish between private and public land uses and values; (b) elicit consumers' preferences and willingness to pay or willingness to accept compensation for alternative land uses and landscapes; (c) reconcile competing private and public objectives through consensus building; (d) abstract ideas about possible and actual uses of land; and (e) account for interregional dependence and spillovers. In the long run, questions and concerns about the irreversibility of land conversions must be addressed if decisions in retrospect prove to be shortsighted. Examples of such shortsightedness include building the "wrong" housing stock, facilitating the "wrong" patterns of development, allowing long-term food security to become an issue, or irrevocably destroying species that could have provided benefits in the future or prevented future costs.

2 What are homebuyers' residential preferences and how do they compare with the actual residential choices available?

Current patterns of development available to homebuyers need to be inventoried, categorized and formally described, recognizing potential regional differences. Patterns of development include urban in-fill, New Urbanism-type development, planned development (e.g., Seaside, Florida, USA), cluster development, development on quarter-acre lots, development on one-acre lots, large lot (down zoning) development, country estates, farmettes, etc. While potentially appealing to many homebuyers, modern planned developments tend to offer only relatively high-cost housing.

Homeowners clearly vote with their incomes and their feet as they move into sprawling subdivisions. More information is needed, however, about whether consumers' housing preferences and demands are being met. Are the desired bundles of market and nonmarket housing services and benefits available to homebuyers, and if not, why not? Do sprawling suburbs fully meet their demands or would homebuyers rather live in other types of developments that are either not available or not affordable? Builders claim that they "are building what consumers want," while critics counter that homebuyers have only limited choices when they shop for a new home. Once different housing options or bundles have been delineated, we need to better understand how consumers choose among these options. For example, how many minutes is a consumer willing to add to her daily commute to work in exchange for a lot that is one quarter of an acre larger? And, could the market and nonmarket services and benefits provided by this larger lot be provided using less land closer to the place of work?

A subset of questions relates to why homeowners move to where they move, and whether their actual housing choices are consistent with their revealed and stated preferences in terms of land use decisions and patterns. Are they seeking green living environments, or are they moving to escape perceived high taxes, crime and poor educational systems? Most likely, both "pull factors" (e.g., desire for more open or green space) and "push factors" (e.g., desire to get away from high taxes and crime rates) drive consumer housing demands and resulting residential land development patterns. Surveys conducted in states such as California and Oregon in the United States (e.g., Holtzclaw 1997) have been used to gather information on homeowners' preferences, but such surveys have not yet been replicated systematically in other parts of the country or world to determine whether preferences in other regions or nations provide similar information. Most surveys of housing preferences do not enquire about broader community characteristics such as environmental amenities and overall congestion or space-between-people.

3 What are the full benefits and costs of alternative patterns of development?

What benefits and costs are associated with different patterns of development across the nation? Costs and benefits foregone have to be measured precisely if all externalities are to be internalized, with payments for costs and benefits accruing to those who create them (Schmid 2003). Benefits and costs include environmental or ecological factors, population health, social capital, amenities and economic variables such as meeting consumer demands. The full range of impacts of different land uses and patterns of development, including supply and demand issues, is shown in Figure 1.1 (page 4). Patterns of development – and the magnitude and amount of development – have varying impacts on government finances, ecosystems, and population health, as well as economic and social factors.

Many of the links shown in Figure 1.1 are only hypotheses at this time, although some have been analyzed in simulation studies (e.g., Rodier and Johnston 1997). Rigorous qualitative and quantitative studies are needed to affirm and quantify these links at the county and sub-county levels of government. In addition, a much better understanding is needed of the magnitude and patterns of land developed for residential housing.

4 Which public policy objectives can be met by different portfolios of land use policies?

Once private and public land use preferences and objectives have been identified, we need to determine which portfolio of institutions will allow these preferences and objectives to be satisfied and met. For example, increases in consumer incomes translate into private preferences and demand for second or vacation homes. The private real estate market generally works well to satisfy private preferences and demand for these types of homes and there is little the government can do to stop these market transactions short of outlawing second home ownership. However, government rules and regulation such as zoning and setbacks may need to be implemented to meet public preferences and demand for, say, protection of lake or river quality from potential pollution problems caused by residential development (e.g., sediment runoff from construction sites). Likewise, continued growth in the population and number of households affects land use. The National Association of Home Builders forecasts that 1.2 million new single-family units will have to be built each year between 2001 and 2010 to accommodate growing demand from new households in the United States. The sheer size of this increase in housing development will bring about significant future changes in US land use and landscapes.

In this context, how effective are different land use-related policy tools for satisfying and meeting revealed and stated land use preferences and objectives? How effective are they in advancing longer-term societal goals? A systematic assessment of incentives and regulations related to land use in different states, regions and nations is urgently needed. This assessment should consider which specific policies work well individually and together. Unintended consequences of land use decisions and patterns should also be identified and assessed. Potential opportunities for rent-seeking arise whenever the government intervenes in the market for land. Thus, policies or decision making procedures that limit opportunities for rent-seeking by private parties through the land use policy and growth-control system should also be assessed. Another assessment need is to identify gaps between good policy structure (theory) and poor policy implementation. Such a gap arises, for example, in the case of transferable development rights, where there is disagreement about the effectiveness and equity of the policy when these rights are actually implemented (see also Lynch 2004, chapter 19 this volume). Finally, there is a need to assess policies that are not intended to affect land use, but that do so unintentionally. These include taxes or subsidies that influence the relative returns on alternative land uses, and the pricing and provision of transportation, sewer and water, and other public services that shape demands for land use. It is especially important to identify policies that are in conflict with social objectives for land use.

Concurrent priorities and action steps

Two concurrent activities must be carried out as the above long-term research priorities are being implemented.

1 Improve databases and decision support systems related to land use

Centralized archives of comprehensive and consistent (using the same standards) data across jurisdictions are needed to better understand and assess land use problems and conflicts. These data sometimes exist within individual communities, but not at a scale readily usable by researchers. Current local, state and national data collection systems are not sufficiently accurate or reliable sources of land use information. Specifically, we need to compile spatially referenced, GIS-type data that represent variables and information from multiple disciplines (see also Bell 2004, chapter 11 this volume).

Multi-state and regional research is needed with cooperation among rural, urban, and transportation economists and sociologists, environmental psychologists and planners, as well as political scientists, as an essential component. Land use conflicts and problems are so complex that no single discipline has all of the answers (or even the questions), or can develop the comprehensive decision support systems that communities need to have if they are to address the problems effectively. So-called endogeneity issues must be addressed analytically. For example, traffic congestion often leads to more road construction, which in turn invites even more congestion; poor environmental conditions lead to stricter regulations that in turn affect environmental conditions in subsequent periods. Thus, when it comes to understanding and assessing land use problems and conflicts, cause and effect relationships are not always clear and need more careful consideration and analysis. More generally, the human or social sciences dimensions of land use problems and conflicts need to gain greater prominence in existing land use simulation and other studies.

2 Land use projections and longitudinal studies

Future land use outcomes, along with policy mechanisms, need to be better forecast through build-out and other analyses that allow residents to visualize what their communities will look like if they keep on developing the way they have in the past. This includes a retrospective evaluation of policies answering questions such as: Did the policies have their intended effects? What were the unintended consequences? And, what were the equity or distributional fairness effects? New policy structures need to be designed that facilitate and accelerate feedback from objective impact evaluation to contemporaneous policy, allowing policy makers to establish more timely and effective policy. An urgent need exists to produce results that improve our knowledge and policy performance in the short run. Over the longer term, forward-looking research that supports the updating of policies and addresses newly realized private and public preferences and objectives for land and landscapes is a major need. This work should be carried out in collaboration with researchers from the natural and planning sciences, incorporating longitudinal studies on focused issues.

A final word

Unlike most research efforts addressing land use problems and conflicts, the agenda outlined here is intended to be comprehensive and integrated. It addresses economic, social, environmental and human health impacts of land use. These broad perspectives are essential to fully understand the causes and effects of current land use practices and patterns. Because land use problems and conflicts appear to be worsening worldwide and many land use decisions made today cannot be easily reversed in the future, if at all, there is a critical need to pursue a targeted research agenda such as that discussed in this book. Information that addresses the questions and issues included in a comprehensive and integrated land use research agenda will help both prevent and solve land use problems and conflicts currently plaguing scarce land resources outside our backdoors, in our communities and around the world.

Bibliography

Abbott, C. (1997) "The Portland Region: Where City and Suburbs Talk to Each Other – and Often Agree," *Housing Policy Debate*, 8(1): 11–51.

Abdalla, C.W. (2001) "Protecting Farmland at the Fringe: Do Regulations Work? Strengthening the Research Agenda" (ed.) Regional Rural Development Paper no. 7, University Park, PA: Penn State University, The Northeast Regional Center for Rural Development.

Abeles-Allison, M. and Connor, L.J. (1990) "An Analysis of Local Benefits and Costs of Michigan Hog Operations Experiencing Environmental Conflicts," Agricultural Economics Report no. 536, East Lansing, MI: Michigan State University, Department of Agricultural Economics.

Abler, D. (2001a) "Multifunctionality: The Question of Jointness: Applying the OECD Framework, A Review of Literature in the United States," Paris: Organization for Economic Cooperation and Development. Online, available at: http://www1.oecd.org/agr/mf/doc/USA-Abler-revised.pdf (accessed 25 February 2004).

—— (2001b) "A Synthesis of Country Reports on Jointness between Commodity and Non-Commodity Outputs in OECD Agriculture," Paris: Organization for Economic Cooperation and Development. Online, available at: http://www1.oecd.org/agr/mf/doc/agrmf_abler_rev.pdf (accessed 25 February 2004).

—— (2001c) "Elasticities of Substitution and Factor Supply in Canadian, Mexican and United States Agriculture" in OECD (ed.) *Market Effects of Crop Support Measures*, 57–88, Paris: Organization for Economic Cooperation and Development. Online, available at: http://www1.oecd.org/publications/e-book/5101141E.pdf (accessed 25 February 2004).

Abt Associates (1999) *Adverse Health Effects Associated with Ozone in the Eastern United States*, Washington, DC: Abt Associates.

Adams, W.M. (2003) *Future Nature*, 2nd edn, London: Earthscan.

Allan, J.D., Erickson, D.L. and Fay, J. (1997) "The Influence of Catchment Land Use On Stream Integrity Across Multiple Spatial Scales," *Freshwater Biology*, 37: 149–161.

Alonso, W. (1960) "A Theory of the Urban Land Market," *Papers and Proceedings of the Regional Science Association*, 6: 149–157.

—— (1964) *Location and Land Use*, Cambridge, MA: Harvard University Press.

Altshuler, A.A. and Gomez-Ibanez, J.A. (1993) *Regulation for Revenue: The Political Economy of Land Use Exactions*, Washington, DC: Brookings Institution.

American Farmland Trust (1994) *Farming on the Edge: A New Look at the Importance and Vulnerability of Agriculture Near American Cities*, Washington, DC: American Farmland Trust.

—— (1997) *Saving American Farmland: What Works*, Northampton, MA: American Farmland Trust.

—— (2001a) "Status of Selected Local PACE Programs: Fact Sheet," Washington, DC: American Farmland Trust.

—— (2001b) "Status of State PACE Programs: Fact Sheet," Washington, DC: American Farmland Trust.

—— (2001c) "Transfer of Development Rights: Fact Sheet," Washington, DC: American Farmland Trust.

—— (2002) "Cost of Community Services Studies," Farmland Information Center, American Farmland Trust. Online, available at: http://www.farmlandinfo.org/documents/27757/FS_COCS_11-02.pdf (accessed 5 April 2004).

American Institute of Chartered Public Accountants (2001) "The Principles of Good Tax Policy: A Framework for Evaluating Tax Proposals," Jersey City, NJ. Online, available at: http://ftp.aicpa.org/public/download/members/div/tax/3-01.pdf (accessed 30 July 2001).

American Planning Association (1991) "Does Development Really Pay for Itself?" Public Investment/Planning Advisory Service Memo, September, Chicago, IL: American Planning Association.

American Planning Association and American Institute of Certified Planners (2000) "The Millennium Planning Survey: A National Poll of American Voters' Views on Land Use." Online, available at: http://www.planning.org/newsrelease/pdf/APA%20Survey.pdf (accessed 2 September 2002).

Anas, A. (1987) *Modeling in Urban and Regional Economics*, New York: Hardwood Academic.

Anas, A. and Xu, R. (May 1999) "Congestion, Land Use, and Job Dispersion: A General Equilibrium Model," *Journal of Urban Economics*, 45: 451–473.

Anas, A., Arnott, R. and Small, K. (September 1998) "Urban Spatial Structure," *Journal of Economic Literature*, 36(3): 1426–1464.

Anderson, E. (1993) *Value in Ethics and Economics*, Cambridge, MA: Harvard University Press.

Anderson, J.E. (1993) "State Tax Credits and Land Use: Policy Analysis of Circuit-Breaker Effects," *Resource and Energy Economics*, 15: 295–312.

Anderson, J.E. and Bunch, H.D. (1989) "Agricultural Property Tax Relief: Tax Credits, Tax Rates, and Land Values," *Land Economics*, 65: 13–22.

Anselin, L. (1988) *Spatial Econometrics: Methods and Models*, Dordrecht: Kluwer Academic.

—— (1998) "Exploratory Spatial Data Analysis in a Geocomputational Environment," in P. Longley, S. Brooks, B. Macmillan and R. McDonnell (eds) *GeoComputation: A Primer*, New York: Wiley, 77–94.

—— (2001) "Spatial Econometrics," in B. Baltagi (ed.) *A Companion to Theoretical Econometrics*, Oxford: Basil Blackwell, 310.

—— (2002) "Under the Hood: Issues in the Specification and Interpretation of Spatial Regression Models," *Agricultural Economics*, 17(3): 247–267.

Anselin, L. and Florax, R.J. (1995) *New Directions in Spatial Econometrics*, New York: Springer Verlag.

Applegate, A. (15 November 2002) "Using the Marketplace to Slow Sprawl," Stroudsburg, PA: *Pocono Record*.

Arendt, R. (1992) *Rural by Design*, Chicago: American Planning Association.

Arrow, K.J. (1974) "Gifts and Exchanges," *Philosophy and Public Affairs*, 1, Washington, DC: Brookings Institution.

Auer, M.J. (1989) "The Preservation of Historic Barns," Preservation Brief no. 20, Washington, DC: US National Park Service. Online, available at: http://www2.cr.nps.gov/tps/briefs/brief20.htm (accessed 25 February 2004).

Babcock, R. and Bosselman, F. (1975) "Land Use Controls: History and Legal Status," *Management and Control of Growth*, Washington, DC: The Urban Land Institute, 1, 196–210.

Bailey, T.C. and Gatrell, A.C. (1995) *Interactive Spatial Data Analysis*, Harlow, England: Pearson Education Limited.

Ball, E., Butault, J.P. and Nehring, R. (2001) *US Agriculture, 1960–96: A Multilateral Comparison of Total Factor Productivity*, Technical Bulletin no. 1895, Washington, DC: United States Department of Agriculture/Economic Research Service. Online, available at: http://www.ers.usda.gov/publications/tb1895/ (accessed 25 February 2004).

Barnard, C.H. (2001) "Urbanization Affects a Large Share of Farmland," *Rural Conditions and Trends*, 10(2): 57–63.

Barnes, K.B., Morgan, J.M. III and Roberge, M.C. (2001) "Impervious Surfaces and the Quality of Natural and Built Environments," 28, Baltimore, MD: Towson University, Department of Geography and Environmental Planning.

Barrows, R.L. and Prenguber, B.A. (1975) "Transfer of Development Rights: An Analysis of a New Land Use Policy Tool," *American Journal of Agricultural Economics*, 57(4): 549–557.

—— (1976) "Transfer of Development Rights: An Analysis of a New Land Use Policy Tool: Reply," *American Journal of Agricultural Economics*, 58(4): 763–766.

Bateman, I.J., Jones, A.P., Lovett, A.A., Lake, I.R. and Day, B.H. (2003) "Applying Geographical Information Systems to Environmental and Resource Economics," *Environmental and Resource Economics*, 22: 219–269.

Batie, S. and Ervin, D. (1999) "Flexible Incentives for Environmental Management in Agriculture: A Typology," in F. Casey, A. Schmitz, S. Swinton and D. Zilberman (eds) *Flexible Incentives for the Adoption of Environmental Technologies in Agriculture*, Norwell, MA: Kluwer Academic Publishers, 55–78.

Bay Journal (May 1997) "Maryland Enacts Sweeping Growth Management Law," 7(3).

Beasley, S.D., Workman, W.G. and Williams, N.A. (October 1986) "Estimating Amenity Values of Urban Fringe Farmland: A Contingent Valuation Approach: Note," *Growth and Change*, 17(4): 70–78.

Beegle, D.B. (1997) "Pennsylvania's Nutrient Management Act: Who Will Be Affected?" Agronomy Fact Sheet (54), University Park, PA: Penn State University.

Bell, K. and Bockstael, N. (2000) "Applying the Generalized-Moments Estimation Approach to Spatial Problems Involving Microlevel Data," *The Review of Economics and Statistics*, 82(1): 72–82.

Bell, K.P. and Irwin, E.G. (2002) "Spatially Explicit Micro-Level Modelling of Land Use Change at the Rural–Urban Interface," *Agricultural Economics*, 27: 217–232.

Bell, T. (1 December 2002) "Threats to Timberland: Prime Forests Have Been Cleared to Make Way for Development in Another Southern Maine Town – At Risk is the Long-Term Survival of the Nation's White Pine Industry," *Maine Sunday Telegram*, 1A, 6A–8A.

Bem, D.J. (1970) *Beliefs, Attitudes, and Human Affairs*, Monterey, CA: Brooks Cole.

Benfield, F.K., Raimi, M.D. and Chen, D.T. (1999) *Once There Were Greenfields*, Washington, DC: National Resources Defense Council, Surface Transportation Policy Project.

Bergstrom, J.C. (August 2001) "The Role and Value of Natural Capital in Regional Landscapes," *Journal of Agricultural and Applied Economics*, 33(2): 283–296.

Bergstrom, J.C. and Ready, R.C. (2004) "Economic Valuation of Farm and Ranch Land Amenities: What Economists Have Learned about Public Values and Preferences," conference proceedings of the workshop on "What the Public Values about Farmland," State College, PA: Penn State University, The Northeast Regional Center for Rural Development.

Bergstrom, J.C., Dillman, B.L. and Stoll, J.R. (July 1985) "Public Environmental Amenity Benefits of Private Land: The Case of Prime Agricultural Land," *Southern Journal of Agricultural Economics*, 17(1): 139–150.

Berndt, E.R. (1991) *The Practice of Econometrics*, Reading, MA: Addison-Wesley Publishing Co.

Beyers, W.B. (2000) *Service Industries Have Powered Growth of Employment in the US South in Recent Years: A Geographical Perspective*, TVA Rural Studies Program, Contractor Paper 00-15. Online, available at: http://www.rural.org/publications/Beyers00-15.pdf (accessed 25 February 2004).

Bignal, E.M. and McCracken, D.I. (June 1996) "Low Intensity Farming Systems in the Conservation of the Countryside," *Journal of Applied Ecology*, 33(3): 413–424.

Birkback, M. (9 April 2001) "Keystone Development Co. Lures Families by Urging Them to Escape Urban Violence," Stroudsburg, PA: *Pocono Record*.

Blakely, M. (1991) "An Economic Analysis of the Effects of Development Rights Purchases on Land Values in King County, Washington," M.S. Thesis, Washington State University.

Blandford, D., Boisvert, R.N. and Fulponi, L. (2003) "Nontrade Concerns: Reconciling Domestic Policy Objectives with Freer Trade in Agricultural Products," *American Journal of Agricultural Economics*, 85(3): 668–673.

Blewett, R.A. and Lane, J.I. (1988) "Development Rights and the Differential Assessment of Agricultural Land: Fractional Valuation of Farmland Is Ineffective for Preserving Open Space and Subsidizes Speculation," *American Journal of Economics and Sociology*, 47(2): 195–205.

Boarnet, M.G. and Haughwout, A.F. (August 2000) "Do Highways Matter? Evidence and Policy Implications of Highway's Influence on Metropolitan Development," discussion paper prepared for The Brookings Institution Center on Urban and Metropolitan Policy.

Bockstael, N.E. (1996) "Modeling Economics and Ecology: The Importance of a Spatial Perspective," *American Journal of Agricultural Economics*, 785: 1168–1180.

Bockstael, N.E. and Bell, K.P. (1997) "Land Use Patterns and Water Quality: The Effect of Differential Land Management Controls," in R. Just and S. Netanyahu (eds) *International Water and Resource Economics Consortium, Conflict and Cooperation on Trans-Boundary Water Resources*, Dordrecht: Kluwer Publishing.

Bockstael, N.E., Costanza, R., Strand, I., Boynton, W. and Bell, K.P. (1995) "Ecological Economic Modeling and Valuation of Ecosystems," *Ecological Economics*, 14(2): 143–159.

Bohman, M., Cooper, J., Mullarkey, D., Normile, M.A., Skully, D., Vogel, S. and Young, E. (1999) "The Use and Abuse of Multifunctionality," Washington, DC:

USDA/Economic Research Service. Online, available at: http://www.ers.usda.gov/Briefing/WTO/PDF/multifunc1119.pdf (accessed 25 February 2004).

Bosselman, F. and Callies, D. (1973) *The Quiet Revolution in Land Use Control*, Washington, DC: US Printing Office.

Bowen, G. (2000) Calvert County Office of Planning and Zoning, personal communication.

Bowers, D. (2001) "Sonoma, Berks, Lancaster Gain Most Acres; Top 12 Named," *Farmland Preservation Report*, 11(9): 1–6.

Bowers, J.K. and Cheshire, P. (1983) *Agriculture, the Countryside and Land Use: An Economic Critique*, London: Methuen and Company.

Bowker, J.M. and Didychuk, D.D. (October 1994) "Estimation of Nonmarket Benefits of Agricultural Land Retention in Eastern Canada," *Agricultural and Resource Economics Review*, 218–225.

Brandenburg, A.M. and Carroll, M.S. (1995) "Your Place or Mine? The Effect of Place Creation on Environmental Values and Landscape Meanings," *Society and Natural Resources*, 8: 381–398.

Bressi, T.W. (1994) "Planning the American Dream," in P. Katz (ed.) *The New Urbanism: Towards an Architecture of Community*, New York: McGraw-Hill.

Bromley, D. and Hodge, I. (1990) "Private Property Rights and Presumptive Policy Entitlements: Reconsidering the Premises of Rural Policy," *European Review of Agricultural Economics*, 17: 197–214.

Brubaker, R. (1984) *The Limits of Rationality: An Essay on the Social and Moral Thought of Max Weber*, London: George Allen & Unwin.

Brueckner, J.K. (1997) "Infrastructure Financing and Urban Development: The Economies of Impact Fees," *Journal of Public Economics*, 66: 383–407.

—— (2000) "Urban Sprawl: Diagnosis and Remedies," *International Regional Science Review*, 23(2): 160–171.

Brueckner, J.K. and Fansler, D. (1983) "The Economics of Urban Sprawl: Theory and Evidence on the Spatial Sizes of Cities," *Review of Economics and Statistics*, 55: 479–482.

Brunstad, R.J., Gaasland, I. and Vårdal, E. (1999) "Agricultural Production and the Optimal Level of Landscape Preservation," *Land Economics*, 75(4): 538–546.

Brunstad, R.J., Gaasland, I. and Vårdal, E. (2001) "Multifunctionality of Agriculture: An Inquiry into the Complementarity between Landscape Preservation and Food Security," 77th European Association of Agricultural Economists Seminar, Helsinki. Online, available at: http://www.ptt.fi/eaae-njf/papers/brunstad.pdf (accessed 25 February 2004).

Builders Association of the Twin Cities (1996) "The High Costs of Sprawl: Urban Land Supply Analysis and Recommendations for Managing Growth," Minneapolis/St. Paul, MN: Builders Association of the Twin Cities.

Buller, H., Wilson, G. and Höll, A. (eds) (2000) *Agri-Environmental Policy in the European Union*, Aldershot, UK: Ashgate.

Bunnell, G. (1997) "Fiscal Impact Studies as Advocacy and Story Telling," *Journal of Planning Literature*, 12(2): 136–151.

—— (1998) "Analyzing the Fiscal Impact of Development: Lessons for Building Successful Communities," *Journal of the Community Development Society*, 29(1): 38–57.

Buol, S.W. (1994) "Soils," in W.B. Meyer and B.L. Turner II (eds) *Changes in Land Use and Land Cover: A Global Perspective*, Cambridge, MA: Cambridge University Press, 211–229.

Burchell, R.W. and Listokin, D. (1978) *The Fiscal Impact Handbook*, New Brunswick, NJ: Rutgers University, Center for Urban Policy Research.

Burchell, R.W. and Listokin, D. (1980) *Practitioner's Guide to Fiscal Impact Analysis*, New Brunswick, NJ: Rutgers University, Center for Urban Policy Research.

Burchell, R.W. and Listokin, D. (1994) *Fiscal Impact Procedures and State of the Art*, Cambridge, MA: Lincoln Institute of Land Policy.

Burchell, R.W., Listokin, D. and Dolphin, W. (1985) *The New Practitioner's Guide to Fiscal Impact Analysis*, New Brunswick, NJ: Rutgers University, Center for Urban Policy Research.

Burchell, R.W., Shad, N.A., Listokin, D., Phillips, H., Seskin, S., Davis, J.S., Moore, T., Helton, D. and Gall, M. (1998) *The Costs of Sprawl Revisited: Transportation Research Board Report 39*, Washington, DC: National Academy Press.

Burchell, R.W., Lowenstein, G., Dolphin, W.R., Galley, C.C., Downs, A., Seskin, S., Still, K.G. and Moore, T. (2002) *Costs of Sprawl–2000: Transit Cooperative Research Program Report 74*, Washington, DC: National Academy Press.

Bureau of Land Management (2003) "BLM Facts," Washington, DC: Bureau of Land Management. Online, available at: http://www.blm.gov/nhp/facts/index.htm (accessed 23 June 2003).

Burgess, P. and Bier, T. (1998) "Public Policy and Rural Sprawl: Lessons from Northeast Ohio," Working Paper no. WP98PB2, Cambridge, MA: Lincoln Institute of Land Policy.

Burrell, A. (2001) "Synthesis of the Evidence on the Possible Impact of Commodity Price Decreases on Land Use and Commodity Production, and the Incidence on the Provision of Non-Commodity Outputs," Paris: Organization for Economic Cooperation and Development. Online, available at: http://www1.oecd.org/agr/mf/doc/burell.pdf (accessed 25 February 2004).

Calthorpe, P.G. (1993) *The Next American Metropolis: Ecology, Community and the American Dream*, Princeton, NJ: Princeton University Press.

Calthorpe, P. and Fulton, W. (2001) *The Regional City*, 84, Washington, DC: Island Press.

Cameron, E.A. (1996) *Land for the People? The British Government and the Scottish Highlands, 1880–1925*, East Linton: Tuckwell Press.

Capiella, K. and Brown, K. (2001) *Impervious Cover and Land Use in the Chesapeake Bay Watershed*, Ellicot City, MD: Center for Watershed Protection.

Carpenter, J. and Lynch, L. (2002) *Is There a Critical Mass Needed to Sustain an Agricultural Economy? Evidence from Six Mid-Atlantic States*, College Park, MD: University of Maryland, Center for AgroEcology, Inc.

Carpenter, S.R., Caraco, N.F., Correll, D.L., Howarth, R.W., Sharpley, A.N. and Smith, V.H. (1998) "Nonpoint Pollution of Surface Waters with Phosphorus and Nitrogen," *Ecological Applications*, 8(3): 559–568.

Carpentier, C.L., Bosch, D.J. and Batie, S.S. (1998) "Using Spatial Information to Reduce Costs of Controlling Agricultural Nonpoint Source Pollution," *Agricultural and Resource Economics Review*, 27(1): 72–84.

Carrion, C. and Libby, L. (2000) "Development Impact Fees: A Primer," AEDE-WP-0022-01. Online, available at: http://aede.osu.edu/resources/docs (accessed 30 October 2003).

Carson, R. (1962) *Silent Spring*, Boston, MA: Houghton Mifflin.

Case, A. and Katz, L. (1991) "The Company You Keep: The Effect of Family and

Neighborhood on Disadvantaged Youth," National Bureau of Economic Research Working Paper no. 3705.

Center for Urban Policy Research (1992) "Impact Assessment of the New Jersey Interim State Development and Redevelopment Plan," New Brunswick, NJ: Rutgers University.

Center for Watershed Protection (2003) "Impacts of Impervious Cover on Aquatic Systems," *Watershed Protection Research Monograph* (1): 142, Ellicott City, MD.

Center on Urban and Metropolitan Policy (December 2002) *Growth in the Heartland: Challenges and Opportunities for Missouri*, Washington, DC: Brookings Institution. Online, available at: http://www.brook.edu/es/urban/missouri/abstract.htm (accessed 15 August 2003).

Centre for Rural Economics Research (2002) "Economic Evaluation of the Organic Farming Scheme," report to the Department for Environment, Food and Rural Affairs, Cambridge, UK: University of Cambridge, Department of Land Economy.

Chen, A. (Spring 1994) "Heat Islands – And How To Cool Them," *Center for Building Science News*.

Chen, D.D.T. (December 2000) "The Science of Smart Growth," *Scientific American*, 283(6): 84–91.

Chen, R.S. (1998) "Appendix A: An Annotated Guide to Earth Remote Sensing Data and Information Resources for Social Science Applications," in D. Liverman, E. Moran, R. Rindfuss and P.C. Stern (eds) *People and Pixels: Linking Remote Sensing and Social Science*, Washington, DC: National Academy Press, 209–228.

Cheng, A.S., Kruger, L.E. and Daniels, S.E. (2003) "'Place' as an Integrating Concept in Natural Resource Politics: Propositions for a Social Science Research Agenda," *Society and Natural Resources*, 8(2): 87–104.

Chesapeake Bay Commission and the Trust for Public Land (February 2001) *Keeping Our Commitment: Preserving Land in the Chesapeake Watershed*, Annapolis, MD: Chesapeake Bay Foundation and The Trust for Public Land.

Chesapeake Bay Foundation (2000) *Land and the Chesapeake Bay*, Annapolis, MD: Chesapeake Bay Foundation.

—— (2002) "Future Growth in the Washington, DC, Metropolitan Area," Annapolis, MD. Online, available at: http://www.savethebay.org/land/landuse/maps/futuregrowth.html (accessed 2 September 2002).

Chicoine, D.L. (August 1981) "Farmland Values at the Urban Fringe: An Analysis of Sale Prices," *Land Economics*, 57: 353–362.

Chicoine, D.L., Sonka, S.T. and Doty, R.D. (1982) "The Effects of Farm Property Tax Relief Programs on Farm Financial Conditions," *Land Economics*, 58(4): 516–523.

Ciccone, A. and Hall, R. (1996) "Productivity and the Density of Economic Activity," *American Economic Review*, 86(1): 54–70.

Clarion Associates (2000) *The Costs of Sprawl in Pennsylvania*, Executive Summary, Philadelphia, PA: 10,000 Friends of Pennsylvania. Online, available at: http://www.10000friends.org/Web_Pages/News/Costs_of_Sprawl_in_Pennsylvania. pdf (accessed 1 April 2001).

Clark, K.L., Euler, D.L. and Armstrong, E. (1984) "Predicting Avian Community Response to Lakeshore Cottage Development," *Journal of Wildlife Management*, 48(4): 1239–1247.

Clawson, M. (1971) *Suburban Land Use Conversion in the United States: An Economic and Government Process*, Baltimore, MD: Johns Hopkins Press for Resources for the Future.

Cliff, A. and Ord, J.K. (1973) *Spatial Autocorrelation*, London: Pion Publishing.

Clonts, H.A. Jr (November 1970) "Influence of Urbanization on Land Values at the Urban Periphery," *Land Economics*, 46: 489–497.

Coalition of Watershed Towns (1993) "Comments on the Draft Generic Environmental Impact Statement for New York City's Draft Watershed Regulations," Delhi, NY: Coalition of Watershed Towns.

Coase, R. (1960) "The Problem of Social Cost," *Journal of Law and Economics*, 3, 1–44.

Cochrane, W.W. (1979) *The Development of American Agriculture*, Minneapolis, MN: University of Minnesota Press.

Colorado Agricultural Statistics Service (July 2003) *Colorado Agricultural Statistics 2000*, Lakewood, CO: Colorado Department of Agriculture and National Agricultural Statistics Service.

Colorado Conservation Trust (2001) "County and Municipal Revenues for Land Conservation in Colorado," Denver, CO, manuscript.

Colorado Department of Agriculture (1997) "Revenues for Colorado Land Conservation Programs," Denver, CO, manuscript.

Conner, R., Seidl, A., VanTassell, L. and Wilken, N. (June 2001) "United States Grasslands and Related Resources: An Economic and Biological Trends Assessment," consulting report to the National Cattlemen's Association and the Nature Conservancy, 158. Online, available at: http://landinfo.tamu.edu/ (accessed 22 November 2001).

Conrad, J.M. and LeBlanc, D. (1979) "The Supply of Development Rights: Results from a Survey in Hadley, Massachusetts," *Land Economics*, 55(2): 269–276.

Conway, R. (1990) "The Washington Projection and Simulation Model: A Regional Inter-industry Econometric Model," *International Regional Science Review*, 13(1–2): 141–165.

Cook, C. (28 September 1994) "Statement at the Hearings on Proposed New York City Watershed Regulations," Walton, New York.

Coomes, P., Olson, D. and Merchant, J. (1991) "Using a Metropolitan-Area Econometric Model to Analyse Economic Development Proposals," *Urban Studies*, 28(3): 369–382.

Cordes, M. (1997) "Leapfrogging the Constitution: The Rise of State Takings Legislation," *Ecology Law Quarterly*, 24: 187.

—— (1999) "Takings, Fairness, and Farmland Preservation," *Ohio State Law Journal*, 60: 1033–1084.

Correll, M.R., Lillydahl, J.H. and Singell, L.D. (1978) "The Effects of Greenbelts on Residential Property Values: Some Findings on the Political Economy of Open Space," *Land Economics*, 54(2): 207–217.

Cosby, A.G. (1997) "Future of Rural America," in G.A. Goreham (ed.) *Encyclopedia of Rural America: The Land and People*, 2, Santa Barbara, CA: ABC-CLIO, 296–298.

Costanza, R., d'Arge, R., de Groot, R., Farber, S., Grasso, M., Hannon B., Limburg, K., Naeem, S., O'Neill, R., Paruelo, J., Raskin, R., Sutton, P. and van den Belt, M. (1997) "The Value of the World's Ecosystem Services and Natural Capital," *Nature*, 387: 253–260.

Coughlin, R.E., Keene, J.C., Esseks, J.D., Toner, W. and Rosenberger, L. (1980) *National Agricultural Lands Study. The Protection of Farmland: A Reference Guidebook for State and Local Governments*, Washington, DC: US Government Printing Office.

Coupal, R. and Seidl, A. (March 2003) "Rural Land Use and Your Taxes: The Fiscal

Impact of Rural Residential Development in Colorado," Agricultural and Resource Policy Report, Fort Collins, CO: Colorado State University, Department of Agricultural and Resource Economics. APR03-02. Online, available at: http://dare.agsci.colostate.edu/csuagecon/extension/docs/landuse/apr03-02.pdf (accessed 30 January 2004).

Crompton, J.L. (2000) *The Impact of Parks and Open Space on Property Values and the Property Tax Base*, Ashburn, VA: National Recreation and Park Association.

Cronon, William (1991) *Nature's Metropolis: Chicago and the Great West*, New York: W.W. Norton & Company.

Cropper, M., Puri, J. and Griffiths, C. (2001) "Predicting the Location of Deforestation: The Role of Roads and Protected Areas in North Thailand," *Land Economics*, 77(2): 172–186.

Crosson, P.R. (1982) "The Long-term Adequacy of Agricultural Land," in P.R. Crosson (ed.) *Cropland Crisis: Myth or Reality?* Baltimore, MD: Johns Hopkins University Press.

—— (1985) "Agricultural Land: A Question of Values," in *Agriculture and Human Values*, 1–12.

Cushman, J.H., Jr (26 January 1996) "G.O.P. Backing Off from Tough Stand Over Environment," *New York Times*.

Cutler, D. and Glaeser, E. (1997) "Are Ghettos Good or Bad?" *Quarterly Journal of Economics*, 112(3): 827–873.

Czech, B., Krausman, P.R. and Devers, P.K. (2000) "Economic Associations Among Causes of Species Endangerment in the United States," *Bioscience*, 50(7): 593–601.

Dahl, T.E. (1990) "Wetlands Losses in the United States 1780's to 1980's," US Department of the Interior, Fish and Wildlife Service, Washington, DC. Online, available at: http://www.npwrc.usgs.gov/resource/othrdata/wetloss/wetloss.htm (accessed 16 July 1997).

—— (2000) "Status and Trends of Wetlands in the Coterminous United States 1987–1997," 82, Washington, DC: US Department of the Interior, Fish and Wildlife Service.

Daniels, T. (1999) *When City and Country Collide: Managing Growth in the Metropolitan Fringe*, Washington, DC: Island Press.

Daniels, T. and Lapping, M. (13 November 2001) "Farmland Preservation in America and the Issue of Critical Mass," paper presented at American Farmland Trust National Conference, Chicago, IL.

Danielson, M.N. and Wolpert, J. (1991) "Distributing the Benefits of Economic Growth," *Urban Studies*, 28: 393–412.

Danskin, M. (2000) "Conservation Easement Violations: Results from a Study of Land Trusts," *Land Trust Alliance Exchange*, winter edition.

Deller, S.C. (1999a) "The Economic and Fiscal Impact of a Proposed Super-Max Prison in Rural Wisconsin," Madison, WI: University of Wisconsin-Madison/ Extension, Department of Agricultural and Applied Economics, working paper.

Deller, S.C. (1999b) "CPAN Modeling Work Group: The Elements of a Basic CPAN Model," *Western Wire*, spring, 14–15.

Deller, S.C. and Koles, M. (1999) "The Economic and Fiscal Impact of the Oshkosh County Airport," Madison, WI: University of Wisconsin-Madison/Extension, working paper.

Deller, S.C. and Shields, M. (1996) "Clustering Wisconsin Counties for Analytical Comparisons," Center for Community Economic Development Staff Paper no. 96.7, University of Wisconsin-Madison: Department of Agricultural and Applied Economics. Online, available at: http://www.aae.wisc.edu/www/cced/967.pdf (accessed 30 October 2003).

Deller, S.C. and Shields, M. (1998) "Economic Impact Modeling as a Tool for Community Economic Development," *Journal of Regional Analysis and Policy*, 28(2): 76–95.

Department of the Environment, Food and Rural Affairs (2000) *Our Countryside: The Future – A Fair Deal for Rural England*, London: HMSO. Online, available at: http://www.defra.gov.uk/rural/ruralwp/whitepaper/ (accessed 9 February 2004).

Dewbre, J., Antón, J. and Thompson, W. (2001) "The Transfer Efficiency and Trade Effects of Direct Payments," *American Journal of Agricultural Economics*, 83(5): 1204–1214.

Dewhurst, J. and West, G. (1991) "Conjoining Regional and Inter-regional Input–Output Models with Econometric Models," in *New Directions in Regional Analysis: Integrated and Multi-regional Approaches*, London: Bellhaven, 171–186.

Dhillon, P.S. and Derr, D.A. (1974) "Critical Mass of Agriculture and the Maintenance of Productive Open Space," *Journal of Northeastern Agricultural Economics Council*, 3(1): 23–34.

Dimond, P. (2000) "Empowering Families to Vote with their Feet," in B. Katz (ed.) *Reflections on Regionalism*, Washington, DC: Brookings Institution, 249–272.

Ding, C., Knaap, G.J. and Hopkins, L.D. (1999) "Managing Urban Growth with Urban Growth Boundaries: A Theoretical Analysis," *Journal of Urban Economics*, 46: 53–68.

Dobbs, T. and Pretty, J. (2001) "Future Directions for Joint Agricultural–Environmental Policies: Implications of the United Kingdom Experience for Europe and the United States," South Dakota State University Economics Research Report 2001–1 and University of Essex Centre for Environment and Society Occasional Paper 2001–5. Online, available at: http://www2.essex.ac.uk/ces/ResearchProgrammes/CESOccasionalPapers/JP-AGRENVPL-Dobbs Pretty10 UK FINAL.pdf (accessed 25 February 2004).

Donovan, T.M., Jones, P.W., Annand, E.M. and Thompson, F.R. III (1997) "Variation in Local-Scale Edge Effects: Mechanisms and Landscape Context," *Ecology*, 78: 2064–2075.

Dorman, R.L. (1993) *Revolt of the Provinces: The Regionalist Movement in America, (1920–1945)*, Chapel Hill: University of North Carolina Press.

Downs, A. (1992) *Stuck in Traffic: Coping with Peak-Hour Traffic Congestion*, Washington, DC: Brookings Institution.

—— (1994) *New Visions for Metropolitan America*, Washington, DC: Brookings Institution.

—— (1999) "Some Realities about Sprawl and Urban Decline," *Housing Policy Debate*, 10(4): 955–974.

Drake, L. (1992) "The Non-Market Value of Swedish Agricultural Landscape," *European Review of Agricultural Economics*, 19(3): 351–364.

Drucker, P. (1989) *The New Realities*, New York: Harper and Row.

Duany, A. (December 2000) "A New Theory of Urbanism," *Scientific American*, 283(6): 90–91.

Duffy-Deno, K.T. (1997) "The Effect of State Parks on the County Economies of the West," *Journal of Leisure Research*, 29(2): 201–224.

Duke, J.M. and Lynch, L. (June 2003) "Farmland Preservation Techniques: Identifying New Options," Newark, DE: University of Delaware Food and Resource Economics Research Report 03-02.

Duncan, M.L. (1984) "Towards a Theory of Broad-based Planning for the Preservation of Agricultural Land," *Natural Resources Journal*, 24(1): 61–135.

Dunford, R.W. (1983) "Further Evidence on the Conversion of US Farmland to Urban or Transportation Uses," Washington, DC: Congressional Research Service.

Dunford, R.W., Marti, C.E. and Mittlehammer, R.C. (February 1985) "A Case Study of Rural Land Values at the Urban Fringe Including Subjective Buyer Expectations," *Land Economics*, 61: 10–16.

DuPage County Planning Department (1992) "Impacts of Development on DuPage County Property Taxes," DeKalb, IL: DuPage County Regional Planning Commission.

Dwyer, J. and Hodge, I. (1996) *Countryside in Trust, Land Management by Conservation, Amenity and Recreation Organizations*, Chichester, UK: John Wiley and Sons.

Dyckman, J.W. (1976) "Speculations on Future Urban Form," Johns Hopkins University, Baltimore, MD: Center for Metropolitan Planning and Research, working paper.

Eagly, A. and Chaiken, S. (1993) *The Psychology of Attitudes*, New York: Harcourt Brace Jovanovich.

EcoCity Cleveland (1996) *Moving to Corn Fields: A Reader on Urban Sprawl and the Regional Future of Northeast Ohio*, Cleveland Heights, OH: EcoCity Cleveland.

Edelman, M., Harris, H.M., Seidl, A. and Warner, M.L. (1999) *Summary of the 1998 National Survey of State Animal Confinement Policies*, Farm Foundation. Online, available at: http://cherokee.agecon.clemson.edu/confine.htm (accessed 15 January 2004).

Edwards, M. and Jackson-Smith, D. (2000) "Paying for Local Services: The Cost of Community Services for Nine Wisconsin Municipalities," Extension Research Report 2, Madison, WI: University of Wisconsin-Madison, Program on Agricultural Technology Studies. Online, available at: http://www.wisc.edu/pats/abspaying.htm (accessed 13 April 2004).

Edwards, M., Deller, S. and Betts, G. (under development) *Assessing the Impact of Development*, Madison, WI: University of Wisconsin-Madison/Extension.

Egan, A.F. and Luloff, A.E. (2000) "The Exurbanization of America's Forests," *Journal of Forestry*, 98: 26–30.

Elad, R.L., Clifton, I.D. and Epperson, J.E. (1994) "Hedonic Estimation Applied to the Farmland Market in Georgia," *Journal of Agricultural and Applied Economics*, 26(2): 351–366.

Elkinton, L. (1990) "Back Roads Adventures: A Private Enterprise Model for Nature Study on Public and Private Land," in W. Grafton, A. Farrise, D. Colyer, D. Smith and J. Miller (eds) *Income Opportunities for the Private Landowner through Management of Natural Resources and Recreation Access*, Morgantown, WV: West Virginia Extension Service, 301–305.

English Nature (2001) *State of Nature: The Upland Challenge*, Peterborough: English Nature.

Environmental Working Group (2001) *Farm Payment Database*. Online, available at: http://www.ewg.org (accessed 8 December 2001).

Ervin, D. (1999) "Toward GATT-Proofing Environmental Programmes for Agriculture," *Journal of World Trade*, 33(2): 63–82.

Esseks, J.D. and Long, L.M. (2001) "The Political Viability of Agricultural Protection Zoning to Prevent Premature Conversion of Farmland," in L.W. Libby and C. Abdalla (eds) *Protecting Farmland at the Fringe: Do Regulations Work? Strengthening The Research Agenda*, Conference Proceedings, Baltimore, MD, 5–7 September, 2001. Online, available at: http://aede.ag.ohio-state.edu/Programs/Swank/pdfs/protecting_farmland_at_the_fringe.pdf (accessed 15 April 2004).

Esseks, J.D. and Kraft, S.E. (2002) "Are Owners of Urban-Edge Agricultural Land Willing to Provide Environmental Benefits that Urban and Suburban Residents Value?" report for American Farmland Trust. Online, available at: http://www.aftresearch.org/farmbill/docs/FINLEnvirBenefitsFiveStates.doc (accessed 25 February 2004).

Evans, J. (1988) *Musts for USTs*, Washington, DC: US EPA.

Ewing, R. (1997) "Is Los Angeles-Style Sprawl Desirable?" *Journal of the American Planning Association*, 63(1): 107–126.

Ewing, R., Pendall, R. and Chen, D. (2003a) "Measuring Sprawl and Its Impact," Smart Growth America. Online, available at: http://www.smartgrowthamerica.org/sprawlindex/sprawlindex.html (accessed 27 March 2004).

Ewing, R., Schmid, T., Killingsworth, R., Zlot, A. and Raudenbush, S. (2003b) "Relationship Between Urban Sprawl and Physical Activity, Obesity, and Morbidity," *American Journal of Health Promotion*, September/October, 18(1): 47–57.

Falconer, K. and Whitby, M. (1999) "The Invisible Costs of Scheme Implementation and Administration," in G. Van Huylenbroeck and M. Whitby (eds) *Countryside Stewardship: Farmers, Policies and Markets*, Oxford, UK: Elsevier Science, 67–88.

Falconer, K., Dupraz, P. and Whitby, M. (2001) "An Investigation of Policy Administrative Costs Using Panel Data for the English Environmentally Sensitive Areas," *Journal of Agricultural Economics*, 52(1): 83–103.

Federal Home Mortgage Association (1996) *Survey of Residential Satisfaction of Housing Occupants*, Washington, DC: Fannie Mae/Federal Home Mortgage Association.

—— (1997) *National Housing Survey*, Washington, DC: Fannie Mae/Federal Home Mortgage Association.

Federated Farmers of New Zealand (2002) "Life After Subsidies: The New Zealand Farming Experience 15 Years Later." Online, available at: http://www.fedfarm.org.nz/documents/LifeAfterSubsidiesAug02.pdf (accessed 25 February 2004).

Ferre, F. (1988) "Ethics, Assessment, and Technology," in *Philosophy of Technology*, Englewood Cliffs, NJ: Prentice-Hall.

Fields, S.F. (1979) "Where Have the Farmlands Gone?" National Agricultural Lands Study, Washington, DC: US Department of Agriculture, Soil Conservation Service.

Fischel, W.A. (1982) "The Urbanization of Agricultural Land: A Review of the National Agricultural Lands Study," *Land Economics*, 58(2): 236–259.

—— (1985) *The Economics of Zoning Laws: A Property Rights Approach to American Land Use Controls*, Baltimore, MD: Johns Hopkins University Press.

Fischer, C.S. (1982) *To Dwell Among Friends: Personal Networks in City and Town*, Chicago, IL: University of Chicago Press.

Fishbein, M. (1967) "A Behavior Theory Approach to the Relations Between Beliefs About an Object and the Attitude Towards That Object," in M. Fishbein (ed.) *Readings in Attitude Theory and Measurement*, New York: Wiley.

Fishel, W. (1997) "Comment on Abbott's 'The Portland Region: Where City and

Suburbs Talk to Each Other – and Often Agree,'" *Housing Policy Debate*, 8(1): 65–73.

Fisher, L. (1995) "The 'Contract with America': What it Really Means," *New York Review of Books*, 42(11): 20–24.

Fishman, R. (1998) "Howard and the Garden," in E. Richert and M. Lapping (eds) "Ebenezer Howard and the Garden City," *Journal of the American Planning Association*, 64(2): 125–138.

Fitchen, J.M. (1991) *Endangered Spaces, Enduring Places: Change, Identity, and Survival in Rural America*, Boulder, CO: Westview.

Fleming, M. (2002) "A Review of Techniques for Estimating Spatially Dependent Discrete Choice Models," unpublished manuscript, Department of Agricultural and Resource Economics, University of Maryland.

Florida, R. (2002) *The Rise of the Creative Class*, New York, NY: Basic Books.

Flynn, A. and Marsden, T.K. (1995) "Rural Change, Regulation and Sustainability," *Environment and Planning*, 27(8): 1180–1192.

Fodor, E. (1999) *Better Not Bigger*, Stony Creek, CT: New Society.

Foster, J.H., Halstead, J.M. and Stevens, T.H. (1982) *Measuring the Nonmarket Value of Agricultural Land: A Case Study*, Research Bulletin 672, Amherst, MA: University of Massachusetts, Massachusetts Agricultural Experiment Station.

Foster, K., Vecchia, P. and Repacholi, M. (12 May 2000) "Science and the Precautionary Principle," *Science*, 288, 979–981.

Fotheringham, A.S. and Rogerson, P. (eds) (1994) *Spatial Analysis and GIS*, London: Taylor and Francis.

Fotheringham, A.S., Brundson, C. and Charlton, M. (2000) *Quantitative Geography: Perspectives on Spatial Data Analysis*, London: Sage.

Franzen, R. (1994) "Oregon's Takings Tangle," *Planning*, 60(6): 13–15.

Freeman, L. (2001) "The Effects of Sprawl on Neighborhood Social Ties," *Journal of the American Planning Association*, 67(1): 69–77.

Friedland, W.H. (2002) "Agriculture and Rurality: Beginning the 'Final Separation?'" *Rural Sociology*, 67(3): 350–371.

Friedman, M.S., Powell, K.E., Hutwagner, L., Graham, L.M. and Teague, W.G. (2001) "Impact of Changes in Transportation and Commuting Behaviors During the 1996 Summer Olympic Games in Atlanta on Air Quality and Childhood Asthma," *The Journal of the American Medical Association*, 285: 897–905.

Friedmann, J. and Weaver, C. (1980) *Territory and Function: The Evolution of Regional Planning*, Berkeley, CA: University of California Press.

Frumkin, H. (2001) "Beyond Toxicity: The Greening of Environmental Health," *American Journal of Preventative Medicine*, 20: 47–53.

—— (2002) "Urban Sprawl and Public Health," *Public Health Reports*, 117: 201–217.

Fujita, M., Krugman, P. and Venables, A. (1999) *The Spatial Economy*, Cambridge, MA: MIT Press.

Fukuyama, F. (May 1999) "The Great Disruption: Human Nature and the Reconstitution of the Social Order," *Atlantic Monthly*, 283: 55–80.

Fulton, W. (1996) *The New Urbanism: Hope or Hype for American Communities*, Cambridge, MA: Lincoln Institute of Land Policy.

Fulton, W., Pendall, R., Nguyen, M. and Harrison, A. (2001) *Who Sprawls Most? How Growth Patterns Differ Across the United States*, Washington, DC: Brookings Institution.

Furuseth, O. (1987) "Public Attitudes Toward Local Farmland Protection Programs," *Growth and Change*, 18: 49–61.

Gale, F. (2000) "Nonfarm Growth and Structural Change Alter Farming's Role in the Rural Economy," *Rural Conditions and Trends*, 10(2): 2–6, Washington, DC: USDA/Economic Research Service. Online, available at: http://www.ers.usda.gov/publications/RCAT/RCAT102/RCAT102A.pdf (accessed 25 February 2004).

Gale, F. and Kilkenny, M. (2000) "Agriculture's Role Shrinks as the Service Sector Expands," *Rural Conditions and Trends*, 10(2): 26–32, Washington, DC: USDA/Economic Research Service. Online, available at: http://www.ers.usda.gov/publications/RCAT/RCAT102/RCAT102F.pdf (accessed 25 February 2004).

Gale, H.F. (1993) "Why Did the Number of Young Farm Entrants Decline?" *American Journal of Agricultural Economics*, 75: 138–146.

Galli, J. (1990) "Thermal Impacts Associated with Urbanization and Stormwater Management: Best Management Practices," Washington, DC: Metropolitan Washington Council of Governments, Maryland Department of the Environment, 188.

Galusha, D. (17 August 1994) "City, Coalition Talks Resume," *Catskill Mountain News*, 1A.

Gardner, D. (December 1977) "The Economics of Agricultural Land Preservation," *American Journal of Agricultural Economics*, 59: 1027–1036.

Gardner, B.L. (April 1994) "Commercial Agriculture in Metropolitan Areas: Economics and Regulatory Issues," *Agricultural and Resource Economics Review*, 23(1): 100–109.

—— (2002) *American Agriculture in the 20th Century: How It Flourished and What It Cost*, Cambridge, MA: Harvard University Press.

Gaspar, J. and Glaeser, E.L. (1998) "Information Technology and the Future of the Cities," *Journal of Urban Economics*, 43: 136–156.

Gatto, P. and Merlo, M. (1999) "The Economic Nature of Stewardship: Complementarity and Trade-offs with Food and Fibre Production," in G. Van Huylenbroeck and M. Whitby (eds) *Countryside Stewardship: Farmers, Policies and Markets*, Oxford, UK: Elsevier Science, 21–46.

Geoghegan, J. (2002) "The Value of Open Spaces in Residential Land Use," *Land Use Policy*, 19(1): 91–98.

Geoghegan, J., Lynch, L. and Bucholtz, S. (2003) "Capitalization of Open Spaces into Housing Values and the Residential Property Tax Revenue Impacts of Agricultural Easement Programs," *Agricultural and Resource Economics Review*, 32(1): 33–45.

George, K.P. (1997) "Values of Residents," in G.A. Goreham (ed.) *Encyclopedia of Rural America: The Land and People*, 2, Santa Barbara, CA: ABC-CLIO, 743–747.

Getches, D.H. and Pellow, D.N. (2002) "Beyond 'Traditional' Environmental Justice," in K.M. Mutz, G.C. Bryner and D.S. Kenney (eds) *Justice and Natural Resources: Concepts, Strategies, and Applications*, Washington, DC: Island Press, 3–30.

Gitter, D. (11 May 1994) "Groups Pushes for Mediated Talks," in R. Oberlag (ed.) *Catskill Mountain News*, 10A.

Glaeser, E.L. (Summer 2000) "Demand for Density? The Functions of the City in the 21st Century," *Brookings Review*, 18(3): 10–13.

Glaeser, E.L. and Kahn, M.E. (2001) "Decentralized Employment and the Transformation of the American City," in J. Rothenberg Pack and W. Gale (eds) *Brookings-Wharton Papers on Urban Affairs*, 2, Washington, DC: Brookings Institution.

Glaeser, E.L. and Kahn, M.E. (May 2003) *Sprawl and Urban Growth*, Working Paper no. 9733, Cambridge, MA: National Bureau of Economic Research, 55.

Glaeser, E.L. and Shapiro, J.M. (2002) "Cities and Warfare: The Impact of Terrorism on Urban Form," *Journal of Urban Economics*, 51: 1–20.

Glynn, T.J. (1981) "Psychological Sense of Community: Measurement and Application," *Human Relations*, 34: 789–818.

Goetz, S.J. (1993) "Human Capital and Rural Labor Issues," *American Journal of Agricultural Economics*, 75: 1164–1168.

Goetz, S.J. and Kelsey, T. (eds) (June 2003) "Ten Things Members of Every Community Need to Know About Land Use," University Park, PA: Penn State University, The Northeast Regional Center for Rural Development. Online, available at: http://www.cas.nercrd.psu.edu/TenThings.htm (accessed 29 March 2004).

Goetz, S.J., Bergstrom, J.C. and Shortle, J.S. (2002) "Land Use Problems and Conflicts in the US: A Comprehensive Research Agenda for the 21st Century," *Regional Rural Development Paper* no. 10: 6, University Park, PA: Penn State University, The Northeast Regional Center for Rural Development.

Gordon, P. and Richardson, H.W. (1994) "Congestion Trends in Metropolitan Areas," in *Curbing Gridlock*, Washington, DC: National Academy Press.

Gordon, P. and Richardson, H.W. (1995) "Sustainable Congestion," in J.F. Brotchie, M. Batty, E. Blakely, P. Hall and P.W. Newton (eds) *Cities in Competition: The Emergence of Productive and Sustainable Cities for the 21st Century*, Melbourne: Longman, 348–358.

Gordon, P. and Richardson, H.W. (1997) "Alternative Views of Sprawl: Are Compact Cities a Desirable Planning Goal?" *Journal of the American Planning Association*, 63(1): 95–105.

Gordon, P. and Richardson, H.W. (24 January 2000) "Critiquing Sprawl's Critics," *Policy Analysis*, 365: 18. Online, available at: http://www.cato.org/pubs/pas/pa365.pdf (accessed 26 February 2002).

Gordon, P., Richardson, H.W. and Jun, M.-J. (1991) "The Commuting Paradox: Evidence from the Top Twenty," *Journal of the American Planning Association*, 57(4): 416–420.

Graves, P.E. (2003) "Nonoptimal Levels of Suburbanization," *Environment and Planning A*, 35(2): 191–198.

Green, B. (2002) "The Farmed Landscape: The Ecology and Conservation of Diversity," in J. Jenkins (ed.) *Remaking the Landscape: The Changing Face of Britain*, London: Profile Books, 183–210.

Green, G.P. (1997) "Development, Community and Economics," in G.A. Goreham (ed.) *Encyclopedia of Rural America: The Land and People*, 1, Santa Barbara, CA: ABC-CLIO, 191–194.

Greenberg, M. (May 2002) "Should Housing Be Built on Former Brownfield Sites?" *American Journal of Public Health*, 92(5): 703–708.

Greenberg, M., Lowrie, K., Mayer, H., Miller, K.T. and Solitare, L. (2001) "Brownfield Redevelopment as a Smart Growth Option in the United States," *The Environmentalist*, 21: 129–143.

Greenberg, M., Miller, K.T., Lowrie, K. and Mayer, H. (2001b) "Surveying the Land: Brownfields in Medium-Sized and Small Communities," *Public Management*, 83(1): 18–23.

Greider, T. and Garkovich, L. (1994) "Landscapes: The Social Construction of Nature and the Environment," *Rural Sociology*, 59(1): 1–24.

Gunderson, C., Morehart, M., Whitener, L., Ghelfi, L., Johnson, J., Kassel, K., Kuhn, B., Mishra, A., Offutt, S. and Tiehen, L. (2000) *A Safety Net for Farm Households*, Agricultural Economic Report no. 788, Washington, DC: USDA/Economic Research Service. Online, available at: http://www.ers.usda.gov/Publications/AER788/ (accessed 25 February 2004).

Guwitt, R. (June 1998) "The Quest for Common Ground," *Governing*, 16–22.

Haining, R. (1990) *Spatial Data Analysis in the Social and Environmental Sciences*, Cambridge, UK: Cambridge University Press.

Halstead, J.M. (1984) "Measuring the Nonmarket Value of Massachusetts Agricultural Land: A Case Study," *Journal of the Northeastern Agricultural Economics Council*, 13(1): 12–19.

Hamed, M., Johnson, T.G. and Miller, K.K. (May 1999) *The Impacts of Animal Feeding Operations on Rural Land Values*, Community Policy Analysis Center Report, Columbia, MO: University of Missouri-Columbia. Online, available at: http://www.cpac.missouri.edu/library/reports/landvalue-saline/landvalues.pdf (accessed 25 October 1999).

Hamilton, N. (2003) "A Practical Guide to Policy Making in Northern Ireland," Northern Ireland Assembly: Office of the First Minister and Vice First Minister. Online, available at: http://www.ofmdfmni.gov.uk/cpubrochure%20.pdf (accessed 15 August 2003).

Hanley, N. (2001) "Policy on Agricultural Pollution in the European Union," in J.S. Shortle and D. Abler (eds) *Environmental Policies for Agricultural Pollution Control*, Wallingford, UK: CAB International, 151–162.

Hanley, N., Whitby, M. and Simpson, I. (1999) "Assessing the Success of Agri-environmental Policy in the UK," *Land Use Policy*, 16(2): 67–80.

Hansen, D.E. and Schwartz, S.I. (November 1975) "Landowner Behavior at the Rural–Urban Fringe in Response to Preferential Property Taxation," *Land Economics*, 51: 341–354.

Hardie, I.W., Narayan, T.A. and Gardner, B.L. (2001) "The Joint Influence of Agricultural and Nonfarm Factors on Real Estate Values: An Application to the Mid-Atlantic Region," *American Journal of Agricultural Economics*, 83(1): 120–132.

Hays, S.P. (1991) "Three Decades of Environmental Politics: The Historical Context," in M.J. Lacey (ed.) *Government and Environmental Politics: Essays on Historical Developments since World War Two*, Washington, DC: The Woodrow Wilson Center Press, 19–80.

Healy, R.G. and Short, J.L. (1983) "Changing Markets for Rural Lands: Patterns and Issues," in R. Platt and G. Macinko (eds) *Beyond the Urban Fringe: Land Use Issues of Nonmetropolitan America*, Minneapolis, MN: University of Minnesota Press.

Heiman, M.K. (1988) *The Quiet Evolution: Power, Planning and Profit in New York*, New York: Praeger Publishers.

Heimberger, M., Euler, D. and Barr, J. (1983) "The Impact of Cottage Development on Common Loon Reproductive Success in Central Ontario," *Wilson Bulletin*, 95: 431–439.

Heimlich, R.E. and Anderson, W.D. (2001) "Development at the Urban Fringe and Beyond: Impacts on Agriculture and Rural Land," ERS Agricultural Economic Report no. 803, Washington, DC: USDA. Online, available at: http://www.ers.usda.gov/publications/aer803 (accessed 11 January 2002).

Heimlich, R.E. and Barnard, C.H. (April 1992) "Agricultural Adaptation to Urbanization," *Journal of Agricultural and Resource Economics*, 21: 50–60.

Hellerstein, D., Nickerson, C., Cooper, J., Feather, P., Gadsby, D., Mullarkey, D., Tegene, A. and Barnard, C. (October 2002) "Farmland Protection: The Role of Public Preferences for Rural Amenities," Agricultural Economic Report no. 815: 74, Washington, DC: United States Department of Agriculture, Economic Research Service. Online, available at: http://www.ers.usda.gov/publications/aer815/ (accessed 25 February 2004).

Henneberry, D.M. and Barrows, R.L. (1990) "Capitalization of Exclusive Agricultural Zoning into Farmland Prices," *Land Economics*, 66: 249–258.

Hennessy, D.A. (2003) "From Driver Stress to Workplace Aggression," paper presented at 111th Annual American Psychological Association Convention, Toronto, Canada, August 7–10.

Hennessy, D.A. and Wiesenthal, D.L. (1999) "Traffic Congestion, Driver Stress, and Driver Aggression," *Aggressive Behavior*, 25: 409–423.

Herlihy, A.T., Stoddard, J.L. and Johnson, C.B. (1998) "The Relationship Between Stream Chemistry and Watershed Land Cover in the Mid-Atlantic Region of the U.S," *Water, Air, and Soil Pollution*, 105: 377–386.

Hirschhorn, J.S. (2000) *Growing Pains: Quality of Life in the New Economy*, Washington, DC: National Governors' Association.

Hite, D., Sohngen, B. and Templeton, J. (2003) "Zoning, Development Timing, and Agricultural Land Use at the Suburban Fringe: A Competing Risks Approach," *Agricultural and Resource Economics Review*, 32(1): 145–157.

Hite, J.C. (1979) *Room and Situation: The Political Economy of Land-Use Policy*, New York: Burnham Publishers.

Hite, J.C. and Dillman, B.L. (July 1981) "Protection of Agricultural Land: An Institutionalist Perspective," *Southern Journal of Agricultural Economics*, 12: 43–53.

Hodge, I. (1989) "Compensation for Nature Conservation," *Environment and Planning A*, 21(8): 1027–1036.

—— (2001a) "Beyond Agri-Environmental Policy: Towards an Alternative Model of Rural Environmental Governance," *Land Use Policy*, 18, 99–111.

—— (2001b) "Rural Economy and Sustainability," paper presented at Agricultural Economics Society Conference, London, December.

Hofreither, M.F. (2002) "Integrated Rural Development," in F. Brouwer and J. van der Straaten (eds) *Nature and Agriculture in the European Union: New Perspectives on Policies that Shape the European Countryside*, Cheltenham, UK: Edward Elgar, 252–279.

Holtzclaw, J. (1997) "Homebuyer Preferences." Online, available at: http://user.gru.net/domz/prefer.htm (accessed 4 August 2002).

Horbulyk, T.M. (2001) "The Social Cost of Labor in Rural Development: Job Creation Benefits Re-Examined," *Agricultural Economics*, 24(2): 199–208.

Horner, R.R., Booth, D.B., Azous, A.A. and May, C.W. (1996) "Watershed Determinants of Ecosystem Functioning," in L.A. Roesner (ed.) *Effects of Watershed Development and Management on Aquatic Ecosystems*, ASCE Conference Proceedings, Snowbird, UT, 251–274.

Hotelling, H. (1929) "Stability in Competition," *Economic Journal*, 39: 41–57.

Hull, R.B., Robertson, D.P. and Buhyoff, G.J. (2004) " 'Boutique' Forestry: New Forest Practices in Urbanizing Landscape," *Journal of Forestry*, 102: 14–19.

Hulsey, B. (1996) "Sprawl Costs Us All – How Uncontrolled Sprawl Increases Your Property Taxes and Threatens Your Quality of Life," Madison, WI: Sierra Club Midwest Office.

Hushak, L.J. and Sadr, K. (November 1979) "A Spatial Model of Land Market Behavior," *American Journal of Agricultural Economics*, 61: 697–701.

Hylton, T. (19 October 2003) "How Now Brownfields," *Pittsburgh Post-Gazette*, 1–3. Online, available at: http://www.post-gazette.vom/pg/o33292/232285.stm (accessed 29 March 2004).

Ihlanfeldt, K. (1995) "The Importance of the Central City to the Regional and National Economy: A Review of the Arguments and Empirical Evidence," *Cityscape*, 1: 125–150.

Imhoff, M.S., Lawrence, W.T., Stutzer, D. and Elvidge, C. (1998) "Assessing the Impact of Urban Sprawl on Soil Resources in the United States Using Nighttime 'City Lights' Satellite Images and Digital Soil Maps," in *Land Use History of North America*, Chapter 3, published on the web by USGS, Biological Resources Division. Online, available at: http://biology.usgs.gov/luhna/chap3.html (accessed 9 April 2004).

Ingersoll, J.H. (1995) "A Delicate Balance: Can Doing What's Right for the Environment Threaten Our Personal Property Rights?" *Country Living*, 18(2): 84–202.

Intergovernmental Panel on Climate Change (2001) *Climate Change 2001: Mitigation*, report of Working Group III, New York: Cambridge University Press. Online, available at: http://www.grida.no/climate/ipcc_tar/wg3/ (accessed 25 February 2004).

International Labor Organization (2003) LABORSTA online labor database. Online, available at: http://laborsta.ilo.org/ (accessed 15 May 2003).

Irland, L. (7 November 2001) "Fragmentation and Parcelization," *Small Woodlands Owners Association of Maine News*.

Irwin, E. and Kraybill, D. (August 1999) "Costs and Benefits of New Residential Development," unpublished paper. Online, available at: http://www.AEDE.osu.edu/programs/comregecon/htm (accessed 24 November 1999).

Irwin, E. and Bockstael, N.E. (2001) "The Problem of Identifying Land Use Spillovers: Measuring the Effects of Open Space on Residential Property Values," *American Journal of Agricultural Economics*, 83(3): 698–704.

Irwin, E.G. (2002) "The Effects of Open Space on Residential Property Values," *Land Economics*, 78(4): 465–480.

Irwin, E.G. and Geoghegan, J. (2001) "Theory, Data, Methods: Developing Spatially-Explicit Economic Models of Land Use Change," *Journal of Agriculture Ecosystems and Environment*, 85(1–3): 7–24.

Irwin, E.G. and Bockstael, N.E. (2002) "Interacting Agents, Spatial Externalities, and the Evolution of Residential Land Use Patterns," *Journal of Economic Geography*, 2(1): 31–54.

Irwin, E.G., Bell, K.P. and Geoghegan, J. (2003) "Modeling and Managing Urban Growth at the Rural–Urban Fringe: Evidence from a Model of Residential Land Use Change," *Agricultural and Resource Economics Review*, 32(1): 83–102.

Jackson, K. (2000) "Gentleman's Agreement: Discrimination in Metropolitan America," in B. Katz (ed.) *Reflections on Regionalism*, Washington, DC: Brookings Institution, 185–217.

Jackson, R.J. and Kochtitzky, C. (2001) "Creating a Healthy Environment: The Impact of the Built Environment on Public Health," Sprawl Watch Clearinghouse Monograph Series, 1–20. Online, available at: http://www.cdc.gov/healthyplaces/articles/Creating%20A%20Healthy%20Environment.pdf (accessed 6 April 2004).

Jargowsky, P.A. (2002) "Sprawl, Concentration of Poverty and Urban Inequality," in G.D. Squires (ed.) *Urban Sprawl: Causes, Consequences and Policy Response*, Washington, DC: The Urban Institute Press, 39–71.

Johnson, J.H. and Kasarda, J.D. (2003) "9/11 and the Economic Prospects of Major U.S. Cities," *Planning and Markets*, 6. Online, available at: http://www.pam.usc.edu/volume6/v6ia1print.html (accessed 27 June 2003).

Johnson, M.P. (2001) "Environmental Impacts of Urban Sprawl: A Survey of the Literature and Proposed Research Agenda," *Environment and Planning A*, 33(4): 717–735.

Jones, K.B., Neale, A.C., Nash, M.S., van Remortal, R.D., Wickham, J.D., Riitters, K.H. and O'Neill, R.V. (2001) "Predicting Nutrient and Sediment Loading to Streams from Landscape Metrics: A Multiple Watershed Study from the United States Mid-Atlantic Region," *Landscape Ecology*, 16: 301–312.

Jorgensen, B.S. and Stedman, R.C. (2001) "Sense of Place as An Attitude: Lakeshore Owners' Attitudes Towards Their Properties," *Journal of Environmental Psychology*, 21: 233–248.

Josling, T. (1969) "A Formal Approach to Agricultural Policy," *Journal of Agricultural Economics*, 20(2): 175–191.

Kahn, M.E. (2001) "Does Sprawl Reduce the Black/White Housing Consumption Gap?" *Housing Policy Debate*, 12: 77–86.

Kassel, K. and Carlin, T. (2000) "Economic Growth in Farming Areas Lags the Rest of Rural America," *Rural Conditions and Trends*, 10(2): 10–16, Washington, DC: USDA/Economic Research Service. Online, available at: http://www.ers.usda.gov/publications/RCAT/RCAT102/RCAT102C.pdf (accessed 25 February 2004).

Katz, B. (November 2000) "The Federal Role in Curbing Sprawl," *Annals of the American Academy*, 572: 66–77.

Katz, B. and Bradley, J. (December 1999) "Divided We Sprawl," *Atlantic Monthly*, 284(16): 26–42.

Katz, L. and Rosen, K. (1987) "The Inter-jurisdictional Effects of Growth Controls on Housing Prices," *Journal of Law and Economics*, 30(1): 149–160.

Kauffman, G.J., Brant, T. and Kitchell, A. (2000) "The Role of Impervious Cover as a Watershed Zoning and Land Use Planning Tool in the Christina River Basin of Delaware," in *WEFTEC Watershed 2000 Conference Proceedings*, Alexandria, VA: Water Environment Federation.

Keeble, D. and Tyler, P. (1995) "Enterprising Behaviour and the Rural–Urban Split," *Urban Studies*, 32(6): 975–997.

Kelly, E. (1993) *Managing Community Growth: Policies, Techniques and Impacts*, Westport, CT: Praeger.

Kelsey, T.W. (1996) "The Fiscal Impacts of Alternative Land Uses: What Do Cost of Community Service Studies Really Tell Us?" *Journal of the Community Development Society*, 27(1): 78–89.

Kiel, K.A. (1995) "Measuring the Impact of the Discovery and Cleaning of Identified Hazardous Waste Sites on House Values," *Land Economics*, 71(4): 428–435.

Kim, S. (2002) "The Reconstruction of the American Urban Landscape in the Twentieth Century," Working Paper no. 8857, National Bureau of Economic Research.

Kleppel, G.S. and DeVoe, M.R. (2000) "The People Factor," in J.E. Davis (ed.) *A Sense of Place. South Carolina Wildlife*, 47, Columbia, South Carolina: SC Department of Natural Resources, 32–43.

Kleppel, G.S., Porter, D.E. and DeVoe, M.R. (2001) "Implications of Urbanization to Ecosystem Structure and Function in South Carolina's Salt Marsh Estuaries," Aquatic Sciences Meeting, February 12–16, Albuquerque, NM: American Society of Limnology Oceanography.

Kline, J. and Wichelns, D. (May 1994) "Using Referendum Data to Characterize Public Support for Purchasing Development Rights to Farmland," *Land Economics*, 70: 221–233.

Kline, J. and Wichelns, D. (1996a) "Public Preferences Regarding the Goals of Farmland Preservation Programs," *Land Economics*, 72(4): 538–549.

Kline, J. and Wichelns, D. (1996b) "Measuring Public Preferences for Environmental Amenities Provided by Farmland," *European Review of Agricultural Economics*, 23(4): 421–436.

Kline, J. and Wichelns, D. (1998) "Measuring Heterogeneous Preferences for Preserving Farmland and Open Space," *Ecological Economics*, 26(2): 211–224.

Kline, J.D. and Alig, R.J. (1999) "Does Land Use Planning Slow the Conversion of Forest and Farm Lands?" *Growth and Change*, 30(1): 3–22.

Kort, J. and Cartwright, J. (1981) "Modeling the Multiregional Economy: Integrating Econometric and Input–Output Models," *The Review of Regional Studies*, 11(1): 1–17.

Koslowsky, M., Kluger, A.N. and Reich, M. (1995) *Commuting Stress: Causes, Effects and Methods of Coping*, New York, NY: Plenum Press.

Krieger, D.J. (1999) *Saving Open Spaces: Public Support for Farmland Protection*, WP99-1, DeKalb, IL: Center for Agriculture in the Environment. Online, available at: http://www.aftresearch.org/researchresource/wp/99-1/wp99-1.html (accessed 25 February 2004).

Krugman, P. (1995) *Development, Geography, and Economic Theory*, Cambridge, MA and London, UK: MIT Press.

Ladd, H. (1990) *Effects of Population Growth on Local Spending and Taxes*, Cambridge, MA: Lincoln Land Institute of Land Policy.

—— (1994) "Fiscal Impacts of Local Population Growth: A Conceptual and Empirical Analysis," *Regional Science and Urban Economics*, 24(6): 661–684.

—— (1998) *Local Government Tax and Land Use Policies in the United States: Understanding the Links*, Northhampton, MA: Edward Elgar Publishing.

Lalli, M. (1992) "Urban-Related Identity: Theory, Measurement, and Empirical Findings," *Journal of Environmental Psychology*, 12, 285–303.

Land Trust Alliance (2002) "More Than $7.3 Billion Committed To Open Space Protection." Online, available at: http://www.lta.org/policy/referenda2000 (accessed 2 September 2002).

Lapping, M.B. (May–June 1979) "Agricultural Land Retention Strategies: Some Underpinnings," *Journal of Soil and Water Conservation*, 34(3): 124–126.

—— (1982) "Toward A Working Rural Landscape," in C.H. Reidel (ed.) *New England Prospects: Critical Choices in a Time of Change*, Hanover, NH: University Press of New England, 59–84.

—— (forthcoming 2004) "Rural Policy and Planning," in A. Gilg, T. Marsden and P. Mooney (eds) *Handbook of Rural Studies*, London: Sage Publishers.

Lapping, M. and Leutweiler, N. (1988) "Agriculture in Conflict: Right-to-Farm Laws and the Peri-Urban Milieu for Farming," in W. Lockeretz (ed.) *Sustaining Agriculture Near Cities*, Ankeny, Iowa: Soil Conservation Society of America, 209–218.

Lapping, M. and Pfeffer, M. (1997) "City and Country: New Connections, New

Possibilities," in W. Lockeretz (ed.) *Visions of American Agriculture*, Ames: Iowa State University Press, 91–104.

Lapping, M., Penfold, G. and MacPherson, S. (1985) "The Right-to-Farm Laws: Will They Resolve Land Conflicts?" *Journal of Soil and Water Conservation*, 38(6): 465–467.

Larson, J.M., Findeis, J.L. and Smith, S.M. (2001) "Agricultural Adaptation to Urbanization in Southeastern Pennsylvania," *Agricultural and Resource Economics Review*, 30(1): 32–43.

Lauber, D. (1975) "Recent Cases in Exclusionary Zoning," *Management and Control of Growth*, Washington, DC: The Urban Land Institute, 1: 465–476.

Lawson, A.B. (2001) *Statistical Methods in Spatial Epidemiology*, New York, NY: John Wiley and Sons.

Lee, C.M. and Fujita, M. (1997) "Efficient Configuration of a Greenbelt: Theoretical Modelling of Greenbelt Amenity," *Environment and Planning*, 29: 1999–2017.

Lee, C.M. and Linneman, P. (1998) "Dynamics of the Greenbelt Amenity Effect on the Land Market – The Case of Seoul's Greenbelt," *Real Estate Economics*, 26(1): 107–129.

Lehman, T. (1995) *Public Values, Private Lands*, Chapel Hill, NC: The University of North Carolina Press.

Leigh, N.G. (2003) "The State Role in Urban Land Development," discussion paper for the Center on Urban and Metropolitan Policy, Washington, DC: Brookings Institution.

Lenman, B. (2001) "From the Union of 1707 to the Franchise Reform of 1832," in R.A. Houston and W.W. Knox (eds) *The New Penguin History of Scotland*, London: Penguin Books.

Leopold, A. (1949) *A Sand County Almanac*, New York: Oxford University Press.

LeSage, J.P. (2000) "Bayesian Estimation of Limited Dependent Spatial Autoregressive Models," *Geographical Analysis*, 32(1): 19–35.

Lewis, S. (1992) "Goodbye, Ramapo. Hello Yakima and Isle of Palms," *Planning*, 58(7): 9–28.

Libby, L. (1997) "Implementing Good Intentions," *Understanding Public Policy*, Oakbrook, IL: The Farm Foundation, 136–149.

—— (2002) "Farmland is Not Just for Farming Anymore: The Trends," in L. Tweeten and S. Thompson (eds) *Agricultural Policy for the 21st Century*, Ames, IA: Iowa State University Press, 184–203.

Libby, L. and Stewart, P. (1999) "The Economics of Farmland Conversion," in R. Olson and T. Lyson (eds) *Under the Blade: The Conversion of Agricultural Landscape*, Boulder, CO: Westview Press.

Lincoln Institute of Land Policy (1995) *Alternatives to Sprawl*, Cambridge, MA: Lincoln Institute of Land Policy.

—— (2001) *The New Spatial Order? Technology and Urban Development, the 2001 Annual Roundtable*, Cambridge, MA: Lincoln Institute of Land Policy.

Lockeretz, W. (1989) "Secondary Effects on Midwestern Agriculture of Metropolitan Development and Decreases in Farmland," *Land Economics*, 65(3): 205–216.

Logan, J.R. and Molotch, H. (1987) *Urban Fortunes: The Political Economy of Place*, Berkeley: University of California Press.

Loomis, J., Rameker, V. and Seidl, A. (October 2002) "Implicit Prices of Open Space Attributes: A Hedonic Model of Public Market Transactions for Open Space," paper presented at Conserving Farm and Forest in a Changing Rural Landscape: Current and Potential Contributions of Economics, University Park, PA: The Northeast Regional Center for Rural Development.

Loomis, J.B., Rameker, V. and Seidl, A. (2004) "A Hedonic Model of Public Market Transactions for Open Space Protection," *Journal of Environmental Planning and Management*, 47(1): 83–96.

Lopez, R.A., Adelaja, A.O. and Andrews, M.S. (May 1988) "The Effects of Suburbanization on Agriculture," *American Journal of Agricultural Economics*, 70: 346–358.

Lopez, R.A., Shah, F.A. and Altobello, M.A. (1994) "Amenity Benefits and the Optimal Allocation of Land," *Land Economics*, 70(1): 53–62.

Loudoun County Rural Economic Development Task Force (November 1998) "The 200,000 Acre Solution: Support and Enhancing a Rural Economy for Loudoun's 21st Century," Leesburg, VA: Loudoun County Office of Agricultural Development.

Loudoun County, Virginia (1998) "Tipping the Balance Toward a More Profitable Agricultural Future," Office of Rural Economic Development. Online, available at: http://www.rural-loudoun.state.va.us (accessed 5 April 2004).

Lowe, P., Murdoch, J., Marsden, T., Munton, R. and Flynn, A. (1993) "Regulating the New Rural Spaces: The Uneven Development of Land," *Journal of Rural Studies*, 9: 205–222.

Lowenthal, D. and Prince, H. (1965) "English Landscape Tastes," *The Geographical Review*, 55: 186–222.

Lowrie, K., Greenberg, M. and Knee, D. (June 2002) "Turning Brownfields into Ballfields, Open Space and Parks," *New Jersey Municipalities*, 6–8.

Lynch, L. and Horowitz, J.R. (1998) "Comparison of Farmland Programs in Maryland," in *The Performance of State Programs for Farmland Preservation*, proceedings of a conference, 10–11 September, Columbus, Ohio: Ohio State University.

Lynch, L. and Musser, W.N. (2001) "A Relative Efficiency Analysis of Farmland Preservation Programs," *Land Economics*, 77(4): 577–594.

Lynch, L. and Lovell, S.J. (2002) "Hedonic Price Analysis of Easement Payments in Maryland Agricultural Land Preservation Programs," working paper no. 2–13, University of Maryland, College Park: Department of Agricultural and Resource Economics.

Lynch, L. and Carpenter, J.E. (April 2003) "Is There Evidence of a Critical Mass in the Mid-Atlantic Agricultural Sector between 1949 and 1997?" *Agricultural and Resource Economic Review*, 32(1): 116–128.

Lynch, L. and Lovell, S.J. (May 2003) "Combining Spatial and Survey Data to Explain Participation in Agricultural Land Preservation Programs," *Land Economics*, 79(2): 259–276.

McBride, W.D. and Key, N. (2003) *Economic and Structural Relationships in US Hog Production*, Agricultural Economic Report no. 818, Washington, DC: USDA/Economic Research Service. Online, available at: http://www.ers.usda.gov/publications/aer818/ (accessed 25 February 2004).

McCann, L. and Easter, K.W. (2000) "Estimates of Public Sector Transaction Costs in NRCS Programs," *Journal of Agricultural and Applied Economics*, 32(3): 555–563.

McCarthy, G., van Zandt, S. and Rohe, W. (May 2001) *The Economic Benefits and Costs of Homeownership: A Critical Assessment of the Research*, Research Institute for Housing America, working paper no. 01-02, Chapel Hill, NC: University of North Carolina at Chapel Hill.

McConnell, K.E. (October 1989) "The Optimal Quantity of Land in Agriculture," *Northeastern Journal of Agricultural and Resource Economics*, 18: 63–72.

McLeod, D.M., Worihaye, J. and Menkhaus, D.J. (1999) "Factors Influencing Support for Rural Land Use Control: A Case Study," *Agricultural and Resource Economics Review*, 28(1): 44–56.

Marshall, A., Hoag, D. and Seidl, A. (2003) "Landowner Expectations and Experiences with Conservation Easements," Compensatory Programs for Conserving Agricultural Land, 262: 91–106, University of California, Davis, CA: Agricultural Issues Center. Online, available at: http://www.aic.ucdavis.edu/ (accessed 23 January 2004).

Maryland Agricultural Land Preservation Foundation (2001) "Report of the Maryland Agricultural Land Preservation Task Force." Online, available at: http://www.mdp.state.md.us/planning/malpp/final2.pdf (accessed 2 September 2002).

Maryland Department of Agriculture (1998) "Maryland Agricultural Land Preservation Foundation Report." Online, available at: http://www.mda.state.md.us/agland/preserva.htm (accessed 2 September 2002).

—— (2001) "Maryland Agricultural Land Preservation Foundation Annual Report for FY 2001," Annapolis, MD: Maryland Department of Agriculture.

Maryland Department of State Planning (1973) "Natural Soil Groups Technical Report," HUD Project no. MD-P-1008-100, Baltimore, MD: Maryland Department of State Planning.

Mason, R.J. (forthcoming 2004) "The Pinelands," in M. Lapping and O. Furuseth (eds) *Big Places, Big Plans: Large-scale Regional Planning in North America*, Aldershot, UK: Ashgate, 29–54.

Matarese, I. and Graham, L. (1990) "Waterfowl: An Alternative Income Producing Option for Recreational Access," in W. Grafton, A. Farrise, D. Colyer, D. Smith and J. Miller (eds) *Income Opportunities for the Private Landowner through Management of Natural Resources and Recreation Access*, Morgantown, WV: West Virginia Extension Service, 301–305.

May, C.W., Horner, R.R., Karr, J.B., Mar, B.W. and Welch, E.B. (1997) "Effects of Urbanization on Small Streams in the Puget Sound Lowland Ecoregion," *Watershed Protection Tech*, 2: 485–494.

Meyer, M., Woodford, J., Gillum, S. and Daulton, T. (1997) "Shore Land Zoning Regulations Do Not Adequately Protect Wildlife Habitat in Northern Wisconsin," Final Report, USFWS State Partnership Grant P1W, 17.

Meyer, W.B. and Turner, B.L. II (1992) "Human Population Growth and Land Use/Land Cover Change," *Annual Review of Ecology and Systematics*, 23: 39–61.

Meyer, W.B. and Turner, B.L. II (1994) (eds) *Changes in Land Use and Land Cover: A Global Perspective*, Cambridge, UK: Cambridge University Press.

Mieszkowski, P. and Mills, E.S. (1993) "The Causes of Metropolitan Suburbanization," *Journal of Economic Perspectives*, 7(3): 135–147.

Miller, D. (August 1999) "Farming the Wild Side," *Progressive Farmer*, 20–22.

Miller, D.J. and Plantinga, A.J. (1999) "Modeling Land Use Decisions with Aggregate Data," *American Journal of Agricultural Economics*, 81: 180–194.

Mills, E.S. (1972) *Studies in the Structure of the Metropolitan Economy*, Baltimore, MD: Johns Hopkins University Press.

Molotch, H. (1976) "The City as a Growth Machine," *American Journal of Sociology*, 82: 309–331.

Morris, A. (1998) "Property Tax Treatment of Land: Does Tax Relief Delay Land

Development?" in H.F. Ladd (ed.) *Local Government Tax and Land Use Policies in the United States: Understanding the Links*, Cheltenham, UK: Edward Elgar.

Moxey, A., White, B. and Ozanne, A. (1999) "Efficient Contract Design for Agri-Environmental Policy," *Journal of Agricultural Economics*, 50: 187–202.

Mulkey, D. and Clouser, R.L. (1987) "Market and Market-Institutional Perspectives on the Agricultural Land Preservation Issue," *Growth and Change*, 18(1): 72–81.

Munger, M.C. (2000) *Analyzing Policy: Choices, Conflicts and Practices*, New York: W.W. Norton & Company.

Muriel, P. (December 2001) "The Impact on Rural Economies of Reducing Farm Subsidies," paper presented at Agricultural Economics Society Conference, London, UK.

Murphy, R. (1994) *Rationality and Nature: A Sociological Inquiry into a Changing Relationship*, Boulder, CO: Westview Press.

Muth, R.F. (1969) *Cities and Housing*, Chicago, IL: University of Chicago Press.

Myers, C.A.B. and Auchenbach, C. (2002) "Effective Agriculture Preservation Zoning: One Tool to Help Save an Industry," in L.W. Libby and C. Abdalla (eds) *Proceedings of a Conference on Protecting Farmland at the Fringe: Do Regulations Work? Strengthening the Research Agenda*, Columbus, OH: Ohio State University, Swank Program in Rural–Urban Policy, 101–108.

Myers, P. (January 1999) *Livability at the Ballot Box: State and Local Referenda on Parks, Conservation, and Smarter Growth, Election Day 1998*, Center on Urban and Metropolitan Policy, Washington, DC: Brookings Institution.

Nasar, J.L. and Julian, D.A. (1995) "The Psychological Sense of Community in the Neighborhood," *Journal of the American Planning Association*, 61: 178–184.

Nash, R. (1967) *Wilderness and the American Mind*, New Haven: Yale University Press.

National Association of Home Builders (2002) "Housing: The Key to Economic Recovery." Online, available at: http://www.nahb.com/housing_issues/keyrecovery.htm (accessed 12 September 2002).

National Conference of State Legislatures (2001) "Principles of High-Quality State Revenue Systems," Washington, DC. Online, available at: http://www.ncsl.org/programs/fiscal/fpphqsrs.htm (accessed 29 November 2001).

National Council for Science and the Environment (1999) "Congressional Research Service Report for Congress. Air Quality and Motor Vehicles: An Analysis of Current and Proposed Emission Standards." Online, available at: http://cnie.org/NLE/CRSreports/Air/air-36.cfm (accessed 11 February 2002).

National Oceanographic and Atmospheric Administration (15 January 1993) "Report of the NOAA Panel on Contingent Valuation," *Federal Register*, 58(10): 4601–4614.

National Personal Transportation Survey (1995) *Our Nation's Travel: 1995 NPTS Early Results Report*, Washington, DC: US Department of Transportation.

—— (1999) *Summary of Travel Trends: 1995 National Personal Transportation Survey*, Washington, DC: US Department of Transportation.

National Research Council (1999) *New Strategies for America's Watersheds*, Washington, DC: National Research Council.

—— (2000) *Watershed Management for Potable Water Supply: Assessing the New York City Strategy*, Washington, DC: National Academy Press.

—— (2001) *Grand Challenges in Environmental Sciences*, Washington, DC: National Academy Press.

—— (2003) *Air Emissions from Animal Feeding Operations: Current Knowledge, Future Needs*, Washington, DC: National Academy Press.

Natural Resources Conservation Service (1995) "Wetlands: Values and Trends," *NRCS/RCA Issue Brief 4*. Online, available at: http://www.nrcs.usda.gov/technical/land/pubs/ib4text.html (accessed 25 January 1996).

—— (revised December 2000a) *Changes in Land Cover/Use Between 1982 and 1997*, Table 5, 1997 National Resources Inventory, Washington, DC: US Department of Agriculture. Online, available at: http://www.nrcs.usda.gov/technical/NRI/1997/summary_report/table5.html (accessed 9 February 2004).

—— (revised December 2000b) *State Rankings by Acreage and Rate of Non-Federal Land Developed*, 1997 National Resources Inventory, Washington, DC: US Department of Agriculture. Online, available at: http://www.nrcs.usda.gov/technical/land/tables/t5845.html (accessed 9 February 2004).

National Wildlife Federation (February 2001) "Paving Paradise – Sprawl's Impact on Wildlife and Wild Places in California: A Smart Growth and Wildlife Campaign," *California White Paper*. Online, available at: http://www.nwf.org/smartgrowth/pavingparadise.html (accessed 25 January 2002).

Nature Conservancy Council (1983) *Farming and the Countryside*, Peterborough, UK: Nature Conservancy Council.

Ndubisi, F. and Dyer, M. (Fall 1992) "The Role of Regional Entities in Formulating and Implementing Statewide Growth Policies," *State and Local Government Review*, 24: 117–127.

Nelson, A.C. and Moody, M. (June 2003) *Paying for Prosperity: Impact Fees and Job Growth*, Washington, DC: Brookings Institution. Online, available at: http://www.brook.edu/es/urban/publications/nelsonimpactfees.htm (accessed 12 June 2003).

Nelson, A.C., Pendall, R., Dawkins, C. and Knapp, G.J. (2002) "The Link Between Growth Management and Housing Affordability: The Academic Evidence," discussion paper, Washington, DC: Brookings Institution.

Nelson, G.C. and Geoghegan, J. (2002) "Deforestation and Land Use Change: Sparse Data Environments," *Agricultural Economics*, 27: 201–216.

Nelson, G.C., Harris, V. and Stone, S.W. (2001) "Deforestation, Land Use, and Property Rights," *Land Economics*, 77(2): 187–205.

New York City Department of Environmental Protection (1993) *Final Generic Environmental Impact Statement for the Final Watershed Regulations for the Protection from Contamination, Degradation, and Pollution of the New York City Water Supply and Its Sources*, New York: New York City Department of Environmental Protection.

New York State Water Resources Institute (1994) "Chronology of Whole Community Planning for the NYC Watershed," manuscript.

Nickerson, C.J. and Lynch, L. (2001) "The Effect of Farmland Preservation Programs on Farmland Prices," *American Journal of Agricultural Economics*, 83(2): 341–351.

Nolon, J.R. (1993) "The Erosion of Home Rule Through the Emergence of State Interests in Land Use Control," *Pace Environmental Law Review*, 10(2): 497–562.

Norton, B. (April 1994) "A Scalar Approach to Ecological Constraints," paper presented at the Workshop on Engineering within Ecological Constraints, National Academy of Engineering, Washington, DC.

Noss, R.F. and Cooperrider, A.Y. (1995) *Saving Nature's Legacy*, Washington, DC: Island Press.

Oberlag, R. (5 November 1995) "Watershed Agreement has Upstate Smiling," *Catskill Mountain News*, 1.

Obermann, W., Carlson, D. and Batchelder, J. (eds) (September 2000) "Tracking Agricultural Land Conversion in Colorado: An Interagency Summary," Colorado Department of Agriculture, Natural Resources Conservation Service, and Colorado Agricultural Statistics Service.

Odum, H.W. (October 1934) "The Case for Regional–National Social Planning," *Social Forces*, 13, 6–23.

Oelschlaeger, M. (1991) "Contemporary Wilderness Philosophy: From Resourcism to Deep Ecology," Chapter 9, *The Idea of Wilderness*, New Haven: Yale University Press.

Ohio Farmland Preservation Task Force (1997) *Report to the Governor*, Columbus, OH: State of Ohio, Department of Agriculture.

Ohls, J. and Pines, D. (1975) "Discontinuous Urban Development and Economic Efficiency," *Land Economics*, 51(3): 224–234.

Ord, J.K. (1975) "Estimation Methods for Models of Spatial Interaction," *Journal of the American Statistical Association*," 70: 120–126.

Orfield, M. (1997) *Metropolitics: A Regional Agenda for Community and Stability*, Washington, DC: Brookings Institution.

Organization for Economic Cooperation and Development (1996) *Amenities for Rural Development: Policy Examples*, Paris: OECD.

—— (1998) *The Environmental Effects of Reforming Agricultural Policies*, Paris: OECD.

—— (1999) *Cultivating Rural Amenities: An Economic Development Perspective*, Paris: OECD.

—— (2001a) *Multifunctionality: Towards an Analytical Framework*, Paris: OECD. Online, available at: http://www1.oecd.org/publications/e-book/5101041E.pdf (accessed 25 February 2004).

—— (2001b) *Environmental Indicators for Agriculture: Methods and Results*, 3, Paris: OECD. Online, available at: http://www1.oecd.org/publications/e-book/5101011E.pdf (accessed 25 February 2004).

—— (2001c) *Transaction Costs and Multifunctionality: Main Issues*, Paris: OECD. Online, available at: http://www1.oecd.org/agr/mf/doc/Transactioncosts32.pdf (accessed 25 February 2004).

—— (2003a) *Agricultural Policies in OECD Countries: Monitoring and Evaluation 2003*, Paris: OECD. Online, available at: http://www1.oecd.org/publications/e-book/5103081E.pdf (accessed 25 February 2004).

—— (2003b) *Multifunctionality: The Policy Implications*. Paris: OECD.

Paarlberg, P.L., Bredahl, M. and Lee, J.G. (2002) "Multifunctionality and Agricultural Trade Negotiations," *Review of Agricultural Economics*, 24(2): 322–335.

Paden, C. and Shen, A. (1995) "New York City Water Under Pressure," *Inside DEP*, 1(1): 1–8.

Pagano, M. (April 2003) *City Fiscal Structures and Land Development*, Washington, DC: Brookings Institution. Online, available at: http://www.brook.edu/es/urban/publications/paganovacant.htm (accessed 15 August 2003).

Page, G.W. and Rabinowitz, H.Z. (1994) "Potential for Redevelopment of Contaminated Brownfield Sites," *Economic Development Quarterly*, 8(4): 353–363.

Palmquist, R., Roka, F.M. and Vukina, T. (1997) "Hog Operations, Environmental Effects, and Residential Property Values," *Land Economics*, 73(1): 114–124.

Palmquist, R.B. (1991) "Hedonic Methods," in J.B. Braden and C.D. Kolstad (eds)

Measuring the Demand for Environmental Quality, Amsterdam: North Holland, 77–120.

Parks, P.J. and Quimio, W.R.H. (1996) "Preserving Agricultural Land with Farmland Assessment: New Jersey as a Case Study," *Agricultural and Resource Economics Review*, 25(1): 22–27.

Parks, P.J. and Schorr, J.P. (1997) "Sustaining Open Space Benefits in the Northeast: An Evaluation of the Conservation Reserve Program," *Journal of Environmental Economics and Management*, 32(1): 85–94.

Patton, M. and Seidl, A. (January 1999) "Matrix of State Level Policies for Animal Feeding Operations," Agricultural and Resource Policy Report, Department of Agricultural and Resource Economics, APR99-01. Online, available at: http://dare.agsci.colostate.edu/csuagecon/extension/docs/agpolicy/matrix.pdf (accessed 30 January 2004).

Peddle, M. and Lewis, J. (October 1996) "Development Exactions as Growth Management and Local Infrastructure Finance Tools," *Public Works Management and Policy*, 1(2): 129–144.

Peiser, R. (1989) "Density and Urban Sprawl," *Land Economics*, 18(4): 463–478.

Penner, J.E. (1994) "Atmospheric Chemistry and Air Quality," in W.B. Meyer and B.L. Turner II (eds) *Changes in Land Use and Land Cover: A Global Perspective*, Cambridge, UK: Cambridge University Press, 175–209.

Pennsylvania Twenty-first Century Environment Commission (1998) "Report of the Pennsylvania Twenty-first Century Environment Commission," Harrisburg, PA. Online, available at: http://www.21stcentury.state.pa.us/2001/final.htm (accessed 25 January 1999).

Peterson, J.M., Boisvert, R.N. and de Gorter, H. (2002) "Environmental Policies for a Multifunctional Agricultural Sector in Open Economies," *European Review of Agricultural Economics*, 29(4): 423–443.

Pfeffer, M. and Lapping, M. (1995) "Prospects for a Sustainable Agriculture in the Northeast's Rural/Urban Fringe," in H. Schwartzweller and T. Lyson (eds) *Research in Rural Sociology and Development: A Research Annual*, 6, Greenwich, CT: JAI Publishers, 67–93.

Pfeffer, M.J. and Lapping, M.B. (1994) "Farmland Preservation, Development Rights and the Theory of the Growth Machine: The Views of Planners," *Journal of Rural Studies*, 10(3): 233–248.

Pfeffer, M.J. and Wagenet, L.P. (1999) "Planning for Environmental Responsibility and Equity: A Critical Appraisal of Rural/Urban Relations in the New York City Watershed," in M.B. Lapping and O. Furuseth (eds) *Contested Countryside: The Rural–Urban Fringe of North America*, Brookfield, VT: Ashgate, 179–206.

Pfeffer, M.J., Stycos, J.M., Glenna, L. and Altobelli, J. (2001a) "Forging New Connections between Agriculture and the City," in O.T. Solbrig, R. Paarlberg and F. di Castri (eds) *Globalization and the Rural Environment*, Cambridge, MA: Harvard University Press, 419–446.

Pfeffer, M.J., Schelhas, J.W. and Day, L.A. (2001b) "Forest Conservation, Value Conflict, and Interest Formation in a Honduran National Park," *Rural Sociology*, 66(3): 382–402.

Phipps, T. (1983) "Landowner Incentives to Participate in a Purchase of Development Rights Program with Application to Maryland," *Journal of the Northeastern Agricultural Economics Council*, 12(1): 61–65.

Pimentel, D. and Giampietro, M. (1994) *Food, Land, Population and the US Economy*, Washington, DC: Carrying Capacity Network.

Pitt, D.G., Phipps, T. and Lessley, B.V. (1986) "Participation in Maryland's Agricultural Land Reservation Program: The Adoption of an Innovative Agricultural Land Policy," *Landscape Journal*, 7(1): 15–30.

Plantinga, A. and Miller, D. (February 2001) "Agricultural Land Values and Future Development," *Land Economics*, 77(1): 56–67.

Plantinga, A.J., Lubowski, R.N. and Stavins, R.N. (2002) "The Effects of Potential Land Development on Agricultural Land Prices," *Journal of Urban Economics*, 52(3): 561–581.

Platt, R.H., Barten, P.K. and Pfeffer, M.J. (2000) "A Full, Clean Glass? Managing New York City's Watersheds," *Environment*, 42(5): 9–20.

Plaut, T.R. (1980) "Urban Expansion and the Loss of Farmland in the United States: Implications for the Future," *American Journal of Agricultural Economics*, 62: 537–542.

Pomerantz, M., Akbari, H., Berdahl, P. and. Taha, H.G. (1999) "Physics and Public Policy for Urban Heat Island Mitigation," presented at American Physical Society, Atlanta, GA.

Popper, Frank J. (1992) "Thinking Globally, Acting Regionally," *Technology Review*, 95(3): 47–53.

Potter, C. (2002) "Agri-Environmental Policy Development in the European Union," in F. Brouwer and J. van der Straaten (eds) *Nature and Agriculture in the European Union: New Perspectives on Policies that Shape the European Countryside*, Cheltenham, UK: Edward Elgar, 67–87.

Power, M.T. (1996) *Lost Landscapes and Failed Economies*, Washington, DC: Island Press.

Pretty, J. (1998) *The Living Land*, London: Earthscan.

Pruckner, G.J. (1995) "Agricultural Landscape Cultivation in Austria: An Application of the CVM," *European Review of Agricultural Economics*, 22(2): 173–190.

Pucher, J. (1995) "Urban Passenger Transport in the United States and Europe: A Comparative Analysis of Public Policies," *Transport Reviews*, 15(2): 99–117.

Putnam, R.D. (2000) *Bowling Alone*, New York: Simon and Schuster.

Rae, A., Nixon, C. and Lattimore, R. (2003) "Adjustment to Agricultural Policy Reform: Issues and Lessons from the New Zealand Experience," Policy Reform and Adjustment Workshop, Wye, UK: Imperial College London. Online, available at: http://agadjust.aers.psu.edu/Workshop_files/Rae_Nixon_Lattimore.pdf (accessed 25 February 2004).

Ramankutty, N. and Foley, J.A. (1999) "Estimating Historical Changes in Global Land Cover: Croplands from 1700 to 1992," *Global Biogeochemical Cycles*, 13(4): 997–1027.

Rappaport, J. and Sachs, J.D. (October 2002) "The US as a Coastal Nation," Kansas City, MO: Federal Reserve Bank of Kansas City, Research Division, RWP-01-11.

Raup, P. (1975) "Urban Threats to Rural Lands: Background and Beginnings," *Journal of the American Institute of Planners*, 41(6): 371–378.

Ready, R. and Abdalla, C. (2003) "GIS Analysis of Land Use on the Rural–Urban Fringe: The Impact of Land Use and Potential Local Disamenities on Residential Property Values and on the Location of Residential Development in Berks County, Pennsylvania," Staff Paper no. 364, Penn State University: Department of Agricultural Economics and Rural Sociology.

Real Estate Research Corporation (1974a) "The Costs of Sprawl: Environmental and Economic Costs of Alternative Residential Development Patterns at the Urban Fringe," Washington, DC: US Government Printing Office.

—— (1974b) *The Public Service Costs of Alternative Development Patterns*, Madison, WI: State Planning Office, Department of Administration, State of Wisconsin.

Reed, M.G. and Gill, A.M. (1997) "Tourism, Recreational, and Amenity Values in Land Allocation: An Analysis of Institutional Arrangements in the Post Productivist Era," *Environment and Planning*, 29: 2019–2040.

Rees, A. (2004) "New Urbanism: Vision Landscape in the Twentieth-First Century," in M.J. Lindstrom and H. Bartling (eds) *Suburban Sprawl: Culture, Theory, and Politics*, Landham, MD: Rowman and Littlefield, 93–114.

Rehnquist, W.H. (25 June 1994) "Excerpt from Court Ruling Limiting Governments' Power Over Property," *New York Times*.

Reiner, E. (1975) "Traditional Zoning: Precursor to Managed Growth," in R. Scott, D. Brower and D. Miner (eds) *Management and Control of Growth*, Washington, DC: The Urban Land Institute.

Relph, E. (1976) *Place and Placelessness*, London: Pion Limited.

—— (1997) "Sense of Place," in S. Hanson (ed.) *Ten Geographic Ideas that Changed the World*, New Brunswick, NJ: Rutgers University Press.

Renkow, M. (Summer 2001) "Non-Metropolitan Population Growth in North Carolina: Rural Renaissance or Urban Sprawl?" *Southern Perspectives*, 5, Mississippi State, MS: Southern Rural Development Center, 1.

Reschovsky, C. (March 2004) "Journey to Work 2000," Census 2000 Brief, C2KBR-33, 13pp, Washington, DC: US Department of Commerce, Bureau of the Census. Online, available at: http://www.census.gov/prod/2004pubs/c2kbr-33.pdf (accessed 24 March 2004).

Rey, S. (1994) *Integrated Multiregional Modeling for Systems of Small Regions*, Ph.D. Dissertation, Santa Barbara, CA: University of California.

Ribaudo, M. (2001) "Non-point Source Pollution Control Policy in the USA," in J.S. Shortle and D. Abler (eds) *Environmental Policies for Agricultural Pollution Control*, Wallingford, UK: CAB International, 123–149.

Richmond, H. (2000) "Metropolitan Land Use Reform: The Promise and Challenge of Majority Consensus," in B. Katz (ed.) *Reflections on Regionalism*, Washington, DC: Brookings Institution, 9–39.

Rickenbach, M.G. and Gobster, P.H. (2003) "Stakeholders' Perceptions of Parcelization in Wisconsin's Northwoods," *The Journal of Forestry*, 101(6): 18–33.

Rilla, E. and Sokolow, A.D. (December 2000) "California Farmers and Conservation Easements: Motivations, Experiences, and Perceptions in Three Counties," Research Paper no. 4, University of California: Agricultural Issues Center.

Rindfuss, R.R. and Stern, P.C. (1998) "Linking Remote Sensing and Social Science: The Need and the Challenges," in D. Liverman, E. Moran, R. Rindfuss and P.C. Stern (eds) *People and Pixels: Linking Remote Sensing and Social Science*, Washington, DC: National Academy Press.

Robinson, S.K., Thompson, F.R., Donovan, T.M., Whitehead, D.R. and Faaborg, J. (1995) "Regional Forest Fragmentation and the Nesting Success of Migratory Birds," *Science*, 267: 1987–1990.

Rodier, C.A. and Johnston, R.A. (1997) "Travel, Emissions and Welfare Effects of Travel Demand Management Measures," *Transportation Research Record* no. 1598.

Rokeach, M. (1970) *Beliefs, Attitudes, and Values: A Theory of Organization and Change*, San Francisco: Jossey-Bass.

Rolston, H. III (1985) "Valuing Wildlands," *Environmental Ethics*, 7(1): 23–48.

Rome, A. (2001) *The Bulldozer in the Countryside: Suburban Sprawl and the Rise of the American Environmental Movement*, Cambridge, UK: Cambridge University Press.

Roper, W.L., Kraft, M.K., Killingsworth, R.E., Mofson, P. and Starrett, B. (February 2003) "Health and Smart Growth: Building Health, Promoting Active Communities," translation paper no. 11: 20pp, Coral Gables, FL: Funders Network.

Rose, J.G. (1984) "Farmland Preservation Policy and Programs," *Natural Resources Journal*, 24(3): 591–640.

Rosenbaum, W.A. (1991) *Environmental Politics and Policy*, 2nd edn, Washington, DC: Congressional Quarterly Press.

Rosenberger, R.S. and Walsh, R.G. (1997) "Nonmarket Value of Western Valley Ranchland Using Contingent Valuation," *Journal of Agricultural and Resource Economics*, 22(2): 296–309.

Rosenfeld, A.H., Romm, J.J., Akbari, H., Pomerantz, M. and Taha, H. (August 1996) "Policies to Reduce Heat Islands: Magnitudes of Benefits and Incentives to Achieve Them," 9, 177, *Proceedings of the 1996 ACEEE Summer Study on Energy Efficiency in Buildings*, Lawrence Berkeley National Laboratory, Report LBL-38679, Berkeley, CA.

Roth, N.E., Allan, J.D. and Erickson, D.L. (1996) "Landscape Influences on Stream Biotic Integrity Assessed at Multiple Scales," *Landscape Ecology*, 11: 141–156.

Rupasingha, A. and Goetz, S.J. (August 2001) "Land Use Research: Scientific Publications from 1986 to the Present," Regional Rural Development Paper no. 8, University Park, PA: Penn State University, The Northeast Regional Center for Rural Development. Online, available at: http://www.cas.nercrd.psu.edu/Publications/RDPAPERS/LURrdp8.pdf (accessed 31 March 2004).

Rupasingha, A., Goetz, S.J. and Freshwater, D. (2000) "Social Capital and Economic Growth: A County-Level Analysis," *Journal of Agricultural and Applied Economics*, 32(3): 565–572.

Rupasingha, A., Goetz, S.J. and Freshwater, D. (2002) "Social and Institutional Factors as Determinants of Economic Growth: Evidence from the United States Counties," *Papers in Regional Science*, 81, 139–155.

Rusk, D. (1999) *Inside Game, Outside Game*, Washington, DC: Brookings Institution.

Sala, O.E., Chapin, F.S. III, Armesto, J.J., Berlow, R., Bloomfield, J., Dirzo, R., Huber-Sanwald, E., Huenneke, L.F., Jackson, R.B., Kinzig, A., Leemans, R., Lodge, D., Mooney, H.A., Oesterheld, M., Poff, N.L., Sykes, M.T., Walker, B.H., Walker, M. and Wall, D.H. (2000) "Global Biodiversity Scenarios for the Year 2100," *Science*, 287: 1770–1774.

Salhofer, K. (2001) "Elasticities of Substitution and Factor Supply Elasticities in European Agriculture: A Review of Past Studies," in OECD (ed.) *Market Effects of Crop Support Measures*, Paris: OECD, 89–119. Online, available at: http://www1.oecd.org/publications/e-book/5101141E.pdf (accessed 25 February 2004).

Sampson, N. and DeCoster, L. (2000) "Forest Fragmentation: Implications for Sustainable Private Forests," *Journal of Forestry*, 98: 4–8.

Samuelson, P.A. (1954) "The Pure Theory of Public Expenditures," *Review of Economics and Statistics*, 36: 387–389.

Sanford, R. and Lapping, M.B. (forthcoming 2004) "Vermont, the Beckoning

County," in M. Lapping and O. Furuseth (eds) *Big Places, Big Plans: Large-Scale Rural Regional Planning*, Aldershot, UK: Ashgate.

Savitch, H.V. (2002) "Encourage, Then Cope: Washington and the Sprawl Machine," in G.D. Squires (ed.) *Urban Sprawl: Causes, Consequences and Policy Response*, Washington, DC: The Urban Institute Press, 141–164.

Schmid, A.A. (August 2003) "Discussion: Social Capital as an Important Lever in Economic Development Policy and Private Strategy," *American Journal of Agricultural Economics*, 85(3): 716–719.

Schneider, K. (9 January 1995) "Fighting to Keep US Rules from Devaluing Land," *New York Times*.

Schueler, T. (1994) "The Importance of Imperviousness," *Watershed Protection Techniques*, 1: 100–111.

—— (1995) "Site Planning for Urban Stream Protection," Washington, DC: Metropolitan Washington Council of Governments. Online, available at: http://www.cwp.org/SPSP/TOC.htm (accessed 25 March 1996).

Schueler, T. and Gali, J. (1992) "Environmental Impacts of Stormwater Ponds," *Watershed Restoration Source Book*, Washington, DC: Ancostia Restoration Team, Metropolitan Washington Council of Governments.

Schwartz, S.I., Hansen, D.E. and Foin, T.C. (December 1975) "Preferential Taxation and the Control of Urban Sprawl," *Journal of Environmental Economics and Management*, 2: 120–134.

Scott, R. (1975) "Management and Control of Growth: An Introduction and Summary," in R. Scott, D. Brower and D. Miner (eds) *Management and Control of Growth*, Washington, DC: The Urban Land Institute.

Scott, Sir W. (1819, 2000) *The Bride of Lammermoor*, in J.H. Alexander (ed.), London: Penguin Books.

Seelye, K.Q. (27 November 2001) "South's Forests Seen Hurt by Sprawl," *New York Times*, A9.

Seidl, A.F. (2000) "A Niche for Local Voluntary Organizations in an Extended Theory of the Firm," *Indian Journal of Applied Economics*, 8(4): 342–356.

—— (February 2002) "Rural Land Use Outlook," 2002 Colorado Agricultural Outlook Forum, 13–15.

Shabecoff, P. (1993) *A Fierce Green Fire: The American Environmental Movement*, New York: Hill and Wang.

Shamai, S. (1991) "Sense of Place: An Empirical Measurement," *Geoforum*, 22: 347–358.

Shi, Y.J., Phipps, T.T. and Colyer, D. (February 1997) "Agricultural Land Values Under Urbanizing Influences," *Land Economics*, 73: 90–100.

Shields, M. (1998) "An Integrated Economic Impact and Simulation Model for Wisconsin Counties," unpublished Ph.D. dissertation, Department of Agricultural and Applied Economics, University of Wisconsin-Madison.

Shields, M. and Deller, S.C. (1998) "Commuting's Effect on Local Retail Market Performance," *Review of Regional Studies*, 28(2): 71–90.

Shields, M., Stallmann, J.I. and Deller, S.C. (1999) "Simulating the Economic and Fiscal Impacts of High and Low-Income Elderly on a Small Rural Region, *Review of Regional Studies*, 29(2): 175–196.

Shields, M., Stallmann, J.I. and Deller, S.C. (2003) "The Economic and Fiscal Impacts of the Elderly on a Small Rural Region," *Journal of the Community Development Society*, 34(1): 85–106.

Shoard, M. (1980) *The Theft of the Countryside*, London: Temple Smith.

Shortle, J.S., Abler, D.G. and Ribaudo, M. (2001) "Agriculture and Water Quality: The Issues," in J.S. Shortle and D.G. Abler (eds) *Environmental Policies for Agricultural Pollution Control*, Wallingford, UK: CAB International, 1–18.

Shucksmith, M. and Chapman, P. (1998) "Rural Development and Social Exclusion," *Sociologia Ruralis*, 38(2): 225–242.

Sierra Club (2000) *Smart Choices or Sprawling Growth: A 50-State Survey of Development*, San Francisco, CA: Sierra Club. Online, available at: http://www.sierraclub.org/sprawl/50statesurvey/SmartChoices.pdf.

Simmons, I.G. (2001) *An Environmental History of Great Britain*, Edinburgh: Edinburgh University Press.

Simons, R. (1998) *Turning Brownfields into Greenbacks: Developing and Financing Environmentally Contaminated Real Estate*, Washington, DC: The Urban Land Institute.

Singal, D.J. (1982) "Howard Odum and Social Sciences in the South," *The War Within: From Victorian to Modernist Thought in the South, 1919–1945*, Chapel Hill: University of North Carolina Press.

Skaggs, R. and Ghosh, S. (1999) "Changes in Soil Erosion Rates: A Markov Chain Analysis," *Journal of Agricultural and Applied Economics*, 31(3): 611–622.

Slavesen, D. (December 1993) "Contamination and the Reuse of Land," *Urban Land*, 32–36.

Smart Growth America (16 October 2000) *Americans Want Growth and Green: Demand Solutions to Traffic, Haphazard Development*, Washington, DC: Smart Growth America.

—— (2001) *Americans Want Smart Growth: Here's How to Get There*, Washington, DC.

Smith, B. (1997) "A Review of Monocentric Urban Density Analysis," *Journal of Planning Literature*, 12(2): 115–135.

Smith, V.K. and Desvousges, W.H. (1986) "The Value of Avoiding a LULU: Hazardous Waste Disposal Sites," *Review of Economics and Statistics*, 68(2): 293–299.

Smout, T.C. (2000) *Nature Contested: Environmental History in Scotland and Northern England Since 1600*, Edinburgh: Edinburgh University Press.

Society of American Foresters (April 2003) "Forest Fragmentation Increases Lyme Disease," *The Forestry Source*, 14.

Sodoma, J. (15 March 1994) in K.O. Wilson, "Filtrate Now, Watershed Residents Demand," *Delaware County Times*, 1.

Sokolow, A.D. (2002) *Protecting Farmland in the United States: An Outline of Optional Policy Strategies and Techniques*, Davis, CA: University of California, 7.

Solitare, L. and Greenberg, M. (2002) "Is the US Environmental Protection Agency Brownfields Assessment Pilot Program Environmentally Just?" *Environmental Health Perspectives*, 2: 249–257.

Sorensen, A.A. and Esseks, J.D. (1998) *Living on the Edge: The Costs and Risks of Scatter Development*, DeKalb, IL: American Farmland Trust, Center for Agriculture in the Environment.

Squires, G.D. (2002) "Urban Sprawl and the Uneven Development of Metropolitan America," in G.D. Squires (ed.) *Urban Sprawl: Causes, Consequences and Policy Responses*, Washington, DC: The Urban Institute Press, 1–22.

Stallmann, J.I., Deller, S.C. and Shields, M. (1999) "The Fiscal Impact of Aging Retirees on a Small Rural Region," *The Gerontologist*, 39(5): 599–610.

State of Colorado, Department of Local Affairs (2004) Online, available at: http://www.dola.state.co.us/is/statinc.cfm (accessed 14 February 2004).

State of Queensland, Australia (2003) "Queensland Policy and Implementation: A Guide to Improved Outcomes," Department of Education. Online, available at: http://education.qld.gov.au/corporate/doem/guide/intro.htm#whatisgoodpolicy (accessed 22 August 2003).

Stave, K. (1998) *Water, Land, and People: The Social Ecology of Conflict over New York City's Watershed Protection Efforts in the Catskill Mountain Region, New York*, New Haven: Yale University Graduate School.

Stedman, R.C. (2002) "Toward a Social Psychology of Place: Predicting Behavior from Place-Based Cognitions, Attitude, and Identity," *Environment and Behavior*, 34(5): 405–425.

Stedman, R.C. (2003) "Is it Really Just a Social Construction? The Contribution of the Physical Environment to Sense of Place," *Society and Natural Resources*, 16: 671–685.

Stein, C.S. (n.d.) "Radburn and the Radburn Idea," unpublished manuscript, Stein Papers, Cornell University, as quoted in M.B. Lapping (Summer 1977) "Radburn: Planning the American Community," *New Jersey History*, 85–100.

Stigler, G.J. (1966) *The Theory of Price*, 3rd edn, New York: Collier Macmillan.

Swinbank, A. (2001) "Multifunctionality: A European Euphemism for Protectionism?" Reading, UK: University of Reading. Online, available at: http://www.apd.rdg.ac.uk/AgEcon/research/workingpapers/as1.pdf (accessed 30 January 2004).

Texas Transportation Institute (2001) "Urban Mobility Report." Online, available at: http://www.tti.tamu.edu (accessed 31 March 2004).

The President's Task Force on Environmental Health Risks and Safety Risks to Children (2000) "Asthma and the Environment: A Strategy to Protect Children." Online, available at: http://www.epa.gov/children/whatwe/fin.pdf (accessed 11 February 2002).

The Rural Legacy Program Grants Manual 2001 (revision 2001) Annapolis, MD: Maryland Department of Natural Resources.

Thibaut, J. and Kelley, H. (1959) *The Social Psychology of Groups*, New York: Wiley.

Thompson, E. (2001) *Agricultural Sustainability and Smart Growth: Saving Urban-Influenced Agriculture*, Washington, DC: Funders' Network for Smart Growth and Livable Communities.

Thompson, R.P. and Jones, J.G. (1981) "Classifying Nonindustrial Private Forestlands by Tract Size," *Journal of Forestry*, 79: 288–291.

Thurston, L. and Yezer, A.M.J. (1994) "Causality in the Suburbanization of Population and Employment," *Journal of Urban Economic*, 35: 105–118.

Tibbetts, J. (1995) "Everybody's Taking the Fifth," *Planning*, 61(1): 4–9.

Tiebout, C.M. (1956) "A Pure Theory of Local Expenditures," *Journal of Political Economy*, 64: 416–424.

Tinbergen, J. (1952) *On the Theory of Economic Policy*, Amsterdam: North-Holland.

Town of Arbor Vitae (1996) *Northwoods Character: Design Review Standards for Commercial, Multifamily and Industrial Development*, Madison, WI: University of Wisconsin-Extension.

Town of Eagle River (1996) *Eagle Town River Area Vision 2020 Survey Report*, Madison, WI: University of Wisconsin-Extension.

Town of Manitowish Waters Zoning Committee (1995) *Town of Manitowish Waters: Community Planning Survey Report*, Madison, WI: University of Wisconsin-Extension.

Town of Phelps Comprehensive Master Planning Advisory Committee (1998) *Town of Phelps Community Planning Survey Report*, Madison, WI: University of Wisconsin-Extension.

Town of St. Germain Comprehensive Master Planning Advisory Committee (1997) *Town of St. Germain Community Planning Survey Report*, Madison, WI: University of Wisconsin-Extension.

Tregoning, H. (2002) "A Comprehensive Approach to Rural Preservation: Maryland's Smart Growth Initiative," *Protecting Farmland at the Fringe: Do Regulations Work? Strengthening the Research Agenda.* Conference Proceedings, Baltimore, MD, 5–7 September 2001. Online, available at: http://aede.ag.ohio-state.edu/Programs/Swank/pdfs/protecting_farmland_at_the_fringe.pdf (accessed 15 April 2004).

Treyz, G., Rickman, D. and Shao, G. (1992) "The REMI Economics Demographic Forecasting and Simulation Model," *International Regional Science Review*, 14(3): 221–253.

Troughton, M.J. (1996) "Rural Canada and Canadian Rural Geography – An Appraisal," *The Canadian Geographer*, 39: 290–305.

Tuan, Y.F. (1977) *Space and Place: The Perspective of Experience*, Minneapolis, MN: University of Minnesota Press.

Ulrich, R., Simons, R., Losito, B., Fiorito, E., Miles, M. and Zelson, M. (1991) "Stress Recovery during Exposure to Natural and Urban Environments," *Journal of Environmental Psychology*, 11: 201–230.

United Kingdom Cabinet Office (2003) *Better Policy Making: A Guide to Regulatory Impact Assessment*, London. Online, available at: http://www.cabinet-office.gov.uk/regulation/scrutiny/ria-guidance.pdf (accessed 18 December 2003).

US Bureau of Land Management (2003) *BLM Facts*. Online, available at: http://www.blm.gov/nhp/facts/index.htm (accessed 21 November 2003).

US Census Bureau (2000) *Geographic Areas Reference Manual*. Online, available at: http://www.census.gov/geo/www.garm.html (accessed 16 June 2003).

—— (2002) *2000 Census of Population and Housing, Summary File 3: Technical Documentation*. SF3/10 (RV), Washington, DC. Online, available at: http://www.census.gov/prod/cen2000/doc/sf3.pdf (accessed 25 February 2004).

—— (2003) *2002 Statistical Abstract of the United States*, table no. 3. Online, available at: http://www.census.gov/prod/2003pubs/02statab/pop.pdf (accessed 13 June 2003).

US Census Bureau, US Department of Commerce and US Department of Housing and Urban Development, Office of Policy Development and Research (September 1999) *American Housing Survey for the United States, 1997 Current Housing Reports*, H150/97.

US Conference of Mayors and the National Association of Counties (2000) *US Metro Economies: The Engines of America's Growth*. Online, available at: http://usmayors.org/citiesdrivetheeconomy/report2000.pdf (accessed 16 June 2003).

US Congress, Office of Technology Assessment (September 1995) *The Technological Reshaping of Metropolitan America*, Washington, DC: US Government Printing Office.

US Department of Agriculture (1997a) "National Agricultural Statistic Service," *Agricultural Statistics*, Washington, DC.

—— (1997b) *US Census of Agriculture*, 1(1), Washington, DC: US Department of Agriculture. Online, available at: http://www.nass.usda.gov/census/census97/volume1/vol1pubs.htm (accessed 7 April 2004).

US Department of Agriculture, Forest Service (2000) *US Forest Service Strategic Plan* (2000 Revision). Online, available at: http://www.fs.fed.us/plan/stratplan.pdf (accessed 22 August 2003).

—— (2003) *Mission, Motto, Vision, and Guiding Principles.* Online, available at: http://www.fs.fed.us/aboutus/mission.shtml (accessed 15 August 2003).

US Department of Commerce, Bureau of Economic Analysis (2004) Washington, DC. Online, available at: http://www.bea.doc.gov/bea/regional/reis/drill.cfm (accessed 14 February 2004).

US Department of Housing and Urban Development (2000) *The State of the Cities 2000: Megaforces Shaping the Future of the Nation's Cities,* Washington, DC: US Department of Housing and Urban Development. Online, available at: http://www.huduser.org.publication/polleg/soc2000_rpt.html (accessed 16 June 2003).

US Department of Transportation (1998) *1997 Status of the Nation's Surface Transportation System: Condition and Performance Report to Congress,* Washington, DC: US Department of Transportation.

US Department of Transportation (September 2003) *Department of Transportation Strategic Planning 2003–2008: Safer, Simpler, Smarter Transportation Solutions.* Online, available at: http://www.dot.gov/stratplan2008/strategic_plan.htm (accessed 24 February 2004).

US Environmental Protection Agency (December 1997) *National Air Quality and Trends Report,* EPA 454-R-98-016, Washington, DC: US EPA, Office of Air and Radiation.

—— (1999) *From the Mountains to the Sea: The State of Maryland's Freshwater Streams,* EPA/903/R-99/023, Washington, DC: Office of Research and Development.

—— (2001a) *Mid-Atlantic Integrated Assessment: Issues – Urban Sprawl.* Online, available at: http://www.epa.gov/emfjulte/tpmcmaia/html/sprawl.html (accessed 12 April 2004).

—— (2001b) "Our Built and Natural Environments: A Technical Review of the Interactions between Land Use, Transportation, and Environmental Quality," EPA 231-R-01-002, Washington, DC. Online, available at: http://www.smartgrowth.org/library/articles.asp?art=235 (accessed 25 February 2002).

—— (January 2001c) *EPA Guidance: Improving Air Quality Through Land Use Activities, Air and Radiation,* Office of Transportation and Air Quality, EPA 420-R-01-001. Online, available at: http://www.epa.gov/otaq/traq (accessed 25 February 2002).

—— (2003) *2003–2008 EPA Strategic Plan: Direction for the Future.* Online, available at: http://www.epa.gov/ocfo/plan/2003sp.pdf (accessed 24 February 2004).

US General Accounting Office (1994) "Drinking Water: Stronger Efforts Essential for Small Communities to Comply with Standards," Washington, DC: USGAO/RCED-94-40.

—— (April 1999) "Extent of Federal Influence on 'Urban Sprawl' is Unclear," Washington, DC: USGAO/RCED-99-97.

—— (September 2000a) *Community Development: Local Growth Issues – Federal Opportunities and Challenges,* Washington, DC: USGAO/RCED-00-178.

—— (2000b) *Local Government Issues: Federal Opportunities and Challenges,* Washington, DC: USGAO.

VanderWilt, M., Meredith, A., Menard, S. and Eslinger, D.L. (2003) "The Relationship between Impervious Surface Coverage and Water Quality," 3rd Biennial Coastal GeoTools Conference Proceedings, Charleston, S.C.

van Dijk, G. (2001) "Biodiversity and Multifunctionality in European Agriculture: Priorities, Current Initiatives and Possible New Directions," Paris: OECD. Online, available at: http://www1.oecd.org/agr/mf/doc/multfinal22june_.pdf (accessed 2004).

Van Horn, C., Dixon, K. and Lawler, G. (2000) "Turning Brownfields into Job-fields," New Brunswick, NJ: Rutgers University, John Heldrich Center for Workplace Development.

VanTassell, V., Conner, R., Seidl, A. and Wilkins, N. (Spring/Summer 2002) "Grassland Dynamics," *Choices*, 17(2): 24–25.

Varian, H.R. (1984) *Microeconomic Analysis*, 2nd edn, New York: W.W. Norton & Co.

Vatn, A. (2002) "Multifunctional Agriculture: Some Consequences for International Trade Regimes," *European Review of Agricultural Economics*, 29(3): 309–327.

Vernberg, F.J. and Vernberg, W.B. (2001) *The Coastal Zone, Past, Present, and Future*, Columbia, SC: University of South Carolina Press.

Vernberg, W.B., Scott, G.I., Stozier, S.H., Bemiss, J. and Daugomah, J.W. (1996) "The Effects of Urbanization on Human and Ecosystem Health," in F.J. Vernberg, W.B. Vernberg and T. Siewicki (eds) *Sustainable Development in the Southeastern Coastal Zone*, Columbia, SC: University of South Carolina Press.

Vesterby, M. and Heimlich, R.E. (1991) "Land Use and Demographic Change: Results from Fast-Growth Counties," *Land Economics*, 67(3): 279–291.

Vesterby, M. and Krupa, K. (2001) *Major Uses of Land in the United States, 1997*, Washington, DC: Economic Research Service, US Department of Agriculture, Statistical Bulletin No. 973.

Vesterby, M., Heimlich, R. and Krupa, K. (1994) "Urbanization of Rural Land in the United States," AER 673, Economic Research Service, Washington, DC: USDA.

Vitaliano, D.F. and Hill, C. (1994) "Agricultural Districts and Farmland Prices," *Journal of Real Estate Finance and Economics*, 8: 213–223.

Vitousek, P.M. (1994) "Beyond Global Warming: Ecology and Global Change," *Ecology*, 75: 1861–1876.

Vitousek, P.M., Mooney, H.A., Lubchenco, J. and Melillo, J.M. (1997) "Human Domination of Earth's Ecosystems," *Science*, 277: 494–499.

von Thunen, J.H. (1826) "Der isolierte Staat" in Beziehung auf Landwertschaft und Nationalekonomie. Hamburg. English translation by C.M. Wartenberg (1966) *von Thunen's Isolated State*, Oxford, UK: Pergamon Press.

Waggoner, P., Ausubel, J. and Wernick, I. (1996) "Lightening the Tread of Population on the Land: American Examples," *Population and Development Review*, 22: 531–545.

Wagner, J.E., Deller, S.C. and Alward, G. (1992) "Estimating Economic Impacts using Industry and Household Expenditures," *Journal of the Community Development Society*, 23: 79–102.

Wakeford, R. (December 2001) "Agriculture Within the Rural Economy: But What Rural Economy Is That?" Paper presented at Agricultural Economics Society Conference, London.

Wang, L. and Kanehl, P. (2003) "Influences of Watershed Urbanization and Instream Habitat on Macroinvertebrates in Cold Water Streams," *Journal of the American Water Resources Association*, 39(5): 1181–1196.

Washington Post (27 November 1998) "'Slow Growth' on Fast Track in Southern California," A3.

Wassmer, R. (Fall 2001) "Growth and Sprawl in California," *Snap Shots*, Sacramento, CA: California State University, Center for California Studies.

Watson, F. (2001) *Scotland: A History*, Stroud, UK: Tempus Books.

Wear, D.N. and Bolstad, P. (1998) "Land Use Changes in Southern Appalachian Landscapes: Spatial Analysis and Forecast Evaluation," *Ecosystems*, 1(6): 575–594.

Weaver, L.A. and Garman, G.C. (1994) "Urbanization of a Watershed and Historical Changes in a Stream Fish Assemblage," *Transactions of the American Fisheries Society*, 123: 162–172.

Weber, M. (1946) "Politics as a Vocation," in H.H. Gerth and C.W. Mills (eds) Max Weber, *Essays in Sociology*, New York: Oxford University Press, 77–128.

Weber, M. (1978) *Economy and Society*, in G. Roth and C. Wittich (eds), 2 vols, Berkeley, CA: University of California Press.

Weitzman, M. (1999) "Just Keep Discounting, but...," in P. Portney and J. Weyant (eds) *Discounting and Intergenerational Equity*, Washington, DC: Resources for the Future.

Weller, D. and Edwards, N. (2001) *Maryland's Changing Land Use: Past, Present and Future*, Baltimore, MD: Maryland Department of Planning.

Wheaton, D.E. (1986) *Urban Public Finance*, Switzerland: Harwood Academic.

Wheaton, W. (March 1998) "Land Use and Density in Cities with Congestion," *Journal of Urban Economics*, 43(2): 258–272.

Whitby, M. (2000) "Challenges and Options for the Agri-Environment," *Journal of Agricultural Economics*, 51, 317–332.

Whittle, P. (1954) "On Stationary Processes in the Plane," *Biometrica*, 41: 434–449.

Wichelns, D. and Kline, J.D. (1993) "The Impact of Parcel Characteristics on the Cost of Development Rights to Farmland," *Agricultural and Resource Economics Review*, 150–158.

Wiebe, K., Tegene, A. and Kuhn, B. (1996) "Partial Interests in Land: Policy Tools for Resource Use and Conservation," Agricultural Economic Report no. 744, Washington, DC: US Department of Agriculture, Economic Research Service.

Wiesbrod, B. (1988) *The Nonprofit Economy*, Cambridge: Harvard University Press.

Wightman, A. (1996) *Scotland's Mountains: An Agenda for Sustainable Development*, Perth, UK: Scottish Countryside and Wildlife Link.

Wilcove, D.S., Rothstein, D., Dubow, J., Phillips, A. and Losos, E. (1998) "Quantifying Threats to Imperiled Species in the United States," *BioScience*, 48(8): 607–615.

Wilcox, B.A. and Murphy, D.D. (1985) "Conservation Strategy: The Effects of Fragmentation on Extinction," *American Naturalist*, 125: 879–887.

Williamson, O.E. (1985) *The Economic Institutions of Capitalism*, New York: Free Press.

Wilson, E.O. (1992) *The Diversity of Life*, Cambridge, MA: Belknap Press.

Wilson, W. (1987) *The Truly Disadvantaged: The Inner City, the Underclass, and Public Policy*, Chicago, IL: University of Chicago.

Wirth, L. (1938) "Urbanism as a Way of Life," *American Journal of Sociology*, 44: 1–24.

Wisconsin Department of Natural Resources (1991) *Wisconsin Lakes*, Madison, WI: WDNR Publ-FM-800 91.

—— (1996a) *Shoreline Protection Study: A Report to the Wisconsin State Legislature*, Madison, WI: WDNR PUBL-RS.

—— (1996b) *Northern Initiatives Research: A Consolidated Analysis of Phone Survey,*

Open House, and Questionnaire Data, draft report, Madison, WI: WDNR Bureau of Research.

Wolff, T. and Carter, J. (2002) *Growing With Less Greenhouse Gases: State Growth Management Practices that Reduce GHG Emissions*, Washington, DC: National Governors Association.

Wolfram, G. (1981) "The Sale of Development Rights and Zoning in the Preservation of Open Space: Lindahl Equilibrium and a Case Study," *Land Economics*, 57(3): 398–413.

Wordsworth, W. (1822) *A Description of the Scenery of the Lakes in the North of England*, London: Longman.

Young, T. and Allen, P.G. (1986) "Methods for Valuing Countryside Amenity: An Overview," *Journal of Agricultural Economics*, 37(3): 349–364.

Yount, K. and Meyer, P.B. (1994) "Bankers, Developers and New Investment in Brownfield Sites," *Economic Development Quarterly*, 8(4): 338–344.

Index